DEMOSTHENES

The career of Demosthenes extended over a thirty year period, and coincided with the rise to dominance of Macedon under Philip II and Alexander the Great. In spite of the fact that this was a time which saw the loss of Greek autonomy, successive generations have judged him the statesman *par excellence*, and the supreme example of a patriot. His oratory is seen as among the finest to survive from the classical era, and it is still quoted by today's politicians.

In this volume, leading scholars provide a thorough, up-to-date study of the man and his career. They discuss Demosthenes' emergence on the political scene; the validity of his policy against Macedon; how his speeches came to be regarded so highly, and whether their reputation is justified; and his influence as both statesman and orator down to the present day.

Cohesive and comprehensive, this is a landmark study of one of the most important figures in both the history and literature of classical Greece.

Ian Worthington is Professor of Greek History at the University of Missouri-Columbia, USA.

DEMOSTHENES

Statesman and orator

Edited by Ian Worthington

London and New York

First published 2000
by Routledge
11 New Fetter Lane, London EC4P 4EE

Simultaneously published in the USA and Canada
by Routledge
29 West 35th Street, New York, NY 10001

Routledge is an imprint of the Taylor & Francis Group

Typeset in Garamond by Taylor & Francis Books Ltd
Printed and bound in Great Britain by TJ International Ltd,
Padstow, Cornwall

British Library Cataloguing in Publication Data
A catalogue record for this book is available from the British Library

Library of Congress Cataloging in Publication Data
Demosthenes: statesman and orator / edited by Ian Worthington.
Includes bibliographical references and index.
1. Demosthenes–Criticism and interpretation. 2. Speeches, addresses,
etc., Greek–History and criticism. 3. Athens (Greece)–Politics and
government. 4. Politics and literature–Greece. 5. Statesmen–Greece–
Biography. 6. Orators–Greece–Biography. 7. Oratory, Ancient.
8. Demosthenes. I. Worthington, Ian.
PA3952 .D68 2000
885'.01–dc21
[B]   00–031056

ISBN   0–415–20456–9 (hbk)
ISBN   0–415–20457–7 (pbk)

0012892277

CONTENTS

List of contributors   vii
Preface   viii
Speech numbers and titles   x
Abbreviations   xiv

Introduction: Demosthenes, then and now   1
IAN WORTHINGTON

1 **The road to prominence**   9
   E. BADIAN

2 **Demosthenes and Philip II**   45
   T.T.B. RYDER

3 **Demosthenes' (in)activity during the reign of
   Alexander the Great**   90
   IAN WORTHINGTON

4 **Demosthenes and Aeschines**   114
   JOHN BUCKLER

5 **Demosthenes and the social historian**   159
   MARK GOLDEN

CONTENTS

6 Demosthenes as advocate: the private speeches   181
DAVID C. MIRHADY

7 The public speeches of Demosthenes   205
R.D. MILNS

8 Philosophers, politics, academics: Demosthenes'
rhetorical reputation in antiquity   224
CRAIG COOPER

9 Demosthenes in the underworld: a chapter in
the *Nachleben* of a *rhētōr*   246
PHILLIP HARDING

Bibliography   272
Index   286

CONTRIBUTORS

E. Badian Department of History, Harvard University, U.S.A.

John Buckler Department of History, University of Illinois, U.S.A.

Craig Cooper Department of Classics, University of Winnipeg, Canada

Mark Golden Department of Classics, University of Winnipeg, Canada

Phillip Harding Department of Classics, University of British Columbia, Canada

R.D. Milns Department of Classics and Ancient History, University of Queensland, Australia

David C. Mirhady Simon Fraser University, Vancouver, Canada

T.T.B. Ryder Department of Classics, University of Reading, England

Ian Worthington Department of History, University of Missouri-Columbia, U.S.A

PREFACE

In my final undergraduate year at the University of Hull, I elected to take T.T.B. Ryder's 'Demosthenes and Macedon' course. This was not for the faint-hearted: for an entire year we covered the reign of Philip II, and we only touched on Alexander the Great in, I think, the final fortnight! We all got to know Demosthenes very well, but a major problem was the lack of a modern treatment of Demosthenes within two covers. Twenty years later, my own course on Philip and Alexander (which bears an uncanny resemblance to Tim Ryder's – though I hasten to add that any imitation is not plagiarism but my form of admiration) has the same problem. There is of course Raphael Sealey's *Demosthenes and his Time*, which was published in 1993, but that book is really a history of Greece in Demosthenes' lifetime, and Demosthenes is subsumed within other themes. Away from the political sphere, Demosthenes as an orator has also received, generally speaking, little attention. Lionel Pearson published *The Art of Demosthenes* over three decades ago (1976), and although commentaries on individual speeches have started to appear in the last few years with welcome frequency, they necessarily focus on a particular speech or series of speeches rather than treat the rhetorical style of Demosthenes as a whole. In view of Demosthenes' major role in Greek political affairs for thirty years and his immense oratorical prowess, as well as his influence throughout history, the time is long overdue for a new treatment of Demosthenes within the one set of covers; hence the rationale for this book. While it does not presume to cast itself as a biography proper and could not render Schaefer's still unparalleled biography (1885–7) obsolete, it will ask some new questions and offer new insights on Demosthenes as a statesman and as an orator, and also evaluate his reputation both in antiquity and down to the present day.

PREFACE

Three notes: (1) All dates are BC unless otherwise indicated. (2) In deference to the fact that the authors in this book live in North America, Australia and England, I have allowed both American and English spellings rather than imposing one spelling system. (3) Cross-references within chapters to other chapters were inserted by me as editor, not by the individual authors.

I have several people to thank, without whose help and support this book would not have seen the light of day. First and foremost, the other authors, who patiently responded to my requests and worked hard in bringing their chapters to completion. Second, my own institution for a University of Missouri Research Board Grant which allowed me to complete my own chapter and to edit the book. Third, Richard Stoneman, whose enthusiasm and support meant a lot (again), and indeed all the staff at Routledge for their hard work. Finally, my wife Tracy, who put up with my usual complaints and late nights with her customary grace and support, for which I am always grateful.

Ian Worthington
Department of History
University of Missouri-Columbia
April 2000

SPEECH NUMBERS AND TITLES

References to speeches by all orators in this book are by their number only. The following is a list of the numbers and titles of the speeches cited in this book for ease of reference (speeches believed to be spurious but which have survived under the name of a particular orator are listed under that name and cited as such in the chapters).

Aeschines

1   *Against Timarchus*
2   *On the False Embassy*
3   *Against Ctesiphon*

Andocides

1   *On the Mysteries*
3   *On the Peace with Sparta*
4   *Against Alcibiades*

Antiphon

1   *Prosecution of the Stepmother for Poisoning*

Demosthenes

1   *Olynthiac 1*
2   *Olynthiac 2*

SPEECH NUMBERS AND TITLES

3 *Olynthiac 3*
4 *Philippic 1*
5 *On the Peace*
6 *Philippic 2*
7 *On Halonnesus*
8 *On the Chersonese*
9 *Philippic 3*
10 *Philippic 4*
11 *Answer to Philip's Letter*
12 *Philip's Letter*
13 *On Organization*
14 *On the Symmories*
15 *For the Liberty of the Rhodians*
16 *For the People of Megalopolis*
17 *On the Treaty with Alexander*
18 *On the Crown*
19 *On the False Embassy*
20 *Against Leptines*
21 *Against Meidias*
22 *Against Androtion*
23 *Against Aristocrates*
24 *Against Timocrates*
25 *Against Aristogeiton 1*
26 *Against Aristogeiton 2*
27 *Against Aphobus 1*
28 *Against Aphobus 2*
29 *Against Aphobus 3*
30 *Against Onetor 1*
31 *Against Onetor 2*
32 *Against Zenothemis*
34 *Against Phormio*
35 *Against Lacritus*
36 *For Phormio*
37 *Against Pantaenetus*
38 *Against Nausimachus*
39 *Against Boeotus 1*
40 *Against Boeotus 2*
42 *Against Phaenippus*
43 *Against Macartatus*
44 *Against Leochares*
45 *Against Stephanus 1*
46 *Against Stephanus 2*

47 *Against Evergus*
48 *Against Olympiodorus*
51 *On the Trierarchic Crown*
53 *Against Nicostratus*
54 *Against Conon*
55 *Against Callicles*
56 *Against Dionysodorus*
59 *Against Neaera*

Dinarchus

1 *Against Demosthenes*
2 *Against Aristogeiton*
3 *Against Philocles*

Hyperides

5 *Against Demosthenes*
6 *Funeral Oration*

Isaeus

6 *On the Estate of Philoctemon*
7 *On the Estate of Apollodorus*
8 *On the Estate of Ciron*

Isocrates

4 *Panegyricus*
5 *To Philip*
7 *Areopagiticus*
15 *Antidosis*
16 *Concerning the Team of Horses*
17 *Trapeziticus*
18 *Against Callimachus*
19 *Aegineticus*
20 *Against Lochites*
21 *Against Euthynus*

Lycurgus

1   *Against Leocrates*

Lysias

1   *On the Murder of Eratosthenes*
2   *Funeral Oration*
12 *Against Eratosthenes*
16 *Before the Council: In Defence of Mantitheus at his Scrutiny*
21 *Defence against a Charge of Taking Bribes*
24 *On the Refusal of a Pension to the Invalid*
25 *Defence Against a Charge of Subverting the Democracy*

ABBREVIATIONS

Ancient authors:

Aes.	Aeschines
Andoc.	Andocides
AP	*Athenaion Politeia* (attributed to Aristotle)
Arist.	Aristotle
Arr.	Arrian, *Anabasis Alexandri*
Curt.	Quintus Curtius Rufus
Dem.	Demosthenes
[Dem.]	Pseudo-Demosthenes
Din.	Dinarchus
Diod.	Diodorus
Dion. Hal.	Dionysius of Halicarnassus
Hyp.	Hyperides
Isoc.	Isocrates
Lys.	Lysias
Plut.	Plutarch
Plut. *Dem.*	Plutarch, *Life of Demosthenes*
[Plut.] *Mor.*	Pseudo-Plutarch, *Moralia*

The following abbreviations for modern works are used:

FGrH	F. Jacoby, *Die Fragmente der griechischen Historiker*, several vols. (Berlin: 1926–30; Leiden: 1940–58)
IG	*Inscriptiones Graecae*
PA	J.E. Kirchner, *Prosopographia Attika*, 2 vols. (Berlin: 1901–3)
Tod 2	M.N. Tod, *Greek Historical Inscriptions*, Vol. 2 (Oxford: 1948)

INTRODUCTION

Demosthenes, then and now

Ian Worthington

Demosthenes (385/4 or 384/3 to 322) hardly needs an introduction.[1] As a *logographos*, he was highly productive and is regarded as the best of the Greek orators whose works have survived today. He wrote speeches not only for clients in the law courts but also for himself in that arena and in the Assembly. Today, sixty speeches survive in his corpus; however, many of the forensic speeches are spurious and probably by another orator, Apollodorus (at least Speeches 46, 49, 50, 52, 53 and 59). Of his symbouleutic or political orations, Speeches 7 and 17 are by others and Speeches 11 and 13 – and perhaps 10 as well – are possibly later creations. Speech 60, the funeral oration over the dead at the battle of Chaeronea in 338, was regarded as spurious in antiquity (Dion. Hal. *Demosthenes* 44), and it is likely that what survives today is a poor imitation.

Demosthenes also played a major role in the history of Athens – and Greece – in a period of turmoil and great political and military change, which saw Greek autonomy fall before the power of Macedon. His political power stretched over thirty years, and so great was his political influence that from 346 to 324 Athenian policy was virtually Demosthenes' policy. Those offering alternate views received little or no support from the Athenian people. As an imperial power, Athens was the most powerful *polis* that could resist Philip II, and then Alexander the Great. Demosthenes was intimately linked with the successes and failures of that city – and thus of Greece as a whole. However, Macedon did subdue Greece, and with his anti-Macedonian policy in ruins, Demosthenes committed suicide in 322.[2]

In 280/79, a little over four decades after Demosthenes committed suicide, his nephew Demochares persuaded the Athenian people to commission a statue of him and to maintain the eldest member of his family at state expense.[3] Polyeuctus cast this statue in bronze, and it was set up in a prominent place in the Agora, where all could see it. Such a statue was a signal honour for a man who had suffered an ignoble end to a public career lasting over thirty years. However, the statue was not strictly meant to rehabilitate Demosthenes as a statesman in the Athenians' – or for that matter posterity's – mind. Rather, it was the product of its own political background: a rise once more in a nationalistic feeling after a Macedonian rule during which Athens was treated as a mere possession.

As part of his punishment for Athens' revolt against Macedon on the death of Alexander the Great in 323, Antipater abolished Athenian democracy and set up a Macedonian oligarchy in 322.[4] Antipater died in 319; the Athenians then enjoyed a resurgence of their democracy, but this did not last long: from 317 to 307 Athens was governed absolutely by Demetrius of Phalerum, installed there by Cassander during the wars of Alexander the Great's rival generals.[5] In 307, the Athenians eagerly welcomed Demetrius Poliorcetes, who expelled Demetrius of Phalerum, and restored some form of democracy to Athens (Diod. 20.45.2–46). The Athenians had simply exchanged the devil for the deep blue sea, of course; most of the decrees passed by the Assembly in this period honoured supporters of Poliorcetes, and the true power of Macedonian rule was shown from 304 when Poliorcetes moved into the Parthenon and turned it into a brothel. Well might the Athenians have breathed a sigh of relief when Poliorcetes' father, Antigonus Monophthalmus, called him to Asia Minor, and both were defeated at the battle of Ipsus in 301.[6] Athens again fell under the rule of Cassander until late 295 when Poliorcetes once more seized the city. He would again control Athens, this time until 287 when the Athenians were able to expel him.[7] Although his son, Antigonus Gonatas, invaded Attica in 283, the Athenians blocked his entry into the city, and Gonatas was then forced to turn his attention to matters in Macedon itself.

Thus, in 280, with Gonatas repulsed and some form of democracy re-established in Athens, it is understandable why Demochares' proposal would be accepted – Mossé succinctly sums it up: 'The Athenians might well be under the illusion that they had regained their former independence, and the erection of a statue in honour of Demosthenes in 280/79 shows that they now considered themselves free from Macedonian control.'[8] Demosthenes' statue was meant to stand as the ultimate example of Greek patriotism and the cause of freedom against Macedonian oppression, just as Demosthenes himself had stood firm (so he says) against the might of Philip II and then Alexander. All might still not be lost. Of course, Athens would never be fully free of Macedonian – and then Roman – presence, as the subsequent years, indeed centuries, proved – 'illusion', to use Mossé's word, was right.

While representing a patriotic ideal, even a hero, to hard-pressed Athenians, Demosthenes' statue also had another effect: Demosthenes' policies and his very patriotism, however flawed, became vindicated. He came to be seen as more than a powerful statesman who might have taken bribes, misjudged situations and contributed to his city's – and country's – dramatic decline as a political and military power. Successive generations and modern scholars came to judge him the statesman and diplomat *par excellence*. To Pickard-Cambridge in 1914[9] or Clemenceau in 1926[10] or Cloché in 1957[11] (to cite only three scholars), Demosthenes was a hero, one man who stood resolutely alone against the oppression of Philip II and Alexander, and so is worthy to be seen as Athens' – indeed Greece's – staunchest patriot. He was right to see the danger of Philip from the outset; blame for Athens' demise (as Clemenceau would argue) rests squarely on the shoulders of the Athenian people, not on those of Demosthenes.[12] If the Athenians had listened to Demosthenes in the first place, then Athenian, and Greek, history would have been very different! Demosthenes did make mistakes, but he can be forgiven in light of his high moral stand against Macedon.

Although Demosthenes' heroic status has been rightly questioned in recent years, especially by Cawkwell[13] and Ellis,[14] he is still often viewed as a great, even *the* great, example of a patriot. Yet, at least until the mid 340s, Demosthenes may well have been nothing more than a political opportunist, operating at the expense of his country's best interests for his own political advancement. Philip was his stepping-stone to political ascendancy, not some greater ideal of his country's freedom. The purpose of this book is to evaluate Demosthenes' political and oratorical career from a variety of viewpoints, and to try to decide what sort of man he was: patriot or opportunist, or both.

Thus, Badian traces Demosthenes' earlier political career down to 351 (Chapter 1, 'The road to prominence'). He argues that an ambitious Demosthenes used his earlier public court cases not only to take revenge on the enemies of his youth but also to lay the foundations of his career as a political speaker. When his first political speeches (including *Philippic* 1) were unsuccessful, Demosthenes, with no basic policy of his own and no assessment of political and strategic priorities, says Badian, changed his policy to one of activism. It was only the attack on Olynthus, a year or two later, that showed him where his future lay; hence the exploitation of the threat from Philip. Ryder (Chapter 2, 'Demosthenes and Philip II') examines Demosthenes' relations with Philip II and the validity of Demosthenes' anti-Macedonian policy during that king's reign. He portrays a cynical yet politically astute Demosthenes, whose ability to switch policy is especially seen in the events surrounding the Peace of Philocrates and whose exploitation of scare tactic rhetoric was meant not only to excite public alarm but also to give him the edge over rival leaders. The validity of Demosthenes' anti-Macedonian policy during the reign of Alexander is the basis of Worthington's discussion (Chapter 3, 'Demosthenes' (in)activity during the reign of Alexander the Great'). He argues that De-mosthenes pursued a more subtle and successful diplomatic policy, and that by the 330s Demosthenes, unlike Aeschines, had recognized that opposition to Macedon was fruitless. This is one reason why we have no political speeches by Demosthenes in this period, although Alexander's absence from Greece also muzzled him. While Demosthenes thus far has been treated in the context of various chronological periods conforming to the earlier, middle and later years of his career, Buckler rises to the challenge of discussing Demosthenes' relations with his great rival Aeschines, which spanned most of the reigns of Philip and Alexander (Chapter 4, 'Demosthenes and Aeschines'). By analysing their differing policies to Macedon by close analysis of the speeches from the False Embassy and Crown trials, he argues that although personal enmity did keep these two powerful individuals at loggerheads with each other, what really divided them was not so much their own personal differences but their view of Philip's real aims.

The speeches of the orators are an invaluable contemporary source for social history and those of Demosthenes are no exception. How can our understanding of Athenian social life help us read Demosthenes? How can our reading of Demosthenes enrich our perceptions of Athenian society? Golden asks and addresses these questions in his chapter (Chapter 5, 'Demosthenes and the social historian'). He questions one of the normal strategies in using oratory as evidence for Athenian social history, the argument from plausibility. He suggests that it is less than safe to assume that juries or other audiences accepted the likelihood of what speakers said and that orators' statements were at least not absurd, and demonstrates this dictum through a discussion of Demosthenes' presentation of one aspect of Athenian society, the world of the gymnasium. The specific information which Demosthenes gives is less reliable than how he presents it or the fact that he thinks something is worth mentioning in the first place.

As has been said, Demosthenes was a *logographos* by trade, and his oratory is amongst the finest to have survived from ancient Greece. His third *Philippic* (9) of 341 and his speech *On The Crown* (18) of 330 are probably the greatest examples of symbouleutic and forensic oratory we have today. Mirhady deals with Demosthenes' forensic speeches (Chapter 6, 'Demosthenes as advocate: the private speeches'); in particular, the five speeches (27–31) which made up Demosthenes' campaign to recover the squandered inheritance left him by his father and the speech against Conon (54). Demosthenes' oratorical mastery is shown not merely by his use of language but even more so, argues Mirhady, by his mastery of the technical aspects of law, and how he was able to exploit and integrate into his speeches the various forms of documentary evidence such as laws, witness testimony, contracts and challenges. In his discussion of Demosthenes' political speeches, Milns also waxes lyrical about Demosthenes' style and artistry (Chapter 7, 'The public speeches of Demosthenes'). He traces developments in Demosthenes' style from his earlier non-Philippic public speeches to what he calls the 'mature' ones, and argues that such developments were due not only to the natural development of Demosthenes as an orator but also to the increasing threat from Philip as his expansion brought him closer to Athens.

After two laudatory chapters on Demosthenes' rhetorical style, Cooper brings us sharply down to earth with a discussion of Demosthenes' reputation as an orator in antiquity (Chapter 8, 'Philosophers, politics, academics: Demosthenes' rhetorical reputation in antiquity'). While later rhetoricians, especially of the late republic and early imperial period, regarded Demosthenes as the 'consummate orator', his reputation in Hellenistic times (but presumably not in his own time) was (surprisingly) far from complimentary. Cooper argues that philosophers, especially the Peripatetics, equated Demosthenes' political dishonesty with dishonesty in his oratory and delivery, and that this contributed to criticism of his style. It was only when rhetoricians, not philosophers, properly studied Demosthenes' works that his great oratorical reputation was established.

Demosthenes' reputation as an orator and statesman and its exploitation throughout the centuries and into our own era are the

Herculean tasks which Harding faces in his chapter which concludes the book (Chapter 9, 'Demosthenes in the underworld: a chapter in the *Nachleben* of a *rhētōr*'. In the case of Demosthenes the orator, he traces the pendulum of Demosthenes' popularity from Roman times and (as seen in the edition of texts and translations of his speeches) especially in the fourteenth to sixteenth centuries, to a decrease in the seventeenth century, to a renewed interest in the eighteenth century, and then to another slump in the twentieth century. Demosthenes the statesman enjoys similar pendulum swings: he was immensely popular in Elizabethan England as he was in England in the late Victorian era and the early twentieth century, for example, but nowadays not so. 'Why not?' asks Harding. Could it be, he suggests, that his unpopularity reflects our own feelings about the politicians of our day?

The majority of the chapters in the book necessarily use the historical and social information in Demosthenes' (and other orators') speeches, and in doing so raise the problem of the historical veracity of speeches. There is no such thing as an objective presentation of information in oratory, since we are dealing with rhetoric; when dealing with past and even contemporary history in speeches, facts, persons and events were exploited and manipulated in order to persuade the audience, all causing us to doubt the accuracy of the historical information found in the Greek orators.[15] Demosthenes is no exception. Another problem concerning the historical veracity of Greek oratory is that speeches were revised after oral delivery. It does not follow that information now present in speeches was orally delivered; with the outcome of an assembly debate or of a trial not hanging in the balance, the orator was not bound to use material as he might have done in the oral version of a speech. These issues are necessarily addressed by Buckler (Chapter 4) – in particular in his appendix, where his treatment of Demosthenes' and Aeschines' speeches from the trials of 343 and 330 is masterful – Golden (Chapter 5) and, to a somewhat less extent, Milns (Chapter 7).

In a book such as this, some overlap of material and the use of descriptive passages to introduce discussion are unavoidable, especially in the case of the political chapters – for example, the discussions of Badian (Chapter 1), Ryder (Chapter 2) and Milns (Chapter 7) on *Philippic* 1, or of Ryder (Chapter 2) and Buckler (Chapter 4) on the events leading up to the Peace of Philocrates of 346 and the Peace itself, or of Worthington (Chapter 3) and Buckler (Chapter 4) on Demosthenes' activities during Alexander's reign.

However, overlap plays an important role in this book and in consideration of Demosthenes' career. While the complexities of the Sacred War, for example, need to be described, as Buckler properly insists, so that we can understand what Demosthenes and Aeschines were arguing about, Buckler and Ryder have different views on several key points. So do Badian and Ryder to some extent on Demosthenes' first *Philippic*. As such, their discussions ably illustrate an important point: in any study of Demosthenes and his time, there is no single approach and no consensus of opinion. Nor, given the complexity of Athenian political life and the 'wild card' in Athenian politics of personal animosity on top of ideological opposition, can there ever be.

NOTES

1 On the date of Demosthenes' birth, see J.K. Davies, *Athenian Propertied Families* (Oxford: 1971), pp. 121–2; cf. Badian, Chapter 1.

2 The subtitle of R. Sealey's *Demosthenes and his Time* (Oxford: 1993) is *A Study in Defeat*, but this is unfairly exaggerating the impact of Demosthenes' policies and of Demosthenes himself.

3 Plut. *Dem.* 30, [Plut.] *Mor.* 550f.

4 See in detail Diod. 18.8.3–6, 56, 65, Plut. *Dem.* 28–30, *Phocion* 29, 33; on the historical background (the 'Lamian War') see Ian Worthington, *Greek Orators* 2: *Dinarchus and Hyperides* (Warminster: 1999), pp. 12–16.

5 On Demetrius see, for example, W.S. Ferguson, *Hellenistic Athens* (London: 1911), pp. 38–94, and C. Mossé, *Athens in Decline* (transl. J. Sewart, London: 1973), pp. 104–8.

6 On Poliorcetes cf. Ferguson, *Hellenistic Athens*, pp. 95–124, and Mossé, *Athens in Decline*, pp. 108–13.

7 On the background, cf. Ferguson, *Hellenistic Athens*, pp. 124–50, and Mossé, *Athens in Decline*, pp. 113–14 and 120–4.

8 Mossé, *Athens in Decline*, p. 125.

9 A.W. Pickard-Cambridge, *Demosthenes and the Last Days of Greek Freedom* (London: 1914).

10 G. Clemenceau, *Démosthènes* (Paris: 1926).

11 P. Cloché, *Démosthène et la fin de la démocratie athénienne* (Paris: 1957).

12 Clemenceau, *Démosthènes*, p. 10.

13 G.L. Cawkwell, 'Demosthenes' Policy after the Peace of Philocrates I and II', CQ^2 13 (1963), pp. 120–38 and 200–13, 'The Crowning of Demosthenes', CQ^2 19 (1969), pp. 163–80 and *Philip of Macedon* (London: 1978).

14 J.R. Ellis, *Philip II and Macedonian Imperialism* (London: 1976), who even criticises Demosthenes' diplomatic coup with the Athenian–Theban alliance of 339 (pp. 191–3).

15 See further Ian Worthington, 'Greek Oratory, Revision of Speeches and the Problem of Historical Reliability', *C&M* 42 (1991), pp.

55–74 and 'History and Oratorical Exploitation' in Ian Worthington (ed.), *Persuasion: Greek Rhetoric In Action* (London: 1994), pp. 109–29 and M. Nouhaud, *L'Utilisation de L'Histoire par les Orateurs Attiques* (Paris: 1982).

1

THE ROAD TO
PROMINENCE*

E. Badian

1 Introduction

It is unfortunately impossible to do really satisfactory historical work on Demosthenes, as on many other topics in Greek and Roman history. At first sight, the evidence looks extraordinarily promising: a large corpus of speeches, more than sixty actual documents of his time; speeches and fragments by other orators, and biographies (including a long one by Plutarch and a short one in the pseudo-Plutarchean *Lives of the Ten Orators*); plus a body of inscriptions that, although less striking than those from fifth-century Athens, is at least technically less controverted and therefore more usable. To those accustomed to the wastes through which ancient history often has to journey, it might seem a Garden of Eden. But although up to a point this is true, there are certainly snakes about. We cannot charm them away, but must honestly confront them.

First, the text. This will no doubt be discussed by other contributors to this volume,[1] since it is basic for any historical interpretation. But we must at once note that there is no satisfactory modern text. The numerous papyrus fragments are available, but they are not much help: Demosthenes was a 'classic' studied in the schools of Hellenistic and Roman Egypt,[2] and the papyri were often (perhaps usually) produced within this process and cannot necessarily be assigned any scholarly authority. Alexandrian scholars seem to have been much more interested in editing the texts of poets than of prose writers: they normally went no further than to produce lists of what they considered authentic and what they rejected. And the manuscripts have, on the whole, not been sorted or even read since the nineteenth century: our texts, and the supposed lines of descent of the manuscripts, are based on what, in the case of other authors, have turned out to be the very inadequate readings and methods of even the best-known nineteenth-century scholars – or their anonymous students. Characteristically, the Teubner text of 1–19 dates from 1914, the Oxford text of the same speeches from 1903 (the later OCT volumes at least reach the 1930s). The Budé series, as usual of varying quality, did no original work on the texts and had completed the speeches by the 1950s. A promising Italian edition by Canfora, who had done much work on Demosthenes, never got beyond Volume 1 (1–17: 1974) and has slender textual annotation. That there was no canonical edition even in antiquity is shown by the fact that some of the speeches have reached us in two versions, one including passages omitted in the other.

This brings us to authenticity.[3] Again, this is not the place for a full discussion, but I shall set up an arbitrary distinction between 'genuine' and 'authentic': I intend to use the former term for what seems to be actually written by Demosthenes, the latter for what he actually said in his speeches. It will be obvious that a great deal of conjecture must enter into judgements in this area.

On genuineness there is a good deal of agreement. Thus, the 'Letter of Philip' (12) does not even pretend to be Demosthenic, and the reply that precedes it in the manuscripts (11) is not nowadays regarded as genuine. Nor is the 'Apollodorus archive', not even directly relevant to Demosthenes, except that he at one time got involved in one of the cases (on both sides, as his enemies asserted).

Some cases saw ancient scholars divided. Thus 7 (*On Halonnesus*) was accepted by Dionysius of Halicarnassus, but rejected by others. Libanius thought it was written by Hegesippus, and he is now generally followed. In antiquity 17 was widely rejected and is universally rejected now. Here, there is on the whole a modern consensus; 10 (what we call the 'fourth *Philippic*') was rejected by some ancient critics, including (it seems) Dionysius, who does not list it. Others thought it genuine: Didymus (for what that is worth: he is not a great scholar or always trustworthy) had no doubt of its genuineness. When his commentary on that speech appeared on a papyrus in 1904 (a year after Butcher had bracketed it in his OCT), many scholars were converted.[4] That speech and its relation to 8 (*On the Chersonese*) do not concern us in this chapter. But it had to be mentioned because the question of authenticity (if not genuineness) hinges on passages common to the two speeches, and it must be stated in connection with this most discussed instance that the repetition of genuine Demosthenic passages in authentic speeches (as far as we can tell) can readily be paralleled in the period here discussed.[5] We shall mention some disputed cases in this period as we come to them.

A century ago the great German scholar Blass discovered an important technical criterion, called after him 'Blass's law': Demosthenes tends to avoid sequences of three short syllables. There is no other fourth-century orator who does this to the same extent, whereas avoidance of hiatus was common at that period. (In fact, it is more marked in some others than in Demosthenes.) Blass himself used his law rather arbitrarily, accepting as genuine some speeches that contravened it but that could conveniently be written off as 'early'. We shall see that this is not acceptable. However, the law is useful only as a negative criterion. It cannot be used as a positive one, since we simply lack evidence on oratory after the fourth century until well into the Roman Empire (when we find Aelius Aristides following this law). According to George A. Kennedy[6] political oratory had little scope after the fourth century and judicial speeches 'ceased to attract the effort of first-rate minds'. This is the well-known argument writing off periods from which no evidence has survived as 'dark ages'. In fact, any reader of Polybius will know that political speeches were plentiful, and Kennedy himself admits that 'the educational system remained focused on rhetoric'. We must admit that we cannot tell whether Blass's law or any other particular stylistic practice was followed during these centuries.

A more recent work submitted as a Harvard dissertation by Donald F. McCabe[7] found that Blass's sorting of the corpus into speeches that did and did not follow his law was on the whole correct. McCabe added other criteria, which usually lead to the same conclusion, and used up-to-date computer technology and statistical method. His results are set out in a series of tables, which also (unlike Blass) take full account of variations in the manuscripts and different ways of interpreting short syllables and hiatus. He adds a comparison with the works of Isaeus.[8] I shall use his results as the basis for discussion of genuineness (though they are of course irrelevant to authenticity as here defined).

As for chronology, Sealey, in a careful survey,[9] proved that Dionysius' dates seem to be reliable wherever we can check them. (He found two exceptions, explained by special problems.) I shall therefore follow Dionysius' dates in *To Ammaeus* 1 for the speeches he lists. The first *Philippic* (4) will need special discussion.

2 Background and family

Demosthenes was the homonymous son of a citizen of the deme Paiania, one of the larger up-country demes. By his father's time the family undoubtedly had property in the city. The elder Demosthenes was well off. His chief income was derived from a weapons factory, hence he is called 'the sword-maker'. We are so wretchedly informed about Athenian genealogy, even in this fairly well documented period, that a good deal of conjecture must enter into any discussion of his family. I argued long ago[10] that a link can conjecturally be established among all the known bearers of Dem(o)- names in Paiania, down to the period of the elder Demosthenes. The reconstruction is complex, but I still think it highly probable, especially as it was later independently reinforced by Mackendrick, who did not know my work, with persuasive arguments.[11] As we both concluded, the family is probably ultimately linked with the Bouzygae, one of the most aristocratic of old priestly clans. Since (I repeat) the state of our knowledge of even leading Athenian families is a thing of shreds and patches, the argument necessarily depends on some conjecture, but no more than is generally accepted under pressure of necessity in most of ancient history. In the years since I first advanced the argument, I have seen no epigraphic find or scholarly argument that has disproved it.[12] Theopompus − not one to flatter demagogues, or Demosthenes in particular − is cited by Plutarch (*Dem.* 4.1) as paying tribute to his origins. The passage is worth quoting, as a document on fourth-century Athenian social attitudes:

> Demosthenes, the father of Demosthenes, was of the class of gentlemen (τῶν καλῶν καὶ ἀγαθῶν ἀνδρῶν) as Theopompus reports, but had the nickname of 'the sword-maker', since he had a large factory and slave workmen engaged in that trade. [Note the 'but'.]

Demosthenes' best-known sneer at Aeschines confirms both the statement and the average Athenian's attitude to those who had to work for a living. After a perfunctory excuse for having to say it (which he did not), the orator continues (18.256–65) by contrasting his upbringing with Aeschines' youthful activities. He sums it up (265) in a great climax:

> You were a teacher [obviously an occupation very low in social rank!], I was attending school; you were a servant at

> initiations, I was being initiated; you were a public secre-
> tary [a surprising revelation of prejudice in the democracy],
> I was addressing the Assembly; you were a bit-actor, I was a
> spectator; you were hissed off the stage, I was hissing.

No one not socially fully secure could have ventured to speak like
that. Theopompus' account (and to some extent our conjecture
about the family) can be regarded as confirmed.

Like some other aristocratic families, this one is not known to
have been politically very active. The elder Demosthenes had
amassed a tidy fortune (15 talents at his death, so Plutarch, *Dem.*
4.3, reports, perhaps from Demosthenes 27.4). It has been plausibly
suggested that he kept it 'invisible' (ἀφανής: a technical term for
'hidden from the tax collectors') as best he could. At any rate, we
know very little about any real estate, surprisingly for a gentleman.
This must account for part of the trouble Demosthenes later had in
convicting his guardians: it seems to have been difficult to get any
solid records, and the details of Demosthenes' estate are a favourite
topic of discussion among scholars.

The orator's mother was a foreign woman's daughter and there
was something shady about her Athenian father Gylon: Aeschines
3.171–2 says he was in charge of an Athenian garrison on the coast
of the Crimea, which he betrayed; he then went back there into
exile and married a very rich Scythian woman. There is certainly
some truth in this. Demosthenes himself admits that his maternal
grandfather was at one time a state debtor:[13] presumably, therefore,
heavily fined in court. (He does not say how his grandfather ceased
to be a state debtor, as he obviously did, but his wife's dowry may
well have helped.) On the other hand, Aeschines' invective,
describing Demosthenes as not a real citizen, finds no support in
the record. Even Aeschines never prosecuted him for this. His
grandparents' marriage must have taken place at the time during
the Peloponnesian War when Pericles' law on citizenship was
suspended, and before it was reinstated in 403/2 (Dem. 57.30), so
that his mother counted as a citizen.

His father never had any trouble under the Thirty; yet Aeschines,
whose own father had to go into exile, never charges him with
having been a collaborator. The family must have been unmolested
because poor. This was no doubt the time when Gylon was still in
exile as an undischarged state debtor. He must have come home
after the restoration of democracy, with plenty of money and the
legitimate wife to whom he owed it. Yet his reputation was

obviously not unimpaired, and he had two daughters to place. What more obvious than to find an impoverished aristocrat who would confer status in return for wealth? This is surely a constant motive in the history of upper-class marriage.[14] The elder Demosthenes' background begins to emerge: both old aristocrat and *nouveau riche*, and avoiding the tax collectors by careful investment and by keeping out of the political limelight.

To conclude this section, a few words on the family connections that seem to exist between Demosthenes and Aeschines. This will be a useful introduction to what may be developed by other contributors to this volume.

To start with the most obvious: the man who, in the absence of closer relatives (for Aphobus and his circle would obviously not do it), sponsored the young Demosthenes for admission to his deme was a local squire called Philodemus. He must have been at least a distant relative of Demosthenes in order to act in this capacity. He later became the father-in-law of Aeschines (Aes. 2.150–2). Next, Aeschines' father bears the almost unique name Atrometus ('Undaunted'); Aeschines' younger brother is called Aphobetus ('Fearless'), a name unique down to this time. Demosthenes' wicked relative, of course, is called Aphobus (also 'Fearless'), a unique name down to this time and for centuries after. Unfortunately we do not know the name of that man's father who married the elder Demosthenes' sister. The son's name permits a guess as to what family he came from, in view of the accumulation of these unique names; but there is no proof.

Aeschines' mother's brother, one Cleobulus, fought under the general Demaenetus the Bouzyges in a successful naval battle (Aes. 2.78): presumably he was not a colleague (for Aeschines would have mentioned that honour) but a trierarch. Demaenetus should be Demaenetus of Paeania, related to Demosthenes' family: the name is extremely rare before about 390. The name Cleobulus is one of two, or at the most three, instances known before the middle of the fourth century. Now, Demosthenes' mother is called Cleobule – almost unique as a woman's name down to the early fourth century, the period of her birth. (There may be one other instance on a tombstone.) The demes of Demosthenes' mother and Aeschines' uncle are different; but women normally do not marry within their own deme: the extremely rare names are worth noting.[15]

Nothing quite certain emerges, but the facts must be observed, and they are too striking and too numerous to be entirely due to chance. Needless to say, relatives need not always be on good terms

– as is clear from many cases in the Demosthenic corpus and in Isaeus, not to mention their modern equivalents. But Demosthenes and Aeschines seem in fact to have been politically allied when the famous embassy set them at loggerheads.

3 The first steps

Demosthenes was born in or near 384 BC: ancient methods of reckoning in such cases make it impossible to calculate ages within a year, unless there is decisive evidence, and there is really none in this case. (Dionysius, a careful chronologer, miscalculated.) As we know, his father died when he was seven or so, after trying conscientiously to provide for his wife and children. Unfortunately he trusted the wrong men, merely (it seems) because they were relatives by marriage. Aphobus seized the property but refused to maintain the widow (Dem. 27.15), let alone look after the integrity of the estate. Taxes were lavishly paid, for obvious reasons: it avoided official scrutiny of what was going on, or offers of *antidosis* (exchange of properties), a provision always hanging over wealthy Athenians and meant to keep them honest as far as the state was concerned. It was perhaps not noticed (or it might be indifferent to the city) that it would encourage dishonest administrators of estates to pay as much as possible in taxes and impositions in order to avoid a challenge. All the time Demosthenes' estate was shrinking and there was no legal means of forcing an audit. By the time the remnant was handed over to the young man, he claims it amounted to about seventy minae in value: not much over one talent (27.4). That, as we have seen, was a startling loss when compared with what it was claimed to have been when the father died. Plutarch found the statement that as a boy Demosthenes was so delicate that his mother would not let him attend the gymnasium, as a boy of his class should have (*Dem.* 4.4–5). Expense must have played a part. But it is clear from what Demosthenes himself said, in the famous passage quoted above, that he must have attended the proper school at least at some time in his boyhood, even if his mother could not keep him there as the estate diminished. He must also have had private tutoring: he asserts that his teachers were sometimes cheated of their pay (27.46).

He was old enough to appreciate the momentous political revolution that followed Leuctra, when Thebes became the chief enemy and Sparta an Athenian ally, while new minor powers transformed the traditional bipolarity of Greek alignments. He was almost of ephebic age at the time of the Greek envoys' trek to Susa and the king's half-hearted intervention on the Theban side against Athens. In 366 (probably) he was admitted to his deme as a full citizen. It was perhaps before he embarked on his ephebic training that he began to prepare himself seriously for a career as an orator, and the training continued after it. The long account we have in Plutarch is plainly encrusted with legend. The famous story of how he took pebbles into his mouth in order to overcome a speech handicap is better attested than other anecdotes: Plutarch (*Dem.* 11.1) ascribes it and one or two others to Demetrius of Phalerum, who claimed to have heard about them from Demosthenes himself; he was certainly old enough to have known Demosthenes.[16] But it may be relevant to note that Demetrius thought little of Demosthenes' speeches: Plutarch at once informs us that he thought them 'vulgar, ignoble and feeble'.[17] He may not be an entirely reliable source. Whatever the truth about individual stories, we may accept Demosthenes' serious and hard work during these years of training. His immediate aim must have been a firm determination to get his property back, for without success in this it was unlikely that he would be able to follow the kind of career he had in mind. We shall see that he never lost his resentment against those who had deprived him of what was his due.

As soon as his ephebic service was over, he launched the prosecution of Aphobus, the principal villain in his personal misfortunes (364/3). He at once had to contend with his opponent's superior knowledge of the intricacies of Athenian law and with his prominent and powerful connections. Both Aphobus' brother-in-law Onetor, whom Demosthenes was forced to sue as well (30–1, probably 362/1: see 30.33) and their powerful friend Thrasylochus, brother of Meidias, intervened with various subterfuges. Thrasylochus had been 'bribed' (so Demosthenes asserts, but does not say how) to hit him with an offer of *antidosis*, which Demosthenes (foolishly, as it turned out) accepted, apparently not quite aware of the fact that this turned the case against Aphobus over to Thrasylochus, who would let it lapse. His later attempts to explain his naïvety are unconvincing. In the end he managed to escape from the trap he had set for himself by cancelling his acceptance, at considerable cost to himself. (He had to assume an expensive trierarchy, which he could do only by taking up unsecured loans, no doubt at exorbitant interest.)

Whether the speeches against Aphobus and Onetor (27–31) are genuine has long been debated. In antiquity, some ascribed them to

Isaeus, who was one of those most consistently regarded as Demosthenes' teachers.[18] McCabe regards 27–8 as doubtful (p. 196, Table 29) and from his research into style, under the headings of clausulae, total rhythm and hiatus, it is clear that they satisfy only the criterion of hiatus (p. 171, Table 28). So do 29–31, according to his Table 27, though 29 and 31 only as adjusted for margin of error. However, all these speeches are far from the values obtained for the average of Isaeus', so the ancient guess that they were written by Isaeus acquires no support.[19] Speech 29 and (to a slightly lesser extent) 31 may be said to agree with Demosthenic practice in all three respects tested by McCabe. Both 29 and 31 are strikingly different from 30, which scores very low in the test for rhythm (McCabe, pp. 158–9). The *prima facie* conclusion, based on scientific stylistic evidence, is that 27 and 28 are not Demosthenes' own work and that 30 is doubtful; whereas 29 and 31 could be regarded as genuinely Demosthenic. It is not at all surprising that the young Demosthenes sought help with those highly important speeches against Aphobus (29, dealing with the evidence of a witness, was much easier to master) and relied on an experienced speech-writer with legal training (though probably not Isaeus). In the first case against Onetor (30), which contains the basic argument, he may at least have sought help, especially since the law concerning *exoulē* was obviously difficult legal territory. Speeches 29 and 31 are probably the first that Demosthenes actually composed himself for delivery in court. The *least* likely explanation is that he changed his own style backward and forward, which would follow if we regard them all as fully genuine.

There are other differences between 27–8 and 29, best summarily pointed out by L. Gernet in his Budé edition.[20] But perhaps the strongest argument against admitting 27–8 as Demosthenic is the difference between his reference to Thrasylochus in 28.17 and his account of the same events and their consequences in the speech against Meidias (21.77ff.). It has often been noted that in 28 he makes no mention of Meidias or of his and Thrasylochus' breaking into the house, which he had locked against Thrasylochus (so 28.17), and of behaving so badly once they were in it that he successfully (up to a point!) prosecuted Meidias for *kakourgia*.[21] He would obviously make more of Meidias' participation in the case against Meidias, but since Meidias was a more important person, the complete omission of his participation is puzzling. It seems that whoever wrote the speech wanted to stick to the barest essentials for the case.

It proved easier for Demosthenes to obtain verdicts than to obtain redress.[22] But it seems that he ultimately got at least part of his inheritance back. In the process he made enough of a name for himself as an orator to embark on a career as a speech-writer. Various speeches in the corpus are judged to belong to this early period, but we cannot pursue them in detail. Once he could afford it, he laid the foundations of a political career by undertaking a trierarchy in Thrace, on his own well-equipped ship, in 360 – a welcome chance to see the Athenian outposts along the lifeline of the wheat imports from Bosporus. The commander of the expedition, Cephisodotus, chose to travel on Demosthenes' ship, probably because he had been a friend of his father's (Aes. 3.51–2). What is more, he seems to have supported Demosthenes for the award of a decoration (a 'trierarchic crown') for the speed and quality of his outfitting of his trireme.[23]

The campaign turned out badly and Cephisodotus was prosecuted. Aeschines (3.51–2) claims that Demosthenes prosecuted his commander (who was fined five talents), but this is probably false, for in his account of the campaign (23.163–8, especially 167) he shows no hostility to Cephisodotus. Sealey suggests that he may have been called as a witness in the case (which would be likely enough, in the circumstances). His evidence, whatever it was, perhaps helped to convict Cephisodotus, even if not intended to be hostile.

4 Public investment – and revenge

During the next few years we do not hear anything about Demosthenes. He seems to have continued to devote himself to the private practice of speech-writing, which turned out to be lucrative. His income from this was invested in voluntary *leitourgiai*, the expensive public services that wealthy Athenians were required to perform at fixed intervals, according to their wealth. While many tried to escape the imposition, or at least to limit it to the legal minimum, any man who aimed at a public career not only willingly performed what was prescribed, but did so with noticeable splendour, as well as, from time to time, volunteering for one of those services out of turn.

In his speech against Meidias Demosthenes lists his own services and contrasts them with Meidias' alleged stinginess in performance (21.153–67). Whatever may be the truth regarding Meidias (orators in Athenian courts were not held to high standards of veracity regarding their opponents), we must believe what Demosthenes says about himself, and it adds up to a distinguished and expensive list, over the span of a very few years. He himself claims that he was chairman of a tax symmory and paying as much as the wealthiest citizens, not (so he says) on the basis of his actual property, but on the basis of what it ought to have been if he had received his inheritance. (In addition he lists several expensive leitourgies, including a *choregia* for a group of male flute-players; and he implies that his *epidosis* of part of a trireme in the Euboean war of 358/7 was on a level superior to Meidias' gift of a whole trireme: 21.160–7).[24] Since these massive contributions were apparently not based on full recovery of his inheritance, we must conclude that his speech-writing secured a massive income for him by the early 350s.

By that time the international scene in Greece had completely changed. After Sparta's defeat at Leuctra she had ceased to be a major power and Thebes had taken her place as the dominant power in Greece. Thebes' bid for hegemony ended with Epaminondas' death at Mantinea (362), which for a few years left Athens as the only major power, with control of the sea through her Confederacy; Thebes, however, remained the strongest power on land and, since Athens had made her into an enemy, an uncomfortable neighbour. Meanwhile in the north, in semi-barbarian Macedon, a new king, Philip II, had come to the throne in 360 (whether at once as king or at first as regent turned out to be immaterial) and, after ridding himself of a pretender supported by Athens by means of a skilful concession, had within a few years shown himself to be incompara-bly different from his predecessors on that throne.[25] The Athenians, deluding themselves as so often, thought they could use him in order to regain Amphipolis – an aim that had been the King Charles's head of their policy for over a decade and had led to some disastrous decisions in the past.[26] In 357 Philip laid siege to Amphipolis. The Athenians refused to accept the offer of the city to turn itself over to them if they would protect it (Dem. 1.8). Demosthenes later pretended to think that they ought to have accepted. In fact, they would have been ill-advised to undertake to fight Philip in the hope that Amphipolis, which had resisted their attempts to take it for so many years, would keep its end of the bargain.

Instead, some Athenians, inspired by this offer, tried to invert the diplomatic picture: perhaps Philip could be persuaded to hand the city over to them after taking it (as he presumably would), in return for Pydna. Philip encouraged the notion: orators could later refer to a letter of Philip in which he wrote of 'restoring' Amphipolis to Athens ([Dem.] 7.27) and speak of the offer as generally known (Dem. 2.6, 23.116). It seems that the negotiations were initiated by some Athenians (probably the Boule), who sent envoys to Philip to propose the exchange. The letter referred to was presumably Philip's reply, brought back to the Boule by the envoys. As has often been pointed out, there was no binding treaty: that could not have been done without a vote in the Assembly, and we are told (very plausibly) that the Boule negotiated in secret; for the Pydnaeans could not be allowed to hear of the whole affair. It was known as ποτ' ἀπόρρητον (a secret at one time not to be revealed, like the Mysteries) by 349, by which time everyone was talking about it, now that it was used by orators to underline the untrustworthiness of Philip (Dem. 2.6, often mistranslated). In fact, it was one of the more disgraceful incidents in fourth-century Athenian policy, which is not devoid of them.[27] Olynthian interest in a treaty was also rebuffed (Dem. 2.6). The Athenians were obviously now putting their hopes in Philip, and Demosthenes did nothing to dissuade them. One result was that Olynthus allied itself with Philip and Athens lost Potidaea. With Athens distracted by the Social War (see below), Philip also helped himself to Pydna.

For the moment we shall leave high politics and even strict chronological order. I propose to follow a series of public court cases that show Demosthenes seizing opportunities for revenge on the enemies of his youth – and for displaying his proficiency as an orator whom politicians would be ill-advised to ignore.

Androtion, the son of Andron who had been one of the oligarchs who had temporarily overthrown the democracy in 411 and had survived, had himself been in politics since the mid-380s (Dem. 22.66). He served on a Boule at some time before 370.[28] At some time before the Social War (by 358, at any rate) we find him as governor of Arcesine on Amorgos (possibly of Amorgos as a whole), stationed there for two years. He was unusually generous to the inhabitants. The decree in his honour is not a conventional eulogy but gives precise facts.[29]

Earlier, in Athens, he had held some office concerned with ceremonial vessels and with inspecting sacred offerings.[30] In 356 he began a second term on the Boule, in the middle of the Social War. He was clearly shocked by what he saw. As much as 14 talents in property taxes owed had not been collected and during two of the preceding years only nine triremes had been built. (The record of the years just before was little better.) He did his best to improve things. Euctemon, in charge of collecting the tax arrears, was obviously corrupt and seems to have done nothing. Androtion now got the People to dismiss him and to appoint a commission, with Androtion and his friend Timocrates on it, with special powers of search, to collect the arrears. It was moderately successful, collecting half of what was owed: 7 talents.[31] During that year the treasurer in charge of shipbuilding absconded with 2 talents (Dem. 22.17ff.) and the Boule therefore could not build the minimum number of triremes it was by law supposed to. (That all this happened in the middle of a serious war, in which Athens suffered from a shortage of ships, illustrates the moral decline of the Athenian democracy at this time.)

Even though the building of the minimum number of triremes was a precondition for the award of honours (especially a crown) to a Boule, Androtion proposed, and the People voted, the crown for the Boule on which he had served. Presumably he had been chosen to do so because of his reputation for incorruptible patriotism. (That he himself wanted the honour may be taken for granted.) But his tax-collecting activities had made him enemies. Two of them – one Euctemon, whose dismissal he had procured – now (355/4) joined to prosecute Androtion for passing an illegal decree. Demosthenes undertook to write the speech for the second prosecutor. (We do not know who wrote for Euctemon.) The speech, like many Athenian speeches before a jury, is full of personal attacks and attacks on the defendant's policies that were irrelevant to the actual case and most of which were meant to arouse hatred and indignation against him. (We have noted two instances in notes 30 and 31.) But the relevant point was strongly made: that a law prohibited the award of a crown to a Boule that had not fulfilled its shipbuilding requirement, and that this one had not. Demosthenes anticipates various answers to this charge, some of them patently (and intentionally) ridiculous, for example, that the Boule had not requested the honour but that the People had offered it, and that this was not forbidden by the law. The Boule clearly had a good defence for failing to complete its shipbuilding programme, in view of the defalcation of the man in charge of the funds (see above). Whether this was a valid defence in law was for the jury to decide. And it seems that, despite all his arguments, legally valid and purely emotive, his client lost the case. Androtion continued to be active in public life.[32] (Much later, we do not know when, he was indeed exiled and wrote his historical work at Megara.)

Androtion's main argument, as far as we can gather it from Demosthenes, seems to have been that a technical legal point should not be used to override genuine merit and deprive it of the honour due to it (see, for example, 12, 16, 35). It is amusing to reflect that Demosthenes' stand against this argument in his first public speech written for delivery before a jury, to the effect that laws must be strictly enforced in order not to set disastrous precedents (for example, above all, 46: 'remember your oaths and that the point of this charge is … whether the laws should be sovereign'; cf. also 6–7, 18ff.), is precisely the opposite of what, by implication, he argued in his last public speech before a jury, this time delivered by himself. In the case of the crown awarded to him (Demosthenes 18; Aeschines 3), there had obviously been a technical contravention of the law,[33] yet Demosthenes countered the legal case by dilating upon all the services he had done for Athens and the benefits he had bestowed on her. By then, he no doubt had enough experience to know that Athenian juries were given to ignoring the letter of the law for the sake of rewarding merit, and perhaps to see that this had not led to a general collapse of the rule of law in the city.

Some generations ago, scholars accustomed to modern politics tried to find in this speech signs of allegiance to an Athenian party, perhaps that of Eubulus, perhaps more generally that of the wealthy upper class, to which Demosthenes certainly belonged. Schaefer even saw in this speech and the similar ones that followed it a plea for a higher public morality.[34] Blass was more discriminating: he refused to see any Demosthenic programme (which is surely correct) and thought that the speech was written entirely for the client of the moment: 'out of the soul of Androtion's enemy'.[35] In part this is certainly true, and it must apply to all the speeches that Demosthenes wrote for clients to deliver in court. Indeed, it must apply to all speeches written for (or, in our culture, delivered on behalf of) clients in court cases. What Blass did not notice is that Demosthenes, although not propounding a programme, had his own axe to grind. We shall return to this after looking at the next speech of this kind.

Soon after his acquittal, and as a clear signal of the utter defeat of Demosthenes' client, Androtion was sent with two colleagues on a mission to Mausolus, the Carian dynast who had done much to instigate the Social War. Its purpose must have been to try to persuade Mausolus to help in ending it on tolerable terms for Athens.[36] On their way, they came across a ship carrying cargo from Naucratis. Regarding it as an enemy ship, the Athenians seized the cargo. (Whether they completed their mission, and whether the incident occurred on their way out or on their way back, we do not know.) We cannot tell what reasons of law were alleged for this. The situation (for us) is complicated by the fact that Egypt was at this time independent and expecting an attack by King Artaxerxes Ochus, who claimed sovereignty over it and regarded the Egyptians as rebels. If the Athenians considered the King their enemy (he was rumoured to have threatened to intervene in the Social War by attacking Athens, and the rumour was obviously believed by some),[37] they might allege that Egypt was Persian and hence enemy territory; if they were trying to defuse the King's hostility, they might regard the rebellious satrapy as their enemy because it was the King's. In any case, the owners of the cargo failed to secure its return, despite their plea that they were not at war with Athens.[38]

But it proved far from easy for the treasury to secure the proceeds. Late in the same year (354/3) or early in the next, the ambassadors were forced to admit that they still held the cargo seized. They were threatened with imprisonment unless they at once turned it in and paid a heavy fine. Next, Timocrates succeeded in passing a law that state debtors would have until near the end of the year to pay if they could offer sureties; and the wording of the law apparently made it unclear whether the actual fine (a doubling of the sum due to the state) would be remitted.[39]

The two men who had prosecuted Androtion now prosecuted Timocrates for passing an illegal law (the notorious prosecution *para nomon*).[40] Demosthenes again wrote the speech for the second prosecutor. (Euctemon presumably had recourse to the same speech-writer as before.) The speech, as we have it, in fact repeats several passages (some of them quite long) from the earlier one: the first time that this practice of Demosthenes' can be fully documented. The details of the argument do not concern us here, but the outcome was the same: Timocrates was acquitted and continued to be active in politics, and the law remained on the books. Androtion and his colleagues no doubt repaid the sum they owed (whether they had to pay the fine we do not know) before the time limit set.

We owe to Raphael Sealey, who first seriously analysed the structure of fourth-century Athenian politics, the recognition of the fact that Demosthenes had good personal reasons for attacking both Androtion and Timocrates.[41] For one thing, the two men were closely linked as political allies and no doubt friends over a long period. Timocrates had been Androtion's colleague and assistant on both of the commissions we have noted. The law of Timocrates, which Demosthenes attacked, of course benefited Androtion; and Timocrates' son moved a friendly amendment to the decree passed by Androtion on honours for the Bosporan dynasts. Timocrates himself had played a prominent part in the manoeuvres aimed at depriving Demosthenes of what was adjudged to him in his cases against his guardians; at the time, Demosthenes also alleged that he had joined Onetor in suborning false witnesses against him. Years later, both Timocrates and his son were among the supporters of Meidias, Demosthenes' personal enemy.[42]

It is also easy to show what we have already remarked: that Demosthenes did not take the cases in order to enunciate some moral or political principle. In fact, on an important point the two speeches contradict each other. In 22, he pleads for leniency for public debtors and calls strict enforcement 'oligarchical' (22.47–58): he paints a heart-rending picture of the rich tax-evader climbing over his roof to get away or hiding under his bed to escape Androtion's inquisition (53). In 24, a law that offers a measure of leniency to public debtors is attacked (24.190–3 *et al.*) as being dangerous to democracy. Demosthenes clearly seized a chance to attack men linked to a circle of his enemies and get his revenge for what one of them had done to him in his youth. Why did he keep a written copy of the speeches, which later secured entry into the collection of his works? Why preserve a record of two of his failures? I must suggest that he at once circulated carefully revised copies of these speeches (whatever theory we hold about final publication, some speeches were undoubtedly circulated by Demosthenes himself), both to demonstrate his mastery of the genre and to warn his enemies that they could not hope to escape unscathed if they challenged him. These counter-attacks had been unsuccessful. But no Athenian politician would lightly risk prosecution by a brilliant speaker, even if that speaker had lost some of his cases. That such personal feuds had serious political consequences must be left for later chapters to argue.[43]

A different instance of personal involvement appears in the speech against Aristocrates (352/1), delivered when Demosthenes was already known as a young politician. It too was written for a client, but this time one connected with Demosthenes: Euthycles had taken part in Cephisodotus' expedition, when the commander had travelled on Demosthenes' trireme, and we may conjecture that he was to some extent Demosthenes' mouthpiece.[44] The speech was an attack not so much on Aristocrates, who is a mere lay figure in it, as on Charidemus of Oreos, a condottiere who had served various masters (he had even fought against Athenians) and whose activities had been chiefly responsible for Cephisodotus' failure. At this early stage of his career, he had to find paymasters for his troops, and this involved changes of allegiance.[45] But he had finally chosen Athens, been made a citizen and rewarded with a crown, and he would in due course transform Athenian activities in the area he knew best, Thrace and Chersonese. He was to become the architect of the policy that established garrisons of Athenian mercenaries in the area of Thrace and the Hellespont, to shore up the weak kingdom of Cersebleptes against Philip. Aeschines was later to say that he did so without informing the Assembly, or at least that the Assembly never understood what was going on. It certainly seems that the People gave him considerable freedom to pursue his policy in the area, probably in conjunction with Chares, and that the policy succeeded in its aim until Athenian morale collapsed (not without Demosthenes' assistance) on the eve of the Peace of Philocrates.[46] Demosthenes, of course, could not yet know all this; and in any case, Aristocrates' decree went much too far in the special protection it proposed to give Charidemus: that anyone who killed him should be liable to extradition for trial in Athens from any of the cities allied with Athens in the Confederacy, and that any individual or city protecting such a man should without further ado be regarded as an enemy of Athens. Demosthenes has no difficulty in pointing out that the decree is badly drafted and that it contradicts several Athenian laws, hence should be aborted as being *para nomōn*.[47] We do not know whether the decree was in fact passed or given up (it had been passed by the Boule but the People had not yet voted on it): since no one killed Charidemus while he was in Athens' service, there is no way of deciding. Verdicts in such cases were usually political rather than based on legal grounds, but in this case what we know of the political climate and of Charidemus' services to Athens up to this point did not justify the extravagance of the proposal. There is a good chance that Demosthenes got his limited revenge on the man who had caused his commander and paternal friend to suffer disaster.

Nor do we know whether these were the only court cases concerning prominent citizens in which Demosthenes participated as a speech-writer during the 350s. As suggested above, these were the speeches that Demosthenes put into circulation in fully written-up manuscript form because they communicated a message, both about his skill as an orator and about the danger of making him into an enemy. All we can say is that no manuscript of any other case of this kind was preserved. Perhaps he did not bother to preserve any others (if they existed) because they were of no personal importance to him.

5 The young man in search of a cause

As I noted near the beginning of the last section, we have abandoned chronological order for the sake of coherently treating one major aspect of Demosthenes' early career. At the same time as he was staking his ground as an orator and warning potential enemies, he was laying the foundations of a career as a political speaker, to which those speeches were meant to provide a background. The first of his political speeches was in fact the first time he appeared in person before a public jury. It concerned the law of Leptines. And here we must say a little more about the Social War, which we have already noticed as background to other speeches.

The Athenians had never quite got over the loss of their fifth-century empire in the Peloponnesian War.[48] Futile attempts to regain it were terminated by the King's Peace of 387/6. But when all might seem lost, Sparta's (and in particular Agesilaus') arrogance in ignoring the provisions of the Peace and setting up her own interest as the only justification for her actions caused such resentment that Athens could seize the chance of forming a new confederacy while claiming to be the true guardian of the Peace against Sparta. The new confederacy had to be very different from the old empire. The 'autonomy' of the allies was fully guaranteed; a council of the allies, sitting in Athens, had nominally equal powers with the Athenian Boule and, to some extent, the Athenian People and, among other rights, apparently decided on the 'contributions' (which replaced the hated 'tribute' (*phoros*) of the fifth-century empire) to which allies were to be liable.

We cannot follow the ups and downs of the confederacy over the next twenty years. One main problem was that it was difficult for the Athenians to collect enough money for major naval operations without breaking the compact. After keeping at least within the letter of it for a long time, they gradually began to encroach on allied autonomy. This had at times led to rebellion by various allies, most important of them Byzantium, which had been persuaded to leave the alliance when Epaminondas appeared in the Aegean with a new Theban fleet in 364 (Diod. 15.79.1). It continued to follow a course hostile to Athens even when it turned out that nothing further would be heard of the Theban fleet, and indeed when the

Theban bid for hegemony was collapsing.[49] The expulsion of some Samians from their homes and the establishment of an Athenian settlement there (which was finally to lead to the total expulsion of the inhabitants and the annexation of Samos as an Athenian cleruchy) was not contrary to the terms of the confederacy, since Samos had never been a member. But it must have produced a powerful effect on the neighbouring islands. Some time in the early 350s, as we saw, an Athenian governor is found on Amorgos: that he was a model of generous behaviour was legally irrelevant. The allies' fears were aggravated by some irresponsible actions by Chares, apparently endorsed by the People at Athens. The allies had come to fear that Athens was 'plotting against them' (Dem. 15.3), as Demosthenes had to admit.[50]

In 357, the major allies of Chios and Rhodes, joined by Byzantium and Cos (which may have been a member of the original confederacy),[51] obtained promises of support from the satrap of Caria, Mausolus, and decided to rebel.

As we have seen, this came at a low point in Athenian finance and public ethics. At the battle of Embata (355) the three Athenian commanders fatally quarrelled among themselves over whether to join battle. It is clear that Athens no longer had enough triremes to face a relatively small muster of allied forces. The result was a defeat that forced Athens to make peace and recognize the independence of the major allies.[52] The rump of the confederacy continued: it was only dissolved by Philip II after Chaeronea. But the collection of mostly small cities remaining conferred prestige rather than power, and the Athenians increasingly ignored them in the formulation of policy.

As we noted, this was the war that provided the context of Androtion's attempt to collect unpaid property taxes: well-meant, but obviously not sufficiently productive to influence the outcome of the war. Another measure belongs to the same context, and it provided Demosthenes with the first opportunity to appear before the members of a jury in a public case.

In the same year that witnessed Androtion's efforts, one Leptines succeeded in passing a law that would cancel all exemptions from civil leiturgies and forbid the practice of conferring such exemptions for the future. The law was at once attacked as being *para nomon*. But one of the prosecutors died before the case came to trial, so others had to take over. By the time of the trial over a year had passed: Leptines himself could no longer be prosecuted, only the actual law that was by now on the books. Demosthenes' speech (20) was the first speech he chose to deliver himself on a matter of political importance (Dion. Hal. *To Ammaeus* 1.4). By then the emergency of the war was over, and although Athenian finances were in a shocking state and the prospects had been made worse by the effects of the defeat, the chance of removing the law from the books was presumably better than when it was first attacked. But the law was defended by one of the leading politicians, Aristophon (who in fact had been granted such an immunity and, in spite of Demosthenes' attempt to confuse the jury (20.148), must have offered to give it up) and by other eminent orators. If Demosthenes is telling the truth (which in this case is likely since the jury would be aware of the facts), Leptines had failed to follow the procedure laid down for passing new laws. He also tries to show that it would be unjust to cancel benefits conferred on benefactors in the past and that, while producing little new income for the city, it would discourage others from becoming public benefactors in future.[53] He produces a long list of benefactors who would be thus unjustly penalised (he makes much of the fact that they include Leucon and his sons, the dynasts of Bosporus who had given Athens privileged access to their immense harvests of wheat: 20.30–40) and finally joins in proposing a law that would merely mandate a scrutiny of those awarded such exemptions and weed out any who appeared not to have deserved them.

Demosthenes starts by telling the jury that he has taken the case partly out of sympathy for the son of Chabrias (20.1), and Chabrias' exploits and their rewards are later detailed at great length (20.75–87).[54] One of his reasons for participating in this case must have been to attract the favour of the numerous eminent men (and their descendants) whom the law would have saddled with burdensome leiturgies. They would make useful political allies. We do not know whether the attack on the law was successful. Dio Chrysostom (31.128–9) reports that it was. But his short account is so inaccurate that it cannot easily be accepted. It has been noted that no such grants seem to be recorded henceforth and that Ctesippus, son of Chabrias, is recorded as *choregos* in the 320s (*IG* ii² 3040). In view of what is known of his character,[55] the *choregia* is unlikely to have been voluntary.

In the following year (354/3) Demosthenes for the first time appeared before the Assembly. The speech *On the Symmories* (the title is due to Hellenistic bibliographers, so Dionysius informs us, *To Ammaeus* 1.4) was later thought of by Demosthenes as dealing with relations with the King (15.6).[56] It in fact deals with both topics, cleverly interweaving them. The Athenians resented the satrap Mausolus' intrigues, which had contributed to their losing the Social War. The King himself, provoked by Chares' support for a rebel satrap,[57] was said to be mustering a large fleet; indeed, a rumour of this had been spread abroad a year before, we do not know by whom, but probably in an attempt to increase the pressure on Athens to make peace with the allies.[58] It seems that the rumour had persisted, or started up afresh. Since Athens was no longer at war with her allies, it was now said that he was preparing a large fleet in order to attack Greece, and it seems that some orators were calling on Athens to lead a crusade against the King, summoning the other Greeks to join her. We are not told who was behind such a hare-brained idea, at a time when Athens had not yet begun to recover from a state in which she had been unable to defeat the small fleets of rebellious allies. Old Aristophon may have been anti-Persian, but he was probably too sensible to come up with this scheme: he knew the state of Athenian finances and had supported Leptines' law, to his own disadvantage. Chares was certainly opposed to the King. But his experience in supporting the rebel Artabazus should have taught him that, if the King really had a major fleet at his disposal, Athens could not fight against it. Since Demosthenes does not name names, we must conclude that only minor political figures had come up with the idea: it looks as if it provided an opportunity for Demosthenes to be an advocate for common sense.

Demosthenes rightly points out that Athens' reputation was not at its highest. She would not be believed if she told the Greeks that the King was going to attack them; and if she was, some would welcome the King in preference to Athens. (This, of course, has to be put very tactfully: Demosthenes suggests the King would bribe many Greeks into supporting him: 14.4–5; but cf. 12, 36–7!) Athens, in any case, was in no position to be a credible leader in a war, especially a naval war; hence he proposed a reform of the symmory system, which had been funding the Athenian navy. Hitherto 1,200 wealthy citizens had provided the class liable to 'trierarchic' service, which now meant partial payment for a trireme. It is clear from his arguments that nearly half of them managed to get exemptions on various grounds, and that was why the system was no longer working (14.16). He now proposed to add another 800 to the register, so that there would in fact be 1,200 men available for the leiturgy. Proceeding to details of organisation, he finally showed how 300 triremes could be funded per year under his proposed system and how they could be manned with citizen crews. If this were carried out, Athens would be strong enough to deter the King from attack; though even then Athens must not try to attack the King.

In view of the widespread tax evasion, adding further taxes on a new segment of the population was rather naïve. The proposal had no chance of passing, and Demosthenes no doubt knew it. On the other hand, the appeal for war against the King almost certainly also had no chance of passing. As we have seen, Demosthenes could not find a single man worth naming who supported it. But in his first appearance he had shown himself a man advocating common sense and with ideas on what needed to be done in order to restore Athens to the status of a major power. The old idea that Demosthenes' early speeches protect the interests of the rich finds no support in anything approaching careful analysis. In 20, some of the wealthiest Athenians would indeed profit if they could retain their exemptions; but that would increase the burden upon the others. The real point was, rather, that those who had been given the exemptions were on the whole the most important people, not the wealthiest. That was the class Demosthenes tried to attract. In 14, when he states that wealth is more useful in the hands of its owners than when drawn off by the state in taxes (an argument not unknown, and not uncontested, in our own day), it is clear that he is not referring only to the possessions of the wealthiest: he speaks in terms of a property tax imposed on all who possessed property, which made up the 6,000 talents estimated to be the total of Athenian wealth (14.27–8; cf. 19 for the total estimate); and his proposed reform of the symmories would not relieve anyone liable to taxation: it would merely extend taxation to men not normally affected by it.

What is interesting to observe is that, at the very time when (according to Cawkwell's convincing chronology) Eubulus was beginning to formulate his own programme,[59] Demosthenes' approach shows no contact with Eubulus': it is far more limited and (one may say) quite unaware of the problems of Athenian decline in public morality among the wealthy and of the constant illusion on the part of the poor that war would give them a chance to improve their fortunes. Those were the main problems that Eubulus made it his business to solve.

About a year later Demosthenes delivered his first speech wholly devoted to foreign policy: that in support of Megalopolis (16). This time there is no sign of moderation or restraint. His main point appears to be that Athens must aim at a balance of power between Sparta and Thebes (16.4–5). But in fact he is much more suspicious of a Spartan revival than of Theban power; and that although Sparta had been an ally for close to twenty years, while Thebes had been an enemy on Athens' borders and had inflicted harm on Athens during that same time. Megalopolis had been firmly allied with Thebes. It was appealing to Athens only because Thebes, under severe strain from its war against the Phocians, was at the time unable to assist. There had not been any Spartan attack on Megalopolis, merely a perceived threat of one. The picture of a restoration of Spartan hegemony over the whole of Peloponnese, which Demosthenes conjures up, was totally unrealistic, in view of Sparta's chronic and increasing manpower shortage. Even if successful in a local war against Megalopolis, she would, if anything, be further weakened by the losses that such a victory would have imposed on her, and less able to pursue any further increase in power. Demosthenes seems aware of all this: he leaves the topic with an artful aposiopesis (16.18) to disguise the implausibility of his assumptions. To posit a Spartan reconquest of Messene was nothing less than absurd.

After a speech, most of which seems aimed at immediate alliance with Megalopolis at the risk of fatally alienating Sparta, the actual motion is almost an anticlimax: the Spartans are to be called upon not to attack Megalopolis and the Megalopolitans to abrogate their treaty with Thebes (16.27); Athens is to act against whichever of the two refuses to comply. But the Megalopolitan ambassadors had already given a very ambivalent reply when questioned about their policy: that they did not care about treaties, but regarded those who aided them as their friends. They could hardly be described as allies who would be trustworthy if Athens needed their help! If Athens turned out to be too weak to help them, they would readily turn to Thebes again. Having forsworn action against the King, Demosthenes seemed to be desperately looking for an area where Athens could pursue an activist policy, whatever the likely political outcome.[60]

The People rejected his idea. The experienced politicians by whom they were guided could never take such a scheme seriously – nor indeed its author, when he made proposals in future. The speech must have counteracted any gain that *On the Symmories* had achieved for him.

What follows did not improve his image. His next major speech was the first *Philippic*. We shall return to it after following him just a little further. In 351/50 he delivered the speech *For the Liberty of the Rhodians* (15). In this speech (securely dated by references to events in Caria) he strongly urges assistance for the Rhodian democrats against the ruling oligarchy installed by Mausolus. Mausolus was now dead and his widow Artemisia had succeeded him, while the King had been disastrously defeated in his attempt to reconquer Egypt and was battling rebellion in Phoenicia and Cyprus (Diod. 15.40.3–51, telling the whole story down to the reconquest of Egypt in 343; but see 48.1 for the events of 351/50). This gave the Rhodian democrats hope that they could regain power.

Demosthenes' plea to support them was hampered by the recent memory of *Symmories*. He is at pains to show that he is not contradicting himself (15.6–8). Under the King's Peace, still legally in force as far as boundaries were concerned, Asia belonged to the King, but the islands (except for Clazomenae and Cyprus) were free. Intervention on Rhodes would not be an attack on the King. Demosthenes rightly stresses that, when Timotheus drove a Persian garrison (which had no right to be there) out of Samos, the King did not intervene (15.9–10). Another contradiction would not be obvious to his audience. In the speech on Megalopolis he had declared in ringing tones that Athens had always helped victims of injustice and had never abandoned the principles of justice when others had (16.14–15). It was this that induced older commentators like Schaefer to read a declaration of moral principles in politics into Demosthenes' early policy speeches. They did not notice (it seems) that in 15 he now departs from that high principle: when all others are acting justly, Athens also must do so; but when all others (ἁπάντων τῶν ἄλλων!) are preparing to act unjustly (i.e., without waiting for them actually to do so), 'for us alone to profess what is just and take no initiative seems to me not justice but cowardice'. He continues: 'For I see that all are judged to deserve their rights in accordance with the power they wield' (15.28). The moralist has turned into an unashamed *Realpolitiker*.[61] There is a confused argument to the effect that Artemisia is unlikely to intervene (15.11–12: he does not say why she should fail to keep Carian collaborators in power) and that the King perhaps will not, in his present position. There follows the astonishing declaration that if he does intervene, Athens will have to treat it as an attack on all the Greeks and act accordingly (15.13)! A great deal of rhetorical embroidery on the theme of Athens' natural hostility to oligarchies, which cannot be trusted to be friendly, and affinity for democracies, which would make peace with Athens whenever Athens wanted it (15.17–18: the audience must have wondered about democratic

Thebes), is meant to support forgiveness towards Rhodes' defection in the Social War; and for the first time in Demosthenes we find a reference to the sinister citizens who give advice against Athens' best interests because they are paid by a foreigner (32–3): that theme had a great future in Demosthenes' oratory. There is a passing reference to inaction against Philip because some think him not worth worrying over (24): they are contrasted with those who think the King too formidable to challenge. Demosthenes seems to disapprove only because each course leads to inaction. He does not say which action would be more appropriate: against Philip, as he had recently advised in the first *Philippic*, or against the King, which he had tried to dissuade the Athenians from taking but seems now at least conditionally advocating (see above). Even after the first *Philippic*, Demosthenes shows no particular concern about Philip, who had been seizing Athenian possessions ever since 357. Considering the speech for Megalopolis and the speech for the Rhodians, which frame the first *Philippic*, we can see that the last must not be judged in the context of later speeches agitating against Philip: it belongs in a context of a young and ambitious orator's seeking a cause in which he can advocate Athenian activism: against Sparta, against Philip, against Caria or even the King. The advocacy of moderation in *Symmories* had proved ineffective in terms of his career, and so (it seems) had the wooing of important Athenians in *Leptines*. Demosthenes had cut his losses and decided that the advocacy of activism in foreign policy held out the greatest promise.[62]

This brings us to the first *Philippic*, a fitting conclusion to this chapter.[63] Even though (as we saw and shall see in greater detail) it belongs in the context of the speeches on behalf of Megalopolis and the Rhodian democrats, it is a fact that Demosthenes' posthumous fame rested chiefly on eleven years' opposition to Philip II. (The brief period of co-operation in 346, to be noted in later chapters, is usually ignored.) This, of course, accounts for the (modern) title given to the speech, which is seen as a prelude to that decade of struggle.

The date and actual configuration of the speech were debated even in antiquity.[64] Dionysius used a manuscript that divided the speech into two: the first speech consisting of our sections 1–29, and a different (later) speech starting with section 30. (None of the manuscripts we have offer that division, although the placing of the speech varies – a fact not intended, and not to be regarded, as of chronological significance.) He must also have found that division

in the Hellenistic bibliographers he followed (see *To Ammaeus* 1.4).
It is certainly not his own idea: he simply takes it for granted and
agrees. As it stands, the date for the second part as a new speech in
Dionysius (347/6) is unacceptable and shows that the division is
worthless. In his list of occasions on which the Athenians came too
late to rescue a besieged city, Demosthenes mentions Methone,
Pagasae and Potidaea, but not Olynthus. Yet that most striking
example (also the most recent, and of greater interest to him than
any other) could not have failed to appear, if the speech had been
delivered after the fall of that city. Since it would be arbitrary to
accept the division and alter the date, the division as such must be
rejected.[65]

One would therefore think that there is no good reason to reject
Dionysius' date for the first part and that it should be applied to the
whole. Yet that has been done, and with astonishing success. Over a
hundred years ago, in an essay in a *Festschrift* honouring Theodor
Mommsen on his *Doktorjubiläum*, the great German scholar Eduard
Schwartz argued at some length that the whole speech should be
dated to 349, when the attack on Olynthus was just beginning.[66]
He took 4.17, a reference to Philip's sudden moves towards
Thermopylae, the Chersonese and Olynthus (all obviously recent
and about contemporary), to refer to this war of 349. Although the
theory seems clearly untenable (the events belong to 353/2), the
author's eminence secured considerable success for it. Indeed, in
Germany and to some extent beyond, it became the only recognized
interpretation. It was the great merit of Jaeger, in a book in which
there is otherwise little to praise,[67] to have swung the German
tradition back towards acceptance of Dionysius' date, which now
appears to be generally accepted.

The speech is much longer than the two, on Megalopolis and on
Rhodes, which surround it. Although at times impassioned, it is no
more so than the speech on the Rhodians. It was the first time that
Demosthenes had shown concern about Philip, even though Athens
had been at war with him since he took Amphipolis and refused to
hand it over. For the first few years the Social War had prevented
serious reaction, and even in its aftermath Athenian finances were so
depleted, with no immediate way of replenishing them, that
Athens' navy was no longer a major instrument of war. Meanwhile
Philip had taken Pydna and Methone, had handed Potidaea over to
the Chalcidic League as a bribe, had twice entered Thessaly at the
invitation of Larissa (which had made him a citizen) and, by 352,
had annihilated a Phocian army and had seized the whole of

Thessaly, gaining election as its *tagos* (military head).[68] He had seriously weakened the Thracian king Cersebleptes, despite Charidemus' efforts (he was saved only by Philip's unexpected illness), and on his way back had made a raid on the territory of Olynthus, since Olynthus had, contrary to her treaty with him, now made peace with Athens and was perhaps even ready to make an alliance with her. Quite recently, he had harassed Athenian shipping on the vital Black Sea route and had organized a raid on the Attic coast at Marathon, the living pride of Athenian history, and had the sacred galley *Paralos* towed away (Dem. 4.34), the crowning demonstration of the state to which the once powerful Athenian navy had been reduced. Demosthenes' main proposal was to establish a strike force, both by land and by sea, manned by a considerable proportion of citizens and not relying entirely on mercenaries, which could be sent anywhere it was needed at short notice. It was a long way from his ambitious proposal for three hundred triremes in *Symmories*, but it was perhaps realistic. (Unfortunately the actual proposal for financing this, read after our section 29, has dropped out.) Nonetheless, it was never carried out. Demosthenes had apparently failed to achieve credibility as a politician, and as was to appear even more than it had, he had powerful enemies.

What is surprising, in an ambitious young politician, is that Demosthenes had for so long ignored Philip, even though Philip had reduced Athens to a second-rank power in the space of a very few years. In the speech against Aristocrates, he is mentioned several times: once (ludicrously, we may think) compared with Charidemus (23.107–9; cf. 116), once (no less absurdly, in the circumstances of recent events) to tell the Athenians that Philip had put himself in danger by incurring their enmity and occupying Thessaly (111–13), taking the risk of losing what he had in his desire for more! It is odd that this speech was delivered in the same year as the first *Philippic*, although presumably in an earlier month. However, even Philip's exposing the helplessness of the Athenian navy, probably after this speech and stressed in the later one, had no permanent effect on Demosthenes' thinking. A year later, as we saw, in the speech on behalf of Rhodes, all that can be said about Philip is that, unlike the King of Persia, he is regarded by Athenians as too weak to be worth an effort. By then, of course, Demosthenes himself no longer depicted him as a menace: he was advocating new adventures in the eastern Aegean. That speech, so soon after the first *Philippic*, clearly did not help him to gain credibility.

The conclusion is inevitable, and Athenian politicians must have seen it, just as we do: Philip, as an enemy, was no more serious in Demosthenes' eyes than Sparta or the Rhodian oligarchs. The impassioned rhetoric of the *Philippic* could not be taken any more seriously than his wild forecasts of a revival of Spartan power or his vague hints about the King's intentions (15.12–13) and optimism about Athens' ability to defeat him (15.23–4), contrasting with what he had advised a few years earlier, in *Symmories*. They were all patently devoid of real conviction. He wanted to become a leader in glorious action, but had no basic policy of his own, no assessment of political and strategic priorities. It is little wonder that, when a real emergency, the Olynthian War, called forth more outbursts of passionate rhetoric, he was not taken as seriously as, at that point, he possibly should have been.[69]

Finally, we may well ask *why* Demosthenes had for so long taken little notice of the one enemy with whom Athens was actually at war, a war in which he had used his power and his initiative to increasingly restrict Athens' possibilities of political and military action. He must surely have been at the centre of Athenian attention all these years, even when the Athenians knew that they were too weak to do much about him.

There is no certain answer to this question. The answer lies buried in the intricacies of Athenian politics, which, with all our scholarship and empathy, we can never quite grasp. But perhaps a clue appears in the opening of the first *Philippic*: a preface that throws an interesting light on the circle of established Athenian politicians (πολιτευόμενοι) into which the aspiring young politician without (as far as we can see) important political connections had to make his way. He would normally (he says) have listened to his elders and remained silent; only if he found something to correct in what they had said would he have expressed his own opinion. And he adds that Philip was an issue that had often been discussed; what is more, what they had been saying had now proved unsatisfactory. It is this that provides his excuse for being the first speaker on this occasion.

To put it in our own words: those who commanded respect had delivered themselves of all possible opinions over several years. There was nothing new to be said, and no point in his echoing opinions expressed by his elders. They would have resented it, and it would not have impressed anyone. Only now, when Philip's actions at sea had injected a new element into the situation, could he seize a chance of coming forward – and he had to seize it quickly, before his elders could speak. In the end, as we saw, he was still not taken seriously. He had tried to advocate policy on a matter in which nobody was very interested (the appeal of Megalopolis) and had got nowhere. But he probably thought he had sufficiently made his mark to have a chance of breaking into the inner circle. He turned out to be mistaken. Hence his return to a passionate performance on a matter (the Rhodian appeal) in which, again, probably no one was very interested. It was only the attack on Olynthus, a year or two later, that showed him where his future lay.[70]

NOTES

* This chapter is based on part of my Martin Lectures delivered at Oberlin College. I was hoping to work the lectures up into a book on Demosthenes, when Raphael Sealey's *Demosthenes and his Time* (Oxford: 1993) appeared. This made it impossible to proceed with the project. The invitation to contribute to this volume offered a welcome opportunity to return to the subject. Needless to say, this chapter is only distantly based on the old lecture.

1 See Milns, Chapter 7, for example.

2 On Demosthenes' reputation at this time see Cooper, Chapter 8.

3 Authenticity, in the sense which I here give to the term, has been much discussed. It cannot be dissociated from theories about the transmission of Demosthenes' speeches. For the latter, see the brief summary in R. Sealey, *Demosthenes and his Time* (Oxford: 1993), pp. 221–9. On the relation of the speeches delivered to our manuscripts and on the origin of the double versions of some of the speeches in our tradition (a longer and a shorter version, the latter omitting passages found in the former but almost certainly genuine) see Ian Worthington, 'The Authenticity of Demosthenes' Fourth Philippic', *Mnemosyne*[4] 44 (1991), pp. 425–8 (cf. his 'Greek Oratory, Revision of Speeches and the Problem of Historical Reliability', *C&M* 92 [1991], pp. 55–74). C. Tuplin, 'Demosthenes' *Olynthiacs* and the Character of the Demegoric Corpus', *Historia* 47 (1998), pp. 276–320 at pp. 292–5, drew attention to Aristotle's assumption that *dēmēgoriai*, unlike forensic speeches, were unwritten and that some (for example, Alcidamas) were against writing out speeches before delivery. In any case, there must originally have been at least two different collections, one containing the shorter versions (perhaps close to the speeches delivered) and the other containing the longer versions (either based on drafts or, on the contrary, on revised work by Demosthenes himself: we cannot usefully guess which). See further Milns, Chapter 7; cf. Buckler, Chapter 4 and Golden, Chapter 5.

4 On Didymus see (briefly) Sealey, *Demosthenes*, pp. 227–8 – much too favourable; cf., for example, E. Badian, 'The King's Peace' in M.A. Flower and M. Toher (eds), *Georgica: Greek Studies in Honour of George Cawkwell* (London: 1991), pp. 29–30, with further references in n. 30. The appearance of a new source (unusual in ancient history) is often

hailed by scholars with uncritical enthusiasm. (On Didymus' quotation of Philochorus, see, for example, K.J. Beloch, *Theopomps Hellenika* [Halle: 1909], p. 54.) It is a sound principle that not all lost sources suddenly in part retrieved are necessarily superior to long-familiar surviving sources. It might be noted that the Loeb editor, J.H. Vince, deserves no credit for still bracketing the fourth *Philippic* in 1930: he had not heard of the Didymus discovery. I do not think that Didymus' faith has settled the question. But detailed discussion is outside our purview; cf. Milns, Chapter 7.

5 For a rather weak treatment of Demosthenes' repetitions see S.G. Daitz, 'The Relationship of the *De Chersoneso* and the *Philippika quarta* of Demosthenes', *CP* 52 (1957), pp. 145–62. The distinctions he tries to establish (between conscious and unconscious repetition; between speeches delivered by Demosthenes and speeches written for others; between speeches delivered after a longer interval and speeches delivered within a year) are unrealistic and do not explain much.

6 'Oratory' in P.E. Easterling and B.M.W. Knox (eds.), *Cambridge History of Classical Literature* 1 (Cambridge: 1985), p. 526 and elsewhere.

7 Donald F. McCabe, *The Prose Rhythm of Demosthenes* (New York: 1981). I learned a great deal from McCabe while associated with the writing of his dissertation, no doubt more than I could teach him. Milns, Chapter 7, also discusses Blass's law and the impact of McCabe's work.

8 Note especially Tables 19–23 on clausulae (after long and detailed discussion of manuscript transmission and determination of length of syllables), pp. 139–52; 24–6, pp. 153–9, on overall rhythm; and 27, pp. 161–2, on avoidance of hiatus. Table 28, pp. 170–2, collects the results under these three headings, for all the speeches in the Demosthenic corpus and the speeches of Isaeus. McCabe's is the first scientific, and not merely subjective, approach to these questions. It should be noted that he does not use his evidence for purely mechanical judgements.

9 R. Sealey, 'Dionysius of Halicarnassus and Some Demosthenic Dates', *REG* 68 (1955), pp. 77–120. He concludes, correctly and usefully, that Dionysius' dates were not his own conjectures, but based on researches by Alexandrian scholars.

10 E. Badian, 'Harpalus', *JHS* 81 (1961), p. 34 n. 134. This must now be slightly, but not significantly, amended in the light of entries in the *Lexicon of Greek Personal Names* (see n. 15 below).

11 P. Mackendrick, *The Athenian Aristocracy 399–31 B.C.* (Cambridge, Mass.: 1969), p. 69 n. 33. It is odd that he omits Demades from this circle, although Demades' close connection with Demosthenes is in fact attested well before the Harpalus affair (see Plut. *Dem.* 8.7, clearly not from an anti-Demosthenic source).

12 By the standards of evidence applied by those who reject the reconstruction, one might argue that we (and that includes them) have no business writing Athenian history at all. It is certainly not admissible procedure to base rejection of Demades' connection with Demosthenes, against good sources, on the hostile reports of his disreputable origins, as one standard British work of scholarship has done. Such aspersions are the common coin of ancient political invec-

tive and prove nothing. We might as well regard Demosthenes as a Scythian.

13 See the embarrassed passage at 28.1–2.

14 We do not know who married the other daughter, but it may be presumed that she was similarly placed.

15 For the names discussed see M.J. Osborne and S.G. Byrne (eds.), *Lexicon of Greek Personal Names 2* (Oxford: 1994), s.vv., pp. 77, 81, 103 and 265.

16 On the story see Cooper, Chapter 8.

17 Cf. Philodemus, *Rhet.*, p. 197 Sudhaus: 'a rambling actor, not straightforward and in the noble style, but descending into the feeble and vulgar'. Enthusiasm for Demosthenes was apparently not universal even in the Hellenistic age, when the canon of orators had long been established.

18 On his supposed teachers see Plut. *Dem.* 5.5–7, [Plut.] *Mor.* 844b–c. Isaeus is the best attested (cf. the *Suda* under both their names), and he was the best expert to turn to for the kind of cases that Demosthenes handled in his earliest years. The tradition is found in extreme form in Pseudo-Plutarch, *Mor.* 839f and 844b: Demosthenes paid Isaeus 10,000 drachmas for instruction (at a time when he could hardly have afforded it) and took Isaeus into his house, apparently for four years! References to McCabe here are to *The Prose Rhythm of Demosthenes*. For a stylistic analysis of these speeches see Mirhady, Chapter 6.

19 Isaeus does not appear in the index to Sealey, *Demosthenes*.

20 *Démosthène, Plaidoyers civils* 1 (Paris: 1954), pp. 64–9. However, he takes the genuineness of 27 and 28 for granted and tries to defend that of 29. After McCabe's work this no longer seems acceptable.

21 On these passages see D.M. MacDowell, *Demosthenes against Meidias* (Oxford: 1990), pp. 1–4. and commentary on *Meidias* 77–80, 83–96. He shows that, contrary to what has sometimes been maintained, the two accounts are not positively contradictory (pp. 296–8): Thrasylochus and Meidias broke down the door that had been locked against them, as they had a right to do after the acceptance of the *antidosis*. (He notes that Demosthenes never prosecuted them for this action.) However, he does not try to explain the omission of all mention of Meidias in 28.

22 This cannot be discussed in detail here. For a convenient brief summary of the whole affair see Sealey, *Demosthenes*, pp. 97–8. We know nothing about Demosthenes' prosecution of the other guardians, except that he started it (29.6). Pseudo-Plutarch, *Mor.* 844c–d, asserts that he won all the cases but did not collect the sums awarded. The passage, however, is too inaccurate to be used as serious evidence.

23 Speech 51 was assigned to Apollonius by Libanius: as has often been pointed out, he must have connected it with the series of Apollonian speeches surrounding it in our (and probably his) manuscripts. McCabe thinks that Demosthenic authorship is not 'in serious doubt' (*Prose Rhythm of Demosthenes*, p. 169; cf. p. 196). Blass and Sealey also accepted it as Demosthenic: see Sealey, *Demosthenes*, pp. 100–1 with n. 126 (p. 293), giving references to acceptance by Blass and J.K. Davies. It corresponds with Demosthenes' practice in McCabe's survey of clausulae and style, but has far less avoidable hiatus. However, the speech is probably too short (only six OCT pages) for statistical tests to

be significant. For the actual events and the chronology, see J. Heskel, *The North Aegean Wars 371–360 B.C.* (Wiesbaden: 1997), pp. 54–9, summarised at pp. 60 and 62.

24 E. Ruschenbusch, 'Demosthenes' erste freiwillige Trierarchie und die Datierung des Euböaunternehmens vom Jahre 357', *ZPE* 67 (1987), pp. 158–9, rightly argued that since Demosthenes had been a trierarch in 360/59 (see above: the Attic year of the war is given by the Scholiast on Aeschines 3.51, p. 115 Dilts), he would be exempt in the following two years; hence his voluntary trierarchy must be in one of those years, that is (in view of the date of the Euboean war), in 358/7. H. Wankel's argument ('Demosthenes' erste freiwillige Trierarchie und die Datierung des Euböaunternehmens vom Jahre 357', *ZPE* 71 [1988], pp. 199–200) that the two-year exemption (attested by Isaeus 7.38) was recent, perhaps only part of Periander's law of 358/7, is baseless. Demosthenes may have furnished another half-trireme in the Social War: see J.K. Davies, *Athenian Propertied Families* (Oxford: 1971), p. 136.

25 For a treatment of Philip's reign and of Demosthenes' activities during it, see especially Ryder, Chapter 2; cf. Buckler, Chapter 4.

26 On this see, in detail, Heskel, *North Aegean Wars, passim*.

27 The Athenian ambassadors to Philip, Antiphon and Charidemus, cannot be identified, as the names are not rare at this time. Two men named Charidemus served as trierarchs (Davies, *Athenian Propertied Families*, s.v.). That the envoy is 'otherwise unknown' (Sealey, *Demosthenes*, p. 110) is an overstatement, serving as a basis for his theory that the envoys may have been sent by Cersebleptes. (This identifies Charidemus as the well-known condottiere, who was at that time serving under Cersebleptes. Sealey, like us, cannot identify Antiphon.) The theory contradicts the sense of the Theopompus passage, as quoted, which implies that the embassy was an Athenian one; and the name Charidemus is too common, and too well-known in Athens at this time, for the conjecture to be necessary or acceptable. That *we* cannot precisely identify the two envoys, while Sealey suggests one (of several) possible identifications for one of them, does nothing to support his suggestion. I briefly discussed the incident in 'The Ghost of Empire: Reflections on Athenian Foreign Policy in the Fourth century' in W. Eder (ed.), *Die athenische Demokratie im 4. Jahrhundert v. Chr.* (Stuttgart: 1995), pp. 95–6. G.E.M. de Ste. Croix's attempt to explain the incident away as unhistorical ('The Alleged Secret Pact between Athens and Philip II concerning Amphipolis and Pydna', *CQ*[2] 13 [1963], pp. 110–19) should now be buried. For other examples of incidents that seem disgraceful see Badian, 'Ghost of Empire', pp. 87–8, 99 and 103–4.

28 On Androtion see Jacoby, *FGrH* 3b *Suppl.* 1, pp. 87–8, with references to his text. His conjectures are in part outdated: see P. Harding, 'Androtion's Political Career', *Historia* 25 (1976), pp. 186–200, for his public career, citing recent interpretations with acute discussion.

29 The Amorgos decree: *SIG*[3] 192, translated by P. Harding, *From the End of the Peloponnesian War to the Battle of Ipsus* (Cambridge: 1985), no. 68, with discussion of the date.

30 The date of this should be in the mid-360s (see Harding, 'Androtion's Political Career', pp. 190–2). He apparently had defective crowns and sacred vessels melted down, perhaps in part in order to bolster public finances; but he also laid down rules concerning sacred vessels, which were still referred to as authoritative twenty years later (see Harding, 'Androtion's Political Career', pp. 190–1). Demosthenes' pathetic lament for the reminders of Athenian glory lost in this action (22.69–74) ignores the positive aspects of Androtion's activity and does not seem to have aroused much of a response in the jury.

31 For the date see Harding, 'Androtion's Political Career', pp. 192–4. Demosthenes complains about his entering citizens' houses in his enforcement of his task (22.47–58) and calls this oligarchic and unconstitutional; but he cannot deny that this power was conferred by the People and that the Eleven went with him when it proved necessary to make such searches (22.49–50); and Androtion was never prosecuted for this decree. Demosthenes gives the figure of 7 talents collected (22.44); later, when he could assume memories had faded, he reduced the figure to 5 (24.162) to make it seem less significant.

32 For his embassy see below. What he had to do (if anything) with the discourteous decree replying to the King's message in 344/3 is uncertain. It depends on heavy restoration in Didymus 8.14–15 (where his name, in the nominative or genitive, is the only certain name). The fanciful restoration proposed early in the twentieth century was rightly challenged by Harding, 'Androtion's Political Career'. It is repeated without comment in the latest text of Didymus, by Pearson and Stephens, apparently unaware of Harding's doubts. In 347/6, Androtion proposed a decree honouring the ruling family of Bosporus.

33 This, the general interpretation, has recently been challenged by E.M. Harris, 'Law and Oratory' in Ian Worthington (ed.), *Persuasion: Greek Rhetoric in Action* (London: 1994), pp. 130–50 – not entirely convincing.

34 A. Schaefer, *Demosthenes und seine Zeit*², 1 (Leipzig: 1885), p. 449.

35 F. Blass, *Die attische Beredsamkeit*², 3.1 (Leipzig: 1887), p. 231.

36 As suggested by Sealey, *Demosthenes*, pp. 105–6. All that we know about the embassy and the complicated legal manoeuvres concerning the proceeds of the cargo seized is based on Demosthenes 24.

37 See Sealey, *Demosthenes*, p. 104, accepting the King's threat as forcing the Athenians to make peace with the allies. This is not a necessary interpretation. With the treasury empty and (as we saw) few triremes built for some years past, Athens had no resources with which to continue the war after the disastrous defeat at Embata.

38 Dem. 24.12. As the passage refers to a speech 'reminding' the People of this, it does not mention the grounds on which the decision was reached. Perhaps it was best not to ask. The odd wording (μὴ φίλια εἶναι τότε) invites speculation, not to be pursued here.

39 This is a major item in Demosthenes' complaint about the law (24.79–83). If he is quoting accurately (he may well be guilty of distortion by omission), his interpretation is correct.

40 This is clearly the substance of the charge: not that the law was 'not advantageous to the city', as some have construed the charge. The speaker naturally tries to point to the financial loss to the city that the

law would cause, but that is one of the incidental developments. The main stress is on illegality, both of procedure and of substance (17–67, 70–107). The themes recur throughout. Sections 68–9 link the two demonstrations, providing the transition from one to the other. For the same scheme in 23, cf. Sealey, *Demosthenes*, pp. 130–1.

41 Sealey's great contribution to our understanding of Athenian politics at this time is set out in 'Athens after the Social War', *JHS* 75 (1955), pp. 74–81 and 'Callistratos of Aphidna and His Contemporaries', *Historia* 5 (1956), pp. 178–203. Both these are reprinted in his *Essays in Greek Politics* (New York: 1967). The relevant points are repeated in his *Demosthenes*.

42 The evidence for the whole association is set out in Sealey, *Demosthenes*, pp. 119–20. For Meidias see Demosthenes 21.139. For Timocrates' earlier intervention, see Demosthenes 30.7–12.

43 See Buckler, Chapter 4, with Worthington, Chapter 3.

44 But there is no support for Sealey's suggestion (*Demosthenes*, p. 131) that the name of his client given by Dionysius (*To Ammaeus* 1.4) may be mistaken and that Demosthenes himself may have delivered the speech. Euthycles' name was not an easy one to get in by mistake.

45 On Charidemus' early career and his dealings with Athenian commanders see Heskel, *North Aegean Wars*.

46 On this see my analysis in 'Philip II and Thrace', *Pulpudeva* 4 (1983), pp. 62–6. He moved to Athens a little later (cf. Dem. 23.126–8).

47 See the long exposition in Demosthenes 23.19–91. Sealey rightly points to some distortions due to Demosthenes' eagerness. The section on expediency again follows this treatment of the legal issue (cf. n. 40 above).

48 See my treatment of this in 'Ghost of Empire', pp. 81–106.

49 For a clear exposition of this see J. Cargill, *The Second Athenian League* (Berkeley: 1981), p. 169. Unfortunately the fact has not penetrated into some major recent reference works; it is only hesitantly mentioned as a possibility in *CAH* 6², p. 202 and is unknown to the contributors to the *Neue Pauly*.

50 For more detailed discussion see my 'Ghost of Empire', pp. 94–5, following G.L. Cawkwell, 'Notes on the Failure of the Second Athenian Confederacy', *JHS* 101 (1981), pp. 51–2. As I noted, Cargill's attempt to defend Athens against this interpretation has on the whole been rejected: see, for example, S. Hornblower's review of Cargill, *CR* 32 (1986), pp. 235–9 with detailed refutation. C.J. Tuplin concisely sums up in *OCD*³, p. 1376: 'The slippage towards 5th-century behaviour is unmistakable.' Cargill's attempt to make the Samian cleruchy seem harmless ('*IG* ii² 1 and the Athenian Kleruchy on Samos', *GRBS* 24 [1983], pp. 321–32) is unconvincing.

51 I am less convinced than I once was by S.M. Sherwin-White's attempt to argue that Cos was never a member of the confederacy (*Ancient Cos* [Göttingen: 1978], pp. 41ff.). There would be room for it on a vacant space on the stele of Aristoteles, and one has to ask: If it never had been a member, what prompted Cos to what would be an act of quixotic unselfishness in joining Byzantium and the others in 357, when their victory was by no means certain?

52 See n. 37 above with p. 23.

53 The only exemptions Leptines had allowed were those for the descendants of Harmodius and Aristogeiton. They were probably secured by oaths.

54 Late commentators produced the statement that he was aiming at marrying Chabrias' widow (Plut. *Dem.* 15.3). It is doubtful whether this rests on anything but speculation based on this initial statement.

55 See Davies, *Athenian Propertied Families*, p. 561.

56 For a stylistic analysis of this speech and the others discussed here see Milns, Chapter 7.

57 Artabazus: see Sealey, *Demosthenes*, pp. 104–5 for a brief summary.

58 Cf. n. 37 above with text.

59 G.L. Cawkwell, 'Eubulus', *JHS* 83 (1963), pp. 47–67. Remarks on the chronology are scattered throughout, but see especially p. 48. Cawkwell's is the standard treatment of Eubulus.

60 Sparta did attack Megalopolis a little later (Diod. 16.39). It is an amusing comment on Demosthenes' efforts to persuade Athens to break with Sparta and on the Megalopolitan envoys' statement that Thebes did actually send a force to assist Megalopolis, which in fact was instrumental in securing her successful defence. Any Athenians trying to help would probably have been sent home. See also the comments of Ryder, Chapter 2, on Demosthenes' earlier political speeches and his aims at this time.

61 Schaefer and his followers (for example, W. Jaeger, *Demosthenes: The Origin and Growth of his Policy* [Berkeley: 1938; repr. New York: 1977], p. 86) were impressed by Demosthenes' moral standpoint in the speech for Megalopolis (Schaefer, *Demosthenes* 1, p. 518). The contradiction, a few years later, was readily ignored, with the help of mistranslation (p. 548). Treated after 15, it impressively ends Volume 1.

62 Contrast Jaeger, *Demosthenes*, p. 76: 'The idea [fear of Philip] flares up momentarily, only to vanish again. But *no one can doubt* that it already underlies the arguments on the Rhodian question *as a fundamental determining motive*' [my emphasis]. Not many who read the speech, with the passing mention of Philip (see text), will have much difficulty in doubting it.

63 For other discussions of this speech see Ryder, Chapter 2, Buckler, Chapter 4, and Milns, Chapter 7.

64 See Sealey, 'Dionysius of Halicarnassus and Some Demosthenic Dates', p. 81.

65 There is no need to document these events: they will be found in all the general histories. As for the division of the speech, I have found only one quixotic effort to defend it, by an Austrian Gymnasialprofessor: E. Eichler, 'War Demosthenes' erste Philippica doch eine Doppelrede?' in J. Hauser (ed.), *Jahresbericht über das k.k. Staatsgymnasium im II. Bezirke von Wien* (Vienna: 1883), pp. 1–29. It is not a bad effort. He succeeds in neutralizing some of the reasons that have been advanced against the division, for example the lack of a preface if a new speech was to start at section 30, and he makes much of the plural verb (δεδυνήμεθα) at the beginning of that section, which is indeed difficult to explain in the light of Demosthenic usage. But he fails to meet the decisive difficulty over Olynthus (see my text). He does succeed in showing that the Hellenistic scholars who accepted the division of the

speech that they found in manuscripts, and Dionysius who also found it in his and took their word in believing it, were not utter fools.

66 'Demosthenes' erste Philippika' in P. Jors, E. Schwartz and R. Reitzenstein (eds.), *Festschrift Theodor Mommsen zum fünfzigjährigen Doctorjubiläum* (Marburg: 1893), pp. 1–44.

67 See my discussion in 'Jaeger's Demosthenes: An Essay in Anti-History' in W.M. Calder (ed.), *Werner Jaeger Reconsidered* (Atlanta: 1992), pp. 289–313. (Unfortunately I was not allowed to proofread the essay as set up, and no one else bothered to do so.) The history of the book and of its translation into German documents Jaeger's lingering attachment to Germany even under Hitler. Sealey, 'Dionysius of Halicarnassus and Some Demosthenic Dates', pp. 81–9, later respectfully demolished Schwartz.

68 On this last see Demosthenes 23.107–9. This obviously called forth Philip's retaliatory raid alluded to in 4.17 (see text). On Philip and Thessaly see now E. Badian, 'Philip II and the Last of the Thessalians', *Ancient Macedonia* 6 (Thessaloniki: 1999), pp. 109–22.

69 Although we must not forget that a Euboean war partly overlapped with Philip's attack on Olynthus, perhaps not by accident. Euboea was much more important to Athens than Olynthus. Demosthenes later proudly proclaimed that he had opposed intervention in Euboea (5.5), and that that was so unpopular that he actually incurred physical danger. It is likely that Eubulus and Demosthenes' enemy Meidias supported intervention.

70 I have not mentioned Demosthenes 13, *On Organization*, since I am not at all convinced of its authenticity, even though much of it is genuinely Demosthenic. In McCabe's investigation, it complies with all his Demosthenic criteria (*Prose Rhythm of Demosthenes*, p. 196; yet he too calls it doubtful). For strong arguments against authenticity see Sealey, *Demosthenes*, pp. 235–7. There is only one that seems to me in favour of (at least) genuineness, possibly authenticity. Both 13 and 23 name Menon of Pharsalus and (mistakenly) Perdiccas of Macedon as men whom the Athenians had honoured for services rendered to them (Sealey, *Demosthenes*, p. 235). In 23.199–200 Demosthenes asserts that the Athenians had granted these men citizenship, even though not the special protection now proposed for Charidemus. In 13.23–4 it is stated that they were not given citizenship, but only immunity from taxes and duties. Each of the statements fits into the context in which it is made. In 13, the speaker is upbraiding the Athenians for having such a low opinion of themselves that they now give the citizenship to all and sundry; hence the point that Meno and Perdiccas did not get it. In 23, the point is that citizenship was never conferred with the special protection now proposed. Hence those chosen as examples must have received citizenship. Since the Athenians obviously had no memory of those cases (else the mistake that Perdiccas was king of Macedon at the time of Xerxes' invasion could never have been made in front of them), the speaker was free, in each case, to fashion his story in accordance with the requirements of his case. The change in 13 is not due to ignorance of 23. However, I find Sealey's other arguments strong enough to show that the speech cannot be authentic, no matter to what date we would assign it. (Dionysius does not list it.)

2

DEMOSTHENES AND
PHILIP II*

T.T.B. Ryder

Opposition to Philip II is the political cause with which Demosthenes' name is most clearly associated. From 351 right through to the Macedonian king's death in 336 Demosthenes used his oratorical and diplomatic skills in support of his unrelenting belief that Philip was a dire threat to the freedom of the Greek world in general and of the Athenians in particular and should be resisted. For the last ten of those years the Athenian people, who were still as free and liable to change their minds about public policy as they had been in certain phases of the Peloponnesian War, were persuaded with a remarkable degree of consistency to share his belief. Other politicians are known to have joined him in promoting this cause, but the tradition is emphatic in assigning the major role to him.

In the 1940s, when emotions were stirred by the trials of World War II and its immediate aftermath, facile comparisons were made between Demosthenes' stand against Philip and that of Winston Churchill against Hitler, but unlike Churchill, who was warning of the threat posed by Hitler as early as 1933, Demosthenes cannot be said on the available evidence to have identified the menace to his people from Philip in advance of other political figures.

1

The earliest episode in the Athenians' relations with Philip to which Demosthenes refers in any extant speech is Philip's successful attack in 357, two years after he took over the kingdom of Macedon, on Amphipolis, which the Athenians had founded as a colony in 437/6, had lost in 424 and had been trying to recover since 370.[1] Both the comments he made eight years later (1.8 and 2.6) are critical of the Athenians' reactions. In the first he asserts that, if they had responded to the appeal for help from two

Amphipolitan envoys, they would have secured Amphipolis and been spared all their subsequent difficulties, and in the second he refers to their simple-mindedness in rejecting the overtures from the Olynthians (who were better able to help the Amphipolitans than they were) and in being beguiled by Philip's promise (which he did not fulfil) to hand the city over to them, when he had taken it, and by the reports of a secret pact between him and Athens.[2] There is no reason, though, to suppose that he expressed disapproval of those Athenian decisions at the time – indeed, for what it is worth, he refers to the rejection of the Olynthians as a product of 'our simple-mindedness'; and it is likely that his view of Philip was like that of many Athenians, who, while sceptical of his ability to establish his authority more securely than had his immediate predecessors, were reassured by his withdrawal two years earlier of the garrison placed in Amphipolis by his predecessor Perdiccas (Diod. 16.3.3) and his abrogation of all claim to that city in the peace-treaty he then made with Athens (Diod. 16.4.1).

Two or three years later, when Demosthenes made his first known speech before the Athenian Assembly, his edited version of it, *On the Symmories* (14), suggests that the threat from Philip was not at the forefront of his mind.[3] The debate was about a proposal to declare war on the King of Persia,[4] to which Demosthenes was strongly opposed. He acknowledged that the King was 'the common enemy of all the Greeks' (3) and recommended preparation against a possible Persian attack, making concrete proposals about reforming the financial support of the fleet, but urged the Athenians not to provoke him to the point where, preferring diplomacy to open warfare, he might beguile their enemies with offers of support. These enemies, among whom only the Thebans are mentioned (33–4), are clearly other Greek states and nowhere is there any reference to a threat from Philip, who in Demosthenes' eyes was no Greek. Yet since spring 357 Philip had taken Amphipolis without handing it over to the Athenians, and then Pydna and Potidaea, which were both effectively Athenian possessions, and had defeated a coalition of Illyrian, Paeonian and Thracian kings (Diod. 16.8, 16.22.3). By midsummer 355, it seems, he was menacing Neapolis, one of Athens' naval allies along the north coast of the Aegean,[5] and in the latter part of the year he was besieging Methone, the last remaining Athenian foothold in the north-west Aegean. The Athenian people, despite being preoccupied and increasingly impoverished by their war with secessionist allies, had reacted by declaring war on Philip over his retention of Amphipolis,[6] and by voting first to send help to the Potidaeans which was too late (Dem. 4.35), then to conclude an alliance with the three barbarian kings, recorded in an inscription of July 356 (Tod 2, no. 157) but evidently not implemented, and finally to send a message of encouragement to the Neapolitans. They had certainly shown themselves aware of the need to check Philip and it is surprising that Demosthenes in his speech does not exploit that awareness either when recommending caution with regard to the Persians or when promoting his scheme for improving naval finance.

The crucial state of Athens' finances at the end of the war with the allies in 355 induced Eubulus and his associates, who were the most influential politicians of the next few years, to oppose unnecessary foreign commitments while pursuing a positive policy of retrenchment. One of the instruments of this policy was the use of the protected status of the theoric fund, which, as its name shows, was originally set up to enable poorer citizens to attend the city's festivals, as a means of preventing accumulated reserves from being raided by demagogic politicians to finance dubious enterprises.[7] Demosthenes was later to protest with due caution against its inviolability.

As for foreign commitments, the Athenians notably kept clear of involvement in the Sacred War which in 355 the Thebans had induced the Amphictyonic Council to declare on the Phocians, doing nothing until 352 to implement the formal alliance which they had made with the Phocians in 356 or early 355 when the Thebans had first begun to use the Amphictyonic machinery against them (Diod. 16.27.5). In 354, though, the Athenians at last decided to send help to the besieged Methoneans, but it was too late to prevent their surrender. Demosthenes, who is the source for this failure (4.35), gave it as an example of the way in which the Athenians' decision-making process frustrated effective response to overseas emergencies, but it should not be supposed from that criticism that he had himself been vainly urging action in the preceding months.

Athenian action in the north-east Aegean was more prompt and more effective. In 353 Chares, although unsuccessful in an enterprising attempt to ambush Philip's small naval squadron off Neapolis (Polyaenus 4.2.22), took Sestos on the Hellespont (Diod. 16.34.3) and the Thracian king Cersebleptes, who had perhaps flirted with the notion of co-operating with Philip (Dem. 23.183), reaffirmed his earlier treaty with the Athenians (Dem. 23.170) by handing over the Chersonese to them (Diod. 16.34.4).

Philip meanwhile in the same year (353) had taken an army into Thessaly in response to a request from the Thessalian federation for help against Lycophron, the tyrant of Pherae, and probably with no intention of being involved further south. As the Thessalians had backed the Thebans in the Sacred War, Lycophron received support from the Phocians, and Philip, though at first successful, was twice defeated in battle by the Phocian leader Onomarchus, and withdrew to Macedonia.

This setback for Philip, the worst that he suffered in his reign, leading, says Diodorus (16.35.2) to mutinous despondency amongst his troops, may very well have encouraged Demosthenes to take up the cause of the Megalopolitans. Probably in autumn 353,[8] they appealed unsuccessfully to Athens for protection against the Spartans, who were evidently threatening to take advantage of the Thebans' difficulties in the Sacred War and reassert their authority in the Southern Peloponnese. In his speech *For the Megalopolitans* (16) Demosthenes argues skilfully about interstate relations in central and southern Greece, but makes no mention of Philip, whose conquests in the north and evident willingness to become involved in Greek affairs could well have been used by Demosthenes' opponents as good reason for not making more commitments in the Peloponnese. There is certainly no sign that Demosthenes foresaw how Philip would work to replace the Thebans as backers of Megalopolis and within five years, according to both him (19.10–11 and 303–6) and his great rival Aeschines (2.79), assist influential friends to power there.

Any Greeks who thought that Philip's defeats in Thessaly were a decisive check on his ambitions were speedily disillusioned. In the following year he returned to defeat Onomarchus and the Phocian army at the battle of the Crocus Field (Diod. 16.35.3–6). According to Diodorus (16.35.5), Chares was 'by chance sailing by with many Athenian triremes' at the time of the battle and many Phocians tried to escape by swimming towards them, but Demosthenes put Pagasae along with Potidaea and Methone (see above) as places to which the Athenians sent help too late (4.35), and it is much more likely that Chares had been sent to assist Lycophron and Onomarchus. Demosthenes makes no other reference to this episode,[9] so that again we cannot know whether he had been pressing for more prompt action or greater readiness. At all events, he must have been impressed by Philip's victory, which gave him control of Thessaly. He must too have been alarmed by the way in which, whatever his original intention, he had identified himself with the prosecutors of the Sacred War against the Phocians (Diod. 16.35.6, Justin 8.2.3).[10]

Clearly, as Diodorus says (16.38.1), it was with the intention of carrying the war with the Phocians into their homeland that Philip now advanced towards the Pass of Thermopylae. How soon it was after his victory in Thessaly cannot be known,[11] but this time the Athenians were sufficiently prompt in decision and action to forestall him. They sent 5,000 infantry and 400 cavalry to block his way through the Pass. Philip made no attempt to force a passage and withdrew first to Thessaly and then to Macedonia. Six years passed before he tried again. Here too it is not known what role, if any, Demosthenes played in the debates which led to the sending of this force, although he was later, in 343, to commend the action in dramatic language (19.319).[12] The appointed naval commander was Nausicles, who later certainly was a supporter of Aeschines (Aes. 2.18, 184). Diophantus proposed a decree of celebration following the expedition's success (Dem. 19.86), and it is likely that Eubulus was also influential in its dispatch.[13]

Back in Macedonia Philip this time had no wounds to lick and he quickly turned his attention to the eastern frontiers of his power. What he aimed to do and how much he achieved is obscure. Demosthenes' brief statement in his *First Olynthiac* (1) of 349 that 'he went to Thrace, then expelled some of the kings there and established others, but fell ill' (13) suggests that he took some action against Cersebleptes to make him think again about the wisdom of his support of the Athenians in the previous year. That he wanted to develop a threat to Athens' corn-supply route from the Black Sea is less likely, given that he did not return to this area until 346.

However, in his *Third Olynthiac* (3), delivered to the Assembly in winter 349/8 a few months after the first, Demosthenes told how news came to Athens in November 352 that Philip was besieging Heraion Teichos (4–5), the location of which he gave as 'in Thrace' and is commonly thought to have been on the shore of the Propontis (the Sea of Marmora) north of the Chersonese.[14] The Athenians, he said, reacted with a long and noisy debate at the end of which they voted to send a fleet of forty ships, manned by citizens under the age of forty-five, and to raise forty talents for the force by a special tax (*eisphora*). This reaction suggests that the Athenians did see Philip's activities as a threat to the Chersonese and the corn-route through the Hellespont and that the euphoria engendered by the success of the expedition to Thermopylae was still stirring their adrenaline. But it soon settled when further news came that 'Philip was ill or dead' and the expedition was abandoned, no force being sent to the area until some eleven months later, when they dispatched Charidemus with 'just ten ships, no citizen troops and only five silver talents'.

This Charidemus, a man of Oreus in Euboea who had been given Athenian citizenship, was the chief target, in his role as chief adviser to the Thracian king Cersebleptes, of a surviving forensic speech which Demosthenes wrote in 352. His client was the prosecutor of one Aristocrates, who was indicted, under the *graphē paranomōn* procedure, for having illegally proposed a decree giving special protected status to Charidemus. In the speech he does not come over as a man who thought that the war against Philip should be the prime concern of his fellow citizens, but it should be remembered that Demosthenes was making the best case for a client and that the views expressed were not necessarily his. Thus it cannot be said that it was his judgement that Philip had chosen to take 'small profits, untrustworthy friends and a dangerous course instead of a life of security' (Dem. 23.112) in preferring as allies the Thessalians, who, he said, had betrayed all their friends, over the Athenians, who had betrayed none of theirs and were the friends of his ancestors, although he certainly returned later in 349 (Dem. 1.22, 2.11) to what he saw as the unstable nature of Philip's alliance with the Thessalians.

Three years later Demosthenes saw the decision not to send the force to Heraion Teichos as a lost opportunity. 'If we had gone eagerly to help these then', he said (3.5), 'as we had voted, Philip would not have survived and he would not be troubling us now.' Whether he had pressed for action at the time or was offering the wisdom of hindsight cannot be known, but either way his judgement was unsound. Philip certainly did fall ill, and withdrew home, leaving Heraion Teichos untaken,[15] so that on arrival the Athenian force would have found nothing to do; and it was far too small to have done Philip any damage nearer home, still less to have caused his overthrow or whatever was implied in Demosthenes' rhetoric.

Rather more than two years before Demosthenes passed his judgement on the Athenians' decision not to send the force they were preparing to Heraion Teichos, and at the time when the dispatch of the small force which Charidemus took to the area of the Chersonese and the Propontis in September 351 was being discussed, he delivered his *First Philippic* (4).[16] This was the first of his surviving series of speeches before the Assembly devoted to the threat of Philip. His chief concern in this speech was to persuade the Athenians to pursue their war with Philip with greater vigour. To this end, he chided their complacency (9, 43, 49), but he was much more concerned to correct what he saw as a feeling of helplessness in the face of Philip's confidence and speed of action, arguing that Philip had grown powerful through the Athenians' own folly and sloth and was not invincible (4–12). He was critical of their reluctance to undertake personal service on military and naval expeditions (7, 44–5), with the consequent reliance on mercenaries (24–5), and of the political and administrative procedures which had made their expeditions sent to help at Potidaea (356), Methone (354) and Pagasae (352) all arrive too late, whereas their great festivals, the Panathenaea and the Dionysia, were always held at the right time (35–6). In addition to this mixture of criticism and exhortation, he put forward detailed proposals for improving Athens' fighting capability. First he proposed the equipment of a fleet of fifty triremes in a high state of readiness to sail to meet emergencies with citizen troops on board, if necessary, and transports to carry up to half their cavalry (16); this force would provide a necessary deterrent, stirring in Philip's mind the thought that the Athenians might shake off 'excessive apathy' and take action as they had the previous year at Thermopylae (17). Then he called for the dispatch of a force to the north Aegean to carry on continuous small-scale warfare and cause harm to Philip (19); this force should consist of 2,000 infantry and 200 cavalry, of whom in each case a quarter should be Athenians, serving for limited periods in rotation, with ten fast-sailing triremes for protection (21–2). He backed these recommendations with an estimate of cost, supported by a document, which is not included in the manuscripts of the speech, explaining how the money would be raised.

Demosthenes' first suggestion was, one assumes, designed to produce a more rapid response than had been made even in the recent emergencies of Philip's threat to win control of the Pass of Thermopylae and his attack on Heraion Teichos. There is no evidence for supposing that it was adopted. Although in July 346 Demosthenes evidently believed that the Pass could be secured by a strong enough force at a very few days' notice, no attempt was then made; and in the summer of 348, when speed was essential to save Olynthus against Philip's unexpectedly swift assault, the Athenian force arrived too late (see below). As for his second suggestion,

Charidemus was, as has been seen, sent out with ten ships and was still based in the north Aegean in early 348 (Philochorus, *FGrH* 328 F50), but he had no citizen troops with him and was given little money (Dem. 3.5) and the sources provide no information about his activities in 350 or 349.

The *First Philippic*, then, had little obvious effect, but the lack of response is not surprising. On the one hand, Demosthenes was still not an established leading politician, as his apology for speaking so early in this debate shows (4.1). On the other, Philip had not made a major move so far since abandoning the siege of Heraion Teichos the previous autumn.[17] Demosthenes did refer to raids by Philip's ships on Lemnos and Imbros, where Athenian citizens were taken prisoners, and nearer home at Geraestus, the extreme south-eastern tip of Euboea, and at Marathon, where *Paralus*, the sacred trireme, was seized (4.34), but these raids had not necessarily happened within the past year and the people's memories were probably focused chiefly on the successful expedition to Thermopylae and on Philip's illness and withdrawal from Heraion Teichos. They were less concerned by the failure to support Lycophron at Pherae, as he was widely seen as a tyrant, and about anything Philip had done to Cersebleptes, a barbarian king, of whom after all a client of Demosthenes had in the previous year evinced profound mistrust.

This is not to say that Demosthenes was not right to urge the Athenians to take serious precautions against Philip's threat. Having committed himself to the support of the god of Delphi, Philip would have been expected to try again to enter central Greece sooner rather than later and, if he looked like relegating the Sacred War to the back of his mind, his Thessalian allies and the Thebans too would be sure to jog his memory. Much the same can be said about the defence of the Hellespont, where, although there was no assumed call of religious duty working on Philip, Cersebleptes filled the Phocians' role as the Athenians' first line of defence and his rival princes that of the Thessalians and the Thebans. It is not likely that in 351 thinking Athenians believed that it would be over four years before Philip began to prepare to move south or east again.

That said, Demosthenes' thoughts and energies seem not yet to have been focused entirely on the Macedonian menace. What internal evidence there is for the date of his speech *For the Liberty of the Rhodians* (15) does not contradict the date of 351/0 given for it by Dionysius of Halicarnassus, who put the *First Philippic* in 352/1. In *For the Liberty of the Rhodians* Demosthenes supported an appeal from exiled Rhodian democrats for help in securing their restoration and the removal of the oligarchic regime set up at Rhodes either at the time of the island's secession from the Athenian confederacy in 357 (Diod. 16.7.3) or just after its independence was recognised in the peace-treaty of 355 (Diod. 16.22.2). Demosthenes convincingly discounted the risk of action at Rhodes provoking a reaction from the Persian king (5–10), but in urging the Athenians to intervene he was asking a lot more of them than he had in the case of Megalopolis before, namely, their commitment to a naval and military action that would require substantial resources. Had he, then, altered his view that the top priority was to prepare against Philip's aggression? He did at one point (24) remind his listeners of the threat from the north when he criticised some of them for frequently expressing contempt of Philip as worthless, while being frightened of the King of Persia as a formidable enemy. It is also notable that, whereas in the *First Philippic* he went into great detail about the formation and financing of his North Aegean task force, he said nothing at all here about the practical problems of restoring the Rhodian exiles. So, it could be that he was more concerned with making debating points in the Assembly than with promoting Athenian intervention.[18]

At all events the Athenians took no action against the Rhodian oligarchy and the year 350 passed with no known development in the war with Philip, who may have been involved in campaigns against his northern and western neighbours. Speaking in late summer of the following year, Demosthenes gave a brief list in chronological order of Philip's activities since 357 ending with his intervention in Olynthus in 351 and expeditions against the Illyrians, the Paeonians and Arybbas, king of Epirus.[19]

This lull continued through the spring and early summer of 349, but around midsummer Philip began a war in Chalcidice which a year later was to end with the capture of Olynthus and the enslavement of its people. Whether those were his original aims must be uncertain. His first moves were against smaller members of the Chalcidian federation, which Olynthus dominated (Diod. 16.52.9, Philochorus, *FGrH* 328 F50), and, as he did not attack Olynthus itself until midsummer 348 (Diod. 16.53.2), he was perhaps hoping that the Olynthians would come to terms without a fight. But Justin (8.3.10) has the war arising from the Olynthians' refusal to hand over to Philip two exiled stepbrothers of his whom they were sheltering, and Philochorus' account of the war starts with them at war with Philip and successfully appealing to the

Athenians for help, all as his first episode in 349/8 (*FGrH* 328 F51).[20]

Most cogently, it is clear from Demosthenes' *First Olynthiac* (1) that he thought that the crisis affected the Olynthians and was urgent. He depicted the Olynthians as feeling imminently threatened and fully aware that they were about to fight 'not for glory or a piece of land, but to prevent their overthrow and enslavement' (5). The speech certainly belonged to the time before the Athenians decided to accept the Olynthians as allies and send them military aid, very probably indeed to the debate in the Assembly over those issues (late summer 349). 'My opinion', he said, 'is that you should vote for an expedition now, prepare the quickest way to send it from here and send envoys who will tell them [the Olynthians] what you intend and be there to see what happens' (2).

To persuade the Athenians to follow that advice he used the same lines of argument that he had used in the *First Philippic*: that Philip's ambition was formidable and a serious danger to Athens, but could be defeated, given that many of his successes were due to Athenian folly and sluggishness – and not surprisingly in the crisis of the moment he put them over with greater emphasis. Thus, if Philip was not stopped in the Chalcidice, his army would soon be in Attica (11, 25–6). After a long list of Athenian failures, he summed up with the judgement 'we have increased Philip's strength and we have made him more powerful than any king of Macedonia has yet become' (9). This time, though, he could also offer a more positive incentive to action, in that an alliance with an Olynthus that he thought was fully committed to fighting Philip offered a heaven-sent opportunity to win the war (7–8, 10–11), and later in the speech he speculated that Philip had not expected defiance from the Olynthians and reported that he was having trouble with his allies in Thessaly and from his old enemies the Paeonians and the Illyrians (21–3). Again, as in the *First Philippic*, he backed up his exhortations with precise advice about what naval and military resources should be deployed. He called for two distinct and substantial expeditionary forces, one to help the Olynthians defend their Chalcidian allies and the other to do damage to Macedon (16–18). This time he did not suggest numbers of ships and men, but he did again demand the personal service of Athenian citizens (20, 24) and he did indirectly suggest that the people might dip into the theoric fund to finance the expeditions, although he did not dare either to name the fund or to make any proposal about it (19–20).

Demosthenes' *Second Olynthiac* (2) followed closely on the first and could well have been a further contribution to the same debate in the Assembly. His words 'I say that we must help the Olynthians and the best and quickest way that anyone suggests wins my approval' (11), strongly suggest that no help has yet been sent and it seems that he is sensing reluctance and seeking to overcome it. In particular, he enlarged on the theme of Philip's present difficulties, suggesting this time that embassies be sent to encourage Thessalian opposition to him (11–13) and that his own subjects in Macedonia were restive and unreliable, the latter point being backed up with a colourful account of life at Philip's court drawn from the evidence of an alleged eyewitness (14–20); indeed, he said, it was only good fortune that kept him successful (22).

In the event the people did vote to accept the Olynthians as allies and to send them military aid, which was fairly speedily dispatched. No doubt other politicians had spoken in favour of this course of action, but Demosthenes may well have played an important role, if his second speech was necessitated by continuing public hesitation; it is noteworthy that he ended it by what seems to be an attack on established politicians who rely on their reputations rather than offering the best advice (31). Demosthenes, though, did not get all he wanted. The force sent to help the Olynthians consisted of a fleet of thirty ships which evidently Chares already had somewhere in the north, augmented by eight to be manned at the Piraeus, and 2,000 peltasts. These men were mercenaries, not citizens, and there is no evidence of any separate operations against Macedonia.

Whether that part of Demosthenes' strategy could have been successful is doubtful, but Chares' presence may have helped to persuade Philip to postpone any direct attack on Olynthus. What Diodorus says (16.52.9) is that after his initial success in winning over Chalcidian towns (*polismata*) he went off to Thessaly to set things right again in Pherae. Demosthenes had been correct in forecasting trouble for Philip in that quarter, but his reports of discontent in Macedonia were apparently groundless.[21]

Evidently, though, Demosthenes was not satisfied with Chares' efforts. In his *Third Olynthiac* (3), delivered at some point in the winter of 349/8, he was a lot more vehement than before in his criticism of his fellow citizens' reluctance to undertake personal military service and to make adequate financial contributions and of the politicians who gratified their slothful inclinations (27–36); and he was more explicit in his suggestions about tapping the theoric fund, proposing the appointment of legislative commissioners (*nomothetai*) to consider amending the laws about the fund and also those about the avoidance of military service (10–11). Nothing, it seems, was done as a result, and when early in 348 Apollodorus proposed that the surplus money should be put at the year's end into the stratiotic (military) fund instead of the theoric, he was prosecuted and found guilty of making an illegal proposal ([Dem.] 59.4–6).

Apollodorus' proposal was connected with the need to send out two expeditionary forces, one under Charidemus to bring further aid to the Olynthians, the other to secure the leading position of one Plutarchus in Eretria, which with other Euboean cities had rejoined the Athenians' naval confederacy in 357. The latter force was dispatched in mid-February[22] under the command of Phocion and is described by Plutarch (*Phocion* 12.1) as 'no great force'. However, it was enough for Phocion, a competent general, to defeat an army collected by Callias of Chalcis 'from all of Euboea' and supplemented by Phocian mercenaries (Aes. 3.87), despite the premature flight of Plutarchus and his contingent. Phocion then expelled Plutarchus from Eretria, but, after he returned to Athens, the situation deteriorated under his successor and the Athenians had to allow the Euboean cities to withdraw from the naval confederacy.[23]

Not surprisingly, there has been speculation about Philip's part in promoting this opposition to the Athenians in Euboea. Back in 351 Demosthenes claimed to have a copy of a letter Philip had sent to the Euboeans, which he felt was significant enough to read out in the Assembly (4.37). Years later in 330 Aeschines in an attack on Callias of Chalcis asserted that he had sent to Philip for reinforcements, but, if true, that does not prove that he supplied any troops, let alone that he had helped stir up the trouble in the first place.[24] Demosthenes' only comment on the Euboean affair was his claim two years later (5.5) that he had been the only speaker to oppose the sending of an army in the first place and this might be taken to indicate that he did not see Philip's hand in the opposition to Plutarchus.[25]

In any case, their distractions in Euboea did not prevent the Athenians from sending out the expedition to Chalcidice a month or more after Phocion had left for Eretria (March–April 348). By then, it seems, Phocion had won his victory, as some of his cavalry were included in the 150 which, according to Philochorus (*FGrH* 328 F50), were assigned to Charidemus along with 4,000 peltasts and eighteen ships.[26] Some of his force at least seems to have been still in Chalcidice, when Philip eventually moved against Olynthus after midsummer 348.[27] The confidence Demosthenes had expressed in the *First Olynthiac* (1.5, 7) in the reliability of the Olynthians proved misplaced. First, traitors surrendered to Philip Torone and Mecyberna, the port of Olynthus (Diod. 16.53.2), then 500 men of the Olynthians' cavalry (Diod. 16.53.2) deserted before Philip won two engagements outside Olynthus (Dem. 19.265, Diod. 16.53.2), and finally, when Olynthus itself was under assault, two of the city's leaders, Euthycrates and Lasthenes, were bribed to end its resistance (Diod. 16.53.2). In the final crisis the Olynthians sent an appeal to the Athenians for more help. They responded by sending Chares back, this time with 2,000 citizen hoplites and 300 cavalry (Philochorus, *FGrH* 328 F51), but a storm prevented him reaching Olynthus before it was betrayed (*Suda*, s.v. *Karanos*).

Amid all the uncertainty about the size and the duration of the Athenian war effort in Chalcidice, two things are clear: first, that it failed; second, that from the citizen body only a very small number of cavalry was ever engaged. Demosthenes could then have argued that, if the Athenians had followed his advice in the *First Olynthiac* more thoroughly, things would have gone better. Whether he did so argue is not known, but, as has been seen, he was critical of those who had persuaded the people to send an army to Euboea in February 348, if the way he spoke about it in late summer 346 is anything to go by (5.5). In that matter, at least, he was surely mistaken, as it was clearly of prime importance for the Athenians to keep the Euboean cities, their closest neighbours to the north, in friendly hands. It is arguable too that it would have been pointless to send citizen hoplites to the Chalcidice at any time before midsummer 348, for while Philip held off from attacking Olynthus there would have been little for them to do. When he finally closed in on the city, they might have helped, but Philip was much nearer to the theatre of war and was in sole charge of making decisions and carrying them out. Granted the help he received from the traitors, it is not surprising that the Athenians were too late.[28]

When Olynthus was surrendered to him, Philip sacked the city and enslaved the inhabitants, selling both men and property as booty (Diod. 16.53.3). It was not his first act of barbaric cruelty, as he had sold the Potidaeans into slavery eight years earlier, while sending home the Athenian settlers there without ransom (Diod. 16.8.5), and he may well have dealt the same way now with other Chalcidians, although Demosthenes was surely exaggerating when seven years later in the *Third Philippic* (9) he listed the wrongs done by Philip against the Greeks and spoke of 'Olynthus and Methone and Apollonia and the thirty-two cities in Chalcidice, all of which Philip has destroyed so ruthlessly that it would not be easy for someone coming to them to say whether they had ever been inhabited' (26). Philip's prime motives here were probably, as Diodorus suggests (16.53.3), material advantage, as he acquired a lot of money from selling slaves and land, and the intimidation of 'the other cities that were opposed to him', among them surely Athens.[29]

It is indeed a fair surmise that it was as much fear of what Philip might do, if somehow he reached Attica, as sober calculation that, having failed to save Olynthus, they were not going to stop him reaching it that persuaded the Athenians to respond when Philip began to talk of peace.[30] That he did begin to do so is at first slightly surprising, but, given that there is no evidence that he was in any political or economic difficulty at home, it must be that he had decided that he ought soon to try to bring the Sacred War to a successful conclusion, and that he would do that more easily if he could secure at least the neutrality of the Athenians. Further, it is likely that he thought it would be better still if he had their co-operation, and that in working out his longer-term objectives he had come to prefer an accommodation with the Athenians to the prospect of war à l'outrance. Maybe he was already thinking of leading the Greeks in a great war against the Persian empire for which it would be poor preparation to have humiliated or even subjugated the most famous city in Greece, but it is not necessary to believe that he was in order to explain what he now did.[31]

2

The negotiation of the peace-treaty concluded between Athens and Philip in spring 346 and its immediate consequences during that summer form the crucial episode in Demosthenes' political career. By the end of it Demosthenes had reached an assessment of Philip's ambitions in Greece that was not going to change over the rest of the king's life, and he had also established his own standing with the Athenian people to the extent that he won all the important debates over the next ten years.

Philip's first peace-feelers almost certainly preceded his capture of Olynthus, being conveyed, according to an account in Aeschines (2.12) which there is no reason to distrust,[32] by Euboean envoys negotiating at Athens for an end to the fighting which had started in February. Aeschines did not report any Athenian reaction, but went on to tell how Philip sent a second conciliatory message through Ctesiphon, an Athenian ambassador, sent to help another citizen, Phrynon, recover ransom money which he had paid to some allegedly Macedonian-based pirates, who had kidnapped him during the Olympic truce (late July/August). Ctesiphon reported that 'Philip said he had gone to war with the Athenians unwillingly and even now wanted to be rid of the war' (Aes. 2.13). This time the people expressed their approval and formally congratulated Ctesiphon *nem. con.*, whereupon Philocrates' motion that Philip be invited to send a herald and ambassadors to discuss peace was passed – unanimously, says Aeschines. But there was still some opposition to negotiations: Philocrates was charged under the *graphē paranomōn* procedure with making an illegal proposal and his motion was put in abeyance pending his trial. When the trial came up, probably quite soon (although Aeschines provided no indication of time), Philocrates was ill, but Demosthenes spoke for him and he was acquitted, his accusers not even receiving enough votes to avoid the penalty. Strangely, there is no indication that Philocrates' motion was reactivated and the invitation sent to Philip. Eventually Aristodemus, who had been sent as an envoy from Athens to plead for the release of citizens captured at Olynthus, returned with another message of goodwill from Philip, in which he now expressed a desire to become Athens' ally. For some reason Aristodemus was slow to make his report and he had to be summoned to do so by the Boule. It was now past midsummer 347 and a whole year since Philip's first message. Aeschines makes a point of saying that Demosthenes was now a member of the Boule and the Attic year 347/6 is known to have been his year on that body (2.82, 3.62). Demosthenes then again showed his support for negotiating with Philip by proposing that a crown be awarded to Aristodemus. It was still some months, though, before the Athenians made their first really positive move for peace by voting on the proposal of Philocrates to send a delegation of ten ambassadors to Philip in Macedonia.

Why did this vote not come until well over a year after Philocrates' original proposal had been so strongly supported? The most likely explanation is that most Athenians were at least still reluctant to concede that Philip had got the upper hand and that, as long as he was still king of Macedon, they were not going to recover lost possessions. It is notable that the two really significant votes seem to have followed substantial setbacks for the city's fortunes.

Philocrates' original proposal probably followed very soon after the news arrived of the failure of Chares' expedition and the fall of Olynthus; the decision to send the ten envoys to open negotiations almost certainly came when in February 346 the Athenians heard that their attempt to take control of the Pass of Thermopylae had failed. The Phocian authorities had offered to hand over to them, in exchange for some help, three places, Alponus, Thronion and Nicaea, which controlled the roads to Thermopylae, and they decided to send the general Proxenus to take them over with fifty ships and 'the citizens up to the age of forty' (a force comparable with that which Nausicles had taken to bar Philip's way in 352), but Phalaecus, the local Phocian commander, declined to co-operate. He may indeed have already agreed with Philip to let him through, as he did a few months later. Aeschines, who is the source for this episode (2.132–3), added that Proxenus' report of this setback arrived on the day when the Athenians were discussing peace (2.134).

The importance of securing Thermopylae in any continuation of the war with Philip had been made even clearer in the months since the fall of Olynthus by two developments. First, Aeschines with the support of Eubulus persuaded the Athenians to send envoys to neutral Greek states calling on them to send representatives to a conference at Athens to discuss joining in the war against Philip. Aeschines himself went to Megalopolis, where Philip's friends were already influential, but failed to win them over (Dem. 19.10–11, 303–6) and the other envoys were evidently no more successful, as there was no conference and no new allies were enrolled. The Athenians, then, would in future have to rely on existing allies, such as the Phocians, and on their own existing resources. Then, at some point in 347, Philip at last demonstrated renewed interest in the Sacred War, responding to an appeal for help from the Thebans by sending 'a few soldiers' (Diod. 16.58.2–3), but obviously arousing fears that next year he would do more, fears that would have become more intense, if, as has been suggested, he concluded a formal alliance with the Thebans in winter 347/6 rather than a few years earlier,[33] and if the signs of increasing Phocian weakness were being correctly read.[34]

It does not necessarily follow that Demosthenes had been opposed to the diplomatic approach to neutral Greek states because it was initiated by his later political enemies and because he himself later described it with an element of mocking exaggeration, but his positive moves to bring about negotiations with Philip suggest that he had decided that peace was necessary and the sooner the better. That is not to say that he believed Philip's expressions of goodwill: for him, as for many Athenians, what was seen as his treachery over Amphipolis was very hard to forget. But a formal treaty which restricted his expansion could do very well for the present.

Demosthenes, Philocrates and Aeschines, but not Eubulus, were among those elected to serve on the delegation of ten usually called the First Embassy, which left for Macedonia probably at the beginning of Anthesterion, the eighth month of the Attic year (then usually starting in late January or early February, but sometimes later, if intercalation of an extra month had been necessary). What happened between this point and Philip's successful entry into central Greece in late Scirophorion (late June/early July) is particularly difficult to establish as the only sources are the edited versions of the two pairs of speeches delivered by Demosthenes and Aeschines at two trials in which they were antagonists – Demosthenes *On the Embassy* (19) prosecuting and Aeschines *On the Embassy* (2) defending in 343 and Aeschines *Against Ctesiphon* (3) prosecuting and Demosthenes *On the Crown* (18) defending in 330 – and all delivered after the whole process of negotiating and ratifying the Peace had been discredited. Demosthenes, having in 343 explicitly excluded Aeschines' conduct on the First Embassy from his accusation of treacherous misconduct, said nothing about what occurred on it in either speech. His silence, though, is not surprising in view of what Aeschines said in 343 about his address to Philip when the envoys went before him (2.34–5):

> Now when I had said this and more beside, at last came Demosthenes' turn to speak. All were intent, expecting to hear a masterpiece of eloquence. For, as we learned afterwards, his extravagant boasting had been reported to Philip and his court. So when all were thus prepared to listen, this creature mouthed forth a proem – an obscure sort of thing and as dead as fright could make it; and getting on a little way into the subject he suddenly stopped speaking and stood helpless; finally he collapsed completely. Philip saw his plight and bade him take courage, and not to think, as though he were an actor on the stage, that his collapse was an irreparable calamity, but to keep cool and try gradually to recall his speech, and speak it off as he had prepared it. But he, having been once upset, and having forgotten what he had written, was unable to recover himself; nay, on

making a second attempt, he broke down again. Silence followed; then the herald bade us withdraw.[35]

As the youngest envoy Demosthenes had to speak last and just after Aeschines, the next-to-youngest, had spoken at great length (to judge from what he says about his speech) and largely on a topic, the Athenian claim to Amphipolis, that Demosthenes clearly realised was entirely irrelevant in Philip's eyes (Aes. 2.36–7). In that situation he could well have thought that much of what he had prepared to say was inappropriate and have failed to improvise, rendering the confrontation a sad disappointment to historians, but fertile ground for psychologists (on Demosthenes' ability to extemporize, cf. Cooper, Chapter 8).

A short time later Philip called in the envoys again, and according to Aeschines 'undertook to say something in answer to each of the arguments put forward' (2.38). Unfortunately, just as Aeschines had said nothing about any of the arguments put forward by other envoys than himself, so too he said nothing about Philip's answers, preferring to point out that he 'naturally' spent most of his time on his arguments while saying nothing about Demosthenes' speech. It must be supposed that the envoys raised the subject of the Sacred War and Philip's expected intervention and he very probably indicated that he would not accept a peace which stopped him intervening; it is unlikely that he went further and said how he thought the Phocians should be treated in defeat, although he could have encouraged associates to drop hints to some of the envoys to help them keep the Athenian public quiet while he carried out his plans, just as in the letter which he gave to the envoys to be read to the Athenian people he told them that he would explain the benefits he intended to confer on them, once he was sure that they agreed to an alliance as well as peace with him, a promise which, as Demosthenes pointed out, he did not fulfil (19.40). Similarly his preparations for a campaign in Thrace against Cersebleptes were obvious; indeed he left Pella, his capital, for it on the same day as the envoys set out for home (Aes. 2.82). In this case he did make a clear undertaking not to attack the Chersonese (Aes. 2.82), but is unlikely to have revealed his plans for Cersebleptes' future. Whatever the truth about these questions, Philip felt that, despite the lack of realism displayed by Aeschines and perhaps others over Amphipolis, it was still worthwhile to pursue peace and, as well as giving the envoys the letter with its beguiling promise, agreed to send representatives to finalise the agreement with Athens. He subsequently appointed a delegation which included Antipater (Aes. 3.72), who was later Alexander's 'regent' in Macedon and Greece, and probably another of his chief lieutenants, Parmenion (second hypothesis to Dem. 19, 5), and they arrived in time for the important debate in the Assembly.

Back at Athens there was still a strong feeling that no peace should be accepted unless it protected the Phocians, to whom the Athenians were bound by oaths of alliance. One way of doing that which was being explored was the possibility of closing the war with Philip – and the Sacred War – with a multilateral treaty somewhere along the lines of the King's Peace and the series of Common Peace agreements which followed it (the most recent concluded in 362),[36] which would of course include the Phocians. At some time in early 346, probably before the First Embassy was sent to Philip, the Athenians had sent another series of ambassadors to the neutral Greek states, this time inviting them to a conference at Athens, in the hope, as Aeschines said, that, if the war had to be continued, they might join them against Philip, and that, if the peace should seem preferable, they would participate in the peace (Aes. 2.57). A little later Aeschines quoted a resolution of the *synhedrion* of Athens' naval confederacy, passed at a time when the Athenians were deliberating about peace, which called on the Athenians not to put anything to the Assembly until envoys sent out to the Greek states had returned and reported (2.60).

The idea, though, was surely a forlorn hope. Evidently the Greek states were not so enthusiastic about it, although, according to Demosthenes (19.16), representatives of some states did travel to Athens and were present when later the Assembly debated peace-terms.[37] More important, Philip was not going to accept any treaty that limited his freedom of action in central Greece. Demosthenes, it seems, realised the futility of pressing for one, for there is no reason to doubt Aeschines' well-documented assertion (2.61) that he persuaded the Assembly not to wait for the return of the envoys from the Greek states, as the allies had suggested, but to fix the dates for debating peace-terms. Aeschines was highly critical (2.62), but the Assembly had agreed with Demosthenes.

The allies, however, did not give up, and when the first day of the debate came (18 Elaphebolion, the ninth month), the Assembly had before it a resolution of the *synhedrion* that, whatever terms were agreed, any Greek state should be permitted to participate in the resulting treaty, if it registered within three months (Aes. 3.69–70). Alongside this resolution was a proposal from Philocrates of terms for a straightforward bilateral peace between the two principals and their allies from which the Phocians were explicitly excluded (Dem. 19.159). In the first day's debate opinion ran strongly against Philocrates and in favour of the allies' proposal. In 330 Aeschines (3.71), in acknowledging his own support for the latter, asserted that all those who spoke that day did so too, while Demosthenes claimed thirteen years earlier that he had not only spoken for the allies' proposal, but had carried a motion that it be confirmed as the Athenians' position (19.144).

Aeschines may have been right in saying (2.65) that the original decree proposed by Demosthenes had provided for speeches to be confined to the first day of the debate with only voting on the second, but it seems that overnight some of the leading politicians came to realise, perhaps with help from Philip's envoys, that the allies' proposal was unacceptable to Philip, who wanted a free hand over the Phocians, and the discussion in the Assembly was resumed. Aeschines now made the speech in which, Demosthenes said (19.13–16), he urged the people to forget their glorious past and to give up helping any state from which they had received no help, a clear reference to the Phocians. Aeschines' explanation of his speech (2.74–7) shows that he was addressing a situation in which opposition to Philocrates' proposed terms was developing into a movement to reject peace altogether. Such a movement of opinion was obviously also the target of Eubulus' warning, mentioned by Demosthenes in 343 (19.291) that, if the people did not vote for peace, 'they should at once go down to the Piraeus (to man the fleet), make financial contributions and use the theoric fund for military purposes'.

In this crisis words and actions attributed to Demosthenes by Aeschines make sense. First in 343 he said that, when Philocrates' proposal was voted down, Demosthenes had ready a new decree to move in its place (Aes. 2.68). This decree cannot have laid down, as Aeschines asserts, exactly the same terms as in Philocrates' original proposal and must have offered an amended version very likely identical with that subsequently embodied in a new proposal from Philocrates, which omitted any reference to the Phocians, referring simply to the Athenians and their allies, and was in fact the one finally approved by the people (Dem. 19.322). Writing in 330 Aeschines added the detail that Demosthenes called Antipater before the Assembly and put to him a question which he answered (3.72). Although Aeschines went on to allege that Demosthenes, having forewarned Antipater of the question, instructed him in the answer, he did not say what the answer was, relying, it seems, on sixteen-year-old memories and tradition. Thirteen years earlier Demosthenes had said (19.321), though without giving a precise context in the debate, that 'Philip's ambassadors forewarned you that Philip did not accept the Phocians as allies' (of the Athenians in the peace-treaty). That Antipater may not have been quite so frank and have said merely that the conditions proposed by the allies were unacceptable to Philip is suggested by the persistent belief of most Athenians that the Phocians were protected by the treaty as allies of Athens, simply through the deletion of the original clause excluding them. Leading politicians, however, cannot have been under any illusions.

Demosthenes went on to say that after the intervention of Philip's ambassadors Aeschines and his associates began making speeches to the effect that Philip could not accept the Phocians as Athens' allies because of his own allies, the Thebans and the Thessalians (who wanted the Sacred War to be concluded with the punishment of the sacrilegious temple-robbers), but 'if he becomes master of the situation and of the peace, he will then do whatever we ask to be arranged' (19.321). Whether they had any solid evidence on which to base this prediction beyond the very vague promise in Philip's letter (see above) or whether it was only an optimistic hope of what might be achieved in negotiations after the peace was agreed will be discussed later. Demosthenes himself, having facilitated the passing of Philocrates' new proposal, was as inextricably linked with the making of the peace as were Philocrates, Aeschines and Eubulus.[38] Where he later claimed to have differed from them was in his eagerness to secure its ratification in the hope either that Philip would be forced to rein in on some of his expansionist policies in Thrace, where he was known to be campaigning against Cersebleptes (Aes. 2.82), or that his dishonesty would be disclosed and the Athenians galvanised into saving the Phocians by taking over Thermopylae (19.151–2).

This claim had some plausibility. He had made some significant moves, first to accelerate an Athenian response to Philip's overtures and then to prevent any delay in arranging for the Assembly to discuss terms. He now joined again with Philocrates in persuading the people to agree that their representatives and those of their allies in the naval confederacy should give their oaths to observe the peace to Philip's ambassadors on the sixth day after the terms were agreed, 25 Elaphebolion (Aes. 3.73–4). When the day came, Critobulus of Lampsacus, representing King Cersebleptes, asked to be allowed to give the oath on his behalf, as one of Athens' allies, although not a member of the confederacy. According to Aeschines (2.83–5), Demosthenes, one of the presiding *proedroi* of the Boule, refused to accept a motion in support of Critobulus, saying that he would not break the peace with Philip, but was forced by public clamour to put it to the vote. What Aeschines did not say was that Critobulus' friends then lost the vote. Nor in either speech did he say anything about any attempt to have the Phocians included in the oath-taking ceremony, presumably because no such attempt was made (the argument from silence being unusually strong here). It is quite likely that the contention attributed by Demosthenes (19.321) to Aeschines and his friends that Philip would prove lenient to the Phocians once he had secured the peace-treaty had made some impression; also, both politicians and their associates had no doubt worked hard at lobbying citizens in the five days since the peace-terms had been approved.[39]

This oath-taking ceremony completed, the Athenians could now press on to obtain the oaths of Philip and his allies. To this end, the same ten envoys who had formed the First Embassy, which included Demosthenes, Aeschines and Philocrates, were appointed very soon after the vote on the peace-terms and before 25 Elaphebolion (Aes. 2.82) to go again to Macedonia. Three years later Demosthenes claimed that his fellow envoys in this Second Embassy were reluctant to depart and he had to draft and see through the Boule a decree instructing them to do so as quickly as possible (19.154). Aeschines in his defence ignored this criticism of himself and his colleagues, but confirmed that such a Boule decree was passed on 3 Munichion (2.91–2). Demosthenes, it seems, should be credited for believing that the sooner Philip gave his oath the better for the city, as he claimed again in 330 (18.30). His actions here could also have been related to a growing feeling that it could be to his benefit in the future to begin to distance himself from Aeschines and Philocrates and any of the others who were closely associated with them.

The Boule's decree had ordered the general Proxenus to convey the envoys 'to wherever he learned Philip was'. Demosthenes wanted them to sail to Thrace, locate Philip and extract his oath, thereby, he thought, stopping his campaign against Cersebleptes, but was frustrated, he said, by Aeschines and the others, who instead took a circuitous route to Pella, taking twenty-three days on the journey (19.154–5), a lack of urgency which he later described (19.166) as proof that they were acting on Philip's behalf. Aeschines

agreed that he had refused to go to Thrace and argued that it was far
too late by then to save Cersebleptes, citing a letter sent to the
Athenian people by Chares which reported that Cersebleptes had
been decisively defeated on 24 Elaphebolion, the day before the
allies of Athens had give their oaths (2.90). What Aeschines did not
say was when that letter had reached Athens. Maybe it did not
arrive before the envoys left, but, if it had, Demosthenes could still
have feared that after defeating Cersebleptes Philip might move on
to extend his control over the coast of the Propontis and his
potential threat to Athens' corn-supply route.

When they eventually reached Pella, the envoys had to wait a
further twenty-seven days, according to Demosthenes (19.155),
before Philip returned. Demosthenes had a certain amount to say
about his quarrels during that time of waiting with Aeschines and
other envoys (19.156–7, 174) and made much of his own unaided
efforts to effect the ransoming of Philip's Athenian prisoners, while
the others, especially after Philip's return, accepted generous
entertainment at his expense (19.166–71). However, he said
nothing about the formal meeting of the envoys with Philip, on
which Aeschines in his defence spoke at length (2.108–18),
concentrating, naturally, on what best helped his case. According to
him, Demosthenes shamelessly usurped the right to speak first and
then spoke at length about his own role in accelerating the
Athenians' acceptance of the peace and in looking after Philip's
ambassadors. It is hard, though, to see how as the youngest of the
envoys he could have assumed the role of first speaker without the
support of at least a few of his colleagues, while his exposition of his
role could have been directed to establishing his own credentials
with Philip and may well have led into a plea for the speedy
ratification of the peace, which Aeschines in 343 ignored. As for his
own contribution, Aeschines said that he had spoken at length
about the history and traditions of the Delphian Amphictyony in
accordance with which Philip should act; he had agreed that the
motive of Philip's proposed expedition against the Phocians was
'holy and just' (2.117), but he had submitted that only those
individuals who had plotted and carried out the seizure of the shrine
at Delphi should be punished and not their communities, and had
gone on to say that Philip should not confirm the misdeeds of the
Thebans against other Boeotians: 'Thebes should be Boeotian, and
not Boeotia Theban' (2.119).

How Philip reacted to this advice is not revealed. It is unlikely
that he made any public response that was at all explicit, but quite

probable that he told his associates to make encouraging noises in private to Aeschines with a view to securing Athenian acquiescence, as Aeschines said they did (2.137). According to Demosthenes (19.35–8), Aeschines was certainly not discouraged, but, addressing the Assembly at Athens on 16 Scirophorion three days after the return of the envoys, gave a persuasively optimistic account of what Philip would do to the benefit of Athens: he would punish the Thebans rather than the Phocians on the grounds that they had originally planned to seize control of Delphi and would re-establish their neighbours Plataea and Thespiae as independent cities, and the Euboeans were expecting him to hand them over to Athens. Aeschines in reply (2.120) claimed that he had not promised anything, but merely reported what he had said to Philip. However, it was, one might think, the sort of Assembly meeting that would be remembered by many jurors only three years later and Aeschines could well have decided to convert hopes into expectations after Demosthenes' success with the Boule three days earlier. On that occasion, according to Demosthenes' account, which he backed with documentary evidence, he denounced Aeschines and Philocrates, going back to Aeschines' speeches in the debates on the peace-terms, but including also their conduct in Macedon,[40] and urged the Boule not to abandon the remaining positions with regard to the Phocians and Thermopylae – the Boule, he said, was convinced (19.18, 31).

Demosthenes is emphatic that the Boule neither passed a vote of thanks to the envoys nor invited them to public hospitality, but what it resolved is not clear. Enough, evidently, to enable Demosthenes to cite the resolution as evidence of his denunciation of fellow envoys (19.31), but did it recommend to the Assembly action at Thermopylae or in Phocis? If it did, was there any possibility that Thermopylae could be held at this late stage when Philip was, as Demosthenes later admitted (19.58), already at the western end of the pass (although news of his advance may not yet have reached Athens)? The only hope was that the Phocian Phalaecus, who held the pass and had refused to hand it over to the Athenian force earlier in the year, might change his attitude now that Philip was at hand. But, if he did, it would take some days for the Assembly to approve an expedition and for a force to be prepared and transported, and in the meantime the Thebans, who were in better shape than in 352, might move north to attack his rear (Aes. 2.137). As for the Phocians in their homeland, Demosthenes later claimed (19.123) that they might have offered

Philip some stern resistance if they had been given any sign of support from Athens.

In the event, however, Phalaecus handed over the pass to Philip in return for safe-conduct for himself and his men to depart under truce (Diod. 16.59.3) and the Phocians then surrendered to Philip, having heard from their envoys of the outcome of the debate in the Athenian Assembly on 16 Scirophorion, when the people had been so carried away by Aeschines' confident predictions that they had refused to discuss the resolution of the Boule passed three days earlier in accordance with Demosthenes' advice, but had agreed to Philocrates' proposal that they should re-emphasise their support for Philip and promise to join in any necessary action to force the Phocians to hand the shrine at Delphi over to the Amphictyonic Council (Dem. 19.47–50). Whether they could have resisted effectively, if the Athenians had resolved otherwise, is doubtful. Aeschines' contention (2.131–2) that the Phocians were by now gravely weakened by lack of money and internal discord is backed by elements in Diodorus' narrative (16.56).[41]

Now in control of Phocis, Philip took no action against the Thebans, but agreed with them and the Thessalians to entrust the matter of punishment to the Amphictyonic Council (Diod. 16.59.4). The news of this reversal of the Athenians' hopes was heard first by members of a third embassy of ten (who did not include this time either Aeschines or Demosthenes), when at Chalcis on their way to meet Philip, presumably at Thermopylae. This embassy at once returned home, where its report caused a panic and the people voted to put Attica on a war footing in anticipation of an imminent invasion (Aes. 3.80). Philip, however, had recently given his oath of peace and alliance with Athens and there is no evidence to suggest that he intended to break it, although he did look to the Athenians to fulfil their side of the agreement. According to Aeschines (2.137), he now called on the Athenians to send a force to support him, but they were dissuaded from doing so by Demosthenes and his associates, who expressed fears that Philip would hold any troops as hostages. They did, though, send the ten envoys, with Aeschines now included, to join Philip in the deliberations over the punishment of the Phocians and the end of the Sacred War.[42]

Aeschines claimed (2.142) that he was able to secure the Phocians a hearing when the Oetaeans were calling for all their men of military age to be killed. In the event their punishment, although represented by Demosthenes as extremely severe (19.64–5, 81), was less harsh than it might have been, given the precedents of Potidaea, Methone and Olynthus: their cities were to be destroyed, but only those directly responsible for the sacrilege at Delphi were to be individually punished, while the rest remained on their land (Diod. 16.60.1–2).

So the Sacred War was brought to a close, but whether Philip had intended that it should be ended in that way has been a matter of some dispute.[43] Some argue that his original plan was what Aeschines hoped it was, to humble the Thebans, while letting the Phocians off lightly, but he was frustrated by the failure of the Athenians to send him the military help he asked for, without which he could not face Theban opposition.[44] Others contend persuasively that the commitment he had made to Delphi in 352 and the importance to him of his Thessalian allies could not let him consider anything less than the severe punishment of the Phocians, which meant victory for the Thebans.[45] On this interpretation his request to the Athenians for troops was not motivated by the military situation, but had a political purpose: to make them acknowledge their status as his allies and to obtain their moral support for his settlement.

Where did these events leave Demosthenes? Certainly they justified the apprehensions about Philip's plans that he had expressed since his return home from the Second Embassy; and, although he could not deny that he had been as much responsible for making the Peace as Aeschines or Philocrates, he could and did argue that he had always been wary of Philip, but had been frustrated by the failure to secure his rapid ratification of the terms. He had accepted the necessity of agreeing to Philip's request for an alliance, but, when it came to the crisis, was not willing to see it implemented. Nor, of course, were most Athenians; and there must remain a suspicion that Demosthenes' strong line in those last few days owed something to a realisation that the people were not going to enjoy seeing the hopes they had placed in the Peace disappointed, and that he would do well to distance himself from it as quickly and emphatically as he could.

Demosthenes' wariness of Philip's intentions continued and to his fellow citizens' advantage. Despite their support of the Phocians, the only penalty imposed on the Athenians was the loss of their privilege of precedence in consulting the oracle (Dem. 19.327). This loss was a significant blow to their prestige, but the Spartans were expelled from the Amphictyonic Council (Pausanias 10.8.2), and it has been suggested that there was an attempt to expel the

Athenians too. The evidence is inconclusive but it is fair to surmise that, if an attempt was made, it was Philip who frustrated it.[46] The Athenians then pushed their luck by refusing to recognise the Amphictyons' grant of membership to Philip (Dem. 5.19) and by boycotting the Pythian Games which were now celebrated for the first time since 358, with Philip as president (Dem. 19.128). Philip responded by sending envoys to demand formal Athenian recognition of his membership and probably of the whole settlement. According to Demosthenes (19.113), Aeschines alone supported Philip's demand and was shouted down, but either during the same debate in the Assembly or very soon after, Demosthenes delivered *On the Peace* (5), recommending the people to back down and do what Philip wanted.

In the first half of this speech (5) he reminded his listeners of three recent occasions on which he had given them good advice, the most recent being when he denounced as nonsense what some unnamed members of the Second Embassy promised Philip would do in the Athenians' interests (10), a detailed list of benefits similar to that ascribed by him to Aeschines three years later (Dem. 19.20–3). He then emphasised that, however unsatisfactory the peace had turned out to be, the Athenians should not do anything to break it or to provide 'those who say that they are Amphictyons' with an excuse for a 'common war' against them (14). Here he seems to have meant the Thebans and the Thessalians, for he went on to observe that Philip had been less concerned with restoring Theban power in Boeotia than with securing the pass and the routes to central Greece, winning the glory of finishing the Sacred War and presiding over the Pythian games (22). In this Demosthenes correctly understood Philip's mind. The Athenians evidently complied with his demands and he withdrew with the bulk of his army to Macedonia, having achieved all that he had aimed for in making the Peace, except a genuine and lasting reconciliation with the Athenians. His chances of achieving that were now no better than they had been before the making of the Peace. His treachery, as it was regarded, over Amphipolis still rankled at Athens and was now compounded by his failure to live up to Aeschines' predictions in his treatment of the Phocians and the Thebans. That Demosthenes had never believed those predictions did not make Philip's threat any less dangerous in his eyes; to him, it seems, no co-operative relationship with Philip was possible without the Athenians being very much the junior partner. If there was speculation about Philip's ultimate ambition being an attack on the

Persian empire,[47] it did not alter Demosthenes' view of his attitude to southern Greece in general, and Athens in particular.

3

The immediate crisis for the Athenians had passed with Philip's return home to the north, but their situation was still uncomfortable. The Thebans, who, while not, it seems, actively hostile since the battle at Mantinea sixteen years earlier, were still unfriendly, were now relieved of the burden of the Sacred War and again in control of Boeotia; the Euboean cities had ceased to be their allies; and above all Philip now controlled Thermopylae and could readily move troops down into Phocis and thence across the Gulf of Corinth into the Peloponnese. There the influence he had established at Megalopolis was seen to presage further penetration (Isoc. 5.73–5, written in summer 346), and in summer 344 the Athenians were so alarmed that they sent Demosthenes and other envoys to Argos and Messene and probably other cities to counteract his influence. In his *Second Philippic* (6), delivered later in 344, Demosthenes quoted extensively from the speech he had made at Messene, in which he had sought to demonstrate how unreliable the Olynthians and the Thessalians had come to find Philip after initially benefiting substantially from their alliances with him; if their object was to preserve their freedom, Philip was not the man to rely on: 'For every king and every despot (*tyrannos*) is the enemy of freedom and the laws' (20–5).

Demosthenes admitted that he and his colleagues had had no success on this mission (25), and earlier in the speech had painted an even grimmer picture, alleging that Philip was already sending mercenaries and money to the Argives and the Messenians and that he was expected to arrive himself with a large force (15). He did not materialise, although he did come as far south as Pherae in Thessaly, where he probably dealt with recurring trouble by installing a garrison (Diod. 16.69.8, Dem. 9.12); and if, as has been suggested,[48] his Peloponnesian friends were facing a renewed threat from Sparta and had appealed for help, his intervention could well have seemed likely. But he had done nothing against the letter of his treaty with Athens and Demosthenes' allegation that he had violated the Peace and was plotting against all Greeks (6.2) was justified only by the argument that any attempt to extend his influence in southern Greece was a breach of its spirit.

It has to be said that exciting public alarm about Philip served Demosthenes' purpose in his internal political rivalries, and elsewhere in this speech he reminded the Athenians of the misleading predictions that Aeschines and others had made about Philip in 346 (30) and put forward the dubious argument, which he was to use the next year at Aeschines' trial, that, if they had not been then misled, Philip would not have come through Thermopylae into Phocis (36).

Libanius' *hypothesis* to this speech, written in the fourth century AD, links it to a debate occasioned by the arrival of envoys from Philip and from Argos and Messene complaining about Athenian support of Sparta, but it does not say how the debate ended. Fourteen years later, in 330, Demosthenes spoke of a debate which took place at a time when 'Philip sent Python of Byzantium and with him ambassadors from all his allies with the purpose of putting the city to shame' (18.36). Although there can be no certainty, chronological indications do not preclude the suggestion that these two debates were in fact one and the same, and that the *Second Philippic* is the edited version of what Demosthenes said in response to Python's message from Philip.[49] What he said in 330 was that he stood up against Python, when he was in full flow, and 'proved Philip to be so clearly in the wrong that even his own allies rose up and agreed', whereas Aeschines supported Philip and put forward false evidence against Athens. It is strange that Aeschines had nothing to say about this episode either at his trial in 343 (when Demosthenes also was silent about it),[50] or in his attack on Demosthenes in 330, particularly as the speech *On Halonnesus* by Hegesippus ([Demosthenes] 7), a close associate of Demosthenes, delivered in 342, shows that Philip's message had positive elements which found support at Athens.

Python, it appears, in a speech before the Assembly represented Philip as preferring the friendship of Athens to that of any other Greek state and urged Athenians not to condemn the peace out of hand, but to suggest suitable amendments 'on the understanding that Philip would do whatever they voted for' ([Dem.] 7.21–2). Hegesippus contended that two years later in his letter to the Athenians, which was the context for his speech, Philip denied having ever agreed to consider amendments ([Dem.] 7.18), but it is very unlikely that Python could have said that Philip would consider them, unless Philip so instructed him. On the other hand, it is inconceivable that Philip ever undertook to do whatever the Athenians wanted. Compromise and common sense suggest that he indicated a readiness to negotiate on some issues and called on the Athenians to make proposals.

Certainly he is said to have accepted one of two substantial amendments which the Athenians put forward, that 'all the other Greeks who do not share in the Peace should be free and independent and, if anyone attacks them, those who share in the Peace should go to their help' (7.30–2),[51] a formulation which echoed the wording of the earlier Common Peace treaties and virtually converted the Peace into another one. Evidently he saw such an agreement as not unduly restrictive, given his control of the Amphictyony and his influence in a number of Peloponnesian cities, and even attractive in view of the opportunities it might offer of joint action with the Athenians. The other Athenian proposal, that the clause in the Peace which gave to each side 'what they held' (included probably in the last Common Peace of 362[52]) should be replaced by the potentially more contentious stipulation that all should possess 'their own territory' (7.18), was never likely to attract Philip; for it would have enabled the Athenians to renew their claims to Amphipolis and Potidaea and to bring up the question of Olynthus and other Chalcidian cities, as indeed Hegesippus admitted (7.9, 26–8). It is indeed difficult not to conclude that this amendment was designed by people who were disturbed by the amount of goodwill so far established and wanted to bring negotiations to an end, a purpose which would seem to have been very shortsighted even in those who did not have the benefit of knowing later history.

Python, the diplomat, may not have expressed disapproval (7.20), but Philip's reaction became clear a few months later with his inhospitable reception of an Athenian delegation led by Hegesippus (Dem. 19.331). Even so he did not completely close the door on negotiations. In 342 his letter (already referred to, which was the subject of Hegesippus' speech), although unyielding on the matter of places which he held but which the Athenians claimed as theirs, included a continuing commitment to conclude a treaty with Athens regulating legal procedures for disputes between individual Athenians and Macedonians ([Dem.] 7.9). He also undertook to submit disputes between his allies the Cardians and the Athenian settlers in the Chersonese to arbitration and to give to the Athenians the small island of Halonnesus off Thessaly, which he regarded as part of his own territory since his expulsion of the pirates there. Hegisippus recommended rejection of all these offers, supported, it seems from Aeschines' comments (3.83), by Demosthenes, who, he said, told the people not to accept Philip's gift of Halonnesus, unless he agreed that he was 'giving it back'. The result was that now Philip took 'No' for an answer and made no further conciliatory offers. Modern commentators have been harsh in their condemnation of Demosthenes, Hegesippus and their associates for their intransigence.[53]

It should not escape notice, however, that making apparently friendly overtures about amending the Peace and resolving disputes was not the only thing that the Athenian public perceived Philip doing in these two years between summer 344 and summer 342. According to Demosthenes (18.136), it will be recalled, Python, who brought Philip's first offer, also launched into strong criticism of the Athenians' conduct, while Philip's rejection of Hegesippus' embassy, however justified his exasperation, would not have brought him good report back at Athens. Moreover, he was, it was constantly reported, continuing to seek to extend his influence in the Peloponnese and in Megara and the Euboean cities, which were uncomfortably close to Attica. Demosthenes' speech *On the Embassy* (19), his contribution to the prosecution's case, when Aeschines' trial on the charge of misconduct on the Second Embassy of 346 came up in summer 343, includes references to the activities of Philip's friends or agents or even troops in all these areas. In Elis his agents were said to have helped in the overthrow of democracy (260, 294).[54] In Euboea his troops were threatening Porthmus, where pro-Athenian Eretrians had established themselves, and Carystus, and were setting up bases for attacks on Attica (87, 204, 326, 334); and a military threat to Megara (87, 204) had nearly succeeded in effecting a takeover by pro-Macedonian politicians, one of whom had twice travelled to Pella (295, 334). This last report was probably a reference to an episode described in greater detail by Plutarch (*Phocion* 15), in which the Megarians sent urgently to Athens for help and Phocion, no blinkered supporter of Demosthenes, persuaded the citizens to send troops and led them in a successful stabilising mission. Further away, an expedition Philip undertook in Epirus, put by Diodorus (16.72.1) in 343/2, was seen as a threat to Ambracia and Acarnania and Athenian troops were sent to the latter during that same year (Dem. 48.24). The people were also ready to authorise the sending of Demosthenes, Polyeuctus, Hegesippus and others on a diplomatic tour of the Peloponnesian cities in the first half of 342, which had some success (Dem. 3.72).[55]

The depth of the mistrust which Philip's attempts to negotiate had to overcome at Athens is well illustrated by the two political trials of 343. Neither Philocrates, who was condemned and escaped death by exile (Aes. 2.6, 3.79), nor Aeschines, who was acquitted by the narrow margin of thirty votes by a jury which may have numbered as many as 1,501 ([Plut.] *Mor.* 840c), would have even been indicted with misconduct on the Second Embassy if the Peace had turned out favourably for Athens. As it was, the main arguments of Demosthenes and Aeschines at the latter's trial rest on the premise that the Peace had been turned by Philip into one bad for the city, so that anyone connected with its implementation was suspected of treacherous dealing. Discussion of Aeschines' trial is undertaken in detail by Buckler (Chapter 4), but my own view is that Aeschines' acquittal should not be taken as a sign of any significant softening of the people's view of Philip.[56] In any case, they still backed Hegesippus and Demosthenes in rejecting Philip's final offers in 342.

Demosthenes' two speeches of spring 341, *On the Chersonese* (8) and the *Third Philippic* (9), make several references to Philip's continuing interference in Euboea. His general Hipponicus was said to have crossed to the island with 1,000 mercenaries, taken Porthmus, destroyed its defences and expelled the anti-Macedonian Eretrian exiles (9.33, 58), and to have then gone along to Eretria itself where he set up Cleitarchus and two colleagues as tyrants (9.57–8). Philip, Demosthenes said, was setting up Euboea as a fortress (*epiteichisma*) against the Athenians (8.66). He could not have been straining the truth overmuch, as these places were very close to Attica and a good many of those exiled would have come there. Both Diodorus (16.74.1) and the contemporary Philochorus (*FGrH* 328 F160) refer to Cleitarchus as a tyrant, Diodorus adding that he was installed by Philip. Demosthenes also reported a similar story from Oreus in northern Euboea, important to the Athenians as a watching and listening post close to Thermopylae and southern Thessaly, where, he said, Macedonian-led mercenaries set up Philistides as tyrant (8.59, 9.33, 59–62).

The autumn of 342 also saw Philip himself operating for the first time since the Peace in the other area over which the Athenians were always nervous, Eastern Thrace and the environs of the Chersonese and the Propontis. Diodorus says that he took a large force to protect 'Hellespontine cities' against Cersebleptes, whose kingdom had survived his defeat in 346, adding that he won several battles and 'founded strong cities at key places' to secure the position (16.71.1–2). Given that Diodorus typically gives no names of either the threatened cities or the new foundations, it is difficult to assess how far in the early months of his campaign he might have seemed to menace Athenian interests,[57] but it cannot have been reassuring that he was reported to be still operating in the area when Demosthenes delivered *On the Chersonese* in the following spring (8.2).

The context of *On the Chersonese* (8) was a debate on a demand from Philip that the Athenians should recall from the Chersonese their general Diopeithes, whom they had sent the previous year to support their settlers in the peninsula. Like many Athenian commanders at this period, he was, according to the speech, inadequately funded, and he had tried to remedy his deficiency by using his mercenaries to raid the lands of the Cardians, Philip's allies at the neck of the Chersonese, and other small cities nearby which were now under his protection (9). From the start Demosthenes sought to widen the discussion, asserting that what speakers should be talking about was not Diopeithes' activities, but the position of the Chersonese and Philip's campaign in Thrace 'now in its eleventh month' (2), which, as he saw it, threatened to win him control of the Hellespont before the Athenians could do anything to stop him (3). His opponents had apparently been saying that the people should either keep the peace by recalling Diopeithes or decide to go to war (6), to which his answer was that Philip was not likely to leave the choice to them. If they opted for appeasement, were they going to wait until he attacked Attica and the Piraeus and in the meantime let everything else go (7–8)? Other echoes of the *First Philippic* and the *First Olynthiac*, such as his criticism of the people's reluctance to take action (32–7) and his recommendation of the equipping and financing of a permanent force to protect Greek states against Philip (46–7), show Demosthenes' thoughts centred now on the likelihood of war. Indeed at one point he told the people: 'First, men of Athens, you must realise this firmly in your minds that Philip is at war (*polemei*) with the city and has broken the peace … He is ill disposed and hostile to the whole city and the ground on which it stands' (39). A new note is a feeling that other Greek states are beginning to see Philip's threat and to look to Athens for leadership, to be heard in the critical remarks about the Athenians' inertia he put into the mouths of the other Greeks (35–7) and in his claim that what Philip fears most is Athens' reputation as the defender of democracy (41–3).

The military preparations Demosthenes suggested were not put in hand, but on the main subject of the debate he won the argument. Diopeithes, as far as is known, was not recalled. Certainly his small force remained in the Chersonese, for in the *Third Philippic* (9), delivered about two months later, Demosthenes stressed the necessity to send money and supplies to it (73). Earlier, after arguing strongly that Philip's attempt on Megara, his setting-up of tyrants in Euboea, his intrigues in the Peloponnese and his invasion of Thrace were acts of war (17), he had developed the theme of his threat to the freedom of all Greeks. In thirteen years, he asserted, Philip had committed more crimes against Greek liberty than the Athenians had in the seventy years of their hegemony or the Spartans in the thirty years of theirs (25). A vivid depiction of Philip's present strength (32–5) was followed by a diagnosis of Greek weakness as due to a failure of spirit and disunity (36–46). The speech ended with a call for vigorous military and naval preparations and energetic diplomacy: it was the Athenians' duty to 'summon, convene, instruct and advise the other Greeks', who would respond, if they saw the Athenians setting an example of awareness and action (70–3).

It was soon apparent that Demosthenes had judged right the mood at Athens and elsewhere. Very soon after this speech was delivered, an alliance was concluded with Chalcis in Euboea, the proposal in the Assembly being moved by Demosthenes (Aes. 3.71), and before midsummer a joint expeditionary force from the two allies liberated Oreus from the tyrant Philistides (Philochorus, *FGrH* 328 F159, under 342/1), after Demosthenes, according to his own account (18.79), had again moved the empowering motion at Athens. This was the first military action authorised by the People against Philip's interests since the Peace and it was soon followed in the next Attic year by the expulsion of Cleitarchus from Eretria (Philochorus, *FGrH* 328 F160, Diod. 16.74.1). At some point Demosthenes went to Byzantium, which had been estranged from Athens since leaving the naval confederacy in 364, but now felt threatened by Philip, and negotiated an alliance with it (Dem. 18.244). His associate Hyperides visited Cos and Rhodes, both of which had been hostile since 357, but were ready to send help to the Byzantines against Philip in 340 (Hyp. frags. 5, 6, Diod. 16.77.2). Later in 341 Demosthenes and Callias of Chalcis went to Acarnania and several Peloponnesian cities, where they secured promises of military support from the Acarnanians and the Achaeans (Aes. 3.95–7), but Aeschines was probably right when he claimed that a conference at Athens proposed for 16 Anthesterion (mid-February 340) never met (3.98, 102).[58] Even so, a 'crown' was awarded to Demosthenes at the Great Dionysia of March 340 for his services to the city (Dem. 18.83).

Whether Philip was provoked by the Athenians' action in Euboea and their continuing support of Diopeithes' force in the Chersonese or was pressing on with an already formed plan is not known, but in 340 he moved vigorously to extend his power along the north shore of the Propontis. His first attack was on Perinthus (Diod. 16.74.2). That the Athenians had reason to harbour a grudge against the Perinthians (Plut. *Dem.* 17) would not have mattered to Demosthenes.[59] What concerned him was the threat to Athens' corn-supply route from the Black Sea, a threat made more immediate when Philip first put his troops into the Chersonese to help a squadron of ships pass through the Hellespont to blockade Perinthus from the sea and then sent a strong letter to the Athenians protesting against their recent infractions of the Peace, a version of which has been preserved in the Demosthenic corpus (12).[60] Possibly as a result of this letter the Athenians seem to have given no help to the Perinthians, who nonetheless held fast against Philip's vigorous assault. He then upped the stakes by attacking Byzantium, which was not only situated on the Bosporus through which the Athenian corn-fleet had to pass, but also now an ally of Athens (Diod. 16.76.3). Although there was a chance that the Athenians might still back off, Philip must have felt ready now for an Athenian declaration of war and he made sure by attacking and seizing the corn-fleet,[61] a coup which was a useful first shot in the ensuing war, causing difficulties at Athens and compensating to some extent for the losses of reputation, morale and material sustained through the failure to take Perinthus and Byzantium.[62] For Demosthenes, this action confirmed all that he had said about Philip's intentions and his bad faith and, according to Philochorus (*FGrH* 328 FF55a and b), it was he who proposed that the *stele* recording the Peace of 346 be destroyed.[63]

The Athenian people clearly agreed with him that this was the point at which diplomacy had to be put aside and warfare undertaken, whatever the risks. Despite Philip's setbacks at Perinthus and Byzantium, from which he was soon forced to withdraw (Diod. 16.77.2), he was still a dangerous enemy, who could bring an army against Attica. He still controlled Thermopylae, and the Thebans were his allies. At least, though, the situation in central Greece was better than in early 341, when

Philip's friends still ruled Eretria and Oreus, and perhaps Demosthenes and others were now hearing things from Thebes that
suggested the beginning of the mistrust of Philip which was to lead
to the Theban seizure of Nicaea and with it control of Thermopylae
by summer 339.

In any case Philip decided to make no move south in the remaining weeks of 340, but went north towards the Danube to fight
a campaign against a Scythian king (Justin 9.2) and, according to
Philochorus (*FGrH* 328 F56b), was still there when the Thebans
took Nicaea from his garrison, an act of open hostility to Philip
designed to deny him passage through the pass.[64]

It was now more difficult for him to bring the war to Attica and
apply to the Athenians the military pressure he had been able to
exert in 346. The pass was not, however, the only route to Boeotia
and Attica. There was another one going south from by the head of
the Malian Gulf leading to Doris and then to Amphissa in western
Locris. It was a good deal less easy for an army than the route by
Thermopylae, which was certainly narrow, but at sea-level, because
it involved initially crossing a high pass to reach Doris. In 352 the
Phocians must have been guarding it, while the Athenians held
Thermopylae, and were probably still doing so in 346. With their
defeat it was now unprotected. Philip, though, still needed a
diplomatic excuse for taking an army that way. It was provided by a
dispute in the Amphictyonic Council which had broken out at its
meeting in autumn 340, with an attack on Athens by the Locrians
of Amphissa. According to Aeschines (3.107–29), he intervened
with a powerful denunciation of the Locrians for cultivating sacred
land and successfully diverted the anger of the Amphictyons onto
them. Their refusal to pay a fine led to the declaration of a Sacred
War on them, in charge of which Philip was appointed after the
Thessalian Cottyphus had failed.[65] Whether Philip engineered the
affair is not known, but the original move of the Locrians came
remarkably soon after the Athenians had declared war on him and
was an issue calculated to keep Athens and Thebes divided.
Demosthenes alleged unconvincingly that the Locrians' initiative
was a fiction fabricated by Aeschines and maintained that his attack
on the Locrians was delivered after he had taken a bribe from Philip
(18.149–50). But, while the eventual result of his actions was
Philip's penetration of central Greece, at the time Aeschines may
have thought that, if the Locrians did not back down, the Athenians
would be protected by joining in or even leading any Sacred War
that might ensue. Demosthenes, however, thwarted his attempt to

send Athenian representatives to the special Amphictyonic meeting called to consider the Locrians' misbehaviour, probably because he was anxious that the Athenians should not be aligned against the Thebans, who had supported their loyal allies of the last Sacred War and were also boycotting the special meeting.

When in autumn 339 Philip came south to take up his command of the Amphictyonic forces, he took the unguarded route into Doris and then unexpectedly turned east down the Cephissus valley and seized Elatea near the border of Boeotia and the main road from Thermopylae to Thebes. When news of Philip's move reached Athens, there was panic (Dem. 18.169). Not surprisingly, most citizens thought more of the Thebans' longstanding hostility towards them and of their alliance with Philip than of their recent seizure of Nicaea and expected them to facilitate the passage of his army into Attica. Demosthenes, though, read the signs differently and persuaded the people to vote *nem. con.* to send ten envoys including himself to offer the Thebans an alliance on generous terms (Dem. 18.177–9) and to have a citizen force ready to march to their aid.

At Thebes the envoys faced a hard task: Philip evidently was not insisting that the Thebans join him in invading Attica, only that they allow him passage through Boeotia (Dem. 18.213) and hand over Nicaea to the Opuntian Locrians (Philochorus, *FGrH* 328 F56b). Demosthenes and his colleagues, however, won the argument, an alliance was concluded, and Athenian troops joined the Thebans in the defence of Western Boeotia (Dem. 18.215) and in sending a force of 10,000 mercenaries under a joint command to protect Amphissa against invasion from Doris. No further move by Philip during the following winter is recorded in the sources, but Demosthenes talked in 330 of two battles in which Athenians fought successfully alongside the Thebans, 'the battle of the river and the winter battle' (18.216) and the war was going so well that Demosthenes, who earlier had won the Assembly's approval of his proposal that all surplus money now be paid into the military rather than the theoric fund (Philochorus, *FGrH* 328 F56a), was awarded a crown by the people at the Great Dionysia of March 338 (Dem. 18.222).

It was probably still spring when Philip lulled the generals charged with defending Amphissa into a false sense of security and took it (Polyaenus 4.2.8), thereby opening up a possible invasion route into southern Boeotia. He did not, however, exploit this advantage, but instead made an offer of peace to the Thebans and the Athenians (Aes. 3.148–51, Plut. *Phocion* 16.1). Aeschines suggested that he was troubled by the thought that, if it came to a decisive battle, he might lose, but it is more likely that he still hoped to win without bloodshed the compliance of the Athenians – and so of the Thebans too – with his plans.[66] Aeschines also claimed that the Thebans had been readier to listen to Philip's offer than the Athenians and that Demosthenes went to rhetorical extremes to prevent them. What the sources do not reveal are the details of Philip's offer, but it cannot have been much, if at all, different from what he had been offering since 346, an alliance in which, as Demosthenes saw it, he would call the tune.

Demosthenes' contribution to the decisive battle near Chaeronea in August of this year (338) was his considerable role in forming the alliance of Greek states, whose forces were comparable in numbers with their opponents,[67] not only Athens and Thebes, but also the Euboean cities, Megara, Corinth, Achaea and perhaps the island states of the north-west Leucas and Corcyra (Dem. 18.237).[68] He had no experience of military command and can be held responsible for the shortcomings of those who exercised it in this battle only if one contends that he should have long before appreciated the city's shortage of effective generals and fundamentally altered his policy towards Philip. It is certainly arguable that it was Philip's tactical skill rather than the quality of his troops that was the decisive factor in his victory.[69]

Be that as it may, Philip's victory was decisive. He encountered no more resistance as he brought southern Greece under his control until he came to deal with the Spartans, whom he was content to leave outside his arrangements for Greece once he had seen to the security of their neighbours.[70] He would almost certainly have been sternly resisted by the Athenians, who urgently prepared for a siege (Lycurgus 1.37–41), had he not decided to persist in his preference for winning their co-operation rather than forcing their surrender. In sharp contrast to his treatment of the Thebans, his renegade allies, who were forced to ransom their prisoners and accept both a Macedonian garrison in their citadel and the rule of a pro-Macedonian oligarchic regime, he released his Athenian prisoners without ransom and renewed his treaty of peace and alliance with the city on terms which left the Athenians with their democratic institutions and their land free of Macedonian occupation (Diod. 16.87.3).

Demosthenes, then, who like many others had safely escaped the battlefield at Chaeronea,[71] and his associates Hyperides and

Lycurgus could continue to operate in Athens. It was they who initiated the defensive measures adopted after the news of the battle arrived (Lycurgus 1.37–41), but they were not the people to negotiate the peace with Philip. That task was entrusted to Aeschines, Demades and Phocion.[72] But their success in the negotiations and the Assembly's ratification of the peace terms and of Philip's subsequent general settlement did not lead to the eclipse of Demosthenes and his colleagues. Demosthenes himself was chosen to deliver the funeral oration for those who perished at Chaeronea (Dem. 18.285). A proposal to elect him as one of the city's representatives on the *synhedrion*, set up to supervise the maintenance of the Common Peace treaty on which Philip's general settlement was based, did fail – indeed his election would have been an extravagant gesture of defiance against Philip at this juncture,[73] but he was elected as one of the Commissioners for Walls and as a Theoric Fund Commissioner for 337/6 (Aes. 3.24, 27, Dem. 18.113). It was in that year that Ctesiphon proposed that Demosthenes again be awarded a crown for his services to the city. The Boule passed the proposal, but before the Assembly could vote on it, Aeschines gave notice of prosecution against Ctesiphon for making an illegal proposal. The prosecution did not come to trial until six years later and will be discussed elsewhere in this book (Buckler, Chapter 4; cf. Worthington, Chapter 3).

4

The people's confidence in Demosthenes, then, was not greatly diminished by the defeat at Chaeronea nor is it likely that his mistrust of Philip's policies and ambitions was modified by his generous treatment of Athens or by his appointment by the Greek *synhedrion* as commanding general in charge of a panhellenic invasion of the Persian empire. Macedonian supremacy was clear. Demosthenes was surely not deceived by the guarantee of the independence of all Greek states taken over from earlier Common Peace treaties and set as the basis of Philip's general settlement. The treaty also guaranteed the existing constitutions of participating cities, many of which were controlled by his friends. The *synhedrion* was always likely to do his will and he had been elected *hegemon* in charge of any action for which it voted. Most cogently, there were now Macedonian garrisons not only at Thebes, but also at Acrocorinth and in Ambracia.[74] As for Philip's Asian project, his declared object was revenge for the profanation of Greek shrines

(Diod. 16.89.2) and the Athenians had suffered particularly badly in 480 and 479. Demosthenes makes no comment in 330 on Philip's plan, which by then Alexander had been carrying out with great success for four years, but it is a fair guess that he was not greatly impressed by Philip's panhellenic declarations. More likely, he saw the projected expedition as potentially helpful, both for the possible dangers it might produce for Philip and for the better chances of obtaining Persian help in Greece.

There may, though, have been a more favourable reaction from other Athenians. Diodorus (16.92.1) records that large numbers of Greeks from all directions gathered in Macedonia for a festival to seek divine approval for the invasion of Asia and to celebrate Philip's daughter Cleopatra's marriage with Alexander the king of Epirus (summer 336): most of the important cities, Diodorus says, including Athens, sent Philip golden crowns and the Athenians declared that anyone who plotted against him and fled to Athens would be handed over to him.

However, when the news came to Athens of Philip's murder at the celebratory games, it was heard with rejoicing as providing an opportunity to strike for freedom (Diod. 17.3.2). According to Aeschines (3.77), Demosthenes was so carried away that, although he was still mourning for his daughter, who had died only seven days before, he put on a garland and a white robe and offered thank-offerings, claiming that Zeus and Athena had brought him the news in advance of the human messengers; he then caused a shrine to be set up to Philip's murderer (Aes. 3.160). Plutarch (*Phocion* 16.6) preserves a warning from Phocion that the army arrayed against the Greeks at Chaeronea was diminished by just one man. Phocion may have been more aware of Alexander's talents, but Demosthenes fully understood the essential role of Philip in building up his kingdom and in conquering Greece; with him gone things must be different. How much or how little different will be discussed in the next chapter.

NOTES

* My thoughts on this subject were enriched by my teaching an optional course on Greek history in the time of Philip II and Alexander the Great in most years between 1978 and 1995, first at the University of Hull, then at the University of Reading. My students, Ian Worthington among the first, and I greatly benefited from the works of G.L. Cawkwell, J.R. Ellis and G.T. Griffith. Professor A. John Graham made very helpful comments on a draft of the first half of this chapter,

and I also thank Ian Worthington for his; they should not be held responsible for its sundry remaining imperfections.

1 Timotheus had led an expeditionary force against it without success in 360/359 (Scholiast on Aeschines 2.31, Polyaenus 3.10.8); see J. Cargill, *The Second Athenian League* (Berkeley: 1981), pp. 166–8.

2 The two envoys may well not have been sent by the Amphipolitan state, but by a faction in it; cf. J.R. Ellis, *Philip II and Macedonian Imperialism* (London: 1976), pp. 63–4. On the alleged secret pact, see G.E.M. de Ste. Croix, 'The Alleged Secret Pact between Athens and Philip II concerning Amphipolis and Pydna', CQ^2 13 (1963), pp. 110–19 (S. Perlman (ed.), *Philip and Athens* [London: 1973], pp. 36–45), G.T. Griffith in N.G.L. Hammond and G.T. Griffith, *A History of Macedonia* 2 (Oxford: 1979), pp. 238–42, and T.T.B. Ryder, 'The Diplomatic Skills of Philip II' in Ian Worthington (ed.), *Ventures Into Greek History: Essays in Honour of N.G.L. Hammond* (Oxford: 1994), pp. 256–7.

3 On Demosthenes' earlier political career and non-policy towards Philip, with a discussion of his first political speeches, see Badian, Chapter 1. On the style and artistry of Demosthenes' public speeches see Milns, Chapter 7.

4 Dionysius of Halicarnassus assigns the speech to Attic year 354/3; cf. R. Sealey, *Demosthenes and His Time* (Oxford: 1993), p. 128.

5 Tod 2, no. 159, with comments by Griffith in Hammond and Griffith, *Macedonia* 2, p. 256.

6 Aeschines refers to the subsequent war as the war over Amphipolis (2.70, 3.54), as does Isocrates (5.2).

7 Cf. G.L. Cawkwell, 'Eubulus', *JHS* 83 (1963), pp. 47–67.

8 On the date see Sealey, *Demosthenes*, p. 129.

9 Apart from 19.319, where he gave the context of the sending of Nausicles' force to Thermopylae (see below).

10 On Philip's espousal of Apollo's cause see Griffith in Hammond and Griffith, *Macedonia* 2, pp. 274–7.

11 Diodorus has the whole sequence of events from Philip's first invasion of Thessaly to his defeat of Onomarchus in 16.35 under 353/2, the march on Thermopylae under 352/1.

12 Demosthenes' claim that only the Athenians came to the aid of the Phocians is belied by Diodorus' references (16.37.3) to 1,000 Spartans and 2,000 Achaeans, but these contingents more likely joined the Phocians in Phocis than helped in the defence of Thermopylae.

13 Sealey, *Demosthenes*, p. 118, plays down Eubulus' links with Nausicles and Diophantus.

14 There is no ancient evidence for the location of Heraion Teichos. Ellis, *Philip II*, p. 87, and Griffith, in Hammond and Griffith, *Macedonia* 2, p. 283, both put it on the coast of the Propontis between the Chersonese and Perinthus.

15 The sources are silent on the outcome of Philip's attack. Griffith's surmise (Hammond and Griffith, *Macedonia* 2, p. 284) that it failed is more convincing than Ellis's (*Philip II*, p. 88) that it succeeded and the place was handed over to Perinthus.

16 On the date of the first *Philippic* see G.L. Cawkwell, 'The Defence of Olynthus', CQ^2 12 (1962), pp. 122–7 (Perlman, *Philip and Athens*, pp.

48–53); cf. Badian, Chapter 1. For a discussion of this speech in the light of Demosthenes' policy and ambition see further Badian, Chapter 1; see too Buckler, Chapter 4.

17 Demosthenes 1.13 puts the intervention in Olynthus after his withdrawal from Thrace, but it was political rather than military (cf. Griffith in Hammond and Griffith, *Macedonia* 2, pp. 297–9, Ellis, *Philip II*, pp. 88–9) and consequent upon the Olynthians, his allies, making a separate peace with Athens, probably in 353 (Dem. 23.107–9).

18 Suggested by Sealey, *Demosthenes*, p. 134, and see especially Badian, Chapter 1.

19 Demosthenes' phrasing does not in fact compel the conclusion that these last three expeditions were more recent than the intervention in Olynthus referred to in n. 17 above, but at 4.48 he referred to current rumours about Philip besieging towns in Illyria.

20 For a discussion of Philip's motives see Griffith in Hammond and Griffith, *Macedonia* 2, p. 315.

21 The first internal dissent reported in the sources is in the narrative of events leading up to Philip's death in 336 (Plut. *Alexander* 9.5–10.5).

22 According to Demosthenes 39.16, shortly before the Choes festival in the middle of the month of Anthesterion.

23 The cities' withdrawal is not explicitly referred to by Plutarch (*Phocion* 14.1), but is clear from the events of 344–341 (see below).

24 Cawkwell, 'Defence of Olynthus', p. 129 (Perlman, *Philip and Athens*, p. 55), was in favour of emending the text of Aeschines to have Callias sending the Phocian Phalaecus; but, as P.A. Brunt observed ('Euboea in the time of Philip II', CQ^2 19 [1969], p. 250), emendation may be right, but is not necessary.

25 So Cawkwell and Brunt; *contra* Griffith in Hammond and Griffith, *Macedonia* 2, p. 318.

26 Transfer of the cavalry at about the time of the Dionysia of 348: Dem. 21.197.

27 Philochorus (*FGrH* 328 F51) says that the third expeditionary force sent by the Athenians included 'seventeen *further* triremes'; that is, over and above those there already, with Chares as 'general of the whole force' (including others beside those he took from Athens).

28 For an assessment of the Athenians' strategy in the defence of Olynthus see especially Cawkwell, 'Defence of Olynthus', pp. 134–8 (Perlman, *Philip and Athens*, pp. 60–4).

29 Cf. Griffith in Hammond and Griffith, *Macedonia* 2, pp. 324–8.

30 The conditions of 'fear and tumult' described by Aeschines in 2.72–3, but without chronological indications, probably belong at this point.

31 With the advantage of hindsight Diodorus sees Philip's Asian ambitions as already formed in autumn 346 (16.60.5). Ellis (*Philip II*, p. 92) sees them developing, probably before his war with Olynthus, from the presence as a refugee at his court of the rebel satrap Artabazus (Diod. 16.52.3). J. Buckler, 'Philip II's Designs on Greece' in R.W. Wallace and E.M. Harris (eds.), *Transitions to Empire: Essays in Honor of E. Badian* (Norman: 1996), pp. 84–6, rightly warns against assuming that Philip at this stage had a 'master plan'. Did Isocrates know

something of Philip's ideas for the future when calling on him in 346 in *To Philip* to lead a panhellenic war against Persia?

32 This episode starts a long stretch of continuous narrative recording a series of public events in the Assembly, the Boule and the law courts. For other discussion of the events leading up to the Peace of Philocrates, and the Peace itself, see Buckler, Chapter 4.

33 As argued, for instance, by J. Buckler, *Philip II and the Sacred War* (Leiden: 1989), pp. 126–7, and see also his discussion of the war in Chapter 4 (this volume). The alliance treaty was put by Griffith in Hammond and Griffith, *Macedonia* 2, p. 266 n. 4, in winter 354/3 before Pammenes took a Theban army through Macedonian territory on his way to Asia (Diod. 16.34.1), passing through Maronea in Thrace (Dem. 23.183).

34 On these signs see Aeschines 2.131–2, Diodorus 16.56.1–5, Buckler, *Sacred War*, pp. 118–19, Griffith in Hammond and Griffith, *Macedonia* 2, p. 333.

35 The translation is that of C.D. Adams in the Loeb Classical Library's edition of Aeschines.

36 Cf. T.T.B. Ryder, *Koine Eirene* (Oxford: 1965), pp. 34–86.

37 Cf. T.T.B. Ryder, 'Ambiguity in Aeschines', *LCM* 2 (1977), pp. 219–23.

38 Note Aeschines' frank admission at 2.79.

39 According to Aeschines (2.84) Demosthenes said that another meeting had been allocated for discussion of cases like that of Cersebleptes, but no such meeting is referred to by either orator. Aeschines also said (2.86) that Demosthenes had accused him of driving Critobulus out of the ceremony, but no such charge was included in the edited version of Demosthenes' speech. Given Aeschines' promotion of the peace-terms as finally agreed, his opposition to Critobulus is intrinsically likely.

40 Demosthenes' words were: 'I recounted the whole story, beginning with those first hopes, aroused in you by the reports of Ctesiphon and Aristodemus, and going on to the speeches which Aeschines delivered during the time of the peace-negotiations, and the position into which they had brought the city.' Clearly 'the whole story' came right up to the time when he spoke.

41 Cf. n. 34 above.

42 This delegation is variously described as a continuation of the Third Embassy (as by Aes. 2.86; cf. Sealey, *Demosthenes*, p. 149) or as the Fourth Embassy (as by Ellis, *Philip II*, p. 122).

43 The debate is well summarised by Buckler, *Sacred War*, pp. 121–5.

44 See especially Ellis, *Philip II*, pp. 90–124.

45 See especially G.L. Cawkwell, *Philip of Macedon* (London: 1978), pp. 93–104 and Griffith in Hammond and Griffith, *Macedonia* 2, pp. 343–7.

46 For the suggestion see Ellis, *Philip II*, p. 122; for Philip's likely role see Griffith in Hammond and Griffith, *Macedonia* 2, p. 455.

47 See above, n. 31.

48 By Griffith in Hammond and Griffith, *Macedonia* 2, pp. 476–8.

49 Suggested by G.L. Cawkwell, 'Demosthenes' Policy after the Peace of Philocrates I', *CQ*^{2} 13 (1963), pp. 121–6 (Perlman, *Philip and Athens*, pp. 147–52); cf. Griffith in Hammond and Griffith, *Macedonia* 2, p. 479 n. 1.

50 Apart from his reference in 343 to 'the Peace being unsworn' (Dem. 19.204), seen by Cawkwell, 'Demosthenes' Policy after the Peace of Philocrates I', p. 133 (Perlman, *Philip and Athens*, p. 159), as a reference to what was now agreed.

51 Ellis indeed suggests that it was Philip who proposed this amendment (*Philip II*, p. 145).

52 Cf. Ryder, *Koine Eirene*, pp. 140–1.

53 See especially G.L. Cawkwell, 'Demosthenes' Policy after the Peace of Philocrates II', CQ^2 13 (1963), p. 209 (Perlman, *Philip and Athens*, p. 174), Griffith in Hammond and Griffith, *Macedonia* 2, pp. 491–5.

54 Cf. Ryder, 'Diplomatic Skills of Philip II', p. 242.

55 Scholiast on Aeschines 3.83 lists five states – Argos, Messene, Megalopolis, Mantinea, Achaea – as having become allies of Athens in 343/2; Messene is confirmed by *IG* ii/iii² 225, probably of July 342. Only the Achaeans fought alongside the Athenians in 338, but none of the others then supported Philip. Ellis, *Philip II*, p. 158, points out that, as Athens and Philip were formally allies, these five states' alliances with Athens did not cancel their relationships with Philip.

56 The political significance of the trial is discussed briefly by Ellis, *Philip II*, p. 153.

57 For attempts to put names on Diodorus' threatened cities and new foundations see Ellis, *Philip II*, pp. 166–8 and Griffith in Hammond and Griffith, *Macedonia* 2, pp. 556–9.

58 Griffith in Hammond and Griffith, *Macedonia* 2, p. 551, suggests that Aeschines was strictly correct in saying that the conference did not meet, but that it met a little later in the year, citing Plutarch, *Dem.* 17.3 as evidence of a conference around this time.

59 Perinthus had been a member of the Athenian naval confederacy (Tod 2, no. 123, line 84), but had dropped out, perhaps in 357.

60 On the letter see Griffith in Hammond and Griffith, *Macedonia* 2, p. 567.

61 Philochorus, *FGrH* 328 F162, Dem. 18.73, Justin 9.1.5.

62 On Philip's motive see Griffith in Hammond and Griffith, *Macedonia* 2, pp. 577–8.

63 In 330 Aeschines (3.55) said that Demosthenes proposed the declaration of war, a charge denied by Demosthenes (18.76), but unconvincingly in view of Philochorus' statement.

64 A point stressed by Griffith in Hammond and Griffith, *Macedonia* 2, pp. 587–8.

65 For a full discussion of this episode see Buckler, Chapter 4.

66 Cf. Griffith in Hammond and Griffith, *Macedonia* 2, p. 595.

67 Diodorus (16.85.5–6) has Philip having the advantage in numbers, while Justin (9.3.9) talks of the Athenians (*sic*) being 'far superior in numbers'.

68 In this passage Demosthenes claims to have won the alliance of the states named, but they were not necessarily all represented in the battle. On the evidence of Tod 2, no. 178, lines 11–15 and 22–4, a contingent came also from the Acarnanians, who had been won over by Callias and Demosthenes in 341 (Aes. 3.97).

69 Cf. Polyaenus 4.2.2 with Griffith's discussion (Hammond and Griffith, *Macedonia* 2, pp. 600–3).

70 See C. Roebuck, 'The Settlements of Philip II with the Greek states in 338 B.C.', *CP* 43 (1948), pp. 84–9 (Perlman, *Philip and Athens*, pp. 210–15).

71 According to Diodorus (16.86.5), more than 1,000 Athenians were killed in the battle and at least 2,000 taken prisoner. The size of the Athenian contingent is not known, but a few thousand must have escaped, probably in an organised retreat. The frequent references to Demosthenes as a runaway by Aeschines (for example, 3.152) and by Dinarchus (1.12) are clearly unfair and wrong.

72 For Aeschines see Demosthenes 18.282; for Demades Demosthenes 18.285. Plutarch, *Phocion* 16.3, says that after Chaeronea the people were persuaded 'to entrust the city to Phocion', in a context that suggests that peace had not been agreed and that making it was what was primarily entrusted to him (cf. Nepos, *Phocion* 1.3).

73 Cf. T.T.B. Ryder, 'Demosthenes and Philip's Peace of 338/7 B.C.', *CQ*² 26 (1976), pp. 85–7 and E.M. Harris, 'Demosthenes Loses a Friend and Nausicles Gains a Position: A Prosopographical Note on Athenian Politics after Chaeronea', *Historia* 43 (1994), pp. 378–83.

74 For the settlement see Ryder, *Koine Eirene*, pp. 102–5, Griffith in Hammond and Griffith, *Macedonia* 2, pp. 624–8, and J. Buckler, 'Philip II, the Greeks and the King 346–336 BC', *ICS* 19 (1994), pp. 111–18.

3

DEMOSTHENES' (IN)ACTIVITY DURING THE REIGN OF ALEXANDER THE GREAT*

Ian Worthington

1

Thirty years ago George Cawkwell published a highly influential article on Demosthenes' later career during which he criticised Demosthenes' reputation – 'why should Demosthenes receive so much credit with posterity?', and 'if we find that Demosthenes was not so clearly right as his fame has made him, the conclusion need not shock us when we reflect on Demosthenes' policy in those years about which the *de Corona* maintains so discreet a silence.'[1] Cawkwell was measuring Demosthenes' political success in the period from Alexander the Great's accession to power (336) to the Crown trial (330) by his use of opportunities to unite the Greeks. However, his questions apply to Demosthenes' career as a whole, given the way it ignobly ended with his self-imposed exile. Cawkwell argued that Demosthenes was not able to unite Greece effectively, and especially that he had misjudged the situation in 331 when he did not support the Spartan king Agis III in his attempt to throw off Macedonian rule, an attempt which ended in Spartan defeat. That is why in 330, according to Cawkwell, Aeschines rekindled his earlier charge against Ctesiphon, and why Demosthenes said so little about this period in his speech: because he too realised his error, and thus his vulnerability. In this chapter, I consider not only some of Cawkwell's arguments for the period he considered but also Demosthenes' career during Alexander's reign as a whole. Bound up with this is also the issue of the Athenian mood towards Macedonian domination.

After Alexander the Great re-established his control over Greece in 336, and especially after he had razed Thebes to the ground in 335, Demosthenes' high profile in Athenian political affairs seems to have fallen dramatically. We know of only three major public appearances over the course of roughly twelve years: the debate over Agis' war of 331–330, his prosecution by Aeschines in 330, and his involvement in the Harpalus affair of 324/3, which resulted in his political exile. Demosthenes' profile during the reign of Alexander is a startling contrast to that during the reign of Philip II. Then, his fiery oratory, exhorting the Athenians to resist Philip at all costs, had elevated him to great political power.[2] So great was Demosthenes' influence that in 346, after Philip and the Athenians had agreed to the Peace of Philocrates, the Athenians had refused to attend the Pythian games since Philip had been elected president of them. When the king made them an offer they could not refuse, it had been Demosthenes who, with his speech *On The Peace*, had persuaded them to go. In the mid- to late 340s Athenian policy was that of Demosthenes, and in 339 his power was such that he was able to persuade the Athenians to agree to an unequal alliance with the hated Thebans in a last-ditch effort to defeat Philip.[3]

During the reign of Philip, then, Demosthenes was highly influential. Moreover, the people's confidence in him as a political leader was not shaken by the ill-fated alliance with Thebes in 339 and then the catastrophic battle of Chaeronea in September 338, at which Philip decisively defeated the Greeks and ended their autonomy.[4] He was politically active in the immediate post-Chaeronea period,[5] and although indicted 'every day' in the courts,[6] and needing someone else to move decrees for him (Aes. 3.159, Plut. *Dem.* 21), he was, significantly, selected to deliver the *epitaphios*, or funeral oration, over the Athenian dead from that battle (Dem. 18.285, Plut. *Dem.* 21). As Thucydides tells us (2.34), only the man 'who is regarded as best endowed with wisdom and is foremost in public esteem' was selected by the state to deliver this type of speech.[7] It comes as no surprise that when Philip was treacherously murdered in 336 by an assassin's sword (Diod. 16.93–5, Arr. 1.1.1), it was Demosthenes who marshalled support for a widespread revolt by the Greek states against the new king, Alexander the Great, and thus against the Macedonian hegemony of Greece.[8]

The Greek revolt was short-lived. Alexander marched southwards with unexpected (and later customary) speed (Diod. 17.4.4) and the Greeks were quickly overwhelmed. In a matter of months, the new king had reimposed the Common Peace of the League of Corinth as set up by his father and the invasion of Persia, as put forward by Philip in 337, was again endorsed.[9] Only Sparta again remained aloof from the League.[10] Demosthenes did not take the collapse of the Greek revolt lying down. When in 335 news reached Greece that during a campaign in Illyria Alexander had died (Arr. 1.7.2, Justin 11.2), the Thebans revolted. Demosthenes at first had supported the Thebans, despite the opposition in Athens of Phocion, even to the extent of persuading the Assembly to supply them with arms (Diod. 17.8.6). Later, when Alexander showed himself to be very much alive, the Assembly reversed its decision to support the Thebans, and left them to fend for themselves. They were no match for an annoyed and impatient Alexander, who had marched some 250 miles in just thirteen days (Arr. 1.7.4) and was eager to invade Persia. Alexander, cynically operating through the League of Corinth, razed Thebes to the ground, and those of the population who were not killed or enslaved fled into exile.[11]

Alexander had been much denigrated since his accession to power by various orators in Athens, as a remark by Libanius testifies (*Or.* 15.42). Demosthenes was one of the orators, and no one, therefore, could doubt his anti-Macedonian stance, which is also evidenced by the fact that shortly after the destruction of Thebes Alexander ominously demanded the surrender of several orators including Demosthenes.[12] However, thanks to the diplomatic intervention of Demades, the king relented in this demand, leaving Demosthenes apparently free to continue as before.[13] Shortly afterwards, in 334, Alexander left for Persia, much to Demosthenes' (and perhaps others') surprise – according to Aeschines, he had said that Alexander would prefer to remain in Pella and not leave Macedon (Aes. 3.160). Antipater was left behind as the guardian (*epitropos*) of Greece and Macedon and to act as deputy leader in the League of Corinth (Arr. 1.11.3).

If we expect to find Demosthenes, that tireless advocate of Greek autonomy, to be as vocal in political life during the Alexander years as in those of Philip, then we are disappointed. As one scholar of Demosthenic Athens recently and succinctly said: 'To explain why little is known of what Demosthenes was doing during the reign of Alexander, the best hypothesis is that he was not doing much.'[14] Perhaps the lesson from Alexander's destruction of Thebes had hit home: rejection of the League of Corinth – in other words, rebellion against Macedonian control – would be met with no mercy. There was also the Macedonian garrison on the Theban Cadmea to bear in mind (Arr. 1.7.4–9.10, Diod. 17.9.1–14.4); Thebes, after all, was not very far from Athens.[15] Macedonian troops could move far more quickly than their Greek counterparts, so caution was the order of the day in dealings with Macedon. This was clearly seen in the Athenians' lack of support for Agis' war in 331 (see below). Demosthenes had narrowly escaped being handed over to Alexander shortly after Thebes' destruction, and we can well imagine that he realised the need to maintain a low profile. He seems to have continued his other career as a *logographos*,[16] and he may even have written some rhetorical works if the *exordia* which we have today are by him.

However, could a man who had played such a key role in political and international affairs for over two decades have been content to return to writing speeches for private individuals? After all, he had soon bounced back after Chaeronea when he had left Athens to secure corn (Dem. 18.248), although very likely this was a pretext in case Philip marched on Athens, as Aeschines would later allege (3.159). In the mid-330s, he had not suddenly transformed himself into a 'philomakedon', nor had freedom of speech been abolished in Athens. Athenian – indeed Greek – politics remained volatile. There were opportunities for statesmen such as Demosthenes to speak on political and military matters – Agis' war against Macedon, for example – and there must have been others about which we have no knowledge.[17] At least some opportunities were taken: for one thing, we know of the Athenian debate over Agis (Diod. 17.62.7) and, for another, Aeschines tells us that Demosthenes had hoped that Alexander would be trampled under the hoofs of the Persian cavalry at Issus (3.164). Demosthenes therefore schemed with those who might seriously oppose Alexander, such as the Persians (see below). Even if he did not give formal speeches in the Assembly we are told that it was his wont to walk around the Agora and elsewhere making his opinion known to all and sundry.[18]

Whilst Demosthenes must have delivered formal speeches in connection with the events mentioned above, and presumably in 324 when Harpalus appeared off the Attic coast (see below), we do not have them. Perhaps, however, there was little point in Demosthenes' making formal speeches against Alexander in the Assembly given the king's absence from Greece, and even more pointless directing his invective against Antipater, who, when all was said and done, was Alexander's agent. In fact, Alexander's very absence may well be the reason why Demosthenes did not make speeches, or at least not many. Demosthenes had grown successful in the days of Philip because of his scare-tactic rhetoric, which characterised most of his speeches. In the process, he misrepresented Philip's activities, and his aims; for example, in *On the Chersonese*, Demosthenes portrays Philip's intentions from expansion in Thrace to Greece and then the total destruction of Athens (2, 14, 18, 60). The same can be said for *Philippic* 3, where Demosthenes uses Philip's victories and the destruction of Phocis to argue that Philip aimed to destroy Athens (6–19). That Philip desired this is most unlikely. Demosthenes, however, can argue in this way, and more importantly persuade his audience, because Philip was physically in Greece, and people knew of the places he had captured. Demosthenes cannot do this with Alexander because he was in places most people had never even heard of, let alone knew about. Without an actual Macedonian king active in Greece, Demosthenes was perhaps robbed of the one thing he needed to make his fiery oratory work. Therefore, based on what we do know, what was Demosthenes' policy during the reign of Alexander, and to what extent did he remain in the background?

2

Agis' war of 331–330 and the Crown trial in 330 seem to have been turning-points for Demosthenes' public profile, and thus they deserve some treatment since they are linked to his Macedonian policy. Before 330, Demosthenes had openly opposed Alexander: in 335, as mentioned previously, he had supported the Theban rebellion, and earlier in the same year he had spoken against a Macedonian demand for Athenian ships ([Plut.] *Mor.* 847c; cf. Plut. *Phocion* 21.1), perhaps for Alexander's campaign in the Danube basin (Arr. 1.3.3). Before 333 (battle of Issus) at least he had openly hoped that the Persians would defeat Alexander – the king's gift of 300 Persian panoplies for Athena after the battle of Granicus (Arr. 1.16.7) did nothing to alter the Athenians' attitude to him, as Alexander must have known.[19] Significantly, he did not release the Athenian captives from that battle but kept them as hostages at work in the Macedonian mines (Diod. 17.22.5, Arr. 1.16.6, 29.5–6, 3.6.2). They were not released until 331. It is possible that Demosthenes continued to harbour hopes of a Macedonian defeat even after Issus, and publicly proclaim them. Although Cawkwell believed that Demosthenes' policy lay in ruins after Alexander's victory at Issus,[20] it is important to bear in mind that Darius escaped from the battlefield, and that he was able to regroup his forces and bring Alexander to battle two years later at Gaugamela. Why therefore should Demosthenes abandon all hope after Issus?

At the same time, this is not to deny that news of Issus must have been startling, and disheartening. I wonder also whether the Athenians reacted to news of the battle not only because Alexander won but also because of what Darius did at the battle. He fled. The parallel with Xerxes after the battle of Salamis in 480 is striking. When all was lost at Salamis Xerxes fled back to Persia, leaving behind a demoralised fragment of his army which was soon totally defeated. Would the Athenians have made this link, or indeed remembered Salamis? I believe so, for the Persian wars are amongst the most frequently used historical topoi by the orators.[21] Now, Thucydides tells us that it was the custom of the Athenians to honour their dead in a solemn public ceremony before the whole citizen body, and for a leading statesman to deliver the *epitaphios* (2.34). A great number of Greeks had died from the mid-fourth century onwards fighting against Macedonian imperialism; hence, as well as symbouleutic speeches, there must have been many funeral orations which we do not have. If that of Hyperides (6), delivered in 322 over those who died in the first year of the Lamian War, is anything to go by, the Persian Wars, and thus the great victory at Salamis, are the *sine qua non* of an *epitaphios*.[22] The Persians in 480 were a foreign foe who threatened Greek freedom just like the Macedonians now, as Hyperides states (for example, 6.12, 37). Many Athenians in 333 could not have overlooked the parallel of Darius' flight after Issus with that of Xerxes after Salamis, and the lesson to be drawn from it.

The year 331 was significant for Greece, for in the spring, while Alexander was probably at Tyre, Agis of Sparta attacked Megalopolis and perhaps arranged for some Peloponnesian cities to rebel against the League of Corinth. This action would certainly have earned him reprisals from the League and thus from Antipater, which would soon lead to actual warfare.[23] The reasons for this war and the course of its events do not concern us here.[24] What is important for us is that Agis sought support from the other Greek states, but Demosthenes, along with Phocion and perhaps Demades, advised the Athenians against it.[25] Although a speech from this time exists which urged the Athenians to war, the spurious Demosthenes 17 (*On the Treaty with Alexander*), Demosthenes' caution was, in hindsight, prudent. Only a few states rallied to

Agis, and despite some Spartan victories (the defeat of Corragus being the most notable), in early 330 the Spartan king was brought to battle at Megalopolis by Antipater, defeated and killed.[26] Agis' allies were fined heavily and Alexander himself was to decide the Spartans' fate.[27] Perhaps surprisingly, he pardoned them; however, they now became members of the League of Corinth.[28] There seems little doubt that he would have been less lenient towards the Athenians had they supported Sparta.

Not long after the defeat of Agis, probably in August of 330, Aeschines launched his famous attack against Demosthenes. In the spring of 336 Ctesiphon had proposed a gold crown for Demosthenes as a reward for the latter's great services to the state (Aes. 3.17–23, 49, 236–7, Dem. 18.57). The Boule had endorsed Ctesiphon's motion (Dem. 18.9, 118), but it was blocked by Aeschines at a meeting of the Assembly as illegal under the procedure called *graphē paranomōn*.[29] The case did not come to court until 330, probably because in the wake of Philip's death Aeschines knew that Demosthenes' influence would have harmed his chances of success.[30] It seems reasonably certain that Aeschines rekindled the charge in 330, not Demosthenes (Dem. 18.308).[31] What is important is that personal enmity and internal politics, not the issue of Macedonian hegemony, was the reason for Aeschines' renewed attack on Demosthenes.[32] Although Aeschines properly stated that it was illegal for a serving magistrate to be honoured in this way (3.24), the basis of his indictment was that Demosthenes had not advised the best policy for the people as Ctesiphon had said in his original proposal (3.49–50). Ctesiphon delivered a short speech of defence, and Demosthenes responded more fully. Ctesiphon/Demosthenes were vindicated, and Aeschines was soundly defeated (Plut. *Dem.* 24.2);[33] he withdrew from Athens to Rhodes, where he apparently founded a school of rhetoric (cf. [Plut.] *Mor.* 840c–d).[34]

Cawkwell argued that Aeschines had been waiting since 336 to bring up the matter of his *graphē paranomōn* against Ctesiphon, and that the opportunity only presented itself after news of Alexander's victory at Gaugamela on 1 October 331 and especially after Agis' defeat.[35] By that stage, Demosthenes had lost credibility for his anti-Macedonian policy, and Aeschines believed that the people would favour his case. There is no need to rehearse Cawkwell's arguments, which are based mostly on chronological grounds, and I believe his view is true – as we saw above, Demosthenes remained active and outspoken in the period following Alexander's accession, and he held the confidence of the people. Aeschines would have taken the first real chance he thought he had to attack Demosthenes, and clearly that chance did not present itself until 330; otherwise, we would have had the Crown trial at an earlier (or, for that matter, later) date. The timing of the trial is not arbitrary, nor is it coincidental that it occurred soon after Gaugamela and Agis' war: it must be linked to the two.

Moreover, it is, I think, significant that Aeschines in his speech lamented the fate of Sparta (3.133), and that this follows an even more eloquent lament for Thebes. The lamentation for Sparta is unusual in Athenian oratory since Spartan history tends to be ignored or even devalued as opposed to that of another state. There is no question that Aeschines was exploiting popular sympathy for Sparta, so evidently news of Agis' fate caused upset in Athens, but coming as it does after the lamentation for Thebes adds even more weight to Aeschines' emotional appeal and in the process demonstrates his stylistic artistry. The Greeks have fallen from hegemony to become mere suppliants of Alexander, and Athens has suffered the same indignity, all because of Demosthenes! To Aeschines, Demosthenes had left Sparta out in the cold, and this was not something a *polis* did to another when faced by a common foe – as the days of the Persian wars testify. Aeschines seems to have felt that here was Demosthenes' vulnerability, and so chose this time to renew his attack on him from six years previously.

Cawkwell believes that Demosthenes was vulnerable to attack because he had misjudged the situation: that he ought to have urged the Athenians to support Agis and so presented Antipater, and thus Alexander, with a very real threat to the Macedonian hegemony of Greece. This is why, argued Cawkwell, Demosthenes concentrated mostly on the 340s, 'about which memories were inexact', in his *Crown* oration, and says next to nothing about his role in the events of 336 to 330: because he realised that Athens should have supported Sparta.[36]

Should the Athenians have supported Agis, especially given that Alexander was marching forever further away from the Mediterranean seaboard, and Antipater at that time was occupied in Thrace (Diod. 17.62.4–6, Curt. 5.1.1), as Cawkwell would argue? Why did Demosthenes not seize this apparent golden opportunity to rouse the Athenians to revolt and join Agis? Cawkwell advanced three theories as to why not: firstly, fear of the corn supply since Macedon controlled Egypt, the Hellespont and the Bosporus. Secondly, the Macedonian garrisons at Thebes, Corinth and Chalcis. Thirdly, the potential for Athenians soldiers serving with Alexander to be held as hostages. He effectively refuted each one, and attributed the Athenians' lack of support, as stated above, to Demosthenes' misjudgement of the situation.[37] I wonder whether Demosthenes could err to this extent after so many years in political life? As the saying goes, 'A week is a long time in politics', and this is likely to have been true of the fourth century as much as of the present. Demosthenes was politically 'streetwise' and had been for over two decades: would he really have misjudged the situation like this? It seems unlikely. Plus he knew his geography: with Agis so preoccupied with the southern Peloponnese, and Argos and Corinth loyal to the League of Corinth, Demosthenes knew that Athens was vulnerable to Macedonian attack. Antipater could march through the isthmus and into the Peloponnese at any time convenient to him. A simpler explanation is closer to the truth: Demosthenes knew that Agis never stood a chance and, more importantly, that Athens was first in line if ever there was a Macedonian land invasion.

Demosthenes' anti-Macedonian policy was the gamble that Persia would defeat Alexander. It had to be, because there was no other option. The Greeks (excluding the Spartans) had been joined together in the League of Corinth since 337 (apart from the few months following Philip's death and Alexander's re-establishment of power), and bound in allegiance to Alexander. No matter how involuntary their membership of the League was, resistance to Macedonian rule was futile. If a Greek *polis* attempted an insurrection, it could be faced by the other *poleis* and Antipater bearing hard down on it: *poleis* throughout Greek history did not shrink from fighting each other. Alexander knew this, as did Philip before him, hence the careful construction of the League of Corinth and administration of Greece. The opportunity for a combined Greek effort against Macedon had been an option before Chaeronea, and then again in the wake of Philip's murder, but only at those times (while Alexander was alive, that is). Demosthenes could only turn to Persia: there was no one else, and Athens had a recent history of diplomatic and military contact with Persia. In 344, the Athenians had rejected an offer of friendship and alliance from Artaxerxes. At some later point, perhaps in 340 after Philip seized the corn fleet and the Athenians declared war on him (Diod. 16.77.2–3), they changed their minds and sought money from the Persian king. Not surprisingly, they were refused (Aes. 3.238). Later, Philip's designs on Persia caused the Persians major concern (Diod. 16.75), and if Arrian is to be trusted, in 336 Darius sent money to the Greeks to support a revolt against Macedon, although apparently only the Spartans took some of it (Arr. 2.14.6). Aeschines in 330 and later Dinarchus in 323 accused Demosthenes of keeping at least some of this money for himself, hence, regardless of the truth of the allegation, he had been connected with it.[38] Therefore, it is safe to assume that Demosthenes had had dealings with Darius against Alexander since 336 and that his gamble – it was hardly policy as Cawkwell calls it – was that Alexander would be trampled under the hoofs of the Persian cavalry. That gamble did not succeed at Issus, and later in 331 it would fail completely at Gaugamela.

The writing was on the wall, and perhaps for the first time Demosthenes was reading it – or reading it properly. He saw from the outset that Agis' war was fruitless, and that Athenian involvement in it would lead to severe reprisals at the hands of Antipater, or of Alexander himself. Even more unpalatable for people like Demosthenes and the Athenians as a whole was the realisation that no revolt against Macedon could be successful. This is closer to the truth as to why he spoke so little, and in such general terms, of the 336 to 330 period in his Crown speech (18.253, 270): the fact that Alexander's defeat of the Persians left no other avenue for support. Greek freedom, *eleutheria*, was ended, as was their *autonomia*: ideals which the Greeks cherished the most.[39] No Greek would have wanted to have been reminded of that, nor of the events of those final few years as the Macedonians inexorably ended Greek autonomy. Agis' war had proved how impotent the Greeks were – why should Demosthenes rub salt into wounds, and potentially generate ill-feeling on the part of the all-important jury, by rehearsing at length what happened? He could certainly respond at length to Aeschines' attacks about his earlier policy, for at least in the 340s the Greeks were autonomous and the Athenians steadfastly resisting Philip. Who, then, could blame Demosthenes for focusing on this period in his speech rather than on the immediate past? Aeschines read public opinion, and the minds of the jurors, differently, and it cost him dearly.

If anyone misjudged the situation, it was Aeschines – the outcome of the trial proves that.[40] He talked of the previous few years much more than Demosthenes (3.159–67), and even closed his speech with the appeal to the jurors not to disregard this recent history (3.259). But they did. He attacked Demosthenes for his policy with Persia (for example, 3.156, 173, 239, 259), but that rhetorical strategy ultimately rebounded on him because the Persian empire was no more. He lamented the fate of Sparta in the hope that this would stir ill-will against Demosthenes. But it did not. The Spartans and the Persians were hardly friends of the Athenians, but they had been opponents – significant opponents at that – of Alexander. Aeschines had reminded the Athenians of the impotency of the Greeks and he paid the price; Demosthenes had talked of earlier times, and was exonerated. In 323 Dinarchus also referred to Agis' war as a lost opportunity (1.34); however, the situation then was very different from 330 in the light of the Exiles Decree and Demosthenes' failed strategy to resist it (see below).

As a result of his victory at the Crown trial in 330, his reputation intact and his previous career so resoundingly endorsed, we ought to expect Demosthenes to have hogged the limelight again. Not so. The aftermath of Agis' war saw a very different Greece, one which remained passive under Macedonian rule until Alexander died. Ditto Demosthenes. A six-year period of silence as regards Demosthenes' activities now follows until 324 and the Harpalus affair, hence Agis' war of 331–330 and the Crown trial in 330 were turning-points in his public profile in the reign of Alexander.

3

During the 330 to 324 period, the Athenians, indeed the Greeks as a whole, came to enjoy the period of peace and prosperity which the Macedonian hegemony brought, and may even have reconciled themselves to it.[41] A *Pax Macedonica*, then. This would also account for the friendships which developed or continued between Athenian statesmen and powerful Macedonians, such as Demosthenes, Demades and Antipater, or Phocion and Alexander ([Dem.] 47.21).[42] Perhaps also it explains why Demosthenes sent his friend Ariston to live with Alexander's close friend Hephaestion.[43] During this period too no friction is known between the more influential Athenian political leaders, such as Demosthenes, Hyperides, Demades and Phocion, who controlled policy.

That the issue of Macedonian hegemony was not a burning one at this time is evident from the acquittal of Demosthenes, as we have seen, and also of Leocrates in 330. Leocrates had fled Athens after the Battle of Chaeronea, very likely thinking that Philip would then march on the city, and had returned to the city, perhaps shortly before Aeschines renewed his attack on Demosthenes. Lycurgus seems to have prosecuted Leocrates for treason, presumably for quitting the city in a time of potential danger. Leocrates weakly argued that he had not fled Athens but merely gone to visit people overseas; surprisingly, he was acquitted, but only by the narrowest of margins (Aes. 3.252). If both Leocrates, who had fled in time of need, and Demosthenes, whose policies had brought Greece to its knees, were condemned, then this would be indicative of a hostile attitude towards Macedon. Yet, the fact that both men were acquitted tells us that their trials cannot be linked to the immediate Macedonian background, but more likely arose from personal clashes, as was discussed above. Besides, Leocrates' crime by 330 was not that great anyway, and with Aeschines' speech the jurors recognised at least some of its legal weaknesses, hence Demosthenes' acquittal.[44]

Nowhere was the prosperity afforded by Macedonian rule more evident than in Athens, thanks to the administration of Lycurgus, who had near total control of Athenian finances for a dozen years (Diod. 16.88.1).[45] By careful manipulation of the Athenian tax system, Lycurgus saved Athens from the financial straits of recent years. He inaugurated a building programme (including a naval arsenal, the Panathenaic Stadium and the Theatre of Dionysus) aimed at fortifying and beautifying the city, and introduced the ephebic system, a form of military conscription. It seems clear that since the Athenians did not become actively engaged with Macedon again until 324, and then only diplomatically, and were enjoying the economic benefits of Macedonian rule, the ephebic system was not meant to prepare Athens for war against Macedon.[46] More likely is that Lycurgus was using the opportunity to support his new policy of educating the youth.[47]

What was Demosthenes doing in the period from 330 to 324? The answer is not fully known. Perhaps he merely contented himself with domestic affairs in this period, supporting Lycurgus in his programme, and said nothing about Macedonian matters because there was no need.[48] He was a *katēgoros* in 325/4, and he may have continued his connection with the Theoric Fund, of which he had been commissioner in 337/6 (Aes. 3.24). He was liturgically active, for during the famine in the 320s he contributed a talent from his own wealth ([Plut.] *Mor.* 851b).[49] In 324/3 he was *architheōros* to Olympia, albeit going there for political reasons connected with Harpalus and Alexander's Exiles Decree.[50] I connect Demosthenes' presence at these games with his public attack on Lamachus of Myrina, who had eulogised Philip and Alexander there (Plut. *Dem.* 9, [Plut.] *Mor.* 845c). Demosthenes was back on the Macedonian attack again, and this time in public. The peace and quiet of the period 330 to 324 was broken. What had happened between 330 and 324 to cause that? The answer has to lie in the Harpalus affair and the Exiles Decree.

The Harpalus affair brought with it the opportunity for outright revolt against Macedon.[51] Harpalus, the imperial treasurer, absconded from Babylon to Athens in 324 with considerable manpower and money to be deployed against Alexander (Diod. 17.108.6, Curt. 10.2.1).[52] At first denied entry, he returned to Athens with a much reduced force and less money, and was admitted. Shortly before, Nicanor of Stagira had arrived in Greece bringing with him Alexander's Exiles Decree for proclamation at the Olympic Games of 324.[53] This desperate measure on Alexander's part was in order to reduce the huge numbers of mercenaries roaming his empire after his dissolution decree,[54] who posed a very real threat to him if marshalled by an ambitious satrap or general. The decree caused great resentment amongst the Greeks. Its terms were known before its proclamation: all Greek cities were to receive back their exiles (excluding the Thebans), and Antipater was empowered by Alexander to force any unwilling city to do so (Diod. 18.8.4). The decree was illegal since return of exiles was outlawed under the terms of the League of Corinth ([Dem.] 17.16) – as if that mattered to Alexander by now. More than that, the sudden population increase as exiles returned would upset any precarious economic stability, a situation that applied all the more to those states adversely affected by the recent famine. That is why, along with most other states, the Athenians resisted the decree (Curt. 10.2.6–7; cf. Din. 1.58, 94).

Furthermore, it would seem that the Athenians were also expected to relinquish their control of the island of Samos. All Samians had received Athenian citizenship in 405,[55] and if Diodorus (18.18.9) is to be trusted, an Athenian cleruchy was established there in 365.[56] Athenian control of the island had been granted by Philip after the battle of Chaeronea (Diod. 18.56.7), so a consequence of the Exiles Decree was that the Athenians would have to remove this cleruchy. Nationalistic pride was therefore hurt, and the Samian issue seems to have been considered as important as the desire to retain Amphipolis during Philip's reign. The Athenians later sent an embassy to Alexander over Samos, probably as exiled Samians began to return to their island as a consequence of the Exiles Decree, but this was unsuccessful (see further below).

The situation was further complicated by the notion that Alexander should be worshipped as a god by the mainland Greeks. Whether this was a directive from the king himself or a Greek initiative is irrelevant; our sources indicate that there was some debate among the Greeks over his deification at this time.[57] Such an act, worship of a living being, was blasphemous to the Greeks of course, and many states, including Athens, resisted.[58]

Despite the resentment both the Exiles Decree and the potential worship of Alexander must have caused, Demosthenes persuaded the Assembly not to accept Harpalus' offer, but to imprison him and confiscate the money he had brought with him to Athens. This sum of money, 700 talents according to far from reliable sources (Hyp. 5.9–10; cf. [Plut.] *Mor.* 846b), was deposited on the Acropolis. Some time later Harpalus fled, and when only half of his alleged money was found in Athens, Demosthenes and several other men were thought to have been bribed by him (Diod. 17.108.8). Demosthenes proposed that the Areopagus should enquire into the affair under the *apophasis* procedure (Din. 1.1).[59] So insistent was he on his innocence that he also offered to submit to the death penalty if the Areopagus found him guilty (Din. 1.8, 40, 61, 108). If his strategy was that his past good relations with that body would serve him well, as Badian has suggested,[60] then he was mistaken. Six months later, the Areopagus submitted its report in which it accused Demosthenes and several others of *dōrodokia*. They were tried in about March 323. Demosthenes was found guilty in what could only have been a political trial (see below) and fined fifty talents, but fled into exile, continuing his protestations of innocence (cf. *Epistle* 2.2, 14–16, 21, 26, 3.37–8 and 43).[61] He was not to return to Athens until Alexander was dead.

While Harpalus was in prison, Demosthenes was sent to Olympia to meet with Nicanor (Din. 1.81, 103). The Exiles Decree was obviously high on the agenda, although Nicanor was but a messenger and had no power to negotiate its terms with any *polis*. Upon his return to Athens Harpalus escaped and suspicions were raised; Demosthenes' stance looked even more questionable when he suddenly had a change of heart as far as Alexander's divinity went: he advised the Athenians to accept it. This switch was attributed to Macedonian bribery, and he was so accused by at least two of his prosecutors at his trial, Dinarchus and his former political ally Hyperides (Din. 1.94, 103, Hyp. 5.31–2).[62]

Demosthenes' guilt or innocence in the affair is irrelevant for the purposes of this chapter; what is important is his political activity and influence at this time.[63] It was Demosthenes who had persuaded the Athenians to reject Harpalus, no easy task given the mood of the people over the Exiles Decree and the opposition from

Hyperides, who wanted to deploy Harpalus' manpower and money against Alexander. It was Demosthenes who had proposed Harpalus' arrest and the subsequent moves which the Athenians should make to the king over him. And it was Demosthenes who went to deal with Nicanor at Olympia, not Demades, or the even more reputable Phocion. All of these factors are proof of his political power at this time. So too is the necessity to convict him at his high-profile trial (see below).

What was his policy in 324? To prohibit the implementation of the Exiles Decree – and it would seem to retain possession of Samos at all costs. Of all Alexander's actions, this decree hit the mainland Greeks the hardest and caused the greatest resentment. It was the final straw and had ominous repercussions for any *Pax Macedonica* since we know of contacts of a more military nature between some Greek states at this time.[64] Demosthenes therefore proposed an embassy to Alexander to plead against the return of exiles and the surrender of Samos, and to aid its chances he exploited the Harpalus issue and the king's deification. From his conversations with Nicanor, Demosthenes must have received advice on what would please the king and what would not.[65] Perhaps he hoped that Nicanor would support the Athenian cause, and when he did not a frustrated Demosthenes could not hold his tongue from rebuking Lamachus of Myrina's encomium on Philip and Alexander – not good diplomacy!

However, Demosthenes knew that in 331 Agis did not stand a chance, and he knew that any revolt against Alexander supported by Harpalus in 324 would suffer the same fate – especially if the king were then on his way back to Greece, as the outcome of the Opis mutiny might indicate. This is an important point, which in my opinion needs to be stressed: the presence of Alexander himself. It was only when the rumour reached Greece that Alexander had died in 335 that the Thebans revolted, and the same applies to the Greeks settled by him in Bactria and Sogdiana when in 325 they heard that he had died in campaign against the Malli (Diod. 17.99.5–6). Like Diocletian's tetrarchy, Alexander's empire and power rested on the force of his own personality; people were afraid of him, hence his potential return to Greece was something to be taken most seriously. Therefore, it was up to diplomacy and flattery to counter the Exiles Decree; to have accepted Harpalus' offer would have been suicide for the Athenians. That was why, upon his return from meeting Nicanor, Demosthenes probably did allow Harpalus to flee – if the embassy could take news to the king that this wanted fugitive was no longer being harboured by the Athenians, Alexander might look more favourably on their request. Moreover, after he returned from his meeting with Nicanor he advocated the recognition of Alexander's divinity. He does not seem to have believed in it, as his remark recorded by Hyperides, that Alexander could call himself the son of Zeus and Poseidon if he so wished, shows (5.31). It is more likely that he supported the proposed apotheosis simply to flatter Alexander and so bolster the chances of success of the Athenian embassy to Alexander.[66] What did it matter to call Alexander a god if he ruled in the Athenians' favour? Demades had hit the nail on the head with his remark, if it may be connected to the Samian issue, that the Athenians were so concerned about heaven that they stood to lose the earth (Valerius Maximus 7.2.13).

No newcomer to the political scene could construct such a complex strategy, which revolved around so many issues all at the same time and with so much at stake. No newcomer could face speeches by powerful opponents intent on military resistance and an Assembly filled with furious citizens over the Exiles Decree, and yet persuade the *dēmos* to agree to a diplomatic recourse. Demosthenes in 324 was the Demosthenes of the mid-340s. Athenian policy again was his policy.

Yet, Demosthenes' strategy did not pay off, for Alexander rejected the Athenian embassy's pleas over the Exiles Decree and Samos.[67] This unwelcome news reached Athens about six months later, at the same time as the Areopagus accused him of accepting a bribe from Harpalus against the city.[68] The coincidence is too much. Perhaps the Areopagites were angry that Demosthenes' strategy had failed. Perhaps they hoped that by including Demosthenes' name in their findings Alexander might have been favourably swayed in a future appeal – after all, Alexander had asked for Demosthenes before, in 335. According to one of his later prosecutors, Demosthenes pleaded that he had been sacrificed to please the king (Hyp. 5.14), and Hyperides may not be wholly rhetorical here. Demosthenes challenged the Areopagites to produce the evidence on which their findings had been based (Din. 1.6, 61, Hyp. 5.3). They could not, for there was none. No evidence was cited in its report; only the names of those suspected of receiving a bribe, together with the amounts supposedly taken.[69]

Moreover, others indicted in the affair, against whom no proof of complicity was given, were acquitted, such as Aristogeiton (Dem. *Epistle* 3.37, 42), Hagnonides and Polyeuctus of Sphettus ([Plut.]

Mor. 846c–d); Demades was probably fined (Din. 1.29, 104), and of the remaining men only the *stratēgos* Philocles was probably condemned (Dem. *Epistle* 3.31). The prosecution speeches of Dinarchus (1) and of Hyperides (5) rest on the premise that the reputation of the Areopagus should be sufficient for accepting its report against Demosthenes. This was not enough. Since no evidence was cited for the allegations of bribery, all of the accused should either have been condemned or acquitted – a fact also recognised by the prosecution (Din. 1.113, 2.21, Hyp. 5.5–7). That even one of those accused was exculpated on the same grounds on which all were brought to trial shows the weakness of both the Areopagus' findings and the hidden agenda that governed Demosthenes' trial. On what grounds did the jurors declare who was guilty and who innocent?[70] The verdict was political, designed to remove Demosthenes from the political scene. Demosthenes had given his city his best and then some in 324; hence, Wilcken's comment is particularly apt: '[the trial] vividly exhibits the absolute rottenness of Attic democracy at the time'.[71] After Demosthenes' disgrace, Hyperides came to the political forefront and Athenian policy towards Macedon took on a more militant bent.

4

Thus ends, to all intents and purposes, Demosthenes' political career, and the Harpalus affair for Demosthenes' reputation in posterity becomes his *bête noire*.[72] Then in June 323 Alexander the Great died at Babylon, and with him died the Exiles Decree. When news of Alexander's death reached Athens, perhaps not too long after, Hyperides officially sanctioned the general Leosthenes to raise troops and the Greeks revolted again, in what is known as the Lamian War. Under his own auspices Demosthenes toured various *poleis* marshalling support against Antipater. On the motion of his cousin Demon, he was officially pardoned and returned to Athens, the people turning out *en masse* to greet him (Plut. *Dem.* 27). The details of the Lamian War are not relevant to this chapter,[73] except to say that Antipater decisively beat the Greeks, after some initial successes, at the battle of Crannon in August 322 (Diod. 18.17.3–5).

Antipater was not a man who believed in second chances, as the Athenians were to discover. Amongst other things, he stationed a garrison at Munychia, and by enforcing a wealth requirement of 2,000 drachmas (Diod. 18.18.4) for citizenship he drastically reduced the number of Athenian citizens. According to Diodorus, 12,000 citizens were disfranchised and fled to Thrace, leaving only 9,000 actual citizens in the city (Diod. 18.18.5). The figure of 12,000 in Diodorus, however, is hard to accept, for Plutarch (*Phocion* 28.4) says that 12,000 were disfranchised but that some stayed in Athens, where they eked out a miserable existence, while others migrated to Thrace, where Antipater gave them land and a city (*polis*). Therefore, at least some of the dispossessed remained in Athens, but the point is that the Athenian citizenry was depleted by almost one half by Antipater's action. Rubbing more salt into the wounds, Antipater then took Samos from the Athenians.[74]

At some point earlier Demades had Demosthenes and Hyperides condemned to death, and they fled into exile. Now, both were hunted down. Hyperides had fled to Hermione but was caught there and executed.[75] Demosthenes had taken refuge in the temple of Poseidon at Calauria (modern Poros). He had no desire to be dragged before Antipater. When he was discovered there, he committed suicide by drinking poison which he kept in his reed pen (Plut. *Dem.* 29.7, [Plut.] *Mor.* 847b, ([Lucian] *Encomium on Demosthenes* 28, 43–9).

5

Fordyce Mitchel was not quite right when he said that 'the story of Athens in the age of Alexander is really an account of Lycurgus' administration'.[76] Lycurgus played a significant role in the city's finances and its public works, but it was Demosthenes who dictated the most important policy: foreign affairs. Demosthenes was a political opportunist at least in the early years of Philip's reign; his earlier political speeches had been failures, and even when he turned his attention to Philip, he was not immediately successful. However, that cynical switch to Philip was to be the making of him politically; he used him as a means of attaining and maintaining power. And he learned from his years in politics. When Philip died, Demosthenes saw that the Greeks still had a chance to throw off the Macedonian mantle, and he urged them to do so. By the time of Agis, he had come to know that they never would, at least while Alexander was alive. Hence, acting in what he thought were the best interests of Athens, he urged his fellow Athenians not to support Agis, and in hindsight he was right.

Life under the Macedonian domination was not harsh, and peace and prosperity followed. Six years later, Alexander's Exiles Decree changed the situation dramatically, but even then, with Alexander on his way back to Greece, Demosthenes knew that military resistance was still not an option. And he was right, for it took Antipater, faced by almost every Greek *polis*, only a year to end the Lamian War. The Athenians would have suffered the same fate if they had revolted in 324/3 as they did in 322; at least Demosthenes prevented that, for the time being. Harpalus' arrival in say 346 or 340 would have been greeted with open arms; in 324, it was a problem which Demosthenes solved by making it part of his diplomatic strategy over the Exiles Decree. Here was his undoing, as subsequent events show. Of course, no strategy of resistance to the decree would have worked; the mercenaries who became unemployed thanks to Alexander's dissolution decree presented the king with potentially serious military and political problems, and their return to Greece was his only solution. Demosthenes must have realised this from his meeting with Nicanor; however, he had to do something, not least to prevent Hyperides from persuading the Athenians to revolt. That he persuaded the people to adopt his diplomatic solution rather than revolt is testimony to his political power. For that, he deserves credit. Demosthenes was less active politically during Alexander's reign, and he pursued a more subtle, compromising diplomatic policy. However, he was no less influential, and in many respects his policy towards Macedon was more successful in the reign of Alexander than in that of Philip.

NOTES

* I am grateful to Professors E. Badian, A.B. Bosworth and B.R.I. Sealey, and Dr Noriko Sawada, for their comments on a previous draft.
1 G.L. Cawkwell, 'The Crowning of Demosthenes', CQ^2 19 (1969), pp. 163–80; the quotations are on pp. 164 and 180, respectively.
2 For Demosthenes' career during the reign of Philip II, see especially Ryder, Chapter 2, and Buckler, Chapter 4.
3 Dem. 18.168–88, 211, Aes. 3.140–1, and see J.R. Ellis, *Philip II and Macedonian Imperialism* (London: 1976), pp. 191–3.
4 On the battle see Diod. 16.85.5–86.6, Plut. *Alexander* 9.2, and for modern discussion see N.G.L. Hammond and G.T. Griffith, *A History of Macedonia* 2 (Oxford: 1979), pp. 596–603. On Chaeronea rightly meaning the end of Greek liberty see G.L. Cawkwell, 'The End of Greek Liberty' in R.W. Wallace and E.M. Harris (eds.), *Transitions to Empire: Essays in Honor of E. Badian* (Norman: 1996), pp. 98–121.
5 See J.K. Davies, *Athenian Propertied Families* (Oxford: 1971), p. 137, for Demosthenes' other post-Chaeronea activities.
6 Dem. 18.249; see too Dem. 25.37, Plut. *Dem.* 21, [Plut.] *Mor.* 845f.

7 Speech 60 in the Demosthenic corpus is the funeral oration. However, what survives today is a poor imitation, for in antiquity it was regarded as spurious (Dion. Hal. *Demosthenes* 44).

8 Demosthenes' attitude to the king is ably shown by his reaction to news of his death: he persuaded the Boule to make a public sacrifice of thanksgiving and danced for joy in the streets even though his daughter had died less than a week earlier (Aes. 3.77, 160; cf. Plut. *Phocion* 16.6).

9 Philip's establishment of the League and his Persian plans: Diod. 16.89.2; for the decree: Tod 2, no. 177; cf. T.T.B. Ryder, *Koine Eirene* (Oxford: 1965), pp. 102–5 and 150–62. Alexander's renewal of the League and invasion of Persia: Aes. 3.161, Diod. 17.3–4, 17.4.9, Arr. 1.1.1–3.

10 On the historical background, see A.B. Bosworth, *Conquest and Empire: The Reign of Alexander the Great* (Cambridge: 1988), pp. 28–33.

11 Diod. 17.8.3–14.1, Arr. 1.7.1–8.8, Plut. *Dem.* 23.1, Justin 11.3.8.

12 Diod. 17.115, Arr. 1.10.4–6, Plut. *Dem.* 23.4, *Phocion* 17.2, [Plut.] *Mor.* 841e, 847c, 848e. The sources give varying numbers, of which five are common to all: Demosthenes, Lycurgus, Polyeuctus, Ephialtes, Charidemus: for discussion see A.B. Bosworth, *A Historical Commentary on Arrian's History of Alexander* 1 (Oxford: 1980), pp. 92–6, R. Sealey, *Demosthenes and his Time* (Oxford: 1993), pp. 204–5.

13 Alexander still demanded Charidemus, who fled to Persia (Arr. 1.10.1–6, Diod. 17.15.1–5, Plut. *Dem.* 23.4–6, Justin 11.4.12).

14 Sealey, *Demosthenes*, p. 208.

15 Cf. Sealey, *Demosthenes*, p. 203: 'Patently [the garrison's] task was no longer to watch the Thebans.'

16 Roughly a third of the private orations which survive today in the Demosthenic corpus are spurious and hard to date. Speech 34, *Against Phormio*, may be dated to 327/6: F. Blass, *Die attische Beredsamkeit*² 3 (Leipzig: 1898), p. 578.

17 Cf. the remarks of Cawkwell, 'Crowning', pp. 163–4, on unknown opposition to Demosthenes in the 340s, but his remarks hold good in general for the 330s and 320s too.

18 For example, Aes. 1.94, 3.1, 164, Din. 1.12, 43.

19 F. Mitchel, 'Athens in the Age of Alexander', *G&R*² 12 (1965), p. 191, believes that Alexander's action was 'a slap at the still independent Spartans', though I cannot see any reason for Alexander to act in this way.

20 Cawkwell, 'Crowning', pp. 174–80.

21 S. Perlman, 'The Historical Example: Its Use and Importance as Political Propaganda in the Attic Orators', *SH* 7 (1961), pp. 158–66. Cf. Ian Worthington, 'History and Oratorical Exploitation' in Ian Worthington (ed.), *Persuasion: Greek Rhetoric in Action* (London: 1994), pp. 109–29.

22 On Hyperides 6 see now Ian Worthington, *Greek Orators* 2: *Dinarchus 1 and Hyperides 5 & 6* (Warminster: 1999).

23 The chronology is that of E. Badian, 'Agis III: Revisions and Reflections' in Ian Worthington (ed.), *Ventures Into Greek History: Essays in Honour of N.G.L. Hammond* (Oxford: 1994), pp. 268–71.

24 On the war see, for example, Bosworth, *Conquest and Empire*, pp. 198–204.

25 Aes. 3.165–6, Din. 1.34–5; cf. Plut. *Dem.* 24.1.

26 Badian, 'Agis III: Revisions and Reflections', pp. 272–7, for the date.

27 Aes. 3.133, Diod. 17.63.1–3, 73.5–6, Curt. 6.1.19–21.

28 Cf. Sealey, *Demosthenes*, p. 206.

29 See P.J. Rhodes, *The Athenian Boule* (Oxford: 1972), pp. 15–16, on the law which Ctesiphon apparently broke.

30 Cf. Cawkwell, 'Crowning', pp. 167–9.

31 I still follow the common opinion that Aeschines reopened the case (cf. E.M. Harris, *Aeschines and Athenian Politics* [New York: 1995], pp. 140–2, 173–4), despite the strong arguments of N. Sawada, 'Athenian Politics in the Age of Alexander the Great: A Reconsideration of the Trial of Ctesiphon', *Chiron* 26 (1996), pp. 60–71, that it was Demosthenes who took the initiative. Sawada argues that Aeschines was forced to rekindle the charge or incur *atimia* himself, for if a plaintiff in a *graphē* did not proceed to prosecute he could become *atimos*, and Aeschines' notice of his intent to prosecute Demosthenes in 336 was still outstanding in 330. However, there is no evidence that Demosthenes and presumably Ctesiphon were pressuring a vulnerable Aeschines in 330. Moreover, given Demosthenes' animosity towards Aeschines, why did he 'force' Aeschines into court in 330, and not before? After all, Aeschines was just as 'vulnerable' before 330. The deciding factor was the war of Agis: Aeschines saw the Athenian inaction thanks to Demosthenes as his chance to strike at his old enemy, and did so.

32 E.M. Burke, '*Contra Leocratem* and *De Corona*: Political Collaboration?', *Phoenix* 31 (1977), pp. 330–40, saw the trials of Leocrates and of Ctesiphon/Demosthenes in 330 arising from the Macedonian issue, but his views have been properly refuted by Sawada, 'Athenian Politics in the Age of Alexander', pp. 57–82. See also above note, and on the two trials and the background against which they were set, see further below.

33 On the weaknesses in Aeschines' case see E.M. Harris, 'Law and Oratory' in Ian Worthington (ed.), *Persuasion: Greek Rhetoric in Action* (London: 1994), especially pp. 142–8. See also below, n. 44.

34 On the case see also Buckler, Chapter 4 Section 4, and see further below.

35 Cawkwell, 'Crowning', pp. 170–3; cf. Harris, *Aeschines*, pp. 140–2. On the date of Gaugamela, see Badian, 'Agis III: Revisions and Reflections', pp. 277–8.

36 Cawkwell, 'Crowning', pp. 173–80; the quotation is from p. 180. *Contra* Sealey, *Demosthenes*, pp. 207–8.

37 Cawkwell, 'Crowning', pp. 179–80. Sealey, *Demosthenes*, p. 207, believes that Athenian inaction was owing to the presence of the Macedonian garrison at Thebes. However, I think Cawkwell's point, that the garrison was there only to buy time until the main army arrived and so was not a matter of concern for the Athenians, is more valid.

38 The accusation itself is rhetorical and intended to denigrate Demosthenes at these two trials since the accounts of the orators are

riddled with inconsistency: see Ian Worthington, *A Historical Commentary on Dinarchus* (Ann Arbor: 1992), pp. 139–43 and 164–8. However, the connection of Demosthenes to Persian money is the important factor, as Cawkwell also notes, 'Crowning', p. 177.

39 On these ideals cf. Sealey, *Demosthenes*, pp. 241–4.

40 Note also the criticisms of Harris, *Aeschines*, p. 142 – he very rightly talks of Aeschines being bewildered by contemporary events, and that he had learnt nothing since his earlier judicial triumphs over Demosthenes.

41 On this point see my 'The Harpalus Affair and the Greek Response to the Macedonian Hegemony' in Ian Worthington (ed.), *Ventures Into Greek History: Essays in Honour of N.G.L. Hammond* (Oxford: 1994), pp. 307–30. I note that Sawada, 'Athenian Politics in the Age of Alexander', p. 81, concurs, but quite rightly says 'this is not to say that they [the Athenians] loved Macedonian rule'.

42 I disagree with Sealey's view, *Demosthenes*, pp. 213–15, that Antipater was expecting help from the Athenians and the Aetolians in a potential clash with Alexander, who was out to replace him by Craterus. This was certainly not the case when Alexander died. Moreover, there is no hard evidence for any deterioration in relations between Alexander and Antipater, and Craterus was still in Cilicia when the king died (Diod. 18.4.1): see Worthington, *Commentary on Dinarchus*, p. 67 with n. 110.

43 Aes. 3.162; E. Badian, 'Harpalus', *JHS* 81 (1961), p. 34, believes that once Hephaestion died Demosthenes' position in Athens 'would undoubtedly be weakened'. However, Hephaestion died in about October 324 (H. Berve, *Das Alexanderreich auf prosopographischer Grundlage* 2 [Munich: 1926], p. 173), but Demosthenes continued to remain influential in Athenian politics at least until the return of the embassy to Alexander over the Exiles Decree in approximately February 323 (on which, see below).

44 On the weaknesses in Aeschines' case see Harris, 'Law and Oratory', pp. 142–8. Of course, the jurors probably did not consider only legal issues, and in a case such as that of Aeschines against Demosthenes it is hard to determine from the speeches we have what ultimately convinced the jurors to vote as they did. Demosthenes' burying of the legal issues in his speech may have been more a feature of his rhetorical style than the legal substance of his case, for Aeschines tends to focus more on legal issues in his speeches, especially in their opening sections.

45 See E.M. Burke, 'Lycurgan Finances', *GRBS* 26 (1985), pp. 251–64 with F.W. Mitchel, 'Athens in the Age of Alexander', pp. 189–204 and 'Lykourgan Athens: 338–322', *Semple Lectures* 2 (Cincinnati: 1970), Bosworth, *Conquest and Empire*, pp. 204–15, Sealey, *Demosthenes*, pp. 209–12, and on religion J.D. Mikalson, *Religion in Hellenistic Athens* (Berkeley and Los Angeles: 1998), pp. 11–45.

46 Cf. Mitchel, 'Athens in the Age of Alexander', pp. 202–4, *contra* Sealey, *Demosthenes*, pp. 211–12, who believes that the ephebes were ready for military service if dissension amongst the Macedonians occurred.

47 See Sawada, 'Athenian Politics in the Age of Alexander the Great', pp. 77–8.

48 Sealey, *Demosthenes*, p. 208, believes that Demosthenes stayed inactive because he knew that armed resistance was only possible when the Macedonians became divided, and that this situation did not occur until the last years of Alexander's life. I assume Sealey bases his view on his belief that Alexander and Antipater were at odds and that Craterus had been sent to replace Antipater (for example, *Demosthenes*, p. 213). However, there is no hard evidence for any deterioration in relations between Alexander and Antipater, and Craterus hardly rushed back to the mainland, as might be expected if Alexander had wanted Antipater replaced – he was still in Cilicia when the king died (Diod. 18.4.1).

49 However, see Davies' reservation about this at *Athenian Propertied Families*, p. 137.

50 Din. 1.81 (with Worthington, *Commentary on Dinarchus*, pp. 250–1), Hyp. 5.18, Plut. *Dem.* 9.1, [Plut.] *Mor.* 845c.

51 On Harpalus, see Berve, *Alexanderreich* 2, no. 143; on the affair in detail, see Worthington, *Commentary on Dinarchus*, pp. 41–77 and bibliography cited.

52 On the background to Harpalus' flight, see Badian, 'Harpalus', pp. 16–25; cf. Bosworth, *Conquest and Empire*, pp. 148–50.

53 Diodorus (probably from Duris of Samos) quotes the text of the decree at 18.8.4; cf. 17.109.1, Curt. 10.2.4, [Plut.] *Mor.* 221a and Justin 13.5.2; for discussion of it, see Badian, 'Harpalus', pp. 15–21 with Bosworth, *Conquest and Empire*, pp. 220–8. For the chronology of this period see my 'The Chronology of the Harpalus Affair', *SO* 61 (1986), pp. 63–76.

54 Diod. 17.106.3, 111.1–2, Curt. 10.1.45. On Alexander's treatment of the satraps and leading officers, Badian's analysis, 'Harpalus', pp. 16–25, cannot be bettered.

55 See R. Meiggs and D.M. Lewis, *A Selection of Greek Historical Inscriptions to the end of the fifth century* BC[2] (Oxford: 1989), no. 94; cf. Tod 2, no. 97.

56 The foundation of this cleruchy is known only from the record of its expulsion in 322 (Diod. 18.18.9), and, as Professor Sealey points out to me, there is something odd in the tradition of a cleruchy sent in 365 to be removed under the Exiles Decree; see further J. Cargill, '*IG* ii[2] 1 and the Athenian Kleruchy on Samos', *GRBS* 24 (1983), pp. 321–32 (with caution).

57 For background see Bosworth, *Conquest and Empire*, pp. 278–89, together with G.L. Cawkwell, 'The Deification of Alexander the Great: A Note' in Ian Worthington (ed.), *Ventures Into Greek History: Essays in Honour of N.G.L. Hammond* (Oxford: 1994), pp. 293–306. On the discussion in Athens, see E. Badian, 'Alexander the Great between Two Thrones and Heaven: Variations on an Old Theme' in A. Small (ed.), *Subject and Ruler: The Cult of the Ruling Power in Classical Antiquity* (Ann Arbor: 1996), especially pp. 25–6.

58 Din. 1.94, Hyp. 5.31–2, Athenaeus 6.251b (Ephippus, *FGrH* 126 F5), [Plut.] *Mor.* 187e, 804b, 842d, Aelian, *Varia Historia* 5.12.

59 On this procedure see R.W. Wallace, *The Areopagos Council, to 307 B.C.* (Baltimore and London: 1989), pp. 199–200.

60 Badian, 'Harpalus', p. 33. His view has been followed by many others; for example, Bosworth, *Conquest and Empire*, p. 218, Sealey, *Demosthenes*,

p. 214, and Wallace, *Areopagos Council*, pp. 199–200. Whether Demosthenes considered he had influential supporters among the Areopagites and so could exploit them is, however, unknown. Dinarchus 1.10 reveals that in 335/4 the Areopagus, perhaps out of amity, refused to enquire into Demosthenes' alleged acceptance of money from the Persian king, and so he may have hoped for a similar response in 324.

61 The authenticity of Demosthenes' letters has been ably demonstrated by J. Goldstein, *The Letters of Demosthenes* (New York: 1968).

62 The accusation is certainly rhetorical: see Worthington, *Commentary on Dinarchus*, pp. 262–3.

63 He claimed that he did take money from Harpalus, but as a loan for the Theoric Fund (Hyp. 5.13). I believe this to be true, and that he was a victim of the political background of the Exiles Decree: see further Worthington, *Commentary on Dinarchus*, pp. 58–73.

64 Specifically, Athens, Aetolia (also very badly affected by the Exiles Decree: Diod. 18.8.6, Justin 13.5.1–6), Locris and Phocis: *IG* ii² 370 and *IG* ii² 367; cf. Diod. 17.111.1–4, 18.8.1–7.

65 Cf. Badian, 'Harpalus', p. 33: Demosthenes attained 'a stay of execution of the Exiles Decree until an embassy had been sent to Alexander; perhaps even advice on how to placate him'.

66 A point made over a century ago by A. Schaefer, *Demosthenes und seine Zeit*² 3 (Leipzig: 1887), pp. 318–19, but all too often neglected; cf. A.W. Pickard-Cambridge, *Demosthenes and the Last Days of Greek Freedom* (London: 1914), pp. 458–9.

67 For a discussion of Alexander's ruling and an examination of the background, including the sources, see Ian Worthington, '*IG* ii² 370 and the Date of the Athenian Alliance with Aetolia', *ZPE* 57 (1984), pp. 139–44. Samian exiles seem to have been returning for some time: see E. Badian, 'A Comma in the History of Samos', *ZPE* 23 (1976), pp. 289–94.

68 R.M. Errington, 'Samos and the Lamian War', *Chiron* 5 (1975), pp. 51–7, compellingly argues that Alexander's Samian directive was made only when the embassy met the king at Babylon, not at Susa simultaneous with Nicanor's departure to Greece as is so often assumed (for example, by Bosworth, *Conquest and Empire*, pp. 215 and 221).

69 Din. 2.21, Hyp. 5.6, Dem. *Epistle* 2.1, 15 and 3.42.

70 Cf. Goldstein, *Letters of Demosthenes*, p. 85: 'the acquittal of even one of them overthrew the basis of all the condemnations, and this fundamental argument the letters [of Demosthenes] urge repeatedly'.

71 U. Wilcken, *Alexander the Great* (transl. G.C. Richards, New York: 1967), p. 217.

72 See Harding, Chapter 9.

73 On the historical background see most conveniently N.G.L. Hammond and F.W. Walbank, *A History of Macedonia* 3 (Oxford: 1988), pp. 108–17.

74 For the peace terms in full, see Diod. 18.8.3–6, 56, 65, Plut. *Dem.* 28–30 and *Phocion* 29 and 33, [Plut.] *Mor.* 846e–847b, 847d, 849a–d, Pausanias 1.43.1 and 7.10.1.

75 Plut. *Dem.* 28.4, *Phocion* 29.1, [Plut.] *Mor.* 849b–c.

76 Mitchel, 'Athens in the Age of Alexander', p. 192.

4

DEMOSTHENES AND AESCHINES*

John Buckler

Some historical epochs are distinguished by great political conflicts the poles of which are personified by the major figures who championed them. Examples are abundant. American history provides the debates between Stephen A. Douglas and Abraham Lincoln over slavery, English the division between William Gladstone and Benjamin Disraeli over imperial policy, and German the dispute between Willy Brandt and Rainer Barzel over *Ostpolitik*. Fourth-century Greece presents Demosthenes and Aeschines, whose responses to the rise of Philip of Macedon divided Athenian politics into two broad groups at opposite ends of foreign policy. Added to the political differences of these two Athenians was a personal enmity that was generally unseemly and often vicious. Both features form such basic ingredients in the contest for public approval that they are virtually inseparable.

The works of Demosthenes and Aeschines constitute the best sources for the history of their rivalry, but they also present the historian with several intriguing challenges. The first and ultimately the most important is the nature of the evidence itself, which has not always been properly understood and is here best treated in the Appendix to this chapter. Neither of these veteran politicians pretended to be an historian, and truth was often as valuable to them as sand in a desert. Far more useful could be a half-truth, a plausible lie, or a mere malicious personal insult. Pure rules of evidence, as idealized in a modern court, are often lacking in their speeches. Instead, their primary aim was to persuade their audience at any given time of the wisdom of their policies and the purity of their motives. As important was the need to disparage the worth of their opponent's views, the accuracy of his knowledge, and indeed his honesty and character. Neither Demosthenes nor Aeschines was a high-minded man whose ideals transcended the political cause that he espoused at the moment. Both men were mean, meretricious, and scurrilous. This harsh verdict demands proof, and the best way to provide it is to examine the way in which these men presented their ideas to the public and to survey their careers as seen against the backdrop of contemporary events. Those careers can be divided into several recognizable periods, each to receive individual treatment. The first and easily the most influential was that when they played such significant roles in the framing of the Peace of Philocrates of 346. At the core of this event is a congeries of problems that include whether they accurately understood Philip's real goals and ambitions, and whether they properly appreciated the political and military situation in which Athens found itself. Joined with these matters were the challenges of deciding whether Philip genuinely wanted peace and friendship with Athens or whether he planned to use the treaty guilefully to buy time until he could eventually subdue it. Next come the years between 346 and 343, which saw Athenian confidence in the peace erode and its chief proponents, Philocrates and Aeschines, indicted for it. The third period involved the renewal of war between Philip and Athens, in which Demosthenes triumphed over his rival's program of peace and concert with Macedonia. Lastly came the period after Philip's victory at Chaeronea in 338, when Aeschines unsuccessfully challenged the wisdom and value of Demosthenes' entire political career.[1]

1

As seen elsewhere in this volume (especially Ryder, Chapter 2), relations between Philip and Athens had proved difficult from the outset, largely owing to Athens' interference in Macedonian affairs and its ambitions in the northern Aegean, especially over Amphipolis.[2] Since most of Philip's early efforts were aimed at securing the territory and peoples neighboring his kingdom, he originally collided with Athens only in this distant but nonetheless sensitive area. Indeed, he and Athens soon became involved in the 'War for Amphipolis', as the Athenians called it (Isoc. 5.2, Aes. 2.70). Until 354 he was something of a menace to Athens in that region but not to Athens itself or its vital interests elsewhere. The Sacred War of 356–346 changed that because his allies and later his subjects the Thessalians drew him into the mainstream of Greek politics. That war was at the outset irrelevant to Philip and an embarrassing nuisance to Athens, but the Phocian seizure and plundering of

Apollo's sanctuary at Delphi eventually drew most of the mainland Greeks into a fitful war that spread far beyond Phocis.[3] This war was distinctive because of its religious significance. The sanctuary of Pythian Apollo was a highly venerated panhellenic shrine, and Phocian violence towards it was an insult not only to everyone, Greek or foreigner, who revered the god but also demeaning to the Amphictyonic Council, which was traditionally entrusted with the care of the sanctuary.[4] Among those horrified by the Phocian sacrilege, both for religious and political reasons, were the Thebans, Locrians, and especially the Thessalians, all of whom struggled to liberate Delphi from the Phocians, who received the lukewarm support of Athens and Sparta. For the broader relations of Philip and Athens Thessalian participation in the Sacred War proved crucial. The Thessalians suffered defeat in the opening stages of the conflict, which led to Phocian invasion of their land. Discouraged and hard-pressed, they appealed to Philip for military succor. In 353 at the battle of the Crocus Plain Philip's private rivalry with Athens in the north joined with his and Athenian involvement in the larger war. To support the Phocians at the battle Athens sent a naval squadron under Chares which arrived too late to retrieve Phocian disaster.[5] Nonetheless, Athens had thereby openly opposed Philip in another theater and over a different cause. In the immediate aftermath of victory Philip neglected Athens to consolidate his power in Thessaly.[6] Only then did he march on Thermopylae, to which Athens responded by sending Nausicles and a force to hold the position. Philip refused to force the issue, but he had now clashed with Athens on the borders of central Greece.[7] Thenceforth until 346 the ambitions of Philip and Athens in the northern Aegean and the course of the Sacred War became concomitant.[8]

After the Crocus Plain and his responsibilities in the south, Philip pursued two principal and related lines of foreign policy: the extension of Macedonian power in the north and wariness of Athens in central Greece. During the next few years he campaigned vigorously in Thrace, where he threatened to absorb the kingdom of Cersebleptes, newly allied with Athens, and Athenian gains in the Chersonese. His activity so alarmed the Olynthians that they concluded an alliance with Athens, which immediately aroused Philip's distrust.[9] With the storm looming over Olynthus, Demosthenes began in 349 to deliver his orations on their behalf; and when the storm broke, Aeschines in the following year launched his political career as a staunch opponent of Philip.[10] His previous service was military rather than political, in which he had served conspicuously at Phlius in 366, at Mantinea in 362, and twice won crowns for his valor in the fighting on Euboea in 348. He won the friendship of Eubulus, as prominent for his prudent financial abilities as for his political acumen, and Phocion, who had made his military reputation under Chabrias and whose political career was marked by old-fashioned probity.

In 348 even before the fall of Olynthus and the end of the fighting on Euboea, Philip made the first move to conclude peace with Athens. Accurate knowledge of the subsequent course of events is essential to understand his dealings with Athens and the response of Demosthenes and Aeschines to them. Vital though it is, a firm chronology of these years is, however, unattainable, for both men had strong reasons to obscure or distort the truth about certain vital events. That said, in 348 some Euboean envoys friendly to Philip opened peace negotiations with Athens in the course of which they mentioned that Philip had told them that he too desired peace.[11] The Athenians greeted the news sceptically, but not long afterwards an unrelated event made them reconsider their position. Phryno of Rhamnus was captured by Macedonian pirates during the Olympic truce, was duly ransomed, and upon his return asked his countrymen to send an embassy to Macedonia to win the repayment of his ransom. They obliged by sending Ctesiphon (*PA* 8893), a friend of Demosthenes, to Philip, who took the opportunity to explain that he had unwillingly gone to war and now wanted peace. When Ctesiphon reported his news, the Athenians were overjoyed, whereupon Philocrates won a vote in the Assembly to open peace negotiations with the king. An opponent, however, attacked Philocrates' motion as unconstitutional, which entailed a trial. When Philocrates proved too ill to defend himself, Demosthenes (Aes. 2.14) spoke successfully in his defense, but the fall of Olynthus put a temporary halt to negotiations. Philip's destruction of the city and his taking of many Athenian prisoners alarmed many in Athens, one of the most influential of whom was Eubulus, an enemy of Philip. He responded by proposing a successful decree that the Athenians send embassies to other Greek states inviting them to meet in Athens to discuss a common war against Philip.[12] Demosthenes (19.304) later snidely criticized this diplomatic effort, claiming that Aeschines and Eubulus urged the Athenians to send ambassadors nearly as far afield as the Red Sea. Demosthenes' sarcasm about a policy complementary to his own suggests envy because the idea was not his. During the Athenian peace deliberations of 346 the point was obviously sensitive to him, for he claims (19.16) that no Greek ambassadors were in the city at the time. Aeschines (2.57–62) flatly contradicts him. Both contemporary statements cannot be true, and only later did Demosthenes (18.20, 23) admit the fact of the absence of Greek ambassadors during the deliberations. This admittedly minor detail arouses the suspicion that the high-minded patriot was not always above the small politician. Demosthenes' scorn notwithstanding, Eubulus prevailed, and Aeschines served as a member of the one known embassy that was sent to the Arcadian League, the capital of which was Megalopolis. The embassy failed because of an Arcadian hostility towards Athens that was shared by several other major Peloponnesian powers. Athens and Sparta, its ally since 369, had long threatened the security of these states, and in 362 they had fought against Epaminondas and his Arcadian allies in part to destroy the very Arcadian League that Aeschines addressed. In 351 Sparta attacked Megalopolis itself, only to be repulsed by the Thebans (Diod. 16.39.1–7). No Arcadian sitting in the Thersilium at Megalopolis in 348 had much reason to love Athens and its Spartan friends. Long after the Theban Hegemony Messenia, the Arcadian League, and Argos viewed Sparta and Athens with fear and distrust. Philip, however, had taken advantage of Epaminondas' Peloponnesian policy by befriending these states against their powerful rivals.[13] Furthermore, Philip enjoyed the advantage of being too far removed from the Peloponnese to be seen as any threat there. Philip's support of Thebes and Thessaly in warring against the Phocian temple-robbers also served him well among other Greeks. He stood forth as the champion of Apollo against the sacrilegious with whom Athens and Sparta were allied. Many Greeks saw Athens as a much greater threat than Philip (Dem. 19.259).

Aeschines and his fellow envoys failed in Arcadia, and he took the rebuff very much to heart. Athenian propaganda portrayed Philip as waging war against all Greeks, which they considered arrant nonsense, as even Demosthenes (18.20, 24) in a fit of honesty admitted. He too saw (18.234) that Athens had only the weakest of the islanders for support. In addition, an incident on the return trip to Athens made a vivid impression on Aeschines. Along the way he encountered a band of captive Olynthian women and children who had been sold into slavery (Dem. 19.11, 305–6, Aes. 2.79). Although Aeschines roundly denounced Philip in his report to the Assembly, he now knew the lack of support that Athens suffered and the terrible price that defeat would entail. It may very well have been at this point that he realized that only peace with Philip would preserve Athens from an Olynthian fate. Whatever his private thoughts, he later told his countrymen (Aes. 2.79) that so long as the war for Amphipolis lasted, he tried to unite Arcadia and the rest of Greece behind Athens; but when no one else came forward with aid, he advised them to make peace. Continued war with Philip would be Athenian alone, and Aeschines had no doubts about the outcome.

A second factor influenced Aeschines' attitude towards Philip, one encouraged by the king himself. By his own admission Aeschines (1.169) believed that Philip entertained no aggressive designs against Athens. He apparently thought it possible for Philip to enjoy his Balkan sphere of interest while Athens concentrated on the Aegean. Philip's career to that point lent credence to this view. He had spent nearly all of his time since 359 campaigning in the north, principally against the Illyrians, Paeonians, and Thracians.[14] He had intervened in Thessaly only by request, and even his fruitless move on Thermopylae in 353 could be seen merely as an attempt to secure the southern border of Thessaly. Moreover, it was traditional Macedonian policy to remain on friendly terms with the Thessalians; and it was that connection, not any preconceived plan of his, that had drawn him into Thessaly and the Sacred War. His desire to end the war stemmed from his own self-projected image of piety towards Apollo and the Thessalian expectation that he would free the god's sanctuary from the impious. Nothing in Philip's previous conduct suggested that he entertained any permanent ambitions south of Thermopylae. Even so, he must surely have then realized the future possibilities that the Sacred War offered him.

The topic of captives was also very much on Athenian minds. Again a minor incident provided the impetus for broader events, this one quickly leading to the first official Athenian embassy to Philip to negotiate peace. Iatrocles was one of the Athenian captives, and his family prevailed upon Philocrates and Demosthenes to send Aristodemus to win his release. Although this was an official delegation, its mission was ransom not peace. Nonetheless, both Iatrocles and Aristodemus returned with enthusiastic reports of Philip's good intentions that included his repeated wish for peace. On the strength of their report Philocrates moved to send ten envoys to discuss peace and other common interests, the delegation consisting of Philocrates himself, who nominated Demosthenes; Nausicles, who nominated Aeschines; Ctesiphon, Aristodemus,

Iatrocles, Phryno, Dercylus, and Cimon.[15] The allies also chose Aglaocreon of Tenedos to represent the Athenian League (Aes. 2.20, 97, 126). Aglaocreon's presence in the delegation is extremely important for a proper understanding of the Peace of Philocrates, as is Demosthenes' refusal even to mention him, so much so that the matter deserves further attention. Tenedos was one of the first states to join the Athenian League, the members of which met in a synod that voted on policy independently of Athens.[16] Aglaocreon was the legal delegate of the League alone, and was empowered to speak only for it. He lacked any legal right to represent any other ally that Athens had. Though obvious, the point is fundamental to the proper understanding of the status of Athenian allies in the treaty, for later debate would involve the question of whether Phocis, Halus, and Cersebleptes had the right to be included among the Athenian allies. In fact, none of these three was ever represented by an ambassador in any of these proceedings (Aes. 2.83–93, Dem. 19.174). The presence of Aglaocreon alone of allied ambassadors proves that from the outset the Athenians intended peace only for themselves and the members of their league.

When the Athenian embassy left for Macedonia in 347, events in places as far removed as Thrace and Thessaly made their task all the more urgent, but the scope and the nature of their predicament were unapparent to them. Philip at the moment pursued his goals in the north, which were of far greater significance to him than were the dealings with Athens. From the beginning of his reign he had striven to bring Thrace under his control, and by 347 he had nearly achieved his desire. Of the three kings of Thrace he had reduced Cetriporis to a political cipher, removed Amadocus from his throne, and pushed Cersebleptes into an isolated and precarious position. With complete victory within his grasp, Philip now prepared to crush Cersebleptes, which would give him control of the Chersonese and anchor the eastern flank of his empire on the western side of the Hellespont. By doing so, Philip could threaten the vital Athenian grain route at will. This was the main objective to which Philip bent his efforts as the Athenian ambassadors journeyed to Macedonia.[17]

Despite the primacy of Thrace in his plans, Philip could not ignore Thessaly, where his problem was twofold. The region was fractious, as witnessed by the current dispute between Halus and Pharsalus. To restore internal order Philip had ordered Parmenio to reduce Halus, which was doubly important to him because of its strategic position on the coast between Pagasae and Thermopylae.[18] The siege of Halus would have remained a minor incident, irrelevant to the peace negotiations between Athens and Philip, except that the Athenian ambassadors stumbled upon the scene on their way to Pella. Parmenio treated them handsomely, doubtless provided them with some first-hand information about Macedonian affairs, and sent them on their way (Dem. 19.163). The episode was then unimportant to the Athenians. The city was not allied with Athens, but would later loom large in discussion. Of far greater concern was the Sacred War, in which the Thessalians had urged Philip to intervene ever since they elected him their archon. He had previously been content to let the Thebans conduct the war; but nine years of inconclusive fighting had led only to stalemate and heavy losses. Now hard-pressed, the Thebans too sent an embassy to Philip seeking alliance and assistance. The Thebans naturally received the enthusiastic support of the Thessalians, who applied still more force on Philip to act. Philip in turn was more than happy to succeed where the Thebans had failed (Diod. 16.58.3). The matter stood thus: Philip and Athens wanted to end the war for Amphipolis, while Thessaly and Thebes wanted him to end the Sacred War. Even though the two conflicts were unrelated, they nonetheless involved nearly all of the principals. Philip could not ignore Athens in either case, but he could seek separate settlements of both. The very complexity of these events, the jumble of the various states involved, and the disparate goals of them all served to complicate the peace agreements of 346.[19]

At Pella the Athenians raised the status of Amphipolis, which had fallen to Philip in 357 and which they desperately wanted back. Philip instead argued that the city was his by right of conquest and that the subject was not open to further discussion, which should not have surprised them. Yet he promised not to invade the Chersonese while the Athenians deliberated over the peace. If the envoys raised the question of including Cersebleptes and other states in the peace, nothing came of it. Philip clearly insisted on a treaty solely between Athens and its allies of the League and himself and his allies, whom he would designate. He promised to clarify his intentions in a letter to be read to the Boule and Assembly when the Athenian people discussed the peace. He also made some vague promises about extraneous matters. Even if some envoys did not believe the sincerity of his promises, which is far from certain, the majority did and their enthusiasm was infectious. Furthermore, it was expedient to accept what they could not change. Philip pressed as well for an alliance to accompany the peace. Although Demosthenes later made a huge outcry against this clause, it was actually less important than that limiting the participants of the treaty so narrowly as it did.[20]

Their mission completed, the ambassadors returned to Athens probably in middle or late Anthesterion (about February/March), and gave a brief report and a letter from Philip to the Boule, for which Demosthenes as a *bouleutēs* moved the usual vote of thanks.[21] Immediately thereafter the envoys gave their report to the Assembly, during which Demosthenes read Philip's letter (Aes. 2.47, 50). He then announced his intention to move a decree (*psephisma*) to grant safe conduct to Philip's herald and ambassadors and to reserve seats for them in the theater (Aes. 2.109, 111, Dem. 19.235). He also moved that the *prytaneis* meet on 8 Elaphebolion (about March/April) 346 to arrange the reception of Philip's delegation, which included provisions for two assemblies to be held on consecutive days, 18–19 Elaphebolion, to discuss the treaty (Aes. 2.53, 60–1, 67, 3.67, Dem. 19.58). The matters to be discussed included peace and alliance.

The events of 18–19 Elaphebolion are fundamental to the understanding of Athenian relations with Philip and the political careers of Demosthenes and Aeschines. The decisions made then would determine whether Athens could actually reach a lasting accord with the king. For the two Athenians their disagreements over these issues would divide them venomously for the rest of their lives. The two orators are also the principal historical sources for these events, but their testimony contains so many contradictions and discrepancies that the whole truth is probably irrecoverable (see Appendix). With that warning in mind, one can at least be certain about the essentials of the treaty.[22] The Athenians and the members of the Athenian League voted for peace and alliance with Philip, his descendants, and his allies. Although Demosthenes condemns the clause extending the pact to Philip's progeny, it amounted to an alliance for all time, for which there were several precedents.[23] The protocol did not include Phocis, Cersebleptes, Halus, or any other Athenian ally (Aes. 2.61, 82–93, 3.69–74, Dem. 19.40–1, 174, 181, 321). Loudly complaining later that Aeschines had excluded them all, Demosthenes in this regard is simply lying. In 346 the Athenians fully understood that these states were such liabilities that they could only endanger the peace, a fact that Demosthenes himself knew well enough at the time. Unless the Athenians publicly distanced themselves, especially from Phocis, they could justifiably become the next target of the Amphictyonic Council (Dem. 5.14). Even though the Athenians did not yet know of

Cersebleptes' fate, they had learned that Philip had marched against him while the first Athenian embassy was returning from Macedonia (Aes. 2.82). There were few doubts about the results. Demosthenes and Aeschines further cloud the issue of who was eligible for inclusion in the accord. Aeschines (3.70) later claimed that the treaty contained a clause that would enable other Greek states to join in the peace within three months, and Demosthenes (19.16) claims that some Greeks had actually sent ambassadors for that very purpose. He later (18.20) spoke the truth, when he bitterly admitted that no other Greeks ever helped Athens with men, money, or anything else. In 346 the Athenians knew that they stood alone against Philip, and must either agree to peace or suffer the consequences.

The Athenian demos with all of the official evidence before it, by free and open vote, ratified the treaty. Moreover, by its subsequent vote to send the original envoys on the second embassy (Dem. 19.17, 150), it endorsed their conduct during the first embassy and the results of 18–19 Elaphebolion. If anything were defective in the original draft of the Peace of Philocrates, the fault lay with the Athenian people, not with Aeschines, Philocrates, or the other ambassadors.

The treaty approved, the next order of business was for the Athenians and the delegate of the League to give the oaths to Parmenio and Antipater, Philip's ambassadors (Dem. 19.69, 163, Aes. 3.72), to vote for a board of envoys to receive Philip's oath, and to instruct their legates as to their duties. They agreed to administer their oaths to Philip's ambassadors on 25 Elaphebolion, but events prevented the occasion from being a routine affair. Five days after voting to accept the peace the Athenians received a disconcerting letter from their general Chares reporting that Philip had overwhelmed Cersebleptes and had taken Hieron Oros, a strategically placed position north-west of Perinthus, on 24 Elaphebolion, or about April 346,[24] news that probably came as no great surprise. On the following day at a meeting of the Assembly before the actual giving of the oaths to the Macedonians, Critobulus of Lampsacus, not a member state of the Athenian League, asked that Cersebleptes be included in the peace as an Athenian ally (Aes. 2.82, 86). Though indeed an Athenian ally, Cersebleptes was not, however, a member of the League, had not been represented on the first embassy, and could now only be a liability. The Athenians could not save him and did not try. Putting aside Demosthenes' later, lurid details of the scene (Aes. 2.81–90), the *bouleutai* rightly rejected Critobulus' request out of hand. The slight may have embarrassed many Athenians, but none was prepared to sacrifice the interest of the city for a doomed ally who had until recently been a troublesome enemy. The incident did not prevent the administration of oaths to Parmenio and Antipater. To celebrate the event Demosthenes made them his guests of honor at a magnificent feast, and in grand style escorted them homewards as far as Thebes (Dem. 19.235, Aes. 2.111, 3.76). While Demosthenes returned to Attica, the Macedonians surely informed the Thebans of the latest developments, assuring them as well of Philip's continued friendship with them.

The oaths given, the Athenians gave their same ambassadors as previously instructions on what clauses were to be included in the treaty (Aes. 2.101; cf. Andoc. 3.35). The demos also gave them discretionary powers to obtain whatever additional benefits possible (Aes. 2.104). This too was a normal clause that enabled the ambassadors to deal with any new or unforeseen developments.[25] This power was not plenipotentiary, despite Aeschines' claim (3.63) to the contrary, for the demos always retained the right of final approval.[26]

While Philip completed his reduction of Thrace, the Athenians prepared their second embassy to receive his oath. Demosthenes (19.154, 18.25) moved a *probouleuma* that the ambassadors sail immediately to Philip wherever they could find him. He implies, but never specifically says, that he wanted them to sail direct to Thrace. Aeschines (2.98) flatly denies that anything was said about Thrace, correctly pointing out that such a venture would have been fruitless. The envoys instead decided that the easiest place to find Philip was Pella. The ten Athenian and one allied envoys set out for Macedonia on 3 Mounichion (about April/May) 346 (Aes. 2.91, 97), travelling by way of Oreus in Euboea (Aes. 2.93, Dem. 19.155, 163), reaching Pella 23 days later (Dem. 19.155, 166, Aes. 2.101). Demosthenes (19.58, 158, 18.30) calculates that in all they spent three months on the embassy. At Philip's court they were joined by embassies from Thebes, Thessaly, Phocis, and Sparta, a sure sign that events would prove anything but routine (Aes. 2.104, 136, Dem. 9.11). This may very well have been the point when Demosthenes began to distrust the efficacy of the peace and Philip's designs for it. He admits (19.150, 234–6, Aes. 2.123) that the original draft of the Peace of Philocrates which he and Aeschines had supported, and the oaths that Philip's ambassadors had accepted, had of themselves led to no irreparable harm. Yet he claims that he now perceived how Philip would use the peace, admitted that he himself was impotent to alter the treaty, and dreaded the dire results of war with Philip. Under these circumstances he could only distance himself from the pact (cf. 19.150 with 5.13–25). He felt that Philip had duped him as easily as he had the rest of the Athenians. The thought must have galled Demosthenes all the more, when he remembered his earlier inability to address Philip on the first embassy. First abashed, now outwitted. He began to watch his fellow envoys, especially Aeschines, which only provoked their animosity (Dem. 19.175, 177, 189, Aes. 2.97, 124). To justify his own presence on the embassy he claimed that he served largely to ransom Athenian captives, for which he carried the princely sum of one talent.[27] Aeschines (2.100) caustically points out that Philip had planned to release his captives without ransom once peace was made.

When the Athenian embassy reached Pella, they found Philip returned from Thrace and preparing to march on Thermopylae (Aes. 2.101–3). The Athenian demos had neither addressed nor even considered this eventuality in its instructions (Aes. 2.113–17), and had indeed already stopped its preparations for war (Dem. 18.26). Aeschines, however, realized that the delegation must do something at once, and so invoked its discretionary power 'to obtain whatever good possible'. That meant that he tried to protect the Phocians and limit Theban power in Boeotia, both of which were technically irrelevant to the Peace of Philocrates and thus not covered in the embassy's instructions (Aes. 2.107). According to Aeschines' no doubt exaggerated account, Demosthenes cravenly argued with his colleagues against the move, but his picture of his opponent's temerity is consistent with his conduct throughout these events (Aes. 2.22, 34–5, Dem. 19.23–7, 35, 316). As a clarification of the treaty the Athenians recognized Cardia as Philip's ally (Dem. 19.174). The city had become significant only because of Cersebleptes' defeat and the future of Athenian interests in the Chersonese. At the moment, the city itself was inconsiderable. Despite Demosthenes' assertion to the contrary (19.159), it is quite unlikely that Cersebleptes entered seriously into the discussion. The most that the Athenians did for their Thracian ally was to urge Philip to treat him honorably (Dem. 19.181). Although Demosthenes claims (19.159) that he tried to include Halus in the treaty, the city, already beleaguered before the first embassy, only became significant after mid-Scirophorion (about June/July) 346, when Philip marched on Thermopylae (Dem. 19.58). Halus, not an

Athenian ally but instead part of Philip's Thessalian sphere, as such was extraneous to the Athenian mission. Nonetheless, Philip doubtless with cynical amusement placated the Athenians by inviting them to accompany him when he reconciled the Halians with the Pharsalians (Dem. 19.36).

The only outstanding issue between Athens and Philip was the settlement of the Sacred War, which entailed the fate of the Phocians and the status of the Boeotian cities of Plataea, Thespiae, and Orchomenus. Here Aeschines had a far clearer, more realistic, and more intelligent view of the situation than had Demosthenes. That conflict, as mentioned, was separate from the specific treaty about to be endorsed, and Aeschines fully realized that the Sacred War could be avoided entirely. The solution was simple, as both Philocrates and he saw: exclude the Phocians from the peace under discussion on the perfectly legitimate grounds that they were not members of the League and had never engaged in their war. Therefore, they could not logically make peace in a war in which they had never been belligerents. What the Phocians did in Delphi was irrelevant to the peace about to be concluded. Demosthenes (5.10) seems never to have grasped the significance of this obvious fact, or otherwise he would not continually have insisted upon including the Phocians in this peace. Indeed, his own assessment of the strategic situation was hopelessly incompetent. He fatuously hoped that so long as the Phocians held Thermopylae, Athens was safe from both Philip and Thebes (Dem. 19.83, 99, 153, 180). He argued that Philip could find no supplies in the area and that the Phocian cities were too numerous and strong easily to be reduced by siege (Dem. 19.123). He argued as well that the Athenians could tighten their hold on the corridor with their troops and fifty triremes (Dem. 19.318–22), even though Aeschines (2.37) pointed out that these ships were unmanned. The truth was otherwise and the situation more complex than Demosthenes imagined. In the first place the Phocian garrisons at Thermopylae commanded by Phalaecus were not under the control of the Phocian home government, which was even then working against him.[28] There was no hope of a united Phocian front against Philip. Next, the Phocians at Thermopylae, even if reinforced by the Athenians and Spartans, would have been caught in a pincer movement between Philip's army descending from the north and the Thebans marching from the south. A valiant defense would have slowed, but not stopped them.[29] Demosthenes' stupidity becomes all the more obvious, when he himself admits (19.123, 318, 321) that Philip's own allies had openly warned that the king could not accept the Phocian alliance because it would violate the oaths given to the Thebans and Thessalians. Aeschines, Philocrates, and the others, who obviously had also broached the matter, dropped it as soon as they saw its futility. Yet even in the face of this stark revelation, and although he admitted the fact of Phocian sacrilege (Dem. 18.18, 19.73), Demosthenes pursued the theme of protecting the Phocians despite the consequences. Stark reality proved that in 346 Athens had no effective military alternative to peace and that peace was possible only without Phocis.

Excluding the Phocians from the Peace of Philocrates put them at a further distance from Athens, but it did not remove them altogether. Owing to their own participation in the Sacred War, the Athenians could not simply forget them. The Thessalians especially demanded that Philip liberate Delphi from the temple-robbers (Dem. 19.318, 320). Only Aeschines had a solution to this problem that furthered Athenian interests, gave some small protection to the Phocians, and would not offend Philip and his allies. He urged them all (Aes. 2.114, 117) to let the Amphictyonic Council decide the fate of the Phocians. The suggestion appealed to Philip for several reasons. Although he then held no seat on the Council, his Thessalian, Theban, and Locrian allies did, but so did the Athenians and Spartans. Philip was in an unrivalled position to dictate results, but at least the Phocians would have some votes on their side. The Amphictyony gave Philip two desirable options. Should he wish to be merciful to the Phocians in spite of the desires of the Thessalians and the Thebans, he could manipulate others to follow his lead. If, however, he preferred harsh measures, he would only be honoring the will of his allies. This freedom of choice gave him the opportunity to tantalize the Greeks then in Pella, offering each party the hope that he would fulfill their particular wishes. Aeschines' solution was hardly ideal, but it gave the Athenians the only realistic possibility of saving the Phocians without themselves risking Amphictyonic retaliation.

The topic of certain Boeotian cities was both delicate and complex. The Thebans had militarily suppressed them and abolished their autonomy. Yet Thebes was far too strong and valuable an ally for Philip to offend or punish, especially when he was about to march on Delphi. Aeschines' clever solution to the problem was to suggest to Philip that since he intended to end the Sacred War, he should apply the oaths of the Amphictyons to all of their members, Thebes included.[30] A major article of this convention forbade the destruction of any Amphictyonic city, but Thebes had violated it by its treatment of some of its neighbors, and like Phocis should therefore be punished for sacrilege (cf. Dem. 19.20–1, 49–50). Aeschines asserted (2.119) that Thebes should be Boeotian and not Boeotia Theban. He had thus seized the opportunity, unappreciated by Demosthenes, of giving Philip a legitimate legal weapon against Thebes. If Philip punished the leaders of the Phocians (Aes. 2.117) and re-established the Boeotian cities as a counterweight to Thebes, he might very well please the Thessalians as much as the Athenians (Aes. 2.136). The proposal at least had certain attractions.

Philip met Aeschines' proposals coolly, adroitly, and duplicitously by describing the great things that he would do when establishing a general settlement. He promised everything but wrote nothing specific (Dem. 19.37, 41, 44, 68). Aeschines said (1.169) that if Philip fulfilled his promises, he would give the Athenians every reason to praise him. Agreeing with that, Demosthenes stated (19.321, 328) that Philip averred that if he got his peace, he would do all that the Athenians wanted. The king insinuated that Thebes would be humbled (Dem. 5.10, 19.20, 42, 74, 220, 18.35–6, Aes. 2.119–20), and some of his companions claimed that he would re-establish the Boeotian cities (Aes. 2.137, Dem. 19.21). Philip's promises regarding Phocis were equally magnificent. They included the possibility of recovering Apollo's plundered treasures from Thebes not Phocis (Dem. 19.21). Philip would protect and deliver the Phocians from their plight (Dem. 19.82, 220). He allayed their fears on all these points (Dem. 19.324). Not only was Aeschines cozened, but even Demosthenes also grudgingly admitted (19.106) the possibility that Philip would keep his word. Nonetheless, Demosthenes elsewhere (5.10, 19.23, 44–5, 82) repeatedly denies that he had ever heard of these promises, on which he once contradicts himself (19.160). It is impossible to believe that Demosthenes alone of the entire embassy heard nothing, if only by hearsay, of what was clearly the most prominent and urgent topic of the hour. Philip carried all before him merely by telling the Athenians what they wanted to hear about a matter over which they had no control. Nor should Aeschines and his colleagues be blamed too harshly, for Philip's comments were such as to alarm the Thebans, sow distrust among the Phocians, and cause great uncertainty among his other diplomatic guests (Aes. 2.136, Dem. 19.53, 324).

Left now was only the Athenian acceptance of oaths that would seal the treaty, but Philip delayed the ceremony until he and his army had marched from Pella to Pherae (Dem. 19.152, 158, 175). Philip explained the delay by his request for the envoys to help him settle the issue of Halus (Dem. 19.36, 39), a topic that they themselves had raised. Only when they had reached Pherae, not more than three days' march from Thermopylae, did he and his allies give the oaths that officially sealed the peace and alliance. The fate of Phocis was then also sealed. The Athenian embassy returned home on 13 Scirophorion (about June/July) 346 with Philip following in its footsteps to Thermopylae.

Upon their return, the ambassadors made their usual report to the Boule (Dem. 19.17). As earlier, the exact truth about the ensuing events cannot now be recovered because of the refractory testimony of Demosthenes and Aeschines. There is, however, very good reason to conclude that Demosthenes intentionally clouded the issue because of his own dubious part in the proceedings. Demosthenes claims (19.18) that he denounced his fellow envoys before the Boule and made one last appeal on behalf of the Phocians and mentioned Thermopylae. According to him, he convinced the council of his views, which if true would mean that the *bouleutai* drafted a *probouleuma* that reflected his interpretation of events and endorsed his recommendations. That in turn means that they rejected the official report of the envoys. It will not suffice to suppose that they presented to the Assembly an open *probouleuma*: he either convinced them or he did not.[31] When, however, the Assembly convened on 16 Scirophorion, Aeschines spoke first, according to Demosthenes (19.19), which is dubious, for one would normally expect Philocrates, author of the peace, to enjoy pride of place on that occasion. At any rate, before Aeschines or anyone else spoke the president (*epistatēs tōn prytaneiōn*) as customary read the *probouleuma* to the Assembly. That was done so that the Assembly knew exactly what it was considering for approval, amendment, or rejection. If Demosthenes told the truth about the Boule being convinced of his report, the *epistatēs* read Demosthenes' version of these events. Demosthenes claims (19.19) that Aeschines did not dispute the truth of his report. Instead, he failed both to give a report on the conduct of the embassy and to mention the previous speeches delivered before the Boule. Yet Demosthenes next claims (19.20–3) that his rival spoke of all that he had accomplished during the mission in a speech full of big promises in which he announced that he had won Philip completely over to the Athenian side, that the king had agreed to humble Thebes, restore the Boeotian cities, and to settle the Sacred War with no great harm to the Phocians. This speech can only be a repetition of Aeschines' report to the Boule. Taken literally, both of Demosthenes' assertions about Aeschines' conduct cannot be true. Yet Demosthenes told enough of the truth for one to conclude that Aeschines did in fact repeat the embassy's report to the Boule before the Assembly and spoke in favor of it. Despite Demosthenes' claims, Aeschines behaved in a regular and legal manner. Indeed, the evidence strongly urges that Demosthenes' accusations on this point be rejected. It further indicates that the Boule had not accepted Demosthenes' purported account of the embassy. Pertinent also is the fact that whatever the truth, the demos had not yet voted on the issue, so no one had yet broken the law.

Aeschines' report was made all the more palatable by Philip's enigmatic promises and seductive letter, which Demosthenes himself (19.39) praises for its gracious and generous tone. Although he loudly and frequently claims that he had never heard of the promises (Dem. 19.23, 44, 160, 5.10), he once slips (19.159–60), thus revealing the truth. Philip's enticing professions were clearly sufficient to persuade desperate men, Demosthenes included, that he did in fact intend to bestow certain benefactions on Athens. Both Demosthenes and Aeschines confessed that the peace was disgraceful, and Aeschines was honest enough to summarize the situation bluntly and coldly, when he remarked (2.118, 130) that the outcome was not according to Athenian prayers but to Philip's deeds. A last detail, significant but easily overlooked, concerns Demosthenes' charges (19.101, 144) that Aeschines misled his countrymen. Even if they are true, they matter not at all. The Athenian demos, not Aeschines alone, ratified the treaty.

An astounded Demosthenes supposedly rose to say that everything that Aeschines had professed was news to him, but the quick-footed Aeschines took a stand beside him while Philocrates stood on the other side to silence him (Dem. 19.23). They began to interrupt him with their shouting and jeering, which they did so successfully that the Athenians began laughing. No one would listen to him. Aeschines (2.121) flatly denies that this memorable scene ever took place, but this method of obstructing debate was common enough.[32] Demosthenes repeatedly claims that the Athenians prevented him from presenting his views (19.25–6, 35, 42–5). Nonetheless, there is excellent reason once again to conclude that Demosthenes has lied. He boasts in a speech (5.10), actually delivered in 346, that he had spoken out publicly against these same revelations, which starkly contradicts the rhetorical question that he later (1.25) put into the mouths of the Athenians: 'Why did you not mention these things on the spot and inform us?' The only benefit that Demosthenes could gain by saying that he was not allowed to speak is to exonerate the Athenians from any blame for their decision. They were not responsible because Aeschines and Philocrates prevented them from hearing the truth, a good rhetorical and sophistic trick on Demosthenes' part.

In another attempt to avoid blame for the treaty Demosthenes repeats that he had joined the others primarily to ransom captives, which he also turns to his own malicious ends by associating the captives with the diplomatic custom of gifts and hospitality. It was a courteous, gracious, and standard gesture in Greek diplomacy for the host to bestow gifts upon foreign ambassadors as a mark of respect and a legitimate way to win favor.[33] Envoys sometimes merely enriched themselves with these gifts, as did the Athenian Epicrates, who confessed to taking gifts from the Persian king and merrily suggested that the Athenians annually send nine poor ambassadors to him so that they could all return wealthy men.[34] Others saw the gifts as payment for betraying their *polis*, one of the most notorious of whom was the Athenian Timagoras.[35] Still other ambassadors, notably the Theban Philo, when Philip offered him a boon, answered that the best gift would be the granting of his state's official request (Dem. 19.140, cf. also Plut. *Pelopidas* 30.8). In portraying his fellow envoys as the avaricious sorts who allowed themselves to be bought, Demosthenes tried to erase the distinction between hospitality and bribery. In contrast, he claims (19.222) that although Philip offered him as much money as he had the others, he suggested that the king give it all in a lump sum for the ransom of the captives. This is not one of Demosthenes' better lies, but it served a useful purpose for domestic politics. He could portray himself as selfless and untainted by any desire for personal gain.

Despite the congeries of truths, half-truths, and lies, the results of the meeting of 16 Scirophorion are clear. From all even remotely reliable indications, the Athenian embassy on that day ratified the same peace treaty that it had endorsed at the time of the first embassy (Aes. 2.123). Demosthenes' claim that he insisted on including the Phocians in it is pure fustian. If Demosthenes spoke out against the treaty, which is improbable, he clearly did not press his case vigorously and his countrymen rejected his counsel. That is only to be expected with Philip already at Thermopylae.

The ratification of the peace was a victory for Aeschines, but it did not end his contest with Demosthenes. For the moment he had won because his appreciation of the situation was more accurate, realistic, and sensible than that of his opponent. From personal experience he knew that Athens was diplomatically isolated and unprepared for a major war. Demosthenes' policy, in contrast, is open to severe criticism owing to a stupidity that bordered upon the suicidal. Knowing that most of Greece opposed Athens, which had the support only of a few weak allies, he argued throughout 346, as witnessed by his *On the Peace*, that Athens alone was a match for any individual enemy. He erroneously thought that the city could withstand Philip, and he minimized the possibility of a coalition against it. Success of the peace that Demosthenes envisioned was possible, if at all, only before the victories in Thrace released Philip's full resources for operations against Phocis. Demosthenes' entire policy regarding Philip had failed before the peace (Dem. 5.13), and nothing that he said, did, or could do during the negotiations could salvage the situation. His mistake is that he hoped to win by peace what he could not win in war. Philip was determined to win both.

2

The Peace of Philocrates, the clauses of which Philip scrupulously honored, gave him the opportunity to end the Sacred War. In a gesture of calculated policy and personal irony Philip invited the Athenians to send forces to join him in dealing with the Phocians (Dem. 19.49–50). They refused, a reaction of fear, distrust, humiliation, and good sense. Many of them suspected that even their peace would not necessarily protect them from Amphictyonic wrath (Dem. 5.13–14). It did because Philip had neither need nor desire to trouble them. The peace had given him all that he had wanted. Nonetheless, his resolution of the Sacred War heightened Athenian fears, for he did nothing for which they had fatuously hoped. The punishment that the Amphictyonic Council with Philip's consent meted out to the Phocians was draconian, precisely the same that the Athenians hoped he would hand to the Thebans, whom instead he honored rather than humiliated. He was next elected to the place on the Council previously held by the Phocians.[36] He could thereby deal with the Athenians on a front independent of the Peace of Philocrates that gave him additional options and opportunities to intervene in Greek affairs without violating it. The results of the settlement of the war, none of which benefited Athens, seemed to many Athenians to be a betrayal of their treaty with him, for which its advocates were nearly as responsible as Philip. Demosthenes recognized this reaction at once, and moved immediately to distance himself from the treaty (5.10).

When it became apparent that neither Philip nor the Amphictyons would punish Athens for its part in the Sacred War, Demosthenes began to undermine the Peace of Philocrates. In late 346 he and Timarchus planned to lodge a charge of treason against Aeschines. Though a prominent politician, Timarchus had allegedly led a lewd life, the rumor of which Aeschines used to strike back at Demosthenes to discredit his case.[37] From this point the duel between Demosthenes and Aeschines became as much personal as political, as Aeschines (1.102) freely admitted. The two strands cannot henceforth be separated; and as the strictly political events of 346 have already been covered, the personal elements now deserve some notice. In the trial against Timarchus Aeschines virtually avoids the heart of the political problem, concentrating instead on the morals of the defendant and the character of Demosthenes. For present purposes the case against Timarchus, such as it is, hardly matters. Not a model of jurisprudence nor a useful historical source for the events of the day, Aeschines' speech nonetheless set the tone of future relations with his arch rival. He demonstrates that he was a cultured man in contrast to Demosthenes, whom he portrays as a lout (1.49). He devotes a great deal of his speech to the ideals of gentlemanly behavior, which he illustrates by extensive quotations from the *Iliad*, Hesiod, and some lost plays of Euripides, all delivered in a skilled actor's voice with which Demosthenes could not compete.[38] Aeschines' entertaining performance made a favorable impression on the jurors. By contrast he condemns Demosthenes for being a mere speech-writer and a sophist (Aes. 1.117, 125, 170–5; cf. 3.16), reminding the jury that the sophist Socrates had schooled Critias (1.73). Resorting to guilt by association, Aeschines claims that Demosthenes was no man because of his friendship with Timarchus (1.167). To support his contention he refers to Demosthenes' nickname 'Batalos', the precise meaning of which is now unknown, but probably used in this instance to refer to fellatio (Plut. *Dem.* 4.5–7). Aeschines adroitly turns his accusation of Demosthenes' salacity to his own political credit by contrasting it with his own proper conduct in the presence of Philip and his young son Alexander. Aeschines uses the incident to introduce one of the few political points of his speech. He claims (1.167–9) that Demosthenes, himself lewd and boorish, will accuse Alexander, then a boy, of shameful practices. Aeschines states that he of course did not even speak to Alexander because of his youth, before turning to his principal political point. Though he did not compliment Alexander, he will greatly praise Philip if he will fulfill his promises. The entire case between Aeschines and Demosthenes hinged upon that one point, and on it Aeschines won.

The condemnation of Timarchus prompted Demosthenes to postpone lodging his indictment of Aeschines, but by 343 the situation had changed substantially enough for him to proceed. By then the Phocians were suppressed, the Thebans prospering, and Philip's purported promises unfulfilled. Moreover, Philip had continued his energetic foreign policy, not only in the north as was traditional but also in Euboea, Megara, and the Peloponnese, which was not. None of this activity violated the Peace of Philocrates, for none of these involved was a party to it; but Demosthenes saw these developments as a sign of Philip's plot to isolate and then destroy Athens. Owing largely to Demosthenes and friends like Hegesippus and Hyperides, the Athenians increasingly saw the peace as a betrayal of their interests, a point of view that Philip tried to change by sending them Pytho of Byzantium as an envoy with an offer to amend the treaty. Aeschines, who spoke in favor of Pytho's mission, thereby lost much of his popularity and credibility. The episode was the first substantial blow to the peace and Aeschines' political career. Hyperides next indicted Philocrates for having taken Philip's bribes to commit treason, and Demosthenes took the occasion to accuse Aeschines of complicity (Dem. 19.117–18). Dismayed by the indictment and the popular uproar, Philocrates fled into exile rather than stand trial. His flight convinced many of his guilt. His fears may well have been sparked not by any crime but by the mood of the Athenian people. Emboldened by Philocrates' reaction, Demosthenes finally filed his formal complaint against Aeschines on the same charges of bribery, corruption, and treason; but unlike Philocrates, Aeschines stood his ground. He defended himself in part by reminding the Athenians of their desperate straits three years earlier, and argued that the peace was the best realistic option then open to them all.

In the trial that followed in 343 the proceedings were marked more by vituperation than any laws of evidence. The tawdry details, however, vividly illustrate the mutual hatred of the two men as well as their legal strategies. The core of Demosthenes' indictment is that Aeschines was originally an opponent of Philip who later bribed him to change sides and support the Peace of Philocrates. Yet in a case that is amazingly weak, Demosthenes illogically admits (19.33–6) that he does not condemn Aeschines because Athens made peace, which he confesses (19.96) that it had already decided to do, but complains that Aeschines took Macedonian bribes to support Philocrates. He further admits (19.236) that when the peace was made no harm had yet come to the city. For all that, he vacuously states (19.96) that the real question was what sort of peace Athens should have made. Most of his evidence comes from events subsequent to the original treaty and is therefore *ex post facto*. They could not have been foreseen in 346 and in many instances Athens was hardly an innocent victim of them.[39] So even had Aeschines in fact accepted bribes, which Demosthenes never proves, the crime would have been irrelevant. Demosthenes' argumentation is no exercise in Aristotelian logic.

Demosthenes bases his charge of bribery on his assertion (19.13–15) that on 18 Elaphebolion 346 Aeschines spoke against the peace but for it on the following day, which Aeschines (2.63–6) denies, claiming instead that he had spoken only on the first day and that Demosthenes had made two speeches of his one (see Appendix). Aeschines (3.71–2) lied on that point, which does not eliminate the possibility that Aeschines may have criticized the treaty but urged its adoption, much as Demosthenes himself did in his own *On the Peace*. On the second day Aeschines supposedly made big promises of what Philip would do, if peace were made (Dem. 19.19–21, 35, 74, 112). In his letter to the Athenians Philip, according to Demosthenes (19.39–41), states his desire to gratify the Athenians, if he knew what they wanted. This point needs clarification because Philip sent the Athenians two letters, one that accompanied the ambassadors of the first embassy (Aes. 3.50) and the second for the same envoys who returned after receiving the oaths on the second embassy (Dem. 19.17, 36, Aes. 2.124–5). Demosthenes' knowledge of the second letter and the big promises demands closer scrutiny because of its many contradictions. Demosthenes praises (19.39–41) Philip's seductive letter, which states his desire to gratify the Athenians, if he knew what they wanted. Demosthenes even comments on its gracious and generous tone, but he loudly and frequently claims that he had never heard of any of them (19.23, 44, 160, 5.10) and accuses (19.8, 201) Aeschines of lying about them. Yet he twice slips (19.159–60), thus revealing the truth, once going so far as to state (19.58) that although he did not believe them, he swore to the peace because of them (19.171). A real possibility exists that at Pella Philip spoke expansively of what benefits he would bestow upon Athens, none of which he included in his letter (cf. Aes. 1.169). If so, and if Demosthenes has given an accurate report of this second letter, no one in 346 should have been deceived by it. Given the peril and the urgency of the situation, Demosthenes, like Aeschines, the other envoys, and the Athenians was all too willing to allow himself to be deceived. Demosthenes merely attempts in 343 to deny his own credulity of 346.

Demosthenes also uses against Aeschines the argument of guilt by association by averring (19.115–19, 245) that since Aeschines supported Philocrates, himself accused of bribe-taking, he must also be guilty of the same offense. He confesses (19.120) that no one will testify against the defendant, and asserts (19.216) that all who speak on his behalf have themselves been bribed. Demosthenes uses (19.225) the same argument regarding Pythocles, a favorite of Philip who now avoids Demosthenes but converses freely with Aeschines. He claims (19.230) that by betraying Phocis Aeschines became rich and (19.145) that its estates now brought him a half-talent a year. Yet he also derides (19.282) Aeschines for not providing the Athenians a liturgy. The first thing a newly rich Athenian would do to enhance his social status would be to undertake a liturgy. The accusation of Phocian leases is circumstantial evidence at best, doubts about the veracity of the charge coming from Aeschines' defense of the Phocians before the Amphictyonic Council and the willingness of some Phocians to testify in his defense (Aes. 2.142). This, the best accusation that Demosthenes can make, is dubious and the others unworthy of credence.

Demosthenes bases an unsavory part of his case on his allegations that Aeschines was totally unsuited to be an ambassador, which he bolsters by a demeaning portrait of him. He begins by claiming that Aeschines' career proves him unworthy of high and responsible duties in which he describes (19.199–200; cf. 18.261–5) Aeschines' earlier life and draws a denigrating picture of his entire family. Aeschines began as a student who read books for his mother while she performed bacchanalian rites. From there he rose to become a junior secretary in public service and thence to an actor in small parts that good performers refused (Dem. 19.246–7). Demosthenes characterizes (18.242) Aeschines as a natural tragic ape, a bumpkin who had murdered Oenomaus, presumably in a play at a rural Dionysia. By bellowing like an ox (Dem. 18.127), he could only feign the voice of an actor (Dem. 18.287). Demosthenes was on very weak ground here, for he often grudgingly admits that his enemy possessed a fine voice and an elegant presence (for example, Dem. 18.23, 35, 122, 132), while he himself was a nervous man with a voice no louder than that of another (Dem. 19.208; cf. Aes. 2.187). Nonetheless, owing to these supposed inadequacies, Aeschines played only meagre and unimportant parts (Dem. 19.200) like that of the tyrant (Dem. 19.247), never the principal ones. Demosthenes concludes that a man who was such a bad actor could not possibly be a good envoy or effective politician. Ignorant of public affairs (Dem. 19.103), Aeschines did not understand that ambassadors were responsible for their words (Dem. 19.183).

Demosthenes saved his purest venom for Aeschines' family. He pronounces (19.237–8, 249) in a display of social snobbery that Aeschines' brothers Aphobetus (*PA* 2775) and Philochares (*PA* 14775) were artisans and clerks, which, while respectable occupations, did not entitle them to be ambassadors and generals. In truth, both men led successful and honorable careers, with Aphobetus holding a position on the Theoric commission and serving as ambassador and Philochares elected general for three consecutive years (Aes. 2.149). In Demosthenes' opinion they had risen above their station, despite the contrary opinion of the Athenian democracy. Their repeated successes in public service offended Demosthenes and added prestige to Aeschines' position. Demosthenes likewise gives (19.287; cf. Aes. 2.159–1) short shrift to Aeschines' brothers-in-law, naming Nicias a mercenary with Chabrias, the famous Athenian general, and calling Epicrates 'Cyrebio' (chaff), who went without a comic mask in the processions of Bacchus and Ceres. He dismisses (19.249; cf. 18.130, 284) Aeschines' father as a schoolteacher, and calls his mother Glaucothea the leader of drunken and debauched revels. Even worse, he mentions her by name, which was an insult to honorable Athenian women,[40] something that Aeschines refused to do in return. He instead refers (Aes. 2.22–3, 78, 180) to Demosthenes' mother as a Scythian nomad. Although Demosthenes' remarks about Glaucothea were mere obloquy, Aeschines' accusation actually had a political point. By claiming that she was a Scythian, he denied that Demosthenes possessed full citizenship, which left him no right to play any role in Athenian politics.

In the face of this blast Aeschines presented a simple and straightforward defense. He provided a chronology of events, and noted that the eleven members of the embassy were unanimous about the need for the peace and the contents of its terms. Demosthenes agreed with the others, and as *bouleutēs* moved that they be crowned (Aes. 2.46, Dem. 19.234). He lavishly entertained Philip's ambassadors (2.111), as Demosthenes himself admits

(19.235). Aeschines easily refutes the principal charge that he had betrayed Athens on the second embassy. He merely observes (2.68, 123) that the later embassy simply presented to Philip what the demos had decided, which was nothing more than the treaty that the first embassy had put before him. He thereby proves that Demosthenes' accusations were baseless.

Aeschines displays his growing hatred of Demosthenes by the quantity, quality, nature, and vehemence of his invective, which served a political as well as a personal purpose. He strikes hard at the heart of Demosthenes' vanity, his oratorical ability and his diplomatic skill. He dismisses his enemy as an ordinary speechwriter (2.180; cf. Dem. 19.246), and ridicules (2.157) his shrill voice. He tells (2.21) how on their way to Macedonia Demosthenes promised his fellow ambassadors that in Philip's presence he would display great eloquence. Events proved otherwise. When Demosthenes actually rose to address the king, speech failed him (Aes. 2.34–5, 125). Philip gently reminded him that he was not an actor and encouraged him to start again. Demosthenes fared no better the second time. To his stage fright Aeschines contrasts (2.42) Philip's oratorical prowess, excellent memory, and ability concisely to discuss the issues at hand. Aeschines' account of Demosthenes' oratorical performance on the second embassy is no more flattering. Aeschines claims (2.11–14) that Demosthenes made a fool of himself by his excessive praise of Philip which aroused the laughter of all the ambassadors. He also maintains (2.114) that the grand Demosthenes, the eloquent orator and accomplished diplomat, failed to address a single essential point of the matters in hand. Aeschines repeats (2.105–7) Demosthenes' admission that he feared Philip and would not quarrel with him (cf. Dem. 19.289). By ridiculing Demosthenes' oratory and scoffing at his timorous silence Aeschines pointedly emphasizes his failure as a diplomat.

Aeschines also uses his dismissive appraisal of Demosthenes' oratorical demonstrations to defend himself against his opponent's denigration of his acting ability (cf. also Dem. 18.180, 209). He disposes of Demosthenes' mockery with a good-natured defense of actors.[41] To counter his enemy's feeble disparagement of his voice and public presence Aeschines liberally quotes in all of his speeches (1.128–9, 141–53 2.158 3.135, 184–5) passages from Homer, Hesiod, and Euripides to buttress his case and to flatter the jury, whom he calls men who were not uneducated. He allows the jurors themselves to decide the quality and pleasantness of his voice and elocution. He thereby uses the trial to present a public performance in which he defends himself and entertains the jurors, for like all other Greeks, they enjoyed a good recitation (for example, Diod. 14.109.1–2). He also uses this topic to contrast a good actor, which he has proven himself to be, to a bad grammarian like Demosthenes (Aes. 2.156; cf. 3.173, Dem. 18.232). Finally, he points to the practical value of actors, who naturally make friends (Aes. 2.15–19). He specifically names Satyrus, whose charm and talent won from Philip the release of some prisoners and even Demosthenes' praise (19.193, 196). Aeschines' friend and Philip's acquaintance Aristodemus successfully served on an embassy to the king (2.15–16) and was so esteemed that Demosthenes took especial pains to include him on a second embassy (Aes. 2.19). By using a combination of personal performance and historical examples, Aeschines easily disposes of Demosthenes' criticisms of him, leaving the jurors to draw the conclusion that his opponent possesses the talent of neither an orator nor an actor.

Aeschines also associates Demosthenes' ill-breeding, boorishness, and lewdness with his failure as a diplomat. He maintains (2.40) that his speech was so vulgar that it offended all of the other ambassadors, who avoided his presence, preferring not even to dine with him (2.97). His public rudeness (Aes. 2.39) made him an official embarrassment and the laughing-stock of them all (2.38). Aeschines intensifies his accusations of Demosthenes' homosexual proclivities, repeating the nickname Batalos (2.99) and opining (2.88) that he was impure of body even to his mouth. He calls him (2.127–8) a hermaphrodite who was not even a free man, and contrasts this degenerate with Philo, a good soldier whom Demosthenes had disparaged. These and several other accusations (2.151, 153, 159, 179) against Demosthenes clearly aimed to humiliate him, but they also repeated the successful tactics that Aeschines had recently used against Timarchus. The message is that Demosthenes is a man so debauched that he cannot honestly represent or usefully serve Athens.

Just as Demosthenes' confidence failed him in oratory, so Aeschines ascribes to him physical cowardice, remarking on his lack of military service, as someone who had never handled arms (2.177) and calling him a deserter (2.79). To mark the contrast he parades (2.167–70) his own military career, beginning with his two years as an ephebe, his campaigning at Phlius, the fighting at Nemea Charadra, at Mantinea, on Euboea, and at Tamynae, for which he was twice crowned. His point is not only to paint Demosthenes as a coward but also (Aes. 1.29; cf. also Andoc. 1.74) to remind the jurors of the custom that men who threw away their shields, thus failing to defend the city, had no right to address the Assembly. Hence he alleges that Demosthenes could neither protect Athens by his oratory nor defend it by his valor.

In sum, Aeschines uses Demosthenes' purported oratorical incompetence, poor social breeding, and lack of military service all to disqualify him as an advisor to the city and one whose opinion and testimony should not even be entertained. Aeschines thus uses a clear narrative coupled with personal invective to discredit Demosthenes and his charge.

Aeschines won acquittal in the trial chiefly because he made the stronger case. Whereas Demosthenes presented hollow accusations, which Aeschines easily rebutted, the latter gave a more factual presentation of events. Whereas Demosthenes railed aimlessly against Aeschines and his family, Aeschines used his one point on the topic to broach a practical objective. The political situation was also favorable to Aeschines: the peace with Philip still stood in effect. If the king had done nothing that the Athenians expected, at least he had not attacked them. Moreover, he still professed his friendship. Even so, relations had cooled in the interval, and many Athenians were becoming more suspicious of Philip's sincerity about peace and friendship, and increasingly considered the Peace of Philocrates as his trick to gain time to realize his real ambitions against them. For these reasons Aeschines won a Pyrrhic victory over Demosthenes, which caused him to play a less effectual role in public affairs during the following years. Demosthenes, though the nominal loser, was left with the political field virtually to himself.

3

Three events threw Aeschines further into the shade after the trial. The first concerned events on Euboea that in 341 led to an Athenian alliance with a newly formed league of cities there, for which Demosthenes was primarily responsible and to which Aeschines was fiercely opposed for myopic and insignificant reasons. The latter recalls (3.85–105) the several injuries that the Euboeans had done Athens: that they had sought Philip's help, courted the Thebans, and stolen from Athens the ten talents that Eretria and Oreus owed it in contributions. He ridicules the contention of Callias and Demosthenes that they had built a Greek coalition against Philip, one that could provide some 100 talents to a common fund against him that was capable of financing 100 ships,

10,000 infantry, and 1,000 cavalry. Having learned his lesson from the Peace of Philocrates, Aeschines now turned the tables on Demosthenes by accusing (3.95–6) him of deceiving the Athenians with big promises. He describes Demosthenes' report, which was delivered to the Assembly with his usual pompous air, as longer than the *Iliad* and as empty as both his speeches and his life. He then asserts (3.97–102) that these hopes would never be realized, but that the ten Euboean talents were gone forever. Not surprisingly, Aeschines accuses Demosthenes' betrayal of Athenian interests as the result of his having taken Callias' bribes. The arguments of 343 were in effect repeated in 341, the only difference being the man who advanced them.

Aeschines' attack on Demosthenes' policy was no more successful than Demosthenes' earlier one on him. Demosthenes (18.79–80) later defended himself by correctly pointing out that his proposals had saved Euboea for Athens. He also (18.82) accused Aeschines of duplicity for having understood all of the ramifications of these events but denying their importance. This time the Athenians fully supported Demosthenes because they completely understood that the independent status of the Euboean League and the lost ten talents were negligible when compared with the larger issue of an allied Euboea. Siding with Demosthenes against Aeschines, they voted to crown him in the theater (Dem. 18.83). Demosthenes' victory further diminished Aeschines' political stature in the city.

Demosthenes again triumphed over Aeschines in a curious affair involving Antiphon, an Athenian who had lost his citizenship in 346.[42] From Athens Antiphon went to Philip, to whom he promised to burn down the dockyard at Piraeus. Demosthenes caught him before the act and brought him before the Assembly. Aeschines defended Antiphon by accusing Demosthenes of having violated his rights, alleging that he had assaulted unfortunate citizens contrary to the norm of democracy and had illegally broken into houses without a warrant (*psēphisma*).[43] Aeschines won Antiphon's acquittal, but his victory was ephemeral. Learning of these events, the Areopagus intervened, reversed the Assembly's decision, and ordered Antiphon retried. He was subsequently found guilty and executed. For present purposes the legal aspects of the case are less significant than the intervention of the Areopagus against Aeschines' defense of Antiphon. It went far beyond the usual political clashes and personal feuds of the Assembly. The Areopagus was right, for Aeschines had seriously blundered when he accused Demosthenes of abusing a citizen, which Antiphon was no longer. More importantly, the most distinguished body of the Athenian democracy had supported Demosthenes against Aeschines, a considerable blow to him and his judgement in a crucial matter. The decision was a vote of confidence in Demosthenes' conduct and a rebuke to Aeschines.

Shortly thereafter Aeschines suffered another reversal at the hands of the Areopagus but one not demonstrably instigated by Demosthenes. Probably in 341 the Delians challenged the right of the Athenians to administer the temple of Apollo on the island.[44] The dispute went back to 426, when the Athenians purified the island (Thucydides 3.104), but the Athenian assertion of right was based upon bald military power. Now the Delians appealed to the Amphictyonic Council for a formal settlement based on religious right.[45] The Athenian Assembly elected Aeschines to argue its case, probably owing to his knowledge of Amphictyonic affairs. The Areopagus, however, intervened to declare him unsuitable for the duty, which it instead invested in his enemy Hyperides. Demosthenes attributes (18.134–6) the decision to the Areopagus' suspicion that Aeschines was a traitor, which has nothing to recommend it. The Areopagus had more likely not yet forgotten Aeschines' blunder over Antiphon. Whatever the reason, the august body now delivered another serious blow to Aeschines' political prestige and further diminished his effectiveness. The damage became even worse since Hyperides apparently won the Athenian case (*IG* ii[2] 1652).[46]

Nothing more is heard of Aeschines until 339, when he again came before the Amphictyonic Council over a dispute that led to the so-called Fourth Sacred War.[47] The Athenians elected Aeschines and two others to represent them at the regular meeting of the Council (Aes. 3.115). Aeschines' election was appropriate, for he thoroughly knew the rules, customs, and history of the Amphictyony. Upon arrival he discovered that the Locrian delegation from Amphissa planned to lodge a charge of impiety against Athens for having rededicated the shields that they had captured during the Persian War. The Locrians, probably at the instigation of the Thebans, objected to the inscription accompanying the shields because it mentioned Theban medism (Aes. 3.116). If the motion passed, the Amphictyons would levy a fine against Athens, which, if unpaid, could have resulted in a sacred war. Such a conflict would necessarily have involved Philip, once again in the guise of protector of Apollo, and perhaps also the Thebans. In a spirited speech Aeschines counter-attacked by accusing the Amphissans themselves of a far greater sacrilege. Pointing dramatically down to the Cirrhan plain below the sanctuary, Aeschines accused them of violating sacred land, the accuracy of which was proven the next day (Aes. 3.119–32, Dem. 18.150). The Amphictyons thereupon ordered a special meeting of the Council at Thermopylae later that spring (Aes. 3.124). When he returned to Athens, the Assembly endorsed Aeschines' conduct (Aes. 3.125).

More was at stake here than mere religious convention. The president of the Council was Cottyphus, a Thessalian and friend of Philip. The Amphissans were Theban allies, so the question became whether the Thebans would side with the other Amphictyons against Athens or abstain entirely from the dispute. If the latter, Philip could justly wage war against them also. All that the Athenians needed to do in that case was to attend the special session at Thermopylae, drop the inscription from their dedication, and honor any Amphictyonic decision regarding the sacrilegious. Demosthenes, however, concluded that Athens could not allow Philip and the Amphictyons to destroy Thebes. Athens, in his opinion, would be next. Therefore, he persuaded the Athenians to remain aloof from any Amphictyonic decision (Aes. 3.125–7). When the Amphictyons convened at Thermopylae, both Thebes and Athens were absent, which violated the Amphictyonic decree (Aes. 3.128). Though not allied, both states defied the Amphictyons and their champion Philip.

Such was the historical situation when Demosthenes and Aeschines renewed their war over Athenian policy regarding Philip. Their contemporary speeches concerning the crisis are not preserved. Only their later reflections and rationalizations are recorded in Aeschines' *Against Ctesiphon* and Demosthenes' *On the Crown*. The decisive difference between them on this occasion is whether in 339–338 Athens should have supported Philip against Thebes, which was Aeschines' position, or Thebes against Philip, Demosthenes', which the Athenians endorsed. The essence of Aeschines' case is that Athens should have implemented his proposal to join against Amphissa because it would have preserved the city from future disaster. Athens by its prestige would have led the Amphictyons against the sacrilegious, resolved the dispute, and prevented Philip from intervening in Greece (3.128–9). Yet Demosthenes craftily and secretly drafted a *probouleuma* rescinding Aeschines' motion and substituting for it a decree that restrained Athens from any intervention (3.125–7). The gods sent portents to warn against the dangers of Demosthenes' policy (3.130–1), which suffered from three fatal flaws (3.140–51). The first was Demosthenes' refusal to admit that Philip only nominally waged war against Athens and that Thebes was his real target, a reality that Demosthenes concealed from the Athenians. Next, in making the alliance with Thebes Demosthenes put Athens at a severe disadvantage. He laid two-thirds of the cost of the war on Athens, which further agreed to share equally the command of the naval forces, though again Athens bore all the costs. Demosthenes put the leadership of the combined armies entirely in Theban hands. Far worse than these things, he usurped the powers of the Boule and Assembly by acting imperiously, against which Aeschines himself had objected at the time. Because of his arrogance Demosthenes had made the wrong strategic decisions. Lastly, when Philip sent envoys to Thebes to make peace, Demosthenes urged Athens not to make peace with him, a move that in turn persuaded the Thebans to decide for war against Macedonia. As a result, Philip's war would not be with Thebes alone but now also with Athens.

In contrast with his feeble case against Aeschines over the Peace of Philocrates, Demosthenes now cogently, effectively, and often grandly rebutted his enemy's evaluation of these events on every point. Although as before he accuses Aeschines of accepting bribes, he lays considerably less emphasis on this point, preferring instead to insist upon Aeschines' grossly mistaken understanding of the political situation. Demosthenes' denials of inconvenient facts are also fewer but more effectively used. While admitting the truth of Aeschines' story of the Amphictyonic inspection of sacred land, he rejects (18.150) as a lie the very idea that the Amphissans planned to lodge charges of sacrilege against Athens.[48] He portrays (18.151–2, 156) it instead as a pretext to promote the war against Athens that Philip always wanted, the war that now saw his march to Elateia. The Thebans, however, recognized the trick, joined the Athenians, and temporarily checked Philip, for which his countrymen could thank some friendly god and him. Nonetheless, Aeschines, the architect of the war (18.159, 163), had also aggravated Athenian hostility towards Thebes that Demosthenes must allay if the city were to survive. Encouraged by the mistaken belief that Athens and Thebes would not unite against him, Philip marched on Elateia (18.168). Demosthenes paints a stirring picture (18.169–78) of the Athenian response to that news, which is reminiscent of Xenophon's account (*Hellenica* 2.2.3–4) of the news of Aegospotami. Though doubtless dramatically embellished, its impact is heroic in its portrayal of Athens alone and in imminent danger, and serves better than any sophisticated argument to prove why Athens needed the Theban alliance.

Before countering Aeschines' criticisms (3.140–51) of the terms of the Atheno-Theban alliance, Demosthenes deftly lays the foundation of his defense against it. He begins by defining and discussing the attributes of a statesman and a good citizen. At the outset he maintains (18.189–90) that the statesman gives his advice before the event, for which he accepts sole responsibility whatever the result. The silent man only later criticizes the unfortunate result of a policy already decided upon. Demosthenes then boldly states (18.191–4) that even if ultimately wrong he himself gave his best advice and then challenges Aeschines, whom he claims had not spoken a word (18.99) to tell the Athenians now what they should have done then. He admits that Philip won the battle of Chaeronea, the decision of which was in divine hands, but Demosthenes' counsel was no crime. He next challenges Aeschines and the Athenians themselves to denounce him if he had failed to do everything humanly possible to avert disaster. He asks his fellow citizens what they would have done without the Theban alliance.

Upon that foundation built of arguments from human lack of foreknowledge, divine will, and practical necessity Demosthenes erects the defense of his terms for the alliance with Thebes. He resumes with another dramatic scene, this one set in Thebes. He recounts the alarm at seeing there the Thebans in Assembly and ambassadors from Philip and those of his allies already in attendance (18.211). Philip's envoys rehearsed past Atheno-Theban hostility, but more importantly asked them either to join them in the invasion of Attica or at least allow them free passage through Boeotia, their reward for which would be a share of the booty (18.213). Despite being thus tempted, the Thebans allied themselves with Athens and subsequently stoutly faced Philip in the field (18.215–17, 229–31). Because of Demosthenes' diplomacy, the ill-starred battle was fought at Chaeronea, some eighty miles (700 *stadia*) from Attica, a small price to pay for the concessions that he had made to Thebes (18.230).

4

The events of 338 gave rise to the last great clash between the two men. It forms something of an historical epilogue, for the event that prompted the confrontation was rather insignificant itself. In 336 Ctesiphon carried a proposal in the Boule to honor Demosthenes with a crown in the theater for public services, including his donation of private money to refurbish Athenian fortifications. Aeschines immediately attacked it as unconstitutional, which prevented the measure from coming before the Assembly until 330. The murder of Philip and the unexpected triumph of Alexander, which threw all of Greece into confusion, doubtless prompted the delay (cf. Worthington, Chapter 3). In 330, however, Alexander was in Ecbatana, far beyond caring about a crown bestowed on a defeated politician by a somewhat inconsiderable Greek state. So, the time seemed safe to proceed. When Ctesiphon finally brought his proposal before the Assembly, Aeschines attacked it, using the occasion to denounce Demosthenes' entire career.

Aeschines formally charges (3.11–48) that it was illegal to honor a magistrate while he was still in office and before he had submitted his accounts for audit and official approval. Lastly, he charges (3.49) that Ctesiphon was wrong publicly to honor Demosthenes as a benefactor of the city, when to the contrary his policies had led only to disaster. The first two charges were mere technicalities; the last was the real grievance. Aeschines intended to demonstrate to the Athenians that his policy had been preferable to Demosthenes', that no reason existed to be grateful for the defeat, and that his opponent was no friend of the people. Aeschines bases his formal prosecution on allegations of crimes in public life during four periods: (1) over the war for Amphipolis concluded by the Peace of Philocrates, (2) the period of the peace which ended when Demosthenes introduced the motion for war, (3) the period of war until Chaeronea, and (4) from then to the present (3.54–5). Aeschines defines a friend of the people as (1) a man free-born on both parents' side, (2) one who has left a legacy of some ancestral service to the people, or at least harbored no inherited enmity to them, (3) one who was temperate and self-restrained in his daily life, lest he take bribes, (4) a man of good judgement and an able speaker, and (5) a brave man who would not desert the people (3.169–70). Aeschines thus indicted Demosthenes as a man, a citizen, and a politician, condemning him for his very life. He concludes (3.231) that it was as appropriate to crown Demosthenes as Thersites, the notorious coward and sycophant.

In his indictment Aeschines resorts to the usual complaints about Demosthenes' mother being a Scythian (3.171–2), a repetition of his earlier attack. More substantial is his charge of Demosthenes' bribe-taking and venality, which for once had some appearance of substance. At 3.172, 239–40, Aeschines accuses

Demosthenes of embezzling the King's gold that was meant to finance the war against Alexander, an incident also treated by Dinarchus (1.18–21).[49] By his failure to distribute the money Demosthenes made the fall of the Theban Cadmeia possible and prevented the conclusion of an alliance with Arcadia. For the most part, however, the complaints are just that. More telling is Aeschines' condemnation of Demosthenes' cowardice in battle. Aeschines dwells acidly on Demosthenes deserting his post at Chaeronea in the face of the advancing enemy and then fleeing the city.[50] He concludes that Demosthenes is useless alike in war and peace, which contrasts starkly with his own distinguished military record.

Aeschines actually has little to say about the political events of this final period, simply because larger events had already thrown Athens into the background. He makes a very plausible, but not incontrovertible, case that Ctesiphon's proposed honors were illegal.[51] His principal new complaint is that after Chaeronea Demosthenes lost three opportunities to take advantage of Alexander's difficulties (3.163–5). The argument is a mere quibble that consists only of the claim that Demosthenes did nothing when Alexander invaded Asia instead of trying to conclude an alliance with the King. Demosthenes similarly failed to exploit Alexander's plight in Cilicia in 333 or the Spartan victory over Alexander's general Corragus.[52] Demosthenes was in reality as helpless as Aeschines to turn these episodes to Athenian profit. In his turn, Demosthenes defends himself by praising his own family while denigrating Aeschines' (18.258–60, 284). He ridicules again Aeschines' career, while extolling his own (18.257–69) and praising his own character (18.268–81).[53] With a brilliant stroke Demosthenes glorifies the defeat at Chaeronea in which for Athens there was pride but no blame (18.306–7). Athens had made a valiant and glorious effort to preserve Greece from the day of Macedonian despotism (18.293). Demosthenes was powerless to stop Philip, but he was the better patriot than Aeschines in having tried to prevent a conclusion that was ultimately the will of the gods (18.320).

5

Unlike before, Demosthenes won this trial, upon which Aeschines went into exile, while Demosthenes gamely but unsuccessfully continued his struggle against Macedonia. Despite their political differences, Demosthenes and Aeschines were both patriots, and none of their allegations of treason and perfidy should be taken seriously. Only their interpretation of Philip's real aims divided them. It is still impossible securely to determine whether either of them accurately gauged the king's ambitions for the simple reason that Philip did not leave a record of them. An analysis of his intentions goes beyond the scope of this chapter,[54] but suffice it to say that the vitriol of the two men for each other testifies to the passion in which they held their views and the love they cherished for Athens. At least they gave their fellow Athenians a clear choice of which path to pursue and in that alone they served as valuable servants of the city. As Aeschines sadly said (2.118), 'Tyche and Philip were master of the deeds. Things turned out not as we prayed, but as Philip did.'

Appendix: the speeches as historical sources

The speeches of Demosthenes and Aeschines on the most urgent issues of this period provide later historians with an excellent and almost unparalleled opportunity to determine what happened during these fateful times. Their authors were contemporaries who furnish testimony about the very events in which they themselves had participated. Another reason is that these two politicians and orators used rhetoric to present their version of what happened with little regard to objective truth. Persuasion and victory in the court or Assembly was their only goal, and both were biased and self-seeking in pursuit of it. Historical accuracy meant virtually nothing to them, and their testimony must be received with the utmost suspicion. Limits of space prevent anything but a brief survey of the subject, but several salient topics merit attention. From the outset careful methodology is the essential ingredient in evaluating the worth of their testimony and in establishing the correct course of events. Moreover, these speeches present scholars with numerous serious problems not necessarily found in other ancient testimony. Such matters include the composition, presentation, and publication of the speeches (cf. Golden, Chapter 5, and Milns, Chapter 7). Their length is significant because it involves both the subsequent inclusion of material not originally presented to the audience and also the question of how much information the listeners could absorb. The latter point directly relates to the problem of the contradictory claims that the two orators frequently make. Presented with these uncertainties, one can reasonably ask whether those present could correctly remember all of the details presented to them and whether they even cared for historical accuracy and rules of evidence. Similar concerns arise over those who subsequently read these long speeches on cumbersome book-rolls. Also pertinent in the matter of details are the documents found in the published speeches and the orators' use of historical allusions. The whole investigation points to the basic historical problem of how the speeches should be used as sources and to what extent they are reliable, trustworthy documents.

The first of these difficulties involves the times of composition, presentation, revision, and publication of the speeches, for they were never the same. Demosthenes and Aeschines debated the peace with Philip in early spring (18–19 Elaphebolion) 346, but Demosthenes did not bring his rival to trial until 343. The speeches actually given in the two assemblies in 346 and at the trial in 343 were not recorded. Versions of the speeches purportedly delivered at the trial were published somewhat later, but how much so is unknown. The publications represent revised versions of what was allegedly actually said, but the extent of revision itself can never be known. The obvious and essential point is simply that no one knows what was actually said to the audiences in 346 and 343, and the recorded accounts are demonstrably altered enough to prove tendentiousness. The speeches should not be taken as accurate records of the events of their day or totally reliable statements of facts. To add to the uncertainties there is some legitimate doubt whether all the published speeches were ever delivered. Plutarch (*Dem.* 15.5), whose knowledge of classical rhetoric was considerable, doubts that Demosthenes actually delivered *On the False Embassy*, despite the testimony of the Atthidographer Idomeneus (*FGrH* 338 F10), and questions whether the case ever came to trial, a view repeated in Pseudo-Plutarch (*Mor.* 840c). A similar problem exists in the case of the speeches dealing with the crowning of Demosthenes. Aeschines (3.27, 219) indicted his nemesis in 337/6, but the case did not come to trial until 330.[55] In this instance there is no question about the trial or the delivery of the speeches, but again they were revised for later publication and the length of time for reworking is unknown. Thus, the printed version of Aeschines' *Against Ctesiphon* and Demosthenes' *On the Crown* are not dependable accounts of what was really said at the trial. Consequently, none of these published works can be taken as documents that preserve verbatim reports of the events that they discuss.

The relation between later revisions and the ultimate length of the published speeches is less important than the question of the amount and nature of material added and deleted. All four speeches nowadays seem very long for oral presentation, but even as late as 1863 Edward Everett could speak at the battlefield of Gettysburg for over two hours to Abraham Lincoln's few minutes. For the ancient Greeks, who were so enamored of their language and rhetoric in general, such length would not necessarily seem excessive. Moreover, Aeschines (2.126; cf. also 3.197) specifically states that eleven amphoras of water were allotted to him for his defense in the trial over the embassy. To judge by the *klepsydra* found in the Athenian agora the eleven amphoras would permit him six and one-half hours for his defense.[56] Nor is it always possible to determine what was either included or excluded after the fact. Some clues, however, come from details alluded to in one speech but not found in its counterpart. Here there is some firm ground. For instance, Aeschines (2.10) claims that Demosthenes compared him to Dionysius of Syracuse and gave details of a dream related by a Sicilian priestess, neither of which appears in Demosthenes' published text. Likewise, Aeschines (2.124) ridicules Demosthenes' tale of his sailing down the Loedias river one night clandestinely to meet with Philip, an episode absent from Demosthenes' speech. Aeschines rebuts (2.125–6) this phantom allegation by claiming that Aglaocreon and Iatrocles slept with him during the entire embassy and are able to prove that no such rendezvous could have occurred. In place of the tale of the Loedias, Demosthenes includes (19.175) for publication the melodrama of how Dercylus, a fellow ambassador, spied on Aeschines at Pherae, for which he was rewarded by seeing the culprit sneaking out of Philip's tent. Not only does Aeschines make no reference to this scene, but in another, unrelated, connection he also mentions (2.155) that Dercylus actually testified on his behalf. One last instance proves mutual lying. At 2.20 Aeschines claims that Demosthenes urged him to join in guarding against Philocrates, whereas Demosthenes (19.13) claims that Aeschines proposed that he do precisely the same thing. Neither accusation deserves credence. These episodes suffice to prove that each man sometimes embellished his testimony not for the sake of the truth but rather to counter some anticipated, but now non-existent charge. They also prove the determination of the two to persuade their hearers even at the expense of truth.[57]

Even as published the speeches present other serious questions of historical reliability. One of the most obvious is also the easiest to answer. None of the documents in any of the speeches is authentic. In Aeschines' *On the Embassy* and *Against Ctesiphon* and Demosthenes' *On the Embassy*, the texts of laws, *psephismata*, and depositions are not included in the text, so it is now impossible to determine whether a genuine document was actually read at all, or if so whether in its entirety, in part, or paraphrased.[58] In his *Against Timarchus* Aeschines himself wrote the original depositions (1.66–8), which leaves the matter of authenticity nugatory. In Demosthenes' *On the Crown* all of the quoted *psephismata* are forgeries, as proven by the names of ten spurious archons. The only genuine name, Chaerondas (18.53), also adorns a counterfeit decree. Likewise, the Chaeronea epigram (18.289) is apocryphal. These documents are useful only to indicate how little ancient readers cared or knew about genuine documentation.[59]

Demosthenes and Aeschines similarly marshal abundant assertions of fact to bolster their cases. It is all too easy and misdirected to accept all of their claims as accurate on the premise that the audience would immediately know from personal experience when an orator was speaking the truth or correctly retailing history, even when that history was recent. An excellent proof comes from a fundamental point in the dispute over the Peace of Philocrates. On 18–19 Elaphebolion 346 the Athenians met in Assembly to discuss the treaty. Demosthenes (19.13–15) firmly asserts that Aeschines (2.63–6) spoke against the treaty on the first day but for it on the second. In response Aeschines just as firmly avers that debate occurred only on the eighteenth and that the nineteenth was reserved solely for ratification of the accord. He also flatly denies that anyone spoke on the second day. Many of the jurors in 343 had surely been present in the assemblies of 346; and yet only three years afterwards the two orators told them completely contradictory things about a point of great significance. Both orators cannot have been right, but for the present purpose the truth of their assertions is less important than the simple fact that they were made. It proves that a speaker could say anything to the audience with little fear of the consequences. Although it seems improbable that anyone would have been brazen enough to deny the demos any opportunity to speak at any time, some modern scholars nonetheless believe Aeschines' statement.[60] In this case, the truth is not far to seek. In 330, when the point no longer mattered, Aeschines (3.71–2) let slip that debate continued on the second day. This incident alone should stand as a warning against accepting any rhetorical declaration of fact at face value.

This episode also says something very significant about the audience. Most of them probably did not remember correctly or in any detail what had happened even a short time before. Enough reliable evidence exists to prove that the Athenians sent several embassies to Philip concerning the peace, the contents and details of which sparked much and sometimes heated discussion. It was easy for most listeners to become lost or confused over the precise course of events and the specific details surrounding them. Furthermore, both orators were fully aware of this fact. They frequently remind the audience of the difficulties of remembering events over the course of time, which gave them full and easy scope to mould history as they wished (Dem. 19.3, 17, 25 18.226 Aes. 3.60). Aeschines also (2.96) accuses Demosthenes of intentionally confusing dates and even (2.153) of inventing them, while he himself depends (2.58–9) upon documentary evidence. In defense of the auditors, it must have been virtually impossible for even the most alert and diligent to remember correctly the barrage of details to which they were subjected in these long speeches. It would have been equally difficult to remember when a speaker had contradicted himself along the way. Nor were things much simpler for later readers. Given the difficulty of looking up references in cumbersome papyrus rolls, even conscientious readers could readily overlook contradictions and errors of fact.[61] In sum, the orators enjoyed such huge opportunities to parade even outrageous misstatements as facts that no modern historian should accept them without severe scrutiny.

The orators' use of purely historical examples forms a different pattern in which more attention is devoted to the presentation of authentic lessons from the past. With regard to the Peace of Philocrates, the most singular case involves the so-called Peace of 392 because of the similarity between the two political situations and Aeschines' and Demosthenes' use of it to analyze the situation then before them. For the example properly to be understood, a short historical notice of the earlier aborted peace is necessary. In 392 the Corinthian War had reached a stage where a reasonable peace settlement was possible for the major belligerents, one of which was Athens. In the ensuing negotiations the orator Andocides was the leading Athenian ambassador, and among his colleagues was Epicrates (*PA* 4859), a man of the Piraeus and a compatriot of Thrasybulus. The proposed treaty would have been for Athens a marked improvement over its instrument of surrender in 404 and the later King's Peace of 386, but it nonetheless failed to meet Athenian expectations.[62] Aware of its shortcomings, Andocides advocated it as a practical and reasonable way by which to end the war. In support of his position Andocides included a short sketch of Greek history in support of his position. Yet he failed to win ratification of the treaty in the Assembly, for which he and his fellow envoys, Epicrates included, were condemned. Andocides' speech visibly influenced Aeschines, as witnessed by his inclusion of his predecessor's lesson in history almost verbatim. Like Andocides, he realized that the settlement he advocated fell short of his countrymen's wishes.[63] Each man, so separated in time, knew that he had settled for a sensible treaty that his contemporaries saw as second best, if that.

Equally intriguing is Demosthenes' use of this same episode, whether its choice was by chance or design. Instead of ruminating on the past and its lesson for the future, Demosthenes concentrates on the results of disappointing Athenian expectations. He focuses on Epicrates, not Andocides, and surely not by accident. Andocides was of somewhat dubious character in large part because of his profanation of the Mysteries, but Epicrates was a patriot and a lover of the democracy. Epicrates serves as the perfect foil. If punishment in the failed peace was the fate of this great citizen, a more severe penalty must be given to Aeschines, a far inferior man. Demosthenes supposedly has the clerk read to the court the decree that condemned Epicrates, Andocides, and the others, and applies to Aeschines every charge that had been successfully levelled against them. In this instance, Demosthenes makes much more effective use of the incident than Aeschines because he concentrates on the specific issues of the case rather than dubious lessons from history and vague hopes for a brighter future.

Although Demosthenes also applies the fate of the corrupt ambassador Timagoras to Aeschines, for the most part both orators use other historical allusions in a rather typical way to hold before the audience the memory of a greater and better past.[64] Thus, in Demosthenes Solon appears as the paragon of democracy, and the glory of Miltiades and Themistocles is contrasted with Aeschines, the shyster lawyer and the craven tool of Philip. Aeschines in turn uses many of the same examples to disparage Demosthenes for similar faults. There is nothing new or original in these appeals to a noble past, for Marathon, Salamis, and the other great triumphs of the fifth century had become stock topics by the fourth century, seen as early as 380 in Isocrates' *Panegyricus*. By 339, the date of Isocrates' *Panathenaicus*, the Athenians had used them so lavishly that Theopompus (*FGrH* 115 F153) wrote contemptuously of them. The orators, however, used them to stir up the patriotism of their listeners and to demonstrate that by contrast their opponents were an inferior breed of Athenian.

The conclusions to be drawn from this brief sketch are the obvious ones that both orators use testimony primarily to carry the day. The accuracy and veracity of the testimony is unimportant as compared to its rhetorical effectiveness. Not one unsupported statement of either man should automatically be accepted as truth.

NOTES

* It is a distinct pleasure to thank Professor Ian Worthington and Dr Hans Beck for their valuable help. Any remaining errors are mine alone.

1 P. Cloché, *Démosthène et la fin de la démocratie athénienne* (Paris: 1957), p. 207, N. Sawada, 'Athenian Politics in the Age of Alexander the Great: A Reconsideration of the Trial of Ctesiphon', *Chiron* 26 (1996), pp. 71–2, but see Worthington, Chapter 3.

2 T.T.B. Ryder and A.N.W. Saunders, *Demosthenes and Aeschines* (Harmondsworth: 1975), pp. 18–20, G.L. Cawkwell, *Philip of Macedon* (London: 1978), pp. 69–76, G. Wirth, *Philipp II* (Stuttgart: 1985), pp. 26–39.

3 J. Buckler, *Philip II and the Sacred War* (Leiden: 1989), *passim*.

4 G. Roux, *L'Amphictionie, Delphes, et le temple d'Apollon au IV* siècle* (Lyons: 1979), *passim*, F. Lefèvre, *L'Amphictionie pyléo-delphique: histoire et institutions* (Paris: 1998), pp. 147–71.

5 Buckler, *Sacred War*, pp. 74–8.

6 J.R. Ellis, *Philip II and Macedonian Imperialism* (London: 1976), pp. 82–6. See also Ryder, Chapter 2.

7 Diod. 16.37.3, 38.2, and Justin 8.2.8, and *IG* ii² 1496 lines 49–51, and G.T. Griffith in N.G.L. Hammond and G.T. Griffith, *A History of Macedonia* 2 (Oxford: 1979), pp. 279–81.

8 Buckler, *Sacred War*, pp. 58–81.

9 H. Bengtson, *Die Staatsverträge des Altertums²* 2 (Munich: 1975), nos. 308, 317, 323, and *IG* ii² 211, and E.M. Harris, *Aeschines and Athenian Politics* (New York: 1995), pp. 156–7.

10 R. Sealey, *Demosthenes and His Time* (London: 1993), pp. 137–40.

11 Aes. 2.12, and Dem. 5.5 with Scholiast. Chronology: *IG* i³ 6, 76–87, Ellis, *Philip II*, p. 264 n. 39, and Harris, *Aeschines*, p. 38 n. 57.

12 Dem. 19.10, 303–4, Diod. 16.54.1–2, Ellis, *Philip II*, p. 265 n. 51.

13 J. Buckler, 'Philip II, the Greeks, and the King 346–336 B.C.', *ICS* 19 (1994), p. 102.

14 Cawkwell, *Philip*, pp. 29–49, J. Buckler, 'Philip II's Designs on Greece' in R.W. Wallace and E.M. Harris (eds.), *Transitions to Empire: Essays in Honor of E. Badian* (Norman: 1996), pp. 77–84.

15 Aes. 2.18–20, Dem. 19.12, R. Develin, *Athenian Officials, 684–321 BC* (Cambridge: 1989), p. 319.

16 S. Accame, *La lega ateniese del sec. IV. a.c.* (Rome: 1941), pp. 83–4, J. Cargill, *The Second Athenian League* (Berkeley: 1981), p. 33.

17 K.J. Beloch, *Griechische Geschichte*² 3.1 (Berlin and Leipzig: 1922), p. 500, E. Badian, 'Philip II and Thrace', *Pulpudeva* 4 (1983), pp. 60–6, Z.H. Archibald, *The Odrysian Kingdom of Thrace* (Oxford: 1998), pp. 232–4, and S.M. Burstein, '*IG* I³ 61 and The Black Sea Grain Trade' in R. Mellor and L. Tritle (eds.), *Text and Tradition* (Claremont: 1999), pp. 93–104.

18 F. Stählin, *Das hellenische Thessalien* (Stuttgart: 1924), pp. 177–80, Hammond and Griffith, *Macedonia* 2, pp. 292–3.

19 Buckler, *Sacred War*, pp. 112–14.

20 Amphipolis: Dem. 18.69, 74–7, 19.22, 137, 253–5, 326, Aes. 2.70. Peace and alliance: Dem. 19.12, 40–1, 48, 87, Aes. 2.61, 82, 3.65, 71. Two letters: after first embassy (Aes. 2.50), after second (Dem. 19.36, Aes. 2.124–5). Cersebleptes: Dem. 19.174, 181, Aes. 3.65, 68, 74. Phocis: Dem. 19.18, 73, 278 (which contradicts 19.15, 174), 321–2, Aes. 2.81, 95, 131. Letter and promises: Dem. 19.36–7, 41, 44, 68, 5.10, Aes. 2.124–5.

21 Aes. 2.45, 81, 3.67, Dem. 19.17, 5.10. Although both Ellis, *Philip II*, p. 110, and Cawkwell, *Philip*, p. 98, give more precise dates, neither Aeschines, as indicated in the index of Blass's Teubner text, nor Demosthenes, as witnessed by S. Preuss, *Index Demosthenicus* (Leipzig: 1892), mentions Anthesterion. All Julian equivalents of Attic months are here given according to the formula of E. Bickerman, *Chronology of the Ancient World* (Ithaca: 1968), p. 20.

22 Bengtson, *Staatsverträge*² 2, no. 329.

23 *IG* ii² 14, 2–3; 34, 36; 97, 1–2; 116, 12, and especially 102, 2 (alliance with Amyntas and his son) and 105, 10–11 (Dionysius and his heirs). See also R. Meiggs and D.M. Lewis, *A Selection of Greek Historical Inscriptions*² (Oxford: 1988), no. 10.

24 Aes. 2.82, 90, 3.73–4, Dem. 19.156, 337. On Hieron Oros, cf. C.M. Danov, *Altthrakien* (Berlin: 1976), p. 122 n. 101.

25 *IG* ii² 43, 74–5; 116, 46–7.

26 Cf. also Andocides 3.33 and Philochorus *FGrH* 328 F149. As Andocides' experience in 392 proves, no Athenian delegation actually enjoyed plenipotentiary powers: cf. U. Kahrstedt, *Studien zum öffentlichen Recht Athens* 2 (Stuttgart: 1936), pp. 276–7.

27 Dem. 19.166–71, and Aes. 2.99, and M.L. Cook, 'Timokrates' 50 Talents and the Cost of Ancient Warfare', *Eranos* 88 (1990), pp. 69–97.

28 Buckler, *Sacred War*, p. 139.

29 The campaign could have been effected by a frontal attack by Philip at the western end of the corridor and a Theban assault from inland on Thronium at the eastern end. The Thebans would in fact strike Thronium from its most vulnerable direction. Moreover, these isolated fortified cities, all with their backs to Mt Callidromon, would have been difficult to supply, even if the 50 triremes could destroy Philip's navy. Furthermore, Alponus, Nicaea, and Thronium in the corridor could all easily be outflanked by an easy route considerably east of Heraclea Trachinia that runs into the Cephissus valley: Buckler, *Sacred War*, pp. 93–5, and E.W. Kase, G.J. Szemler, N.C. Wilkes and P.W. Wallace (eds.), *The Great Isthmus Corridor Route* 1 (Dubuque: 1991), pp.

21–55, and G.J. Szemler, W.J. Cherf and J.C. Kraft (eds.), *Thermopylai: Myth and Reality in 480 BC* (Chicago: 1996), pp. 44–57.

30 Aes. 2.107–17, and Pausanias 10.37.6, and Roux, *L'Amphictionie*, pp. 30–5, and Lefèvre, *L'Amphictionie pyléo-delphique*, pp. 147–51.

31 Meaning of an open *probouleuma*: P.J. Rhodes, *The Athenian Boule* (Oxford: 1972), pp. 59–61, and M.H. Hansen, *The Athenian Democracy in the Age of Demosthenes*[2] (Norman: 1999), pp. 38–9.

32 M.H. Hansen, *The Athenian Assembly in the Age of Demosthenes* (Oxford: 1987), pp. 70–1.

33 D.J. Mosley, *Envoys and Diplomacy in Ancient Greece* (Wiesbaden: 1973), pp. 79–80, and F.E. Adcock and D.J. Mosley, *Diplomacy in Ancient Greece* (London: 1975), pp. 156–5.

34 Aristophanes, *Ecclesiazousae* 71, Plato com. fr. 119 in J.M. Edmonds, *The Fragments of Attic Comedy* 2 (Leiden: 1957), Plut. *Pelopidas* 30.12, and cf. also *Hellenica Oxyrhynchus* 10.2, Dem. 19.277–80.

35 Xenophon, *Hellenica* 7.1.33, Plut. *Pelopidas* 30.9 and *Artaxerxes* 22.9, and Athenaeus 2.48d–e, and 6.251a–b, 6.253f.

36 Roux, *L'Amphictionie*, pp. 166–7, and Lefèvre, *L'Amphictionie pyléo-delphique*, pp. 94–5, 108–9.

37 K. Fiehn, 'Timarchos', *RE* 6A (1936), 1234–6.

38 Aes. 1.141–53 and 2.157; S. Perlman, 'Quotations from Poetry in Attic Orators of the Fourth Century B.C.', *AJP* 85 (1964), pp. 156–72 and P.E. Easterling, 'Actors and Voices: Reading between the Lines in Aeschines and Demosthenes' in S. Goldhill and R. Osborne (eds.), *Performance Culture and Athenian Democracy* (Cambridge: 1999), pp. 154–65.

39 Ryder, *Demosthenes and Aeschines*, pp. 39–46, Hammond and Griffith, *Macedonia* 2, pp. 489–516, and Wirth, *Philipp II*, pp. 102–23.

40 D. Schaps, 'The Woman Least Mentioned: Etiquette and Women's Names', *CQ*[2] 27 (1977), pp. 323–30.

41 Easterling, 'Actors and Voices', pp. 154–65.

42 Dem. 18.132–3, and Din. 1.63, and Plut. *Dem.* 14.5, and R. Garland, *The Piraeus* (Ithaca: 1987), p. 44.

43 Hansen, *Athenian Democracy*, p. 77.

44 Dem. 18.134–6, and cf. Hyp. frags. 67–71, 76, and *IG* ii[2] 222.

45 Roux, *L'Amphictionie*, p. 54.

46 Beloch, *Griechische Geschichte*[2] 3.1, p. 533 n., followed by F.R. Wüst, *Philipp II von Makedonien und Griechenland* (Munich: 1938), p. 52, and Ellis, *Philip II*, pp. 130–3, argue for 346/5, while Harris, *Aeschines*, pp. 121–2, without proof or argument, suggests a date 'not long after the execution of Antiphon'. Although Harris is quite probably right, a real case for the date must be attempted. All those urging the earlier date depend upon historical possibilities, an approach that neglects the admittedly sparse evidence. The reasons here for the later date are that Demosthenes (18.134) states that the Areopagus distrusted Aeschines because of his part in the episode of Antiphon. *IG* ii[2] 222, which honors Pisithides of Delos for his benefactions, though undated, can cautiously be placed by epigraphical evidence in the 340s, which lends at least some modest support for Demosthenes' testimony.

47 Wirth, *Philipp II*, pp. 125–30, and P. Londey, 'The Outbreak of the 4th Sacred War', *Chiron* 20 (1990), pp. 239–60.

48 Plut. *Demetrius* 13.1, Pausanias 10.19.4; H.W. Parke, 'Notes on Some Delphic Oracles', *Hermathena* 52 (1938), pp. 71–8, A. Schaefer, *Demosthenes und seine Zeit*[2] 2 (Leipzig: 1886), p. 533, and Roux, *L'Amphictionie*, pp. 31–5.

49 For the falseness of these claims, see Ian Worthington, *A Historical Commentary on Dinarchus* (Ann Arbor: 1992), pp. 139–43, 160–8.

50 Aes. 3.159–61, 175–6, 187, 209, 246, 252–3, and Plut. *Dem.* 20.2. The penalty for cowardice in the face of the enemy was *atimia*: G. Busolt and H. Swoboda, *Griechische Staatskunde* 2 (Munich: 1926), pp. 950–1. Either Demosthenes was not guilty of the charge, which is unlikely, or the Athenians, like the Spartans after Leuctra (Plut. *Agesilaus* 30.2–6), decided not to enforce the law.

51 G.L. Cawkwell, 'The Crowning of Demosthenes', *CQ*[2] 19 (1969), pp. 163–80, and Harris, *Aeschines*, pp. 143–5, and Sawada, 'Athenian Politics', pp. 71–4.

52 A.B. Bosworth, *Conquest and Empire: The Reign of Alexander the Great* (Cambridge: 1988), pp. 55–62.

53 G.O. Rowe, 'The Portrait of Aeschines in the Oration *On the Crown*', *TAPA* 97 (1966), pp. 397–406.

54 Buckler, 'Philip II', *passim*, 'Philip's Designs', *passim*, and T.T.B. Ryder, 'The Diplomatic Skills of Philip II' in Ian Worthington (ed.), *Ventures Into Greek History: Essays in Honour of N.G.L. Hammond* (Oxford: 1994), pp. 228–57.

55 W.W. Goodwin, *Demosthenes On the Crown* (Cambridge: 1957), p. 270 n. 2, and Harris, *Aeschines*, p. 208 n. 29.

56 *AP* 67.1 with P.J. Rhodes, *A Commentary on the Aristotelian Athenaion Politeia* (Oxford: 1981), pp. 719–21; cf. Ian Worthington, 'The Duration of an Athenian Political Trial', *JHS* 109 (1989), pp. 204–7.

57 Cf. Ian Worthington, 'Greek Oratory, Revision of Speeches and the Problem of Historical Reliability', *C&M* 92 (1991), pp. 55–74.

58 R. Thomas, *Oral Tradition and Written Record in Classical Athens* (Cambridge: 1989), pp. 38–40, W.C. West, 'The Public Archives in Fourth-Century Athens', *GRBS* 30 (1989), pp. 529–43, and R.L. Fox, 'Aeschines and the Athenian Democracy' in R. Osborne and S. Hornblower (eds.), *Ritual, Finance, Politics* (Oxford: 1994), pp. 140–1, who emphasizes Aeschines' familiarity with the Athenian archives in the Metroön, which, however, proves nothing about his actual use of the documents that he found there.

59 Spurious archons: 18.37, 54, 75, 105, 115–16, 118, 155, 164, 181; for Chaerondas, cf. H. Wankel, *Demosthenes, Rede für Ktesiphon über den Kranz* (Heidelberg: 1976), pp. 358–60, 1231–3. Cf. also J.K. Davies, 'Documents and "Documents" in Fourth-Century Historiography' in P. Carlier (ed.), *Le IV*[e] *Siècle av. J.-C.: Approches historiographiques* (Paris: 1996), pp. 29–39. These facts should also warn those modern historians who rely upon this kind of evidence to support the authenticity of the decrees of Miltiades, Themistocles, the Peace of Callias, and the Congress Decree. J.P. Sickinger, *Public Records and Archives in Classical Athens* (Chapel Hill: 1999), 168–76, appeared too late for systematic comment here, yet the work errs in assuming rather than proving that Demosthenes and Aeschines actually and accurately read documents from the Metroön in their speeches.

60 For example, Harris, *Aeschines*, pp. 117–18.
61 For such difficulties, cf. S. Hornblower's 'Introduction' in S. Hornblower (ed.), *Greek Historiography* (Oxford: 1994), pp. 62–3.
62 Bengtson, *Staatsverträge*² 2, nos. 211, 242.
63 Aeschines (2.174) even credits Andocides with having successfully made peace; cf. Beloch, *Griechische Geschichte*² 3.1, pp. 81–5.
64 Use of historical allusions: L. Pearson, 'Historical Allusions in the Attic Orators', *CP* 36 (1941), pp. 209–29, and M. Nouhaud, *L'Utilisation de l'histoire par les orateurs attiques* (Paris: 1982), pp. 353–64.

5

DEMOSTHENES AND THE SOCIAL HISTORIAN*

Mark Golden

How can our understanding of Athenian social life help us read Demosthenes? How can our reading of Demosthenes enrich our perceptions of Athenian society? These are the questions I address in this chapter. The subjects are big ones, however, and I have chosen to focus quite narrowly. In the first section, I examine one strategy of modern historians for using Demosthenes and the other Attic orators for their purposes, what I call the argument from plausibility. In the second, I turn to Demosthenes' presentation of one aspect of Athenian society, the world of the gymnasium. Some readers may feel that, like an Athenian advocate, I have put my stress on insignificant or even irrelevant material in order to make my case. Like that advocate, I would reply that I am content to persuade a bare majority.

1

In a speech Demosthenes wrote for him, Diodorus indignantly reproaches Timocrates with the unseemly vigour he and his ally Androtion used to collect arrears of *eisphora*, the special tax imposed on Athens' property owners in times of war. 'You would enter houses along with the Eleven, the receivers and their assistants and you never took pity on anyone. No, you stripped off their front doors and snatched away the sheets from off their beds and, if a man had a maidservant, you seized her as payment of his debt' (Dem. 24.197). The passage makes an appearance in A.H.M. Jones' account of the economic basis of Athenian democracy, where Jones takes it to show that relatively few Athenians, the better-off only, owned slaves. 'The domestic servant probably did not go very far down the social scale.'[1] The maidservant plays a similar part in Jones' Cambridge inaugural lecture, also published in 1952.[2] Just three years later, however, Jones revisited the households of the payers of *eisphora* at Athens, only to find that they had come down in the world. Now, many such taxpayers 'were relatively poor'.[3] These differences in the socioeconomic situation of *eisphora*-payers reflect to some degree the different purposes to which Jones puts this passage of Demosthenes: to argue against the notion that Athenian democracy was based on the labour of slaves and the resulting leisure of ordinary citizens, and to emphasize the predominance of domestics among ancient slaves. But we should also note that Jones was 'the most English and least theoretical of historians' – both terms are meant as compliments – a man who preferred to set out the facts and let them speak for themselves before moving on to interpretation.[4] If they sometimes proved to be bilingual, as in this instance, it is an indication of how tricky it can be even for the best historians to use the speeches of Demosthenes as evidence for Athenian society.

The problems posed by our texts of Demosthenes and the other Attic orators are too well known to need much discussion here.[5] Some speeches were not composed for delivery at all – they are rhetorical exercises, products of the fourth century, or much later.[6] (I take this opportunity to confess that I once translated Lincoln's Gettysburg address into Demosthenic Greek, though as far as I know this has not yet misled historians.) Others, such as Demosthenes 21 *Against Meidias*, may never have been delivered or at least may not have been delivered in the form in which we have them.[7] As for the speeches' contents, the crucial point, as usual, is that nothing we read was composed or delivered or preserved for our benefit. The orators' works are (in Thucydides' phrase) display pieces, to be heard, circulated as advertising for their authors, and then forgotten; it is the taste of ancient rhetoricians and the accidents of history which have turned them into treasures for all time.

Those addressed to the Assembly or the Boule tended to touch only tangentially on social historians' concerns. Of course, even passing remarks may be of interest. In his *First Philippic*, delivered in 351, Demosthenes criticizes his fellow citizens' approach to Philip: 'You wage war like the barbarians box. For whenever a barbarian is hit, he holds the place where he was struck, and if you hit him on the other side, there go his hands. He does not know how to put up his guard or how to keep an eye on his adversary and he does not want to learn' (4.40). Questions come quickly. Where has Demosthenes seen barbarians box? Abroad – say in Macedon itself? But we have no reason to believe that Demosthenes had travelled north as early as this. In Athens, then? If so, this might be one of a very few tantalizing glimpses of slave sparring partners in Greek gymnasia.[8] How far may we press the details of this image? It would be rash to presume that they really reflect an identifiable barbarian style, or even a mirror image of Athenian practices. The particular qualities Demosthenes describes are determined by the parallel he draws: the Athenians have been passive and unperceptive. Still, the burden of Demosthenes' charge, that the Athenians have deployed superior strength unskilfully, plays against the usual assumption of his audience, that Greek heavy athletes triumphed through technique and trickery and not just brute force. Two other aspects call for comment. First, the image packs extra punch because the reversal of roles, in which the Athenians figure as the barbarians in Philip's place, is presented in the very heart of the democracy, the Assembly. Second, the simile stakes Demosthenes' claim to familiarity with the world of sport – that it and references like it are meant to make that link will be one of the subjects of this chapter's second section.

Law court speeches, on the other hand, regularly reveal Athenian social life and attitudes, but their evidence is shaped by their context and conventions. Witnesses in Athenian trials were not cross-examined, presiding officers provided no control over the relevance or admissibility of evidence and no guidance on the law. Juries were very large, neither experts nor necessarily experienced (and less so in Demosthenes' time than in the fifth century, when jurors were allocated to a particular court for a year). They were required to reach verdicts by majority vote immediately after the conclusion of a trial of less than a day's duration.[9] Though they swore an oath to judge according to the laws, this was problematic in practice – jurors might not know the law, and laws might contradict each other or fail to apply to a given set of circumstances – and anyway unenforceable.[10] 'Laws, like other forms of evidence, served to persuade rather than to bind an Athenian court.'[11] And alone among those who held public office, the juror was unaccountable, not subject to *euthynai* – something the comic juror Philocleon glories in (Aristophanes, *Wasps* 587). Such proceedings, though judicial, are likely to be less than judicious at times. Speakers both laboured under these restrictions – they faced strict time limits – and exploited them. Sometimes they are merely vague, counting on the jury's familiarity with facts or institutions of which we are desperately unsure. For example, Athenians were aware of the age at which members of phratries (or at least of their own phratry) made the offering of hair, the *koureion*. Our best contemporary evidence comes from a speech by Isaeus, which recounts the attempts of an elderly Athenian to introduce a young man he alleges to be his son to his phratry (6.18–26). The value of this evidence, however, is vitiated by the imprecision of the terms ('after these events', 'sometime later') Isaeus uses in his narrative.[12] In this instance, the vagueness is probably motivated by the desire to avoid *akribeia*, the precision characteristic of written texts, which was thought to be unsuitable for courtroom speeches.[13] Elsewhere, orators may mean to maintain ambiguity for rather different reasons.

Sometimes the imprecision which puzzles us today was designed to influence juries long ago. In prosecuting his guardian Aphobus, Demosthenes describes himself as seven years old when his father died (Dem. 27.4; cf. 63) and as under his guardians' care for ten years after, until he finally reached majority (27.6, 17, 24, 26, 29, 35–6, 39, 63; cf. 29.34, 59, 31.14). Such numbers must be approximate only, rounded up or down. But which? Is (for example) Demosthenes exaggerating the length of time during which Aphobus and his accomplices managed his affairs (and so the extent of their depredations) or understating it (in order to appear generous in forgiving some of the interest he is owed)? We cannot say for sure.[14] We may consider a more complex instance, the passage of Demosthenes, *Against Timocrates* (24.197) with which this section began. Uncertainty as to the socioeconomic status of *eisphora*-payers arises because this is not something to be established objectively. On the contrary, they, the jurors, and Timocrates' prosecutor, Diodorus, are engaged in a subtle negotiation of identities, a kind of courtroom conference call. Demosthenes' aim in composing this account is to forge links between his client, his audience and the victims of his adversary's actions – at the same time as he insists that their experiences and emotions are relevant, even important, to the wider community. In fact, the jurors, who had to be at least 30, were older than their fellow citizens and had more opportunity to serve (because they were richer or poorer than most or lived closer to the venues where trials took place) or else were more willing to serve in this particular way. Moreover, our success in grasping the social basis for Demosthenes' rhetoric, problematic enough already, is hindered still more by the fact that we know next to nothing about Diodorus' wealth or social standing.

Finally, most frustratingly, the orators lie. That speakers should lie in the political arena perhaps no longer shocks, let alone surprises. 'How can you tell when a politician is lying? When he moves his lips.' The Australian author of a book published in England says this is a Russian joke, but I have heard it told of a Canadian prime minister.[15] Lest Americans feel left out: 'George Washington could not tell a lie, Richard Nixon could not tell the truth, Ronald Reagan could not tell the difference.' (The culture of deceit was so pervasive in the Nixon presidency that the White House published an inaccurate recipe for his daughter's wedding cake.) At Athens, however, lies to the Assembly might meet severe sanctions: the Athenians fined and even condemned to death speakers who they came to believe had misled the people.[16] In a court case, on the other hand, lies were virtually risk-free. Detection might be difficult. It seems to be harder than one might think, at least for the public at large: lying and other forms of deception may be essential for the survival of human and other species and our capacity to recognize them, important though it is, may consequently lag.[17] Athenian litigants' liberty to conduct a case virtually as they liked and the limits on the length of speeches combined to let all but the most damaging slanders and misrepresentations – not always those of most use to social historians – go unchallenged, and the defendant, who spoke last, need fear no rebuttal. As for those who were caught out, witnesses faced a charge under a *dikē pseudomartyriōn*; suborning perjury was also illegal. But it was the litigants' speeches which were at the centre of any Athenian trial, and though both prosecutor and defendant swore an oath at the preliminary hearing, the *anakrisis*, this seems to have guaranteed only the truthfulness of depositions handed in at that time.[18] To cite a non-existent law was (allegedly) an offence punishable by death ([Dem.] 26.24). Otherwise, what was said by litigants or the *synēgoroi* they called on to speak on their behalf was judgement proof. As Harris puts it, 'Since both the plaintiff and the defendant had only a few hours to give their speeches, they had to use any means at their disposal to convince the jury of the justice of their case. If lies, deceptions and innuendo served to further this end, those means would not be shunned.'[19] And let me stress that I am not just talking about, say, events in the past, historical allusions, something about which an Athenian juror might pride himself on knowing little and caring less. As Pearson remarked of the orators long ago, 'Everyone knows that their accuracy does not conform to the standards generally expected of historians.'[20] My claim is a stronger one, encompassing contemporary institutions and customs as well.

How, then, are we to get at the truth? For some social historians, the puzzles our evidence poses are their own answers. Were women forbidden to litigate in their own right or even to appear as witnesses? Does decorum prevent speakers from identifying respectable citizen women by name? For Steven Johnstone, such conventions do not merely reflect the silencing of Athenian women but refigure disputes, whatever their origins or cast of characters, into conflicts between men.[21] From a lofty enough vantage point, the corpus as a whole is a dialogue between élite politicians and the masses, whose ideology and interests they must promote in order to succeed.[22] But most social historians, concerned with smaller-scale questions, must develop strategies for evaluating the reliability of single statements, short accounts, what one speech actually says.

Fortunately, two prominent historians – Raphael Sealey, whose first article on the orator appeared forty-five years ago, and Edward Harris, the leading authority on Aeschines – have recently tackled this problem head-on. Both are chiefly engaged in political history, the intricacies of Athenian policy towards Macedon and its domestic and external consequences above all. But the criteria they propose for determining the reliability of what we find in Athenian speeches are more generally applicable.[23] There are some variations: Sealey alone calls attention to the tendency of speakers to exaggerate their roles in the events they describe. But on the whole their principles, derived independently, are in reassuring agreement: precise dates produce confidence, assertions corroborated by testimony about public events are more credible than mere allegations, about what was said and done in private above all. There is another principle, however, followed by both scholars in practice, which may have seemed too self-evident to need expression: plausibility. Harris's comment on the orators' recourse to deception, quoted above, goes on, 'Nothing aside from the knowledge of the audience and the limits of plausibility restrained' them. Sealey notes of a statement by Demosthenes, 'The assertion was tendentious, unsupported and incompatible with what the same orator had said in 343/2, but it may not have been absurd.'[24] Plausibility has become an accepted touchstone for social historians too. Even if a speaker's statements cannot be believed in every detail (so the argument runs), something similar must have been familiar and credible to an Athenian audience, and so counts as evidence for our understanding of Athenian society.[25] It seems to me, however, that this line of argument needs more attention than it usually gets.

I offer six preliminary considerations. Each has the effect of limiting the force of the argument from plausibility:

1   An audience might well accept that something happened once – for example, that Diocleides came across the mutilators of the Herms when he was up extra early one night for the long walk to Laureion (Andoc. 1.38–9). But this does not mean that such nocturnal journeys were any more regular than the sacrilege itself, and it is normal and customary activities which are most significant for social history.

2   A legal argument made to an audience of experts (such as the *ephetai* in a homicide court, initiates in a case connected to the Eleusinian Mysteries, serving soldiers in a matter of military discipline) is better evidence than one to an ordinary jury. Nevertheless, recent scholarship tends to accept the testimony of Demosthenes 22.25–7, 24.114–15 (on the choice of procedures open to prosecutors) and to reject that of Lysias 1.32–3 (on the relative severity of adultery and rape).[26]

3   The plausibility of a statement in the judgement of one speaker or one audience does not show that the contrary statement would be less plausible. Prosecuting Callistratus, Leodamas argued that the instigator of an act was more guilty than the man who carried it out; prosecuting Chabrias, the man who put Callistratus' plan into effect, he reversed their relative responsibility (Arist. *Rhetoric* 1.7.13). Circumstances alter court cases.

4   Some statements are only meant to be plausible in character – credible in regard to the speaker or defendant or people like them, but not necessarily to many or most others.[27] How many of those who judged Euphiletus for the murder of Eratosthenes liked to think of themselves as so easy for their wives to fool?

5   Some plausible statements are not meant to be taken literally. In the course of his prosecution of Aristocrates (a Demosthenic speech), Euthycles offers jurors a detailed disquisition on the Athenian homicide courts (Dem. 23.65–78). This has become a staple of modern studies on the subject. Its original purpose, however, was rather different. Its amplitude and abundance, *peribolē*, were meant to impress the audience with the awful nature of Aristocles' transgression – in fact, he had proposed that the Athenians take measures to *prevent* Charidemus' murder – and so to stress that case's importance. When, therefore, Demosthenes writes that the Court of the Areopagus is one of the many unique Athenian institutions, and the most distinc-

tive and venerable at that (23.65), and then that the Court of the Delphinium is still more sacred and awe-inspiring (23.74), we should not imagine that this hierarchy would provoke jurors to protest. But neither should we suppose that they paid it a lot of attention – they have been inundated with an overwhelming abundance of material – or that Demosthenes thought they would.[28]

6   Some stories may have been plausible – but just as stories. Jurors in particular were accustomed to repeating tricks of structure and rhetorical tropes; these no doubt afforded the pleasure of recognition quite apart from their contribution to an argument. (So Lysias can both disparage and deploy the credit clients claim for their services to the city.)[29] When Demosthenes praises Phormio's rare virtues, he tells the jurors, 'People engaged in business and banking think it remarkable for a man to be both hard-working and honest' (Dem. 36.44). This is not evidence for the laziness or thievery of bankers or even evidence (good evidence at any rate) for mainstream attitudes – it is the Athenian equivalent of present-day lawyer jokes, often told by lawyers to lawyers, a genre which (whatever its origins) has now taken on a life of its own. As Phillip Harding comments on allegations that ambassadors took bribes, 'Charges of this sort, like Demosthenes' inferences that Euboulos' wealth was proof of corruption, could only seem reasonable because they were expected'.[30] Familiarity bred content in matters of substance, too. As Aristotle observes, audiences like to hear what they think they already know (Arist. *Rhetoric* 2.21.15). Take the account Apollodorus offers of Chabrias' victory party after he won the four-horse chariot race at the Pythian games of 374 ([Dem.] 59.33–4). Phrynion was among the guests, along with his companion Neaera, a famous hetaera and the subject of much of Apollodorus' speech. 'There Phrynion fell asleep and many had sex with her while she was drunk – even Chabrias' servants.' Perhaps this did seem plausible enough to the jurors. But so what? I expect that they had as much first-hand acquaintance with the social practices of pricey hookers and celebrity generals as the reader of a supermarket scandal sheet does today. The main function of Apollodorus' narrative is to make good in part on the promise he made earlier in the speech, to entertain the jurors with spicy scenes of low morals in high life (59.20). Its appeal builds on the fantasies of the middle-aged Athenian male, *nikē* and nooky. And on

flattery: what juror would admit, even to himself, that he was too unworldly to know of such goings-on (cf. Arist. *Rhetoric* 3.7.7)?

This example leads to one last consideration, most relevant to forensic speeches. Along with most historians, I have assumed so far that orators aimed at plausibility. It is worth considering whether this was always so. Indeed, Aristotle argues (rather cryptically) that implausibility might in itself be presented as a token of truth. 'Incredible things which are thought to happen nonetheless are even more likely to be true. For we only believe in what actually is or in what is probable. Therefore, if a thing is incredible and improbable, it must be true' – otherwise no one would say it was (Arist. *Rhetoric* 2.23.22). (Thucydides' Cleon calls the Athenians 'slaves to the paradoxical': 3.38.5.) More fundamentally, truth was no more a transcendent virtue in Athenian courts than in many others; for one thing, it was not an adequate defence against a charge of defamation.[31] For another, part of the legacy of the archaic period was a complex attitude towards lies and deception. Within certain contexts, these 'lose the negative connotations that normally attend them and become representations of intelligence, persuasive power, inventiveness, imagination, and verbal dexterity'.[32] These contexts might include affairs of state. The first return of Pisistratus has been read, most attractively, as a festival procession with Athena in the leading role, the tyrant as her attendant, and the people knowing and appreciative participants in the make-believe.[33] Classical Athenians were perhaps less ambivalent, at least most of the time; the characterization of Odysseus in tragedy seems a sure sign of that. Some, however, may have retained an admiration for the successful scamp, the trickster on trial, the defendant who somehow gets off despite the odds. Here is Demos in Aristophanes' *Knights* (1375–80 [Sommerstein's translation]):

> I mean those adolescents in the perfume-market, who sit and blabber things like this: 'Clever man, that Phaeax; ingenious, the way he escaped death! He's cohesive and penetrative, productive of original phrases, clear and incisive, and most excellently repressive of the vociferative.'

Demos' description of these young Athenians, wet between the ears as well as behind them, is as unflattering about their enthusiasm for trendy slang as it is about their judgement, but does go to show that a taste for verbal ingenuity might sometimes replace respect for the facts of a case or its consequences. We must not suppose that this weakness for wit invariably vanished at the age of majority or of jury duty. The speech Lysias wrote for an invalid claiming a pension (24) seems to be based on the premise that a weak case can in fact be bolstered by making a virtuoso display of its absurdities.[34] And why not? One of the most interesting trends in the study of Athenian law is to stress the courts' engagements with and similarities to another context where male citizens passed judgement on the words of their peers – the theatre.[35] The idea is not a new one. Aristotle observes that contests within the *polis* – he means court cases and political debates – are (unfortunately) decided on the basis of style rather than content, just as actors rule the dramatic stage instead of poets (Arist. *Rhetoric* 3.1.4). Furthermore, speakers in court cases use exordia much as dramatic poets their prologues (*Rhetoric* 3.14.5–6). More recent writers have stressed the overlap between theatre audiences and jurors, the importance of performance (tone of voice, gesture, deportment) in appeals to each, the public nature of the arena in which these appeals were made. Trials were serious play – punishments such as exile and execution were all too real – but a kind of play nevertheless. What kind? Sometimes a tragedy.[36] A client of Antiphon's refers to his stepmother as Clytemnestra, the most famous of ancient husband-killers, in order to encourage the jurors to play the role of their dramatic analogues in Aeschylus' *Eumenides*, and so to vote in his favour (1.17).[37] A comic turn might be more effective yet.[38] Laughter may make an audience lose concentration – and so presumably lose interest in plausibility or the capacity to judge it (Arist. *Rhetoric* 3.14.7). Demosthenes has Euthycles claim that the Athenians acquit even men who are clearly guilty for the sake of a few witticisms (*asteia*).[39] He himself vilifies Aeschines' family through the stuff and vocabulary of comedy – and of Old Comedy, the comedy of hyperbole and invention to boot. It is surely likely, speaking of plausibility, that speakers used such tactics because they worked.

What is most instructive about this trend for my purposes is that some of those responsible for the most insightful and persuasive work on this theme nevertheless accept the force of the argument from plausibility.[40] Lanni goes so far as to argue that spectators acted as a check on litigants and jurors. 'The presence of bystanders may also have inhibited the litigants by giving them reason to avoid wild exaggerations and lies ... The presence of bystanders may have served as an informal *euthyna* for jurors, since it ensured that the jurors could not make collective judgements without the immediate knowledge of a section of the community.'[41] The fairest response to this is, 'Maybe yes, maybe no'. I can see no reason why bystanders should consistently be any more resistant to humour or any other irrational appeal for their favour than jurors, nor any more unanimous in their opinions. The role played by public opinion in the trial of the generals after the battle of Arginusae offers little confidence on either count (Xenophon, *Hellenica* 1.7.12–13). I would prefer to think that the Athenians attended the theatre as spectators and the courts as judges in much the same frame of mind, ready and willing to suspend disbelief. Unlike the editor of this volume, the Athenian juror could not say, 'I am from Missouri'.

This account is meant to be skeptical about the value of Demosthenes' speeches as evidence for Athenian social history, but by no means nihilistic. There are too many examples of their sensitive and successful use for that.[42] In the next section, I will try to add to them by turning to an aspect of society mentioned earlier, the world of the gymnasium. I will suggest that the very fact that Demosthenes thinks something is worth mentioning may be better evidence for Athenian social history than the specific information he imparts.

2

In the course of his speech on the second embassy to Philip, delivered before the Athenian Assembly in 343, Aeschines offers a sketch of his family background. His elderly father Atrometus, he says, competed as an athlete in his youth but lost his property during the Peloponnesian war. After the war, he helped restore the democracy and served bravely as a soldier in Asia Minor; besides, he was by birth a member of the same phratry as the distinguished *genos* of the Eteoboutadae. Like an athletic past, these are claims to status. His eldest brother Philochares (Aeschines goes on) campaigns with Iphicrates, serves as general and spends his free time in the gymnasium (2.147–9). How could anyone cast aspersions on his origins? The point, of course, is that Demosthenes just had, in his speech for the prosecution, depicting Atrometus as a lowly schoolmaster, Aeschines' mother as the devotee of some outlandish cult – the fact that he names her, Glaucothea, is itself an index of contempt – and Philochares as 'a painter of alabaster boxes and tambourines'.[43]

Aeschines was sensitive to such slurs. His speeches, as a consequence, are liberally larded with references to the pastimes of the élite, among them the world of athletic competition. Timarchus addressed the Assembly *'gymnos*, like a pancratiast, so drunk and lewd that those of sound judgement covered their eyes in shame for the city' (1.26; cf. 1.33). Jurors are invited to regard Aeschines and those like him as competing alongside them for Athens' peace and security (2.183). The arduous training of the heavy athlete would be unbearable if he did not know that the crown goes to the best man (3.179–80). The *polis* should counter Demosthenes' trickery like a boxer manoeuvring for position and not let him escape through fancy footwork (3.206). Vivid images. We would like to know more about their basis. What kind of spectacle did Timarchus make of himself? Did he really reveal more of his body than was customary when he spoke – we may think of the tradition about Cleon's unseemly style – or is the use of *gymnos*, 'lightly clad' or, in an athletic context, 'naked', inspired by the charge against him, of addressing the Assembly despite having prostituted himself? A man who has involved his body in questionable conduct in one context may well be accused of flaunting it in others. And why the *pankration*? Did its reputation as an event from which few holds were barred fit so shameless a defendant? Or was it simply popular, as its singling out among combat events at 3.179 implies? Whatever the explanations for the particular words Aeschines chooses, the ambience he evokes is key. 'Apparently' (as Ober puts it) 'he hoped to be perceived as the sort of man who spent a good deal of time in gymnasia and so naturally used athletic turns of phrase.'[44]

Robin Lane Fox has objected to this characterization, on the grounds that 'on closer inspection' athletic metaphors are not unduly prominent or distinctive in Aeschines, nor always applied to the orator himself.[45] However, he adduces no quantitative measures of prominence nor parallels to (say) Aeschines' metaphorical use of *pankratiazein* in the other Attic orators. (There is none.) And his observation that it is the jurors who are called *synagōnistai* seems to miss the point. Aeschines has already established his own credentials as the member of a family of athletes. Now he invites the jurors to share his status with him, to imagine themselves as men of the gymnasium, participants in prestigious pursuits. A select fraternity – from which Demosthenes is later excluded. 'Look to see who among you intends to aid Demosthenes', Aeschines exhorts in the concluding section of his speech against Ctesiphon (3.255).

'Companions of his youthful days as a hunter or men who exercise with him? No way – he has not spent his time hunting wild boars or cultivating bodily vigour but hunting down men of property.'

The origins of the gymnasium are not beyond dispute: that it represented a carry-over from the exclusive world of aristocratic competition we glimpse at the funeral games of Patroclus and among the Phaeacians is only one possible view.[46] Still, those with the leisure to while away hours in talk, exercise or competition on a regular basis were surely a minority at Athens – if not only the *jeunesse dorée* featured in Plato's dialogues – and serious athletes, requiring as they did money for trainers and travel as well as time, must usually have come from the élite.[47] It is interesting, therefore, to find some recent writers on Greek sport emphasizing democratic elements as well. So we may read that (allegedly) Solonian laws excluding slaves from exercise and rewarding victors at Olympia and Isthmia made athletics a positive obligation for all Athenian citizens, that the Olympic festival became more democratic over its first one hundred celebrations ('the competitions were still somewhat elitist but now they were more popular – in both senses of the word'), and that Croton's extraordinary domination of the *stadion* race from 588 to 488 was due to democracy.[48] For our purposes – the use of Demosthenes as a source on Athenian social history – the most instructive example of this tendency is a thoughtful contribution by Nick Fisher, one of a series of studies of the democratization of élite activities and institutions in classical Athens.[49] For Fisher, athletics was a source of social mobility, a way for poorer boys to parlay local prizes and the patronage of an admirer into fortune and fame. At the same time, 'the democratic system gradually, but positively, encouraged much wider participation in athletics and gymnastics' through the full calendar of athletic festivals.[50]

There is certainly evidence which might buttress Fisher's argument. Isocrates, for example, claims that 'our forefathers' compelled those who had sufficient means to devote themselves to horsemanship, athletics (*ta gymnasia*), hunting and philosophy. Unlike nowadays (he goes on, in the mid-fourth century), young men did not waste their time in gambling dens or with flute girls (7.45–8; cf. [Andoc.] 4.22). The implication (if we take this seriously) is that fewer among the élite were involved in athletics, leaving more of the field open to others. In addition, the theft of citizens' property from gymnasia was deterred by the death penalty (Dem. 24.113–14). The ascription of this measure to Solon might be taken to point to the democratic associations of exercise. Nevertheless, Fisher's case seems overstated to me. To consider Panathenaic prizes (the only ones on which we have reliable information): outsiders (to judge from the find-spots of Panathenaic amphoras) must have won many of the prizes for all-comers, only the top two athletes were rewarded (not four, as Fisher says)[51] – second-place earned only one-fifth as much as first – and most of the events reserved for individual Athenians were equestrian, not athletic. Moreover, though the inscription which is our main evidence for the fourth-century programme (*IG* ii^2 2311) is fragmentary, it does seem to indicate that the Panathenaea included more equestrian events than the contemporary Olympic festival and perhaps than the Pythian too. The sport of kings was no more democratic then than now. Finally, Fisher ignores the decidedly undemocratic ethos which pervaded competition even in classical Athens. Plutarch contrasts the spirit of obedience among the Spartans with those who swagger in the excess of their own power, abuse the judges at competitions, revile *chorēgoi* at the Dionysia, jeer at generals and gymnasiarchs ([Plut.] *Mor.* 817b). Is he thinking of democratic Athens? If so, he is wrong: citizens there obeyed officials as they did their naval commanders and chorus trainers (Xenophon, *Memorabilia* 3.5.18; cf. 21). This despite the rough justice they might receive, to be struck like slaves if they committed a foul and naked at that, so that they were all the more vulnerable and the insult was visible to all. Sport was not meant to be democratic: Aristotle notes, as a Socratic analogy which might be used against choosing magistrates by lot, that no one would pair athletes in a competition that way if they were not already known to be capable (Arist. *Rhetoric* 2.20.4). Nevertheless, Fisher's piece rightly raises the questions of ordinary Athenians' experience of athletic competition and training and of their attitudes towards them. Were these more complex than is usually thought or is implied by Aeschines? This brings us back to Demosthenes.

How does Demosthenes situate himself in relation to athletics and to Aeschines' rhetorical appropriation of it? In his biography, Plutarch demonstrates one avenue of approach. He accepts Aeschines' portrayal, but proffers an explanation. Demosthenes did indeed fail to pursue the studies appropriate to a boy of good family, but this was because he was defrauded by his guardians (and so unable to pay his teachers) and also due to his physical fragility: his mother would not let him work hard and his *paidagōgoi* would not force him (Plut. *Dem.* 4.3–5). There was one arena, however, to which Demosthenes did devote himself (Plutarch goes on), exercising himself (*engymnasamenos*) in his lawsuit against his guardians, and this training gave him confidence for public affairs. 'Just as Laomedon of Orchomenus took up running on the advice of his doctors and later became one of the best at the long race, so Demosthenes, entering courtroom competition in his own private interest, eventually came first in competition with speakers on the business of the *polis* just as if he were in the great crown games' (6.1–2). Plutarch's language – in particular, the use of a form of *apodyein*, 'to strip' (as if for athletic exercise) – confirms the parallel and the point: Demosthenes was the equal of any athlete. So too, when he later speaks of Demosthenes' worthy struggle against Philip on behalf of the Greeks, Plutarch uses a word with athletic overtones, *agōnizomenos* (12.7). The author of the *Lives of the Ten Orators* goes further, reporting Philip's comment that Demosthenes' speeches were like soldiers because of their warlike force, unlike Isocrates', mere athletes affording pleasure as in a show ([Plut.] *Mor.* 845d).

The parallel between athletic and rhetorical exercise was a commonplace in Demosthenes' own day as well (for example, Isoc. 15.180–5, 295). But Demosthenes himself does not follow this approach. Instead, he pursues what we might call a democratic strategy. Aeschines is welcome to boast of his athletic associations – though it is Philip, and not the jurors of Athens, who are his team-mates (Dem. 18.41; cf. 67). Demosthenes joins the mass of Athenians who do not compete as athletes (or at any rate not at a very high level), but have a lively interest in those who do. In his speech against Leptines' law, Demosthenes praises his fellow citizens' lack of envy for others. 'For all time', he says, 'you have bestowed the greatest gifts on those who win crowns in athletic competitions. And you have not begrudged them or allotted them less honour because, in the nature of things, only a few can have a share' (Dem. 20.141). Now, this speech, delivered before a panel of *nomothetai* in 355, may have been Demosthenes' first political performance. Like the *First Philippic* and its image of the barbarian boxer, it predates by some years the embassies to Philip and the rivalry with Aeschines which resulted. There can be no suspicion, then, that Demosthenes' self-presentation in these speeches, as a man who knows something of sport but does not compete himself, is called forth solely by Aeschines' rhetoric. It may in fact be rooted in reality; the tradition Plutarch follows may be accurate in its portrayal of a wordy weakling. Surely, however, it must also bespeak a current within the Athenian citizen community. The Demosthenes of *Against Leptines* and the *First Philippic* was a young man, pushing thirty and then just past it, an age when someone of his social standing might still take regular exercise, even compete with some hope of success. (Phaenippus is attacked for his purchase of a chariot when he is still young and vigorous enough to go on foot: Dem. 42.24.) That he had not and did not might make him seem an outsider to some in his audiences – as his reputation as a water-drinker was meant to later on.[52] The mere mention of athletics, a token of interest and knowledge in an area ordinary Athenians thought important, might mollify some he addressed. We may compare contemporary politicians: American presidents like to throw out the first pitch at the World Series, though their actual involvement in baseball varies widely. (George Bush played first base for Yale, while Bill Clinton's interest in playing the field seems to be mainly metaphorical.) The gesture itself is what matters. This consideration may motivate an anecdote about athletes in another early speech by Demosthenes, *Against Meidias* 21 (347/6) and the way the story is told.

This speech deals with a punch Meidias delivered to Demosthenes' cheek in the theatre of Dionysus and Demosthenes' willingness to turn the other one – or at least to seek recompense in the controlled context of an Athenian courtroom. About a third of the way through, Demosthenes offers three examples of similar outrages and their consequences. The first concerns two athletes (21.71):

> Everyone knows – or if not everyone, many people – that on one occasion Euthynus the famous wrestler, the young lad (*ton neaniskon*), defended himself even (*kai*) against Sophilus the pancratiast. (He was a strong man, dark – I am sure some of you know the man I mean.) They were in Samos, just passing the time privately with some friends; and because he thought him insolent, he defended himself so vigorously that he actually (*kai*) killed him.
>
> (MacDowell's translation, adapted)

Recent analyses have done much to illuminate how subtly Demosthenes uses this story.[53] Like the other anecdotes, it is an object lesson on how a good citizen ought not to respond to provocation. Meidias' offence was certainly as serious as any. Men have killed for less, even a wrestler, inured to physical risk and hurt, insulted as a private citizen and not, as Demosthenes was, in the

174

course of civic duties as *chorēgos*. Demosthenes' restraint is all the more remarkable in that he was (like the *neaniskos* Euthynus) a young man and so liable to act rashly. In fact, Demosthenes understates his age in *Against Meidias* (21.154), which makes his self-control seem more striking still. The effect (as of so much else in this speech) is to align Demosthenes with the jurors and the city's democratic institutions and increase his distance from Meidias' extravagance – Meidias' wealth is a constant refrain – and from the upper-crust milieu of the gymnasium, where fights and feuds are frequent.

So far, so good. We may doubt, however, whether all the jurors – a large crowd, as always – would have grasped all these nuances. The narration is casual, even confusing. It is far from obvious, for example, that it was Euthynus who killed Sophilus, and not the other way around. The Greek is grammatically ambiguous; at least one ancient commentator got it wrong.[54] Nor need we believe that the incident was as well known as Demosthenes pretends: it took place some time before, in far-off Samos, out of the public eye. I suspect that there were many jurors who sat through this story more like John Keats ('Darkling I listen') than Douglas MacDowell and the other fine scholars who have examined it so searchingly. Nevertheless, to them (and they may have been the majority) Demosthenes seemed no less a democrat than to their sharper associates. In their case, however, this was simply because (once again) he told them a story about sport like a regular guy, and in the off-hand and allusive way a regular guy might tell it. (Plutarch observes that Demosthenes' manner of speaking was extraordinarily pleasing to the masses [*tois pollois*], though Demetrius of Phalerum and other men of taste held it in low regard: *Dem.* 11.3.) Demosthenes' deployment of athletics, then, indicates that it was contested terrain, open to both élite pitches like Aeschines' and his own democratic spin. And the Samos story – in which a young wrestler beats the odds (note the emphatic use of *kai*) to kill a more seasoned adversary – confirms what I argued earlier: plausibility is sometimes beside the point. The way something is said, the very fact that it is said at all, may matter most. Similarly, Demosthenes' willingness to ignore plausibility in a courtroom context makes our reliance on what he says about any aspect of the world he worked in more dangerous. At the same time, it adds something significant to our understanding of that world.

NOTES

* Thanks for information and advice to Craig Cooper, Nick Fisher, Virginia Hunter, David Mirhady, Lene Rubinstein and Ian Worthington. I am all the more grateful in that some of these scholars hold different views than those I express here.

1 A.H.M. Jones, 'The Economic Basis of the Athenian Democracy', *Past and Present* 1 (1952), pp. 13–31 (quotation, p. 19) = Jones, *Athenian Democracy* (Oxford: 1960), pp. 3–20 (quotation, p. 12).

2 A.H.M. Jones, 'The Athens of Demosthenes' = *Athenian Democracy*, pp. 23–38 (at pp. 36–7).

3 A.H.M. Jones, 'The Social Structure of Athens in the Fourth Century B.C.', *Economic History Review* 8 (1955), pp. 141–55 (quotation, p. 147) = *Athenian Democracy*, pp. 75–96 (quotation, p. 84). Cf. A.H.M. Jones, 'Slavery in the Ancient World', *Economic History Review* 9 (1956), pp. 185–99 (at p. 185) = M.I. Finley (ed.), *Slavery in Classical Antiquity: Views and Controversies* (Cambridge: 1960), pp. 1–15 (at p. 1): 'persons of relatively humble means'.

4 J. Morris, 'A.H.M. Jones', *Past and Present* 47 (1970), pp. 147–50 (at p. 147).

5 See S.C. Todd, 'The Use and Abuse of the Attic Orators', *G&R*² 37 (1990), pp. 159–78 (at pp. 164–7). See also the chapters of Buckler, especially his Appendix (Chapter 4), and Milns (Chapter 7).

6 For example, Pseudo-Andocides 4 *Against Alcibiades* (see now D. Gribble, 'Rhetoric and History in [Andocides] 4, *Against Alcibiades*', *CQ*² 47 [1997], pp. 367–91), Pseudo-Demosthenes 25 *Against Aristogeiton* 1 (see now R. Sealey, *Demosthenes and His Time: A Study in Defeat* [New York: 1993], pp. 237–9), and perhaps Lysias 1 (as argued by J.R. Porter, 'Adultery by the Book: Lysias 1 (*On the Murder of Eratosthenes*) and Comic *Diegesis*', *EMC* 41 [1997], pp. 421–53).

7 See now E.M. Harris, 'Demosthenes' Speech against Meidias', *HSCP* 92 (1989), pp. 117–36 (delivered), D.M. MacDowell, *Demosthenes Against Meidias (Oration 21)* (Oxford: 1990), pp. 23–8 (may have been delivered, but not necessarily in the present form), P.J. Wilson, 'Demosthenes 21 (*Against Meidias*): Democratic Abuse', *PCPS* 37 (1991), pp. 164–95 (at p. 165) (probably not delivered), and J. Ober, 'Power and Oratory in Democratic Athens: Demosthenes 21, Against Meidias' in Ian Worthington (ed.), *Persuasion: Greek Rhetoric in Action* (London: 1994), pp. 85–108 (at pp. 90–2) (delivered). My discussion in the second section of this chapter assumes that the speech was delivered much (at least) as we now have it. On revision of speeches in general, see Ian Worthington, 'Greek Oratory, Revision of Speeches and the Problem of Historical Reliability', *C&M* 42 (1991), pp. 55–74 and 'History and Oratorical Exploitation' in Worthington (ed.), *Persuasion*, pp. 109–29 (at pp. 109–18). On the special problems of Assembly speeches, see C. Tuplin, 'Demosthenes' *Olynthiacs* and the Character of the Demegoric Corpus', *Historia* 47 (1998), pp. 276–320.

8 See Hippocrates, *Epidemics* 6.8.30, cf. Galen, *On Anatomical Procedures* 7.13. (I hope to discuss slaves in Greek sport at greater length elsewhere.)

9 For the possibility that some trials lasted longer than a day, see Ian Worthington, 'The Duration of an Athenian Political Trial', *JHS* 109 (1989), pp. 204–7.

10 On jurors' lack of familiarity with the laws, see now A.W. Nightingale, 'Plato's Lawcode in Context: Rule by Written Law in Athens and Magnesia', *CQ²* 49 (1999), pp. 100–22 (at pp. 105–13). For a different view of the oath's efficacy, see E.M. Harris, 'Law and Oratory' in Ian Worthington (ed.), *Persuasion: Greek Rhetoric in Action* (London: 1994), pp. 130–50 (at pp. 132–7), and Mirhady, Chapter 6.

11 S.C. Todd, *The Shape of Athenian Law* (Oxford: 1993), p. 60. Aristotle offers advice on how to argue in the face of the law and the juror's oath (Arist. *Rhetoric* 1.15.12, 1.15.17): see D.C. Mirhady, 'Aristotle on the Rhetoric of Law', *GRBS* 31 (1990), pp. 393–410.

12 See M. Golden, *Children and Childhood in Classical Athens* (Baltimore and London: 1990), pp. 27–8.

13 See Alcidamas, *On the Writers of Written Speeches* 13, Arist. *Rhetoric* 3.12.2.

14 See Sealey, *Demosthenes*, pp. 247–8, replying to M. Golden, 'Demosthenes and the Age of Majority at Athens', *Phoenix* 33 (1979), pp. 25–38 (at p. 33).

15 J.A. Barnes, *A Pack of Lies: Towards a Sociology of Lying* (Cambridge: 1994), p. 30.

16 See R.A. Knox, '"So Mischievous a Beaste"? The Athenian *Demos* and its Treatment of Politicians', *G&R²* 32 (1985), pp. 132–61.

17 Lying and evolution: see Barnes, *Pack of Lies*, pp. 147–54, L. Rue, *By the Grace of Guile: The Role of Deception in Natural History and Human Affairs* (New York and Oxford: 1994), pp. 82–127; cf. I. McEwan, *Enduring Love* (London: 1997), pp. 180–1: 'Pitiless objectivity, especially about ourselves, was always a doomed social strategy. We've descended from the indignant, passionate tellers of half truths who in order to convince others, simultaneously convinced themselves. Over generations, success had winnowed us out, and with success came our defect, carried deep in the genes like ruts in a cart track – when it didn't suit us we couldn't agree on what was in front of us.' Difficulties in detection: see P. Ekman, M. O'Sullivan and M.G. Frank, 'A Few Can Catch a Liar', *Psychological Science* 10 (1999), pp. 263–6.

18 See A.R.W. Harrison, *The Law of Athens* 2 (Oxford: 1971), pp. 99–100.

19 E.M. Harris, 'Demosthenes' Speech against Meidias', p. 117.

20 L. Pearson, 'Historical Allusions in the Attic Orators', *CP* 36 (1941), pp. 209–29 (quotation, p. 209).

21 S. Johnstone, 'Cracking the Code of Silence: Athenian Legal Oratory and the Histories of Slaves and Women' in S.R. Joshel and S. Murnaghan (eds.), *Women and Slaves in Greco-Roman Culture: Differential Equations* (London and New York: 1998), pp. 221–35; cf. L. Foxhall, 'The Law and the Lady: Women and Legal Proceedings in Classical Athens' in Foxhall and A.D.E. Lewis (eds.), *Greek Law in its Political Setting: Justifications not Justice* (Oxford: 1996), pp. 133–52 (at pp. 143–9).

22 J. Ober, *Mass and Elite in Democratic Athens* (Princeton: 1989).

23 Sealey, *Demosthenes*, pp. 150–1, E.M. Harris, *Aeschines and Athenian Politics* (New York and Oxford: 1993), pp. 15–16.

24 Sealey, *Demosthenes*, p. 152, on Demosthenes 18.23.

25 See, for example, P.C. Millett, *Lending and Borrowing in Ancient Athens* (Cambridge: 1991), p. 3, E.E. Cohen, *Athenian Economy and Society: A Banking Perspective* (Princeton: 1992), pp. 36–40, Todd, *Shape of Athenian Law*, p. 276, J. Roy, 'An Alternative Sexual Morality for Classical Athenians', *G&R*² 44 (1997), pp. 11–22 (at p. 22 n. 24), N.R.E. Fisher, ' "Workshops of Villains": Was There Much Organised Crime in Classical Athens?' in K. Hopwood (ed.), *Organised Crime in Antiquity* (London: 1999), pp. 53–96 (at pp. 55–6, 64, 74).

26 Choices: see, for example, R.G. Osborne, 'Law in Action in Classical Athens', *JHS* 105 (1985), pp. 40–58, Todd, *Shape of Athenian Law*, pp. 160–3, and Fisher, ' "Workshops" ', pp. 63–4. Severity: see E.M. Harris, 'Did the Athenians Regard Seduction as a Worse Crime than Rape?', *CQ*² 40 (1990), pp. 370–7, D. Cohen, *Law, Sexuality, and Society* (Cambridge: 1991), p. 178 n. 20; *contra*: C. Carey, 'Rape and Adultery in Athenian Law', *CQ*² 45 (1995), pp. 407–17. This, however, may be justified on the grounds that the argument to the *ephetai* is based only in part on their area of special competence while every Athenian citizen might have been aware of so fundamental a feature of the legal system.

27 See now D.A. Russell, '*Ēthos* in Oratory and Rhetoric' in C. Pelling (ed.), *Characterization and Individuality in Greek Literature* (Oxford: 1990), pp. 197–212, and C. Carey, 'Rhetorical Means of Persuasion' in Ian Worthington (ed.), *Persuasion: Greek Rhetoric in Action* (London: 1994), pp. 26–45 (at pp. 39–43).

28 Cf. T.L. Papillon, *Rhetorical Studies in the Aristocratea of Demosthenes* (New York: 1998), pp. 30–2.

29 Compare Lysias 12.38 with 16.17, 21.19, 25.12–13.

30 P. Harding, 'Rhetoric and Politics in Fourth-Century Athens', *Phoenix* 41 (1987), pp. 25–39 (at p. 32).

31 See Todd, *Shape of Athenian Law*, pp. 258–62.

32 L.H. Pratt, *Lying and Poetry from Homer to Pindar: Falsehood and Deception in Archaic Greek Poetics* (Ann Arbor: 1993), p. 57.

33 See W.R. Connor, 'Tribes, Festivals and Processions: Civic Ceremonial and Political Manipulation in Archaic Greece', *JHS* 107 (1987), pp. 40–50 (at pp. 42–7).

34 See P. Harding, 'Comedy and Rhetoric' in Ian Worthington (ed.), *Persuasion: Greek Rhetoric in Action* (London: 1994), pp. 196–221 (at pp. 202–6).

35 See, for example, R. Garner, *Law and Society in Classical Athens* (London: 1987), pp. 95–130, Wilson, 'Demosthenes 21 (*Against Meidias*)', pp. 175–80, E. Hall, 'Lawcourt Dramas: The Power of Performance in Greek Forensic Oratory', *BICS* 40 (1995), pp. 39–58, W.J. Slater, 'The Theatricality of Justice', *CB* 71 (1995), pp. 143–57 (at pp. 143–6), A.C. Scafuro, *The Forensic Stage: Settling Disputes in Graeco-Roman New Comedy* (Princeton: 1997), and A. Lanni, 'Spectator Sport or Serious Politics? οἱ περιεστηκότες and the Athenian Lawcourts', *JHS* 117 (1997), pp. 183–9. Compare the remarks of Cooper, Chapter 8.

36 See V. Bers, 'Tragedy and Rhetoric' in Ian Worthington (ed.), *Persuasion: Greek Rhetoric in Action* (London: 1994), pp. 176–95, Hall, 'Lawcourt Dramas', pp. 54–5, P.J. Wilson, 'Tragic Rhetoric: The Use

of Tragedy and the Tragic in the Fourth Century' in M.S. Silk (ed.), *Tragedy and the Tragic: Greek Theatre and Beyond* (Oxford: 1996), pp. 310–31.

37 Cf. M. Gagarin, *Antiphon: The Speeches* (Cambridge: 1997), p. 105.

38 See K.J. Dover, *Greek Popular Morality in the Time of Plato and Aristotle* (Berkeley and Los Angeles: 1974), pp. 23–33, A.S. Halliwell, 'The Uses of Laughter in Greek Culture', CQ^2 41 (1991), pp. 279–96 (at pp. 292–4), P. Harding, 'Comedy and Rhetoric', Hall, 'Lawcourt Dramas', pp. 54–5.

39 Dem. 23.206, cf. Lys. 24.18.

40 So Hall, 'Lawcourt Dramas', p. 43, Lanni, 'Spectator Sport or Serious Politics?', p. 183 n. 7.

41 Lanni, 'Spectator Sport or Serious Politics?', pp. 187, 189.

42 See, for example, C. Mossé, 'The "World of the *Emporium*" in the Private Speeches of Demosthenes' in P. Garnsey, K. Hopkins and C.R. Whittaker (eds.), *Trade in the Ancient Economy* (London: 1983), pp. 53–63, V.J. Hunter, *Policing Athens: Social Control in the Attic Lawsuits, 420–320 B.C.* (Princeton: 1994).

43 Dem. 19.199, 237, 249, 281.

44 Ober, *Mass and Elite*, p. 283.

45 R. Lane Fox, 'Aeschines and Athenian Democracy' in R. Osborne and S. Hornblower (eds.), *Ritual, Finance, Politics: Athenian Democratic Accounts Presented to David Lewis* (Oxford: 1994), pp. 135–55 (at pp. 138–9).

46 See now C. Mann, 'Krieg, Sport und Adelskultur. Zur Entstehung des griechischen Gymnasions', *Klio* 80 (1998), pp. 7–21.

47 See M. Golden, *Sport and Society in Ancient Greece* (Cambridge: 1998), pp. 141–5, 158–62, and D.G. Kyle, 'Games, Prizes, and Athletes in Greek Sport: Patterns and Perspectives (1975–1997)', *CB* 74 (1998), pp. 103–27 (at pp. 120–5).

48 See M.-M. Mactoux, 'Lois de Solon sur les esclaves et formation d'une société esclavagiste' in T. Yuge and M. Doi (eds.), *Forms of Control and Subordination in Antiquity* (Leiden: 1988), pp. 331–54 (at 341–5), D.G. Kyle, 'The First Hundred Olympiads: A Process of Decline or Democratization?', *Nikephoros* 10 (1997), pp. 53–75 (quotation, p. 74), Stephen G. Miller, 'Naked Democracy' in P. Flensted-Jensen and T.H. Nielsen (eds.) *Polis and Politics* (Copenhagen: 2000), pp. 277–96.

49 N. Fisher, 'Gymnasia and the Democratic Values of Leisure' in P. Cartledge, P. Millett and S. von Reden (eds.), *Kosmos: Essays in Order, Conflict and Community in Classical Athens* (Cambridge: 1998), pp. 84–104; cf. 'Symposiasts, Fisheaters and Flatterers: Social Mobility and Moral Concern in Old Comedy' in D. Harvey and J. Wilkins (eds.), *Aristophanes and His Rivals* (London: 2000), pp. 355–96.

50 Fisher, 'Gymnasia', p. 93.

51 Ibid., p. 90.

52 See Demosthenes 6.29–30, 19.46.

53 See especially MacDowell, *Demosthenes Against Meidias*, pp. 288–9, Wilson, 'Demosthenes 21 (*Against Meidias*)', pp. 169–72, Ober, 'Power and Oratory', pp. 95–7, N. Fisher, 'Masculinity and the Law in Classical Athens' in L. Foxhall and J. Salmon (eds.), *When Men Were Men:*

Masculinity, Power and Identity in Classical Antiquity (London and New York: 1999), pp. 68–97 (at pp. 80–1).

54 M.R. Dilts (ed.), *Scholia Demosthenica* 2 (Leipzig: 1986), p. 186 (section 219 *ad loc.*).

6

DEMOSTHENES AS
ADVOCATE

The private speeches*

David C. Mirhady

The title of this chapter is respectfully borrowed from a lecture
published a generation ago by the foremost scholar of Greek law of
his time, perhaps of this century, Hans Julius Wolff.[1] Wolff was
addressing a meeting of Berlin jurists, not specialists in Greek
history, let alone Greek law, so his comments were meant to draw a
general picture of the classical Athenian legal process as much as of
Demosthenes himself. Wolff was also primarily a legal historian and
was little interested in the sort of social aspects of Athenian law that
have become more common in recent scholarship.[2] He and his
listeners were particularly interested in characterizing Demosthenes'
activity as a sort of profession or trade (*Gewerbe, Beruf*). The trade
would of course be closest to that of a modern lawyer, though this
characterization has sometimes been resisted. After all, Demosthenes and the other speech-writers (*logographoi*) of classical Athens did
not as a rule represent their clients in court. They had no special
qualifications and no legally recognized status. Every litigant was
supposed to argue his own case, ostensibly without expert help.
Nevertheless, in the absence of any institutionally recognized legal
experts in Athens at all, the *logographoi* with their rhetorical training
and practical experience writing speeches for others could fulfill
many of the roles played by today's lawyers. They offered legal
advice at various stages of litigation before finally writing up a
speech for their clients to use before the people's court.

Aristophanes' dig in *Clouds* 466–8 about how the trained speech-
writer can earn popularity – as well as considerable sums of money
– through his trade is only the first of a number of texts that
suggest hostility against the perceived corruption of speech-
writing.[3] Isocrates denies ever having had any connection with the

courts (15.36–8) despite our having six forensic speeches (16–21) that are attributed to him on good authority. Aeschines criticizes Demosthenes both simply by referring to him as 'a certain speech-writer' (1.94, cf. 2.180) and by mentioning that Demosthenes teaches techniques of speech that include deception (1.117, 170). He also levels a charge against Demosthenes as private logographer that has vexed every commentator on Demosthenes, namely, that Demosthenes wrote a speech for pay for the banker Pasion, presumably our Demosthenes 36, and then revealed its contents to Pasion's opponent Apollodorus (2.165; cf. Plut. *Dem.* 15.1–2), for whom he wrote our Demosthenes 45. Speeches 36 and 45, if actually both by Demosthenes, do show a remarkable flexibility on the part of a single individual to invent such powerful arguments praising and vilifying the very same individuals. Demosthenes himself appears to have been sensitive to criticisms of his involvement in others' private disputes. At the end of *Against Zenothemis* (32.32), the speaker, Demon, admits that his relative Demosthenes has helped him and quotes what Demosthenes had said to him when asked for help: he denied ever having come forward to plead any private cases since he entered political life. In another speech, however, these scruples do not prevent Demosthenes from using Lacritus' activity as a teacher of forensic pleading against him (35.41). Anaximenes includes advice about how to deal with this issue in his handbook (*Rhetorica ad Alexandrum* 36.37–42).

There is no disagreement, however, that from his debut on the forensic stage, Demosthenes distinguished himself as its master. His own legal campaign to recover the inheritance left him by his father, which is documented by no less than five extant speeches (27–31), is a *tour de force*. It served not only to win his dispute, even if not to recover his entire legacy (Plut. *Dem.* 6.1–2), but also to advertise his skills to a broad range of clients who kept him employed writing speeches for them for much of the rest of his life. What made Demosthenes' forensic oratory so effective was, I will argue, not simply his abilities with the language and with narrative (although these are estimable and were as highly admired in antiquity as they are today)[4] but his mastery of the technical aspects of law. In particular, his success was due to his employment of the various forms of documentary evidence that were available to the Athenian logographer, documents such as laws, witness testimony, contracts and challenges. As Demosthenes himself points out in his first speech, he is competing against opponents who are not only adept at speaking, by which he is presumably referring to their ability with language and narrative, but who are able in preparing their cases (27.2). They understand their position *vis-à-vis* the law, the need to collect witnesses, and the strategies to be employed in documenting maneuvers employed at preliminary hearings. In the democratic courts of the fourth century, as much as character invective, emotional pleas and cogent narrative played their roles, it was the successful preparation and employment of documentary evidence that was the key to success. As Demosthenes says in defense of himself in the political sphere (Plut. *Dem.* 8), 'the man who prepares what he is going to say is the true democrat'.[5]

There is some irony in Aristotle's description of such documentary evidence as 'artless proofs' (*atechnoi pisteis*).[6] The term reveals that for him they are forms of argumentation that lay somehow outside the craft or *technē* of the orator. They were formulated ostensibly by someone other than the speech-writer and delivered only intermittently by the court secretary during breaks in the oral delivery of the litigant's speech.[7] Aristotle's characterization of the documents as 'artless' stems both from the fifth-century sophists, who privileged argumentation based on probability over more formal means of proof and dispute resolution,[8] such as oath-swearing, and from a fairly widespread distrust among élite circles regarding statements committed to writing.

From the end of the fifth century, when the ideology of Athenian democracy saw a pronounced shift away from the unbridled popular sovereignty of the Assembly to one checked by the sovereign authority of law,[9] especially written law (Andoc. 1.87), the written word took on ever increasing importance within the Athenian judicial framework.[10] First and foremost there was the text of the laws themselves, which each juror was sworn to uphold as part of his dicastic oath.[11] As Carey writes, 'the juror's oath, and the strenuous efforts of Athenian litigants to prove that the law supports their stance on the subject at issue, indicate that the jurors did feel bound by the law and that for the most part they consciously sought to make their decisions conform to the law'.[12]

Simultaneously with the shift to the sovereignty of law, the creation of the institution of public arbitration forced a further commitment to the written word.[13] From the end of the fifth century on, almost all private disputes had to be heard first before a democratically selected (that is, by lottery) public arbitrator (*AP* 53.4–5). Unlike the private arbitrator, who was often empowered by the disputing parties to impose a resolution on them, the public arbitrator's decision could be appealed. What gave his role special force, however, was that only the evidence that had been produced before him, committed to writing and deposited in his evidence jar could be brought subsequently before a democratic court (*AP* 53.2; cf. Dem. 54.27). All evidence thus had to be committed to writing and disclosed both to the arbitrator and to the opponents.

This process of committing evidence to writing was completed sometime in the 370s, when it appears that witnesses were no longer required actually to give testimony in court at all.[14] While their presence was still required, they did not speak: their pre-recorded testimony was simply read aloud to the court by the court secretary. Demosthenes describes the situation (29.18):

> having given his testimony with the other witnesses (at the arbitration), he made no denial of the fact, when, standing by the plaintiff's side in the popular court, he heard his testimony read.[15]

From this passage, it is apparent that the witness in court does not even have to affirm what is read.

Among the canon of Attic orators' writings that are preserved for us, Demosthenes' are the first that are all composed only after this final great shift to written evidence is complete. The earlier orators, Antiphon, Andocides, Lysias, Isocrates, and Isaeus, all employed *atechnoi pisteis* to some extent. However, Demosthenes is the first to be able to exploit the full ramifications of the shift.[16] With a convert's zeal, his devotion to the use of these documents far outstrips that of his later contemporaries, Aeschines, Lycurgus, Hyperides, and Dinarchus. The earlier orators all relied on witnesses who would stand before the court and say something – we do not know what exactly – that confirmed the truth of something the litigant claimed. Perhaps they said as little as 'what he said is true'. Demosthenes, on the other hand, had a fixed, written document read aloud, a document whose precise meaning and consequences could be assessed by everyone present and whose contents were known in advance by both parties to the dispute. He emphasizes this point in *Against Stephanus* (45.44–5):

> bear in mind that the reason why the law requires people to give evidence in written form is that it may not be open to them to strike out any part of what has been written, or add anything to it … . Who will ever be convicted of giving false testimony, if he is to depose to what he pleases,

and be accountable only for what he pleases? No, the law does not thus make a distinction in these matters, and you must not listen to such a thing either. The straightforward and honest course is this: 'What stands written? To what have you deposed? Show that this is true. For you have written in your plea in answer to the complaint these words, "I have given true testimony in testifying to what is contained in the deposition" – not "to this or that in the deposition".'

The rhetorical handbooks of Aristotle and Anaximenes lay out systematic advice about how to argue both for and against each item of documentary evidence,[17] but these are somewhat compromised by a sort of sophistic freedom of thought. Their advice is not necessarily practical, since much of it would be unpalatable in an Athenian court. Arguments that Aristotle recommends for use in arguing against written laws, for instance, are not found in the Attic orators at all.[18] The rhetoricians likely took as their starting point the simple list of documents placed in the evidence jar after the arbitration or the *anakrisis*, the preliminary hearing before the magistrate. This list consisted of the written charge (*enklēma*) (and presumably the defendant's formal denial, *antigraphe*), witness testimony (*martyria*) and challenges (*proklēseis*) (*AP* 53.2). In Aristotle's canonical treatment of these documents in *Rhetoric* 1.15, the written charge gives way to a discussion of laws. The discussion of witness testimony expands into a discussion of both witness testimony and contracts (since a contract's credibility depends in any case on its being supported by witness testimony and its persuasive function rests on its being somewhat like a private law between the contracting parties). Challenges give way to discussions of torture and oath, the dispute-ending procedures about which challenges are made.

The practical reality of such argumentation differs markedly in many respects from the prescriptions of the handbooks. The handbooks suggest, for instance, a clear break between narration of the events at issue and the proof for that narration. In the speeches narrative and proof are closely integrated. In the earlier *logographoi*, especially Lysias and Isaeus, narrative and proof appear to be largely directed by the narrative strategies of the writers, documentary evidence appearing in a largely ancillary role. In Demosthenes this independence disappears: the documentary evidence itself provides the roadmap to the narrative. Likewise, Aristotle gives pride of place to his 'artistic proofs' (*entechnoi pisteis*), arguments based on circumstantial evidence (*tekmēria*) and probabilities (*eikota*) educed from the speech, from the character of the speaker and from the emotional response of the listeners; he relegates documentary evidence to the status of 'inartistic proof'. In his private speeches, Demosthenes reverses this order. Indeed, Aristotle himself admits that documentary evidence is found in lawcourt speeches in particular (*Rhetoric* 1.15.1). As Demosthenes says to the judges at the end of his second speech against Aphobus, 'you have heard sufficient proofs from witnesses, from evidence, and from probabilities' (23; cf. 30.25). Written witness testimony is his proof *par excellence*.

In the following pages, I shall retrace Demosthenes' argumentation in the series of speeches that he wrote concerning his own inheritance. Demosthenes' strategies vary according to the situation, but his devotion to the use of documentary evidence is clear throughout.[19]

From the beginning of his first speech against Aphobus (27), Demosthenes has his opponent over a barrel. He attacks him on every material aspect of his case and backs up each line of argumentation, first with admissions (*homologiai*) wrested from Aphobus (10, 24, 34, 39, 42–3), and then with witness testimony that confutes each point in what is left of Aphobus' defense (8, 17, 22, 25–6, 28, 33, 41, 46). Aphobus is one of three guardians to whom Demosthenes' father entrusted his estate until Demosthenes came of age. According to Demosthenes, they have stolen almost everything, so he has initiated litigation against each of them. Demosthenes clearly had to anticipate the need for such witness testimony long before his encounter at the popular court, and he laid the foundation for his case early. The witnesses he provides, despite what has been written by Sally Humphreys and Stephen Todd,[20] are not necessarily partisan. Many of them were admittedly friends and relatives of Demosthenes, but his opponents were supposed to belong to this circle also. Most of Demosthenes' witnesses are not even identifiable from the text of the speech, though of course the text of the testimony itself, which we do not have, did identify them. Like so much else in democratic Athens the identity and status of the witness, besides his being a free male, was irrelevant.[21] A witness was similar to the judges who were to decide the case; he was simply a free man, though one who had some relevant, specific knowledge. Many of the judges in fact know the broad outlines of the case already, so Demosthenes can claim them as friendly to his side, implicitly calling on them as his witnesses (57; cf. 29.49). Where Demosthenes is not in a position to produce witnesses, such as on the point of his maternal grandfather's indebtedness in the second speech against Aphobus (28), he makes clear that this is only because of a trick by his opponents, which left him with no time to locate a knowledgeable witness. Only then does he resort to other forms of evidence (*tekmēria*: 2).

In his construction of the events of his case, Demosthenes must teach (*didaskein*: 27.3) the judges not only about the events themselves, but what sorts of evidence about those events are most significant (*megistos*), accurate or detailed (*akribos*) and clear (*saphos, phaneros*). He thus constructs several hierarchies of evidence, which will vary somewhat according to the circumstances of the case and the sorts of evidence available. In his first speeches against Aphobus (27–8), his opponents themselves are at the top of his list. They are his 'greatest' (*megistoi*) witnesses through having registered Demosthenes in the highest tax bracket (27.7; cf. 28.4), even if they were compelled to do this because the size of the estate made it impossible to hide (27.8). Demosthenes' description of his opponents as 'witnesses' involves, of course, a great conceit; the opponents do not appear as witnesses (*martyres*) in any technical sense at all. No statement from them will be read aloud in court stating that they entered him in the highest tax bracket. Nevertheless they did do so, and nobody denies it. Beyond the significance (namely, probative value) of the evidence, the second hierarchy involves accuracy or extent of detail (*akribeia*), for the judges must gain 'accurate' knowledge (27.1, 7, 9). Thus, after the important but blunt evidence of the tax bracket, Demosthenes goes on to detail his father's precise property holdings (27.9–17). A third hierarchy involves the clarity of the presentation (27.1, 47–8), which results from the accumulation of points that are demonstrated in support of Demosthenes' claims.

Most of the witnesses whose testimony Demosthenes has read aloud are anonymous. The identities of the witnesses who provide testimony in 27.22, 26, 28, 33 and 39, for instance, are never stated. Someone, we do not know who, needs to say, for instance, that Aphobus was in charge of a factory that should have realized thirty minae per year (27.18). It seems likely that in all these cases, which involve partial admissions on the part of Aphobus, the witnesses were people at a preliminary hearing, perhaps the public arbitration, who were there for the express purpose of witnessing what exactly each party said under questioning from the other side, as is suggested in 27.41: 'take and read for them these testimonies of those before whom they answered'. Admissions (*homologiai*) are particularly powerful because of the Athenian principle that those things upon which there is an admission are binding (*kyria*; cf. Dem. 56.2 and Isoc. 18.24).

The first witnesses that Demosthenes identifies, in Speech 27, are the two guardians he has not yet charged, Demophon and Therippides, and his uncle (by marriage) Demochares, though he claims there are many other witnesses (unnamed) (14, 18). Aphobus admitted to Demochares certain facts of the case, to which Demochares now gives witness (15). Demosthenes puts repeated emphasis on the fact that Aphobus gave written acknowledgement to the other guardians of receiving a dowry, though he does not produce this document (14, 16). He is also able to make use of the accounts that were submitted in writing by his guardians (19) and of answers that they gave, in the form of transcribed testimony, at preliminary hearings (42). The fact that his opponents disagree among themselves in the recorded documents adds particular weight to Demosthenes' position (43; cf. 28.3).

Demosthenes ridicules the immateriality of the points supported by Aphobus' witnesses (25–6) and Aphobus' inability to provide witnesses on the material points (21, 49, 51, 54, 28.1): 'demand that he provide witnesses on each point' (51). Aphobus' witnesses' testimony about the baseness of Moeriades' character is a red herring; they ought to be saying where Demosthenes' slaves are. Aphobus also ought to have witnesses for goods delivered (21). It is important to recognize that Demosthenes does not impugn Aphobus' witnesses directly; he simply argues that their testimony is immaterial. Too much has been made of the possible corruptibility of witnesses in Athens;[22] the references to it are relatively rare. Where they occur, as in *Against Onetor* 1 and *Against Conon* (discussed below), the false witnesses are described as having been in league with the opponent throughout; they are co-conspirators against the speaker. Demosthenes argues that while Aphobus has made various statements, he has given no demonstration, no *epideixis*, of them, the *epideixis* consisting of witness testimony (51). Demosthenes makes no demand here for witnesses of a particular status or impartiality; he simply demands witnesses.

While arguing his case, Demosthenes, like all litigants, is constructing a rhetorical epistemology, a system whereby some sources of knowledge are deemed more credible than others for persuasive reasons. In the epistemology that Demosthenes constructs, it is interesting to note that he argues that more accurate or exact (*akribesteron*) knowledge could actually be gained, not just from witnesses' testimony, but from the text of his father's will, which has gone missing (40):

> You would, however, have had more exact knowledge of the matter, if they had been willing to give up to me the will which my father left; for it contained (so my mother tells me) a statement of all the property that my father left, along with instructions regarding the funds from which these men were to take what had been given them, and regarding the letting of the property.

Aristotle strangely makes no provision for wills in his scheme of *atechnoi pisteis*; it is likely that he saw them as a form of contract, which, in turn, he considered a sort of particular law (*Rhetoric* 1.15).

Demosthenes employs arguments about laws twice in *Against Aphobus* 1. The first time he simply refers to a law that expresses the commonly known Athenian principle that dowry monies in arrears are owed 18 per cent interest (27.17). The second time he actually has several laws read aloud (27.58). The interpretation of them has been vexed, but Demosthenes argues, based on inference from them, that his guardians were required to lease out his estate at a rate that would have realized about 12 per cent per annum. (One could wish that all investments won such a high guaranteed return.) On close examination, Demosthenes' employment of these laws appears unclear and hardly to his credit. But the judges do not have the benefit of close examination. Within the overall context of his argumentation it is important for Demosthenes simply that he appear to be faithful to the letter of the law, to be using the law on his side. As Carey says, 'to judge from the surviving oratory, there appears to have been a fundamental inhibition against frontal assaults on the authority of law'.[23]

In response to questioning by Demosthenes and by the public arbitrator, Aphobus appears to have issued Demosthenes a challenge, saying that he was willing to show that Demosthenes' estate was worth ten talents and that if it was not, Aphobus would make up the difference (27.50–2). Aphobus then placed some testimony concerning his challenge into the evidence jar. Demosthenes clearly did not accept the challenge, since it was predicated on a claim by Aphobus that had yet to be demonstrated. In this speech, moreover, he is not interested in arguing on the basis of challenges. He parries the thrust of Aphobus' challenge first by saying that Aphobus should simply demonstrate his claim to the arbitrator, and then essentially by claiming that the challenge was immaterial (27.52), a desperate act by his opponent when he was backed into a corner both by Demosthenes and by the impartial public arbitrator, who had asked a series of tough questions (27.50). But Demosthenes refers to no challenges of his own, since in this case he does not need them. The challenge belongs to the realm of extra-judicial settlement, to which private arbitration also belongs. It is an informal, oral realm of dispute resolution, governed by the traditional rules of aristocratic culture that had existed in Athens for hundreds of years.[24] In the first sentence of his speech, Demosthenes makes clear that Aphobus' actions have precluded a settlement within that realm (27.1). The private arbitrators would have been intimates (*oikeioi*) of theirs and thus have had clear knowledge upon which to decide between them. Since the democratic judges have no accurate knowledge, Demosthenes must construct an epistemology that is not based on intimate familiarity, but on the rules of the democratic court. In the subsequent speeches, of course, he will have to take recourse to argumentation based on challenges, indeed, challenges which he made even before the first speech and which he might have used in it but did not.

Against Aphobus 2 (28) was delivered in response to Aphobus' first speech in defense of himself before the popular court. It therefore raises questions about the extent to which the text that we have actually reflects the arguments that Demosthenes must to some extent have had to extemporize. One result of his extemporization would be, of course, that he could not rely to the same extent on prepared, written testimony. What he does use is recycled: the same testimony that is read at 27.8 is read again at 28.10, and so on. The thrust of Demosthenes' speech is directed at answering a charge by Aphobus that Demosthenes' maternal grandfather had died indebted to the state (thereby making Demosthenes also a state debtor through inheritance). Again, however, the same hierarchy of proofs comes forward. Demosthenes demands witnesses (1): 'This is the pretense he uses; but he offered no witness testimony that my grandfather died indebted to the state.' He also lays even greater emphasis on the missing will, which he now refers to as 'witness testimony' (*martyria*) (5): 'having destroyed such important witness testimony, they expect to be believed by you without any rational support'. Demosthenes clarifies the close relationship between the credibility of the will and witness testimony (5): 'it was necessary, as soon as my father died, to call in many witnesses and call on them to seal the will, so that if anything became disputed it would be possible to go to this text and discover the truth of everything'. Aphobus and the other guardians did actually produce documents to support their claims, lists which had been duly sealed. These Demosthenes dismisses as incomplete, simply memoranda from which many items that should have been in the will were left out (6). We may wonder whether these documents might not have had vastly more credibility than Demosthenes acknowledges.

Against Aphobus 3 (29) was delivered sometime after the first two speeches.[25] Demosthenes won his first confrontation before the popular court. Now Aphobus has countered with a suit for false testimony against one of Demosthenes' previously unidentified witnesses. He has also dispersed his property in an attempt to foil Demosthenes' attempts to get hold of it, so that Demosthenes must also litigate now against Onetor (3; for the speeches against Onetor, see below). In this suit, he is again faced with 'teaching' (*didaskein*) the judges, so that they may learn 'with greater accuracy' (*akribesteron*: 4), and many of the circumstances regarding evidence remain the same. This time, however, the suit concerns false testimony, so Demosthenes must face this issue head-on. Aphobus claims that Demosthenes' witness, Phanus, lied when he testified that Aphobus admitted that Milyas, whom he had wanted to have tortured as a slave, was actually a freedman. Aphobus' brother Aesius had joined in this testimony with Phanus, but now recants (15). Demosthenes' argumentation about his own motives behind using Aesius' testimony and Aesius' current recantation reveal several things about witness testimony in general (15):

> He now denies it, because he has allied himself in the suit with Aphobus; but at that time he gave this testimony along with the other witnesses, for he had no desire to perjure himself, or to suffer the penalty which would straightway follow. Surely now, if I had been getting up false testimony, I would not have put this man in my list of witnesses, seeing that he was more intimate with Aphobus than with anyone else in the world, and knowing that he was going to plead for him in the suit, and that he was my adversary. It is not reasonable that one should call as witness to a false statement one who is an opponent, and a brother of his adversary.

Aesius was clearly a partisan of Aphobus, and yet Demosthenes enlisted his testimony to Aphobus' having admitted that Milyas was a freedman. For Aesius to have refused to give testimony would have required his swearing an oath in which he would have had to claim that he did not know whether Aphobus had made this admission. His perjury would have been manifest and would likely have entailed legal penalties (see 49.20).[26] The arbitrator is likely to have played a role in forcing such testimony (cf. 20).

Demosthenes' discussion of the motives for false testimony (22–4), which, he claims, are absent for his own witnesses in this case, reveals some striking similarities with the accounts in the rhetorical handbooks of Aristotle and Anaximenes.[27] He says that his discussion is based on probabilities (*eikota*). Indeed, it is the sort of discussion one would find in handbooks about how to deal with this topic, since they also deal with probabilities. He lists three motives: bribery, friendship, and enmity, and these same three are mentioned as a group by Anaximenes (*Rhetorica ad Alexandrum* 15.5). He also describes his witnesses as 'respectable people' (29.24), which corresponds with Aristotle's 'reputable' (*Rhetoric* 1.15.19).

Demosthenes has also resorted to a challenge to torture a slave in this speech, which is somewhat necessitated by there being witnesses on both sides whose testimony conflicts (11):

> I knew, men of the jury, that I should find the whole con-
> test centering about the witness testimony written in the
> document, and that it would be regarding the truth or
> falsehood of this that you would cast your votes, and I
> therefore determined that the first step for me to take was
> to offer Aphobus a challenge. What, then, did I do? I of-
> fered to surrender to him for examination by torture a slave
> who knew how to read and write, and who had been pres-
> ent when Aphobus made the admission in question, and
> who wrote down the statement of the witness. This man
> had been ordered by me not to use any fraud or trickery,
> nor to write down some and suppress others of the state-
> ments made by the plaintiff regarding the matters at issue,
> but simply to write the absolute truth, and what Aphobus
> actually said.[28]

The challenge was made in the marketplace, where there were many bystanders, some of whom have provided testimony, and it was directed not only at Aphobus, but also at his brother Aesius (12,

17). Demosthenes has resorted to the challenge not only because of the conflicting testimony of witnesses, but also because the case concerns testimony that dealt with a previous challenge of Aphobus to torture a slave. Aphobus is thus caught equivocating about torture (*basanos*), which was universally approved as the surest form of proof in the ideology of the Athenian courts (14): 'For he surely cannot claim this, that for some matters, which he himself wants, torture is clear, and for others it is not clear.' Aphobus apparently counter-challenged with a different set of questions for the slave (13; cf. 29.50). Demosthenes dismisses this challenge as quickly as possible, emphasizing that the question he would have had put to the slave went to the central issue of the dispute, while Aphobus' fallacious demand concerns 'other things'. As he says later in the speech (39), 'after passing over those who were admittedly slaves, he demanded to torture a free man, whom it would have been impious for me to surrender; he was not seeking to bring the matter to a test, but he wanted to make a specious argument out of the fact that his demand was refused'.

Aphobus apparently still considers Milyas a slave, despite Demosthenes' arguments that he had admitted him to be a freedman, and he has renewed his challenge to have him tortured (25). In response, Demosthenes has offered three female slaves for torture, who are old enough to remember Demosthenes' father having manumitted him. Later, Demosthenes imagines that Milyas were still a slave and gives us one of our only arguments against the torture of a 'slave' in Attic oratory (40): 'let's picture Milyas being racked on the wheel, and let's examine what [Aphobus] would have hoped him to say. Would it not be that he did not know that this man had any of the money?' The key words are 'he did not know'. Any challenge to torture a slave has to be premised with the claim that the slave does know. Demosthenes has provided many witnesses who testified that they did know that Aphobus had the money. Instead of charging them for false testimony, Aphobus has sought to get at this former slave, who does not know, and torture him.

To this Demosthenes added the further challenge, to have his own mother swear an oath regarding the manumission (26). This form of oath-challenge was the strongest way for the statements of a woman to come before a popular court, since women could not act as witnesses. Since women exercised few political rights in Athens, they did not witness as many events as they might in other cultures. Indeed, Athenians must also have been loath to subject the women of their families to public scrutiny by having them swear such oaths. But in this case, the challenge was made in what was essentially a family squabble, since Aphobus was a cousin of Demosthenes (and was supposed to have married Demosthenes' mother according to the wishes of Demosthenes' father). Demosthenes' mention of her is brief and to the point.

Demosthenes refers to the various challenges to torture slaves and to have his mother swear an oath to support his case as 'just measures' (*dikaia*). They are the 'greatest tests' (*megistoi elenchoi*) of what has been testified to by his witnesses (27). Clearly he gives them a greater role here than he had in his first speeches against Aphobus. The suit for false testimony has apparently not been preceded by a public arbitration, however, so after Aphobus introduced testimony from witnesses like Onetor and Timocrates, who gave testimony regarding the monies of the guardianship, Demosthenes excuses himself for not having prepared witnesses to deal with them (28). But his response is fascinating. After reminding the judges that he has already won his case on these matters against Aphobus, he restates his case and says in his own voice what was in documents that had been read aloud by the court secretary in the original case. He begins with his charge (*enklēma*) and goes on with the testimony that has become the basis for the suit for false testimony (31–2). About several parts of his father's legacy, however, Demosthenes does have testimony at hand, so he goes on presenting his case in the normal order, outlining the events and then backing up his narrative with the reading of laws and testimony (33–9). But later Demosthenes returns to his method of stating in his own voice the substance of what normally is the stuff of documentary evidence. At the original arbitration, when Aphobus was being insistent on his challenge to torture Milyas (cf. 14, 39), Demosthenes formulated a complicated counter-challenge (51–2):

> For I, in my desire to refute him in every particular, and in my attempt to make clear to you his tricks and his villain-ies, asked him how large the sum was regarding which he demanded to examine Milyas, as one 'who had knowledge of the facts'. To this he stated falsely, that it was in regard to everything. 'Well then', said I, 'as to this I will give up to you the one who has the copy of your challenge to me. If, after I have given oath that you acknowledged [Milyas] to be free and that you so testified against Demo, you will swear to the contrary with imprecations upon your daugh-

ter, I release to you everything for which you shall be shown by the examination of the slave to have at the first demanded Milyas; and the damages which you were condemned to pay shall be lessened by this much – that is, by the amount in regard to which you demanded Milyas, so that you may be found to have been put to no disadvantage by the witnesses'.

Demosthenes clearly did not formulate the challenge along lines that Aphobus would have favored, since he limited the amount at issue to what Milyas might have been tortured over instead of 'everything'. He also makes the stakes very high over this relatively small amount: the settlement would have entailed the two cousins swearing conflicting oaths. But Demosthenes is taking full advantage of this stock form of argumentation based on refused challenges. The refusal to settle a dispute through swearing an oath amounts to the refusal of Aphobus 'to judge these things for himself' (53; cf. 30.2 and Arist. *Rhetoric* 1.15.30–1).[29] Both Demosthenes and the witnesses he is defending were willing to swear oaths to the truth of their case, and thereby to settle the dispute, but Aphobus did not bite (54).

In the two speeches against Onetor (30 and 31), Demosthenes has apparently not had the benefit of the extensive preparation that went into the speeches against Aphobus, especially Speech 27. There again seems not to have been a public arbitration for this suit, where Demosthenes could have lined up his witnesses and forced Onetor to disclose his. Demosthenes has to rely on recycled testimony and on challenges that serve to bolster it. Under the guise of an *apotimema*, a method by which a wife's family secures a guarantee for her dowry by laying claim to a piece of her husband's land in case of divorce,[30] Onetor has seized some of Aphobus' land that Demosthenes hoped to have as part of his award. According to Demosthenes, Onetor and Aphobus perpetrated a false divorce, which gives Onetor this opportunity. Onetor prevented Demosthenes from seizing the land, so Demosthenes has brought a suit for ejectment against him. Presumably because of his lack of preparation, Demosthenes relies to an even greater extent in Speech 30 on stock forms of argumentation (most clearly at 37) rather than on the witness testimony. He refers to these stock forms of argumentation as 'great and clear evidence' (*tekmēria*: 5). So while he still uses witness testimony (9), he also relies largely on conclusions drawn from Onetor's refusal of his challenges. From the outset, he recognizes that in this dispute his opponent will use witnesses who will give false testimony (3). One of them is Aphobus (38), his previous opponent, who is continuing their dispute through Onetor (4). The other is Timocrates, the former husband of Aphobus' wife, whose testimony Demosthenes himself also uses for his own purposes (9). The challenges are thus needed as a second-order proof, one that backs up witness testimony when the opponents have witnesses who give conflicting evidence.

Timocrates testifies that he returned his former wife's dowry in the form of installments to Aphobus at a rate of 10 per cent per annum (7, 9). These payments covered the interest on the money. It is unclear whether they involved any payment of the capital. Demosthenes' case is based on the assumption that none of the capital was paid to Aphobus. It should thus be Timocrates and not Aphobus who should provide the guarantee in the form of the *apotimēma*. This, however, must be an assumption, which Demosthenes must support 'from probabilities' (10–13), since clearly he was not in a position to provide witnesses regarding arrangements among Aphobus, Onetor, and Timocrates. The 'probabilities' suggest that the dowry was paid by installments only because it was known that Aphobus' property was to be under dispute; they follow from the great wealth of these men (10), its liquidity (11), and the harm to one's reputation that flows from not paying a dowry outright (12). Timocrates could have returned the full dowry and Onetor could have passed one on to Aphobus had they wanted to do this. Demosthenes can also argue from the actions (*pepragmena*: 14) of his opponents, the timing of the marriage in connection with his own litigation, which imperiled Aphobus' estate and made the payment of a dowry to him unlikely (14–18). He relies on anonymous witnesses, presumably three different anonymous witnesses, to affirm the timing of the marriage to Aphobus and its relation to the progression of Demosthenes' claims against him (17).

In a preliminary confrontation, Demosthenes questioned Onetor and Timocrates about the particulars of the case before anonymous witnesses (19 and 30). He makes much of the fact that no witnesses saw Aphobus receive the installments from Timocrates (20–1): 'Is this credible to you, that with a dowry of a talent Onetor and Timocrates handed over to Aphobus so much money without witnesses? ... No one would complete such a transaction without witnesses.' The following passages, for all of their rhetorical charge, are critical for an appreciation of the role of witnesses in Athens. The marriage feast is described as an act of communal witnessing, in which members of one family are entrusted to those of another.[31] Timocrates has already testified himself that he had agreed to pass on the dowry in the form of installments to Aphobus (9). Now Demosthenes challenges whether the installments were ever paid, since no one witnessed them (23).

> As it was, they could not induce their friends, who were more honest men than themselves, to bear witness to the payment of the money, and they thought that, if they produced other witnesses, not related to them, you would not believe them. Again, if they said the payment had been made all at once, they knew that we should demand for examination by torture the slaves who had brought the money. These, if the payment had not been made, they would have refused to give up, and so they would have been exposed. But if they maintained that they had paid the money without witnesses in the manner alleged, they thought to escape detection.

Demosthenes moves in this passage from his opponents' lack of witnesses to a hypothetical challenge to torture slaves. The torture-challenge becomes the second-order proof for witness testimony, even hypothetical witness testimony.

In the next passage (25–30), in which he wants to show that Aphobus' divorce from his wife was a sham, Demosthenes uses three kinds of evidence, which he describes as witnesses, great evidence (*megala tekmēria*) and sufficient proofs (*pisteis*) (25). Even after the purported divorce and Onetor's claim to the land on the basis of *apotimēma*, Aphobus continued living with his wife and working the land. Demosthenes confronted Onetor before witnesses and challenged him by offering him a slave for torture over these points. Onetor declined the challenge but admitted that Aphobus continued working the land. Demosthenes provides witnesses to the challenge, as well as to the fact that Aphobus had stripped the land, as if realizing that he would have to hand it over to Demosthenes. He uses as evidence (*tekmēria*: 31) of there being no ill-will (the likely result of a genuine divorce) between Aphobus and Onetor that the latter had joined in the pleadings for Aphobus against Demosthenes (31–2). Despite this being common knowledge, Demosthenes provides witnesses for this also. As further evidence (33), he notes that while Onetor's sister went straight from Timocrates to Aphobus in order not to remain unmarried even temporarily, she has not remarried after 'divorcing' Aphobus. As if admitting that this inference is weak, Demosthenes also produces as a witness Pasiphon, who cared for Aphobus' wife when they were supposedly divorced and who saw Aphobus attending to her also (34).

Demosthenes also challenged Aphobus to allow three slave women from his house to be tortured on the same point (35–6). The fact that he can point to bystanders who agreed that Demosthenes' challenge to torture the slave women was just suggests strongly that such slave tortures actually took place.[32] Here Demosthenes actually has the challenge read aloud and then turns to a piece of argumentation that is clearly off the rhetoricians' rack, for it copies almost word for word an argument in Isaeus (8.12) and Isocrates (17.54).[33]

In his second speech against Onetor (31), Demosthenes deals with another sort of document, albeit one that could hardly be brought into court. These are the *horoi*, marking stones, which were set up on the disputed property to indicate that it was security for the dowry Onetor had provided, by way of Timocrates, to Aphobus. Demosthenes provides testimony from 'those who know' that Onetor had himself removed *horoi* from a house on the land indicating that it was security for two thousand drachmas (4). He then draws an inference from this removal and Onetor's inconsistency (8) that neither the house nor the land were actually security for anything, that the entire *apotimēma* was a fraud: 'to me it seems that no greater evidence than this could be found' (5). Although he refers to the laws concerning *apotimēma* (8), he does not have them read.

Onetor has apparently offered to settle their dispute by swearing an oath to the effect that he gave a dowry of one talent, for which the disputed land is security (9). Demosthenes counters that he might have sworn earlier that the dowry was one talent plus two thousand drachmas, and thus have committed perjury according to his current claims. Demosthenes extends his argument against Onetor by imagining what sort of oath Onetor might have sworn to support his case if he were challenged to do so (9). Demosthenes accuses Onetor of being a trickster (*technazōn*: 10) attempting to beguile the judges with a sort of shell game played out with the *horoi* (12). These are clearly not the sort of documentary evidence upon which Demosthenes wants the popular court to depend.

There are many other points to be made about Demosthenes as private logographer, and about his employment of documentary evidence. There are several speeches composed for use in cases involving the *paragraphē*, for instance, in which the tables are turned and the prosecutor is put on the defensive for having brought an inadmissible charge (32–8).[34] Various other speeches involve other such legal technicalities. But examination of many of them is greatly complicated by uncertainty of authorship. Many of the private speeches in the Demosthenic corpus are clearly not by Demosthenes but by Apollodorus,[35] the son of Pasion the banker, and the authorship of several others has also been challenged. But clearly many of them are Demosthenic, and their argumentation follows a pattern that Demosthenes sets down already in his speeches on his own behalf. A thorough analysis of all Demosthenes' private speeches is beyond the possibilities of this chapter, so I shall confine myself just to one.

Against Conon (54) has won some of the highest praise among the speeches that Demosthenes wrote for others.[36] It is generally dated to 341 and concerns a case for assault. As in 29 and 30, conflicting testimony from witnesses plays a large role, so Demosthenes must also resort to argumentation regarding challenges. The speech is especially relevant to this chapter since it illustrates what had become conventional argumentation in the popular courts against what is portrayed as outlandish behavior by the opponent regarding his use of evidence. At the beginning of the speech the speaker, Ariston, reports that he has followed the advice of family and friends (and presumably of his logographer) by instituting a private suit for assault instead of a more serious charge. Indeed, this speech shows a remarkable interest in the law and in its purposes.

Ariston first provides unnamed witnesses for the assaults he and his servants received from sons of Conon while they were all on garrison duty two years before (6). He also provides at first unnamed witnesses to the events over which he is litigating, when Conon and several others fell upon Ariston and a friend, Phanostratus, in a drunken brawl. They may be the people who happened by and helped Ariston home afterwards, though it can only be Phanostratus who testifies to the beginning of the actual assault (9). Later in the speech, he will identify the passers-by by name (32). A relative named Euxitheus and friend named Meidias came upon the group as they were making their way to Ariston's home. There he was cleaned up and seen by a doctor before being moved on to Meidias' house. Presumably it is now Euxitheus and Meidias who testify about Ariston's injuries, as does the doctor (10). A doctor (the same one?) and others also testify about the severity of Ariston's injuries and the difficulties of his convalescence (12).

There is a sense in which Ariston's case could now be complete: he has detailed the assault and supported his narrative with witness testimony. But he goes on to anticipate Conon, who will argue, Ariston supposes, that the events over which Ariston is litigating do not meet the threshold for a charge of assault and that Conon was really only a bystander. Ariston anticipates this with an *a fortiori* argument pointing out that even verbal assault is against the law, though he does not actually have the law read aloud at this point (17–19). Instead he goes on to base his arguments on the laws concerning *hubris* and robbery (24), the more serious charges he chose not to bring (1). (In this he is following a tactic pioneered by Isocrates in *Against Lochites*.)

At the arbitration, Conon apparently spent a great deal of time insisting that Ariston's witnesses swear to their testimony (26), a bizarre step since the truth of testimony is supposed to be assured by the suit for false testimony alone. Finally, when things were getting late, Conon challenged Ariston to have some slaves tortured. Ariston argues that this was altogether the wrong time for a challenge of this kind, and has witnesses testify that it was only a delaying tactic (29).

Finally, he deals with the conflicting testimony. He anticipates the testimony that Conon will use by actually quoting from it in his own voice (31). Conon's witnesses are his own drinking buddies (33); they are notorious libertines (34) and brutes (37). He mimics the talk of drunken conspiracy among Conon's gang, in which testimony was simply manufactured to suit Conon's needs (35). Ariston's emphasis is that his own witnesses are independent passers-by and a doctor (36); these are the sorts of independent witnesses one ought to produce before the democratic court. Ariston condemns the attitude of Conon's witnesses towards the written document of witnesses' testimony, the *grammateion* (which he reports using the diminutive *grammateidion* 37 to reflect his opponent's contempt for the written document), and their attitude about false testimony on behalf of *hetairoi*. He goes on to condemn Conon's behavior in bringing in his family and swearing outlandish oaths upon their heads to support his case. Ariston must also swear in response, but his oath is sober and conventional. That is in keeping with his entire presentation.

In conclusion, Demosthenes' private speeches are grounded on argumentation and on rules of evidence, that is, on a judicial and rhetorical epistemology tailored to the needs of the democratic ideology within which it functioned. Gone are the days in which the Greeks simply gathered before a panel of aristocrats and decided their cases through oral argumentation (see for example Homer, *Iliad* 18.497–508 and Plut. *Aristides* 4). Certainly there were still private arbitrators, vestiges of an aristocratic past; they were chosen by agreement of the disputing parties and sometimes empowered to settle their disputes. Before them the rules of argumentation were less formal: slaves could appear as witnesses and women sometimes participated as well. Demosthenes functioned well in these forums too, as well as before the new public arbitrators. But he keeps a coterie of anonymous witnesses on hand on these occasions to commit to writing the events, especially his opponents' admissions, that will serve him in the popular court. In the democratic courts, where only free males could participate, there was only written evidence, which demanded both transparency and accountability.

Demosthenes was a litigious Athenian.[37] He used the courts aggressively himself and he aided and abetted others in the pursuit of their claims through his logography. There has been a long history in the western tradition decrying this litigiousness as 'sycophancy', a sort of 'meddlesomeness' (*polypragmosynē*). In fact, it is a fundamental part of the democratic process, in the modern system as in fourth-century Athens. In the case of Athens, it is perhaps the most significant way in which the *dēmos*, the entire citizen body, can assert social control and 'police' the *polis* through the popular courts: 'The laws, which for you are authoritative, have made these [members of the popular court] authoritative' (Dem. 24.118).[38] In his survey of the ideology of Athenian democracy, M.H. Hansen includes discussion of 'Accountability' and 'Publicity',[39] and he recognizes the role of written laws in this process. The able employment of these written laws, of written testimony, contracts, wills, and challenges in the popular courts contributed no less to the effective running of the democracy.

NOTES

* My thanks are due to Mervin Dilts, Mark Golden, Phillip Harding, Edward Harris and Ian Worthington, who read an earlier draft of this chapter and made many helpful comments. It was also read at a meeting of the Classical Association of the Canadian West in February 1999.

1 H.J. Wolff, *Demosthenes als Advokat. Funktionen und Methoden des Prozesspraktikers im klassischen Athen, Schriftenreihe der juristischen Gesellschaft e.V.* 30 (Berlin: 1968). Wolff was preceded in his characterization of Demosthenes as an *Advokat* by E. Drerup, *Aus einer alten Advokatenrepublik. Demosthenes und seine Zeit* (Paderborn: 1916), who in the midst

of World War I wished to condemn the domination of politics in the powers aligned against Germany by men who were, like Demosthenes, advocates.

2 See for example R. Just, *Women in Athenian Law and Life* (London: 1989), P. Cartledge, P. Millett and S. Todd (eds.), *Nomos: Essays in Athenian Law, Politics and Society* (Cambridge: 1990), and D.J. Cohen, *Law, Violence and Community in Classical Athens* (Cambridge: 1995). See also now S. Johnstone, *Disputes and Democracy: The Consequences of Litigation in Ancient Athens* (Austin: 1999).

3 Cf. Plato, *Phaedrus* 257c, Din. 1.111. See R.J. Bonner, *Lawyers and Litigants in Ancient Athens: The Genesis of the Legal Profession* (Chicago: 1926), pp. 219–22, and K.J. Dover, *Lysias and the Corpus Lysiacum* (Berkeley: 1968), pp. 155–7.

4 See L. Pearson, *The Art of Demosthenes* (Meisenheim am Glan: 1976), pp. 39–74. W. Jaeger, *Demosthenes: The Origins and Growth of His Policy* (Berkeley: 1938), p. 29, puts the stylistic matter quite strikingly: 'there has been a change in the mental and spiritual structure of the men of the time; and this change has led to a complete break with the homely simplicity of their ancestors' way of speech, begetting an unprecedented refinement in the art of persuasion, which reaches its highest point not when it is used to beguile the audience with studied and striking sound effects, but when it apparently employs the most natural means alone'. For Demosthenes' reputation in antiquity see Cooper, Chapter 8; Harding, Chapter 9, discusses Demosthenes' reputation from antiquity to the present.

5 C. Carey, 'Legal Space in Classical Athens', *G&R*^{2} 41 (1994), pp. 172–86, understates the point: 'it was probably very difficult to win a case without any supporting testimony or documentation at all. Rhetoric can only take you so far' (p. 181).

6 C. Carey, 'Artless Proofs in Aristotle and the Orators', *BICS* 39 (1994), pp. 95–106, especially n. 6, points out that Aristotle exaggerates the distinction between artful and artless proofs.

7 See D.C. Mirhady, 'Non-Technical *pisteis* in Aristotle and Anaximenes', *AJP* 112 (1991), pp. 5–28.

8 E. Schiappa, *The Beginnings of Rhetorical Theory in Classical Greece* (New Haven: 1999), pp. 35–9, has now argued against this view, which originates with Plato, *Phaedrus* 267a. I am not so sure that we can dismiss Plato's evidence.

9 See M. Ostwald, *From Popular Sovereignty to the Sovereignty of Law* (Berkeley: 1986), M.H. Hansen, *The Athenian Democracy in the Age of Demosthenes* (Oxford: 1991), pp. 170, 303–20, and E.M. Harris, 'Law and Oratory' in Ian Worthington (ed.), *Persuasion: Greek Rhetoric in Action* (London: 1994), pp. 130–52.

10 See G.M. Calhoun, 'Oral and Written Pleading in Athenian Courts', *TAPA* 50 (1919), pp. 177–93. T.M. Lentz, *Orality and Literacy in Hellenic Greece* (Carbondale: 1989), p. 72, sees a reluctance on the part of the Athenians to introduce writing into their pleadings: 'the use of written evidence in the law courts of Athens is a popular reflection of the attitude towards writing Plato expresses in the *Phaedrus*'. I would argue the opposite aspect: that the integration of writing followed as an integral part of the maturation of the democratic constitution.

11 See D.C. Mirhady, 'Aristotle on the Rhetoric of Law', *GRBS* 31 (1990), pp. 393–410.

12 C. Carey, '*Nomos* in Attic Rhetoric and Oratory', *JHS* 116 (1996), p. 34 n. 8.

13 See H.C. Harrel, *Public Arbitration in Athenian Law* (Columbia: 1936).

14 See R.J. Bonner, *Evidence in Athenian Courts* (Chicago: 1905).

15 The translations of Demosthenes in this chapter are modified from A.T. Murray (transl.), *Demosthenes III–V* (Cambridge, Mass.: 1936–39).

16 Jaeger, *Demosthenes*, pp. 29–30, emphasizes that unlike Antiphon and Andocides, none of the great 'orators' who immediately preceded Demosthenes, Lysias, Isaeus, or Isocrates made a practice of delivering speeches in the Athenian courts. The first two were metics, and Isocrates kept silent.

17 I have sketched the similarities and the putatively common origins of these accounts in Mirhady, 'Non-Technical *pisteis*', pp. 5–28.

18 For the advice on laws, see Carey, '*Nomos*', pp. 33–46, and on challenges to oath and torture see D.C. Mirhady, 'The Oath-Challenge in Athens', CQ^2 41 (1991), pp. 78–83 and 'Torture and Rhetoric in Athens', *JHS* 116 (1996), pp. 119–31.

19 For a further discussion of the background to Demosthenes' dispute and especially how he used it for political ends see Badian, Chapter 1.

20 S.C. Humphreys, 'Social Relations on Stage: Witnesses in Classical Athens', *History and Anthropology* 1.2 (1985), pp. 313–69, and S. Todd, 'The Purpose of Evidence in Athenian Courts' in Cartledge, Millett and Todd, *Nomos*, pp. 19–39; cf. Todd, *The Shape of Athenian Law* (Oxford: 1993), pp. 96–7. The explanation of Cohen, *Law, Violence and Community*, pp. 110–11, seems no more satisfactory: 'witnesses are there to tell whatever needs to be told to support you'. Carey, 'Legal Space', p. 184, points out that in classical Athens the implicit view of the role of witnesses 'places the emphasis on matters of fact'.

21 I argue this point at greater length in 'Athens' Democratic Witnesses' in E.M. Harris and L. Rubenstein (eds.), *The Law and the Courts in Ancient Greece* (London: 2001).

22 See D. Cohen, *Law, Violence and Community*, p. 107.

23 Carey, '*Nomos*', p. 36.

24 It is embraced by Isocrates 15.27. I have traced some of the continuity in the use of the oath-challenge from Homer to the fourth century, in Mirhady, 'Oath-Challenge', pp. 78–80.

25 The authenticity of this speech has been challenged. Cf. F. Blass, *Die attische Beredsamkeit*² 3.1 (Leipzig: 1893; repr. Hildesheim: 1962), pp. 232–4. Several parts of it are repeated from *Against Aphobus* 1.27. To me, the speech is undoubtedly by Demosthenes, although I am willing to believe that it was thoroughly worked over (by him) before reaching its current state.

26 For the procedures surrounding this situation, see C. Carey, 'The Witness's *Exomosia* in the Athenian Courts', CQ^2 45 (1995), pp. 114–19.

27 Cf. Mirhady, 'Non-technical *pisteis*', pp. 14–15.

28 For a similar situation, see Isaeus 8.6–14.

29 For other passages and discussion of this stock argument, see Mirhady, 'Oath-Challenge', pp. 80–1.

30 See E.M. Harris, '*Apotimema*: Athenian Terminology for Real Security in Leases and Dowry Agreements', *CQ²* 43 (1993), pp. 73–95.

31 Cf. A. Scafuro, 'Witnessing and False-Witnessing: Proving Citizenship and Kin Identity in Fourth-Century Athens' in A.L. Boegehold and A.C. Scafuro (eds.), *Athenian Identity and Civic Ideology* (Baltimore: 1994), pp. 156–98.

32 M. Gagarin, 'The Torture of Slaves in Athenian Law', *CP* 91 (1996), pp. 1–18, has proposed that such challenges to torture (*basanos*) were only legal fictions, that torture rarely if ever occurred. In general, he follows the magisterial study of G. Thür, *Beweisführung vor den Schwurgerichtshöfen Athens. Die Proklēsis zur Basanos* (Vienna: 1977). I have argued that torture did take place in 'Torture and Rhetoric in Athens' and in 'The Athenian Rationale for Torture' in J. Edmondson and V. Hunter (eds.), *Law and Social Status in Classical Athens* (Oxford: 2000), pp. 53–74.

33 See Mirhady, 'Torture and Rhetoric', p. 130.

34 S. Isager and M.H. Hansen, *Aspects of Athenian Society in the Fourth Century B.C.* (Odense: 1975), provide extensive analysis of the *paragraphe* speeches.

35 See J. Trevett, *Apollodorus the Son of Pasion* (Oxford: 1992).

36 Commentaries on this speech have been written by F.A. Paley and J.E. Sandys, *Select Private Orations of Demosthenes* Part 1⁵ (Cambridge: 1898), Part 2⁴ (Cambridge: 1910), who also cover 34–7, 39–40, 45–6, 51, 53 and 55, F.C. Doherty, *Three Private Speeches of Demosthenes* (Oxford: 1927), who also includes 34 and 39, and C. Carey and R.A. Reid, *Demosthenes: Selected Private Speeches* (Cambridge: 1985), who also include 37, 39 and 56. L. Pearson, *Demosthenes: Six Private Speeches* (Norman: 1972), deals with 27–8, 30–1, 32 and 36.

37 See M.R. Christ, *The Litigious Athenian* (Baltimore: 1998).

38 See V. Hunter, *Policing Athens: Social Control in the Attic Lawsuits, 420–320 B.C.* (Princeton: 1994).

39 Hansen, *Athenian Democracy*, pp. 310–12.

7

THE PUBLIC SPEECHES OF DEMOSTHENES*

R.D. Milns

Of the seventeen 'symbouleutic' (advisory) speeches or *dēmēgoriai* that have come down to us in the Demosthenic corpus, *Philippic* 4 (10), *Answer to Philip's Letter* (11) and *On Organisation* (13) are, in my opinion, spurious and the creations of later 'forgers', who have incorporated genuine Demosthenic material in the speeches to give them an air of authenticity. *On Halonnesus* (7) and *On the Treaty with Alexander* (17) are genuine political speeches, but wrongly attributed to Demosthenes, with *On Halonnesus* probably belonging to the violently anti-Macedonian Hegesippus, and *On the Treaty with Alexander* to either Hegesippus or Hyperides, the leader of the most radical anti-Macedonian faction at Athens after the defeat of Chaeronea.

I am aware that there are many scholars who argue for the genuineness of *Philippic* 4 and *On Organisation*.[1] I find it hard, however, to believe that two such poorly constructed speeches could have emanated from the same pen that wrote the third *Olynthiac* or third *Philippic*. This is especially true of *On Organisation*, which is so feeble and full of platitudes and empty rhetoric that one could almost imagine that it is the speech delivered early in Demosthenes' career to which Plutarch makes reference in his *Life of Demosthenes* (6), were it not that allusions in the speech seem to set its 'dramatic' date around 350/49.[2] In the case of *Answer to Philip's Letter*, only a person deliberately set on controversy could argue that the speech, with its totally inaccurate assessment of Macedonian power and Philip's relations with his Macedonians, taken almost verbatim from *Olynthiac* 2, is a genuine speech intended for delivery in the Assembly. With respect to *On Halonnesus* and *On the Treaty with Alexander*, not only were they attributed in antiquity to Hegesippus and Hyperides,[3] but both speeches fail modern stylometric tests.[4] *On the Treaty with Alexander*, moreover, is so lacking in vigour and structure that it was even suggested in antiquity that if Demosthenes was the author, he was obviously now senile – a claim which is rejected by the Scholiast with the argument that this speech was delivered early in Alexander's reign, whereas the chief glory of Demosthenes' oratory, the Crown speech (18), was delivered considerably later in the king's reign, 'when Alexander was in India and Persia'.[5] I do not propose to deal with any of these speeches in this chapter.

1 Dating and sequence of the genuine speeches

The fullest treatment of this subject to come down from antiquity is that of Dionysius of Halicarnassus in his *First Letter to Ammaeus*, in which Dionysius is trying to demonstrate that Demosthenes' public speeches owe nothing to Aristotle's *Rhetoric* since they were all delivered before the composition of that work.

Modern opinion has overall tended to agree with the dates given by Dionysius,[6] with the main area of controversy centring around the date of *Philippic* 1 and the sequence of the three *Olynthiacs*. With respect to the first *Philippic*, the most extreme divergence from Dionysius has been that of E. Schwartz,[7] who, on the basis of a reference to Philip's campaign against Olynthus at section 17, would date the speech to 349/8, but after the three *Olynthiacs* (as with the Scholiast on Demosthenes 3.2, who comments 'as he himself [Demosthenes] *later* advised in the fourth speech'). It is, however, likely that the 'campaign' against Olynthus is an otherwise unknown threat, not the actual siege of the city.[8] Ellis has argued for a date 'of about January 350',[9] but there is no solid reason, as Sealey observes, to reject Dionysius' date of 352/1, with perhaps spring of 351 as a more precise date (as argued by Sandys).[10]

As to the sequence of the three *Olynthiacs*, the traditional order of the manuscripts has the support of the majority of scholars, from Blass, Schaefer, Weil and Sandys to Sealey.[11] Ellis argued for a sequence of 2, 1, 3 (the same as Grote) based essentially on two arguments: the Theoric Fund is mentioned in 1, not in 2 and is attacked in 3; and there is a change in the Thessalian situation in 1.22 and 2.11 which favours the order 2, 1, 3.[12] Most discussions ultimately turn on interpretations of ambiguous phrases or of 'the mood' or 'the time' of the three speeches; though there seems to be unanimity amongst modern scholarship that the third *Olynthiac* is precisely that – the third. Overall, the most sensible approach seems to be to stay with the order of the *Olynthiacs* given in our best manuscript.

2 Publication and circulation of the speeches

This is a major question which has long exercised scholars and continues to do so. In the context of fourth-century Athens, what do we mean by 'publication'? If we can agree on a definition of this term, is there evidence to show that Demosthenes 'published' his speeches? If so, what relation do the speeches that have come down to us have with those that were actually delivered in the Assembly?[13]

In answer to the first of these questions, perhaps the minimum definition would be that copies of a speech were made at Demosthenes' instruction and distributed to such people as the orator wished, whether in Athens or in other Greek cities. This would imply the existence of a written version of the speech, approved by the author. This, of course, need not be the *ipsissima verba* of what was said in the Assembly, but it would be reasonable to assume that it was close to it. It is known that the Assembly did not approve of speakers reading from prepared texts; and it is also known that Demosthenes prepared his speeches before he delivered them (Plut. *Dem.* 8), though whether this was in written form and, if so, whether in note form or in full, cannot be said. It is at least highly likely that even a full – and memorised – text would have been revised on the basis of its reception, if the orator intended it for immediate publication; what is not likely in this situation is that major distortions or suppressions were made.

Evidence does exist that texts of Demosthenes' speeches existed in his own time. Plutarch (*Dem.* 11.4) quotes the Peripatetic biographer Hermippus as citing Aesion, a contemporary of the orator, that he had read Demosthenes' speeches. This would certainly strongly imply that there were available copies of the speeches for those who wished to read them; and the argument of Trevett that Demosthenes himself allowed Aesion to read his own text of the speeches seems to be somewhat implausible.[14]

Whilst hardly anyone today would argue that the speeches that have come down to us were both spoken in the Assembly and spoken exactly as we have them, most would incline to the view that each of our speeches does represent a speech delivered to the People but edited or revised afterwards for circulation. Such revision would explain certain difficulties in some speeches; for example, the omission in *Philippic* 1 (after 29) of the promised account of the means of funding the proposed military force; the absence in *Philippic* 2 of the reply to the foreign ambassadors which Demosthenes says he will suggest to the People (28); and the longer and shorter versions of *Philippic* 3, where it has been argued that the longer version was delivered at Athens and the shorter circulated as a pamphlet around the Greek cities.[15] Similarly, the general nature of the speeches, which do not appear to address specific motions, might indicate speeches either revised for wider consumption or written as 'political pamphlets' from the start.[16] These arguments are criticized by Trevett, who tries to demonstrate that the speeches as we have them are nothing more and nothing less than the unrevised drafts which Demosthenes wrote before speaking in the Assembly.[17] This leads Trevett to ask the same question as Hansen:[18] why is it that only eleven symbouleutic speeches (this excludes the spurious speeches) have survived from a public career of at least twenty-two years? Trevett's answer that most of his speeches were improvised, either in whole or in part, is not satisfactory, as it does not explain why *these* speeches have survived, nor why there are no public speeches from the later, post-Chaeronea, period of Demosthenes' public life (on this, see Worthington, Chapter 3).

Hansen, who argues that the speeches represent Demosthenes' general views on Athenian and Macedonian policy, with only *Philippic* 1 actually dealing with a specific motion, does make two points of great importance: Demosthenes was exceptional in publishing several of the speeches which he gave before the Assembly (Andocides, Hegesippus, and Hyperides with three speeches between them, are the only others known to have published *dēmēgoriai*); and the corpus which we have today contains the full complement of the *dēmēgoriai* published by Demosthenes. Hansen's answer to the question 'Why these speeches?' is based on a passage in Plato's *Phaedrus* (257–8), where it is stated that the ambitions of successful politicians were satisfied by the passing of their decree; hence they do not need to publish their speeches. According to Hansen, this is why the published speeches of Demosthenes cover the years 355–341, when Athens often rejected his proposals and publication was the only way to have his policies more widely known; whereas from 341 to 338 almost all his proposals were accepted. This, however, does not take into account, as with Trevett's argument, the absence of speeches from the period after 338.

On the question as to *why* the speeches were circulated, whether in Athens alone or more widely, the answer must be purely and simply for political purposes – to attempt to persuade influential doubters of the validity of Demosthenes' position on the ever-increasing threat posed by Philip. The earlier, non-Philippic speeches may have been circulated by the orator to try to convince powerful politicians that here was a young man with ideas and a persuasive tongue, who was well worth watching. The words of Blass are worth repeating:

> Publication had no other than the practical purpose which the spoken speech had also had. Demosthenes always and everywhere assessed the value of a speech according to its effect. Nowhere in Demosthenes is there any hint that he had valued or loved his writings in and for themselves as the products of his artistry, as did Isocrates his *Panegyricus*.[19]

3 Style and artistry

Before we turn to examine the essentials of Demosthenes' style and artistry, it might be as well to remember that any Athenian politician faced extraordinary difficulties which his modern counterpart does not. Firstly, there were no electronic aids to amplify the voice; hence, the absolute necessity of knowing how to project the voice, especially in an open-air environment. Then there was the problem of dealing with an audience of citizens ten times the number of members of the British House of Commons, who did not always observe the politenesses of a modern-day debating society, as is evident from Demosthenes' frequent appeal to his audience to hear him out until the end.[20] Indeed, it is clear from *Olynthiac* 2 that the major politicians had their organised groups of supporters, whose partisan spirit, one may be sure, was not limited to warm applause of their own political masters (29).[21] To make oneself heard by and to keep the attention of six thousand or more of one's fellow citizens for a significant amount of time sometimes required both courage and determination,[22] but also oratorical powers of the highest order. A mediocre or hesitant speaker would not have lasted long. Nor, for that matter, would a prolix or verbose orator have found a tolerant and patient audience. It is an interesting experience to read a speech of Demosthenes delivered to the Assembly and follow it with a parliamentary speech of Edmund Burke.

That Demosthenes had, at least in his more developed style, these qualities is clear from the enthusiasm and emotion with which Dionysius speaks of the effect that *reading* a speech of Demosthenes had on him (*Demosthenes* 22).[23] What then, he asks, must have been the effect on those who actually *heard* him? Dionysius ascribes Demosthenes' success to the fact that his rhetorical style was fashioned from all three of the main styles (plain, middle and grand, with Lysias, Plato and Isocrates representing each of these styles respectively). Dionysius' account has recently been criticised by Wooten, who argues that Dionysius only vaguely perceived in his discussion what Hermogenes saw very clearly two hundred years later: Demosthenes' style is really a combination of swiftness and brevity (*gorgotēs* and *syndromē*) and fullness or abundance (*pleonasmos* or *peribolē*).[24] The advantages of this style are that it makes the *thought* clear and emphatic by saying the same thing over and over again, but each time with variation; and, that it holds the audience's interest because the speaker uses short, 'punchy' clauses rather than the long, carefully crafted, periodic sentences of an Isocrates. To quote Wooten, this style 'reinforces the ethical appeal. It projects the image of a man who is energetic, concise, straightforward, to the point, but who also can explain problems ... in a clear and distinct manner.' Wooten's choice of Demosthenes 9.36–7 admirably illustrates this concept.[25] To this must be added, at least from the first *Philippic* onwards, the emotional involvement of the orator in his subject and his intense and forceful vigour (*deinotēs*, as Dionysius calls it). The passion leaps out from the printed page and a modern reader can, by reading the Greek aloud, gain some of the experience that Dionysius had (and we should remember that for an ancient Greek 'reading' meant 'reading aloud'). The finest examples, in my view, are *Olynthiac* 3 and *Philippic* 3.

The style of the *Olynthiacs* and *Philippics* did not, however, spring fully made from the forehead of the goddess of Persuasion. It is possible to trace a development from the earlier non-Philippic *dēmēgoriai* to the mature speeches, whose intensity and power would certainly have been helped by both the growing experience of the orator and the increasing seriousness of the situation as Philip's strength and expansion grew ever greater and closer to Athens. Pearson examined the growth of Demosthenes' political oratory;[26] to him, the earlier speeches – especially *On the Symmories* (14) – have a 'Thucydidean' quality about them in that they appear to imitate the language of Thucydides and, like the historian's speeches, require careful reading because of the complexity of the argument;

'the result is somewhat bewildering'.[27] In the more mature speeches, argues Pearson, Demosthenes has decided to model his public speeches on his forensic style, with the result that we get a greater blend of narrative with the argument, thus giving 'a greater directness of argument, a greater speed in the flow of language and the absence of any appearance of hesitation'.[28]

There can be no doubt that much of Pearson's account is correct, though it should be stressed firstly that the deliberative speeches in Thucydides frequently adopt the tactics of the law-courts,[29] and secondly that the orator himself could revert to his 'Thucydidean' style in the later speeches if he thought that it would achieve a desired effect (for example, to catch the audience's attention). The best example of this is the opening of *Philippic* 3, where the syntax and organisation of clauses is highly unnatural, so much so that Dionysius feels obliged to rewrite it in 'conventional' form (*Demosthenes* 9). To reproduce the convoluted and broken syntax of this passage in English is almost impossible. There is, however, an obvious difference in the quality of *On the Symmories* and *For the People of Megalopolis* and *Philippic* 1, delivered at most three years later. Both the two earlier speeches are lacking in the fire and passion of the later speeches and both have exceedingly complex arguments, which it is difficult to imagine an audience following. By contrast, *For the Liberty of the Rhodians*, delivered in the same year as *Philippic* 1, is much clearer in its structure and argument and, though unsuccessful, closer to the style of the later speeches. It is also interesting in that it contains three 'firsts': it contains the first mention in Demosthenes' public speeches of Philip, in a very different light from that of the first *Philippic*; it contains the first mention in the speeches of the orator's concern about the existence of Athenian politicians in the pay of the enemy; and it has the first enunciation of the principle that democracies and authoritarian regimes (in this case, oligarchy) are natural and irreconcilable enemies.[30] Nonetheless, it is remarkable how different the tone and intensity of *Philippic* 1 is by comparison with *For the Liberty of the Rhodians*. We really are on a higher plain of oratory, perhaps caused by Demosthenes' sudden realisation of what a real threat Philip did pose!

The three *Philippic* speeches, the *Chersonese* speech and the three *Olynthiacs* represent the mature Demosthenes, with *On the Peace* being, by virtue of its circumstances, somewhat less fiery and assertive and more defensive.[31] There are many individual features that contribute to their overall effectiveness, some of which are thematic, some of which are stylistic. Among stylistic features it should be pointed out that Demosthenes shows great mastery in capturing and holding the attention of his audience by the frequent use of imaginary dialogue between himself and his audience or by means of an imaginary interjection from a heckler.[32] A good example occurs in *Philippic* 1 when the orator, early in the speech, after vividly describing Philip's restless and constant aggressiveness, turns to his audience and asks them (10–11):

> When, then, Athenians, when will you do your duty? What must first happen? 'When there is a need for it.' What then should we consider what is now happening? For in my opinion the greatest 'need' is a sense of shame at the political situation. Or do you want, tell me, to go around and ask each other 'Is there any news?' Could there be anything more newsworthy than a fellow from Macedonia defeating Hellenes in war and regulating their affairs? 'Is Philip dead?' 'No, he's not, but he's ill.' What difference does it make to you? If anything happens to him, you'll soon create another Philip if this is how you attend to your business.

The dialogue is delivered in short, staccato sentences, mostly written without connecting particles (*asyndeton*) to give it 'punch'. The use of *asyndeton* to achieve this effect is frequent in the mature speeches, sometimes combined with other stylistic effects. Here, from *On the Chersonese*, is a passage in which *asyndeton* is coupled with *anaphora* – the repetition of the same word or phrase at the beginning of a series of clauses (65–6):

> *It was not safe* in Olynthus to urge Philip's cause without at the same time benefiting the masses by giving them Potidaea to enjoy; *it was not safe* in Thessaly to urge Philip's cause without at the same time Philip's benefiting the majority by expelling their tyrants and giving back Thermopylae to them; *it was not safe* in Thebes until he gave Boeotia back to them and destroyed the Phocians. But at Athens [then follows a list of the harm that Philip had done Athens] *it is safe* to urge Philip's cause.[33] (My emphasis)

Again, a series of short, sharp rhetorical questions can build up to a sustained and explosive climax, as can be seen in *Olynthiac* 3.16:

What time or what opportunity, Athenians, do you seek better than the present one? When will you do your duty, if not now? Has not the fellow already seized all our strongholds and if he becomes master of this territory [sc. Olynthus], will not our disgrace be absolute? Are not those people now at war whom we promised we'd save if they went to war? Is he not our enemy? Does he not hold what is ours? Is he not a barbarian? Is he not anything you want to call him?

Another stylistic device that Demosthenes employs with great effect is metaphor and simile.[34] It may be, of course, that some of the metaphors are 'faded', so that the word has virtually lost its metaphorical sense (for example, the use of 'sickness' or 'to be sick' to describe a state that is in a parlous political condition; for example, 9.39).[35] Nevertheless, and despite Pearson's claim that Demosthenes is sparing in his use of imagery,[36] the speeches show a constant and striking use of these two similar figures of speech. A brilliant simile is that in *Philippic* 1 when the orator compares the way that the Athenians are fighting Philip to a barbarian boxing with a Greek:

when one of them [sc. a barbarian] is hit, he always clutches where the blow lands; and if you hit him somewhere else, there go his hands. He neither knows how nor wishes to put up a guard or meet you face-to-face. (40)

The consequence of this is that 'You march up and down with him [sc. Philip] and you have him as your commander-in-chief' (40). Another vivid simile is that found in *Philippic* 3, where Philip is compared to a fever which strikes even those who feel they are at a safe distance from him (29). This simile is followed immediately by one from the law courts, in which Philip, as a non-Hellene, is compared with a slave or a suppositious bastard who damages property that is not his legally by inheritance (30). In *Olynthiac* 3 a metaphor from the symposium is used to show how the political affairs of Athens have been 'pledged away' in return for the pleasure and gratification of the moment (22).[37] This speech also contains the metaphor from ham-stringing (31) – that is, enervating – which is criticised by John the Sicilian (6.227W) and Hermogenes (3.226) as 'harsh' and may be the basis of the expression parodied by Aeschines (3.166).[38]

Another stylistic device often used by the orator in his mature speeches to capture the attention of his audience is paradox. The first *Philippic* begins the discussion section with the statement that:

> What is the worst aspect of your political situation from the past is the best for the future. What is this? It is the fact that your affairs are in a bad way because you have not done your duty in any way; whereas, if they were so if you had done all that you should, there would be no hope of their improving (33).[39]

Likewise, *Olynthiac* 1 states that the most formidable aspect of Philip's situation is also the best for Athens. This is Philip's autocratic position, which gives him a great advantage in planning and executing warlike enterprises, but puts him at a disadvantage in coming to agreements with states governed constitutionally (4).

A common feature of all Athenian orators is the use of historical examples (*paradeigmata*) to support an argument or inspire their hearers. Modern discussions have shown how relatively limited is the range of examples adduced by the orators and how the orators are very careful to avoid giving the impression that they have superior knowledge to that of their audience.[40] Demosthenes is no exception to these generalisations. The very 'Athenian' battles of Salamis and Marathon are adduced in consecutive sections in *On the Symmories* (29 and 30). Argive compassion for Athenian refugees in the face of Spartan threats is used in *For the Liberty of the Rhodians* to urge the Athenians not to fear Artemisia, 'at once a barbarian and a woman' (22). In the same speech the orator refers to two treaties made with the Persian king, one by Athens and one by Sparta. Neither are specified by name and both are said to be 'Known to you all' (8).[41] The first *Philippic* contains three paradigms, one of which refers to the Spartan domination after the Peloponnesian War (3). A second refers to the campaign of Haliartus in 395 (17), and a third to the Corinthian War in 390 (24). Genuine historical examples (that is, events that occurred outside the lifetime of most of the audience) are fewer in the *Olynthiacs* and second and third *Philippics*. In *Olynthiac* 2, Athenian resistance to Spartan domination in defence of the rights of the Hellenes is contrasted with present Athenian inactivity in defence of their own rights (24). In *Philippic* 2, Athenian resistance to Persia at the time of the Persian Wars and refusal to abandon the cause of Hellas, in spite of enticements from the Persian king, gives the orator the opportunity of comparing the heroic behaviour of the Athenians with the treachery of Philip's ancestor, Alexander I – all of which, says Demosthenes, Philip 'is finding out, I think, and hearing about' (10).[42] In *Philippic* 3, the days of the Spartan hegemony are once again adduced to demonstrate how the nature of warfare has been changed by Philip: 'in the good old days there were established rules for conducting wars, all of which Philip disregards and tramples on' (48). Just before this there occurs perhaps the most elaborate and developed paradigm in the public speeches, that of Arthmius of Zelea, in which Demosthenes shows how the Athenians of old dealt with bribery and corruption when the interests of the Hellenes at large, not necessarily their own, were concerned and threatened (41–6).[43]

Another stylistic matter may be mentioned briefly, as it shows so clearly how Demosthenes is prepared to go against rhetorical conventions if he believes it will help to make his speech more forceful. This is the use of – or deliberate non-avoidance of – hiatus (that is, where one word ends in a vowel and the next begins with a vowel), a practice which would have been anathema to that most non-practical orator, Isocrates. Despite the zeal of Blass, who would remove all hiatus from the text of Demosthenes, editors and other critics have been less Procrustean. Sandys, citing Dionysius (*Demosthenes* 43–52) and Cicero (*Orator* 151), cautiously implies that not all hiatus should be removed by emendations and transpositions.[44] Butcher, in his Preface to volume 1 of the Oxford Classical Text of Demosthenes, is more sceptical: 'he does not seem to have been as worried as Isocrates about avoiding hiatus'.[45] Pearson, however, claims that Demosthenes 'skilfully and economically uses hiatus in order to create an effect' and that it should not be assumed that hiatus is a mark of carelessness.[46] Among the passages which Pearson cites to illustrate Demosthenes' virtuosity is that which occupies sections 28–9 of *Philippic* 3, in which there is hiatus at six different places. One may concur with Pearson's view that this is deliberate and with his opinion that 'Only an accomplished orator would dare to write such a sentence for himself ... It is a tremendous *tour de force.*'

As might be expected, there are constantly recurring themes in the mature speeches. The orator frequently exhorts his fellow citizens to rouse themselves from their apathy, to serve in person, to order their priorities correctly and to uphold and emulate the glorious traditions and examples of their ancestors.[47] The fact that he does not hesitate to castigate his fellow citizens for their deficiencies is a mark of his confidence in his ability to handle his audience. Constant is his depiction of himself as a person who is not afraid to speak the truth, unpleasant though it may be to hear – and even dangerous for himself.[48] Those who urge other policies are depicted as self-serving flatterers, speaking only what they think their audience wishes to hear.[49] Increasingly it is hinted and then openly alleged that such people are Philip's friends and Philip's hirelings, and the theme of bribery, corruption and their corrosive effects, not just in Athens but amongst all the Hellenes, rises to a splendid crescendo in the magnificent passages in the third *Philippic*, to which reference has already been made. Insistent, too, are the attacks on Philip's character, especially his ruthlessness, his burning ambition and his treachery and deceit, whereby he has beguiled and then destroyed those states foolish enough to believe his promises.[50] Another frequently recurring argument for the Athenians' taking firm, decisive action in person is the danger that if Philip is not fought 'there' (in the north) he will have to be fought here, in Attica.[51]

One frequent argument used by the orator has already been mentioned[52] and is worth dwelling on for a while, especially because of its modern parallels. This is the idea that monarchy (tyranny) and constitutional government (democracy) are natural and eternal enemies of each other and that kings are always trying to destroy democracy, and especially a democracy like that of Athens, which had always stood forth as the champion of freedom and liberty against would-be tyrants. The germ of the idea is first found in *For the Liberty of the Rhodians*, where the orator urges his audience to regard oligarchies as the common enemies of all who love freedom (20), and states that he believes that it would be more to Athens' advantage to have all the Hellenes making war on her, if they are democracies, than to have them as friends if they are under oligarchies. In *Philippic* 1, the gossips at Athens are quoted (48) as claiming that Philip, in concert with the Spartans, is working for the overthrow of Thebes and the breaking up of the 'free states' (*politeiai*). In *Olynthiac* 1, as already mentioned, Demosthenes argues that Philip's autocracy gives him a great advantage in warfare but a great disadvantage in negotiations for peace, which he would like to enter into with Olynthus, since the Olynthians have before their eyes the examples of what happened to states which, like Amphipolis and Pydna, put themselves into Philip's power. He then generalises with the words: 'And in general I think that tyranny is an object of distrust to free states, especially when they have a common border' (5). But it is in *Philippic* 2 (20–5) and *On the*

Chersonese (41–3) that the concept is spelled out most clearly and most eloquently. In the second *Philippic*, the orator purports to be quoting from the speech which he gave in 344 as an ambassador to the Messenians and Argives, warning them to beware of Philip's approaches and once again using the example of his deceptions of Olynthus. The moral is that 'such close relations with tyrants are not safe for free states'. There is only one secure way for democracies to deal with tyrants: distrust them (24–5):

> Guard this; cleave to it; if you preserve this, you will never suffer any dreadful experience. What are you seeking? Freedom. Then do you not see that even Philip's titles are most alien to this? For every King and every tyrant is an enemy to freedom and a foe to the rule of law?

In *On the Chersonese* 41–2, Demosthenes tells his audience that it is against Athens' constitution above all that Philip is waging war – that he knows he can never hold his gains securely as long as they are a democracy. It is, Demosthenes says, Athens' nature to vindicate all the victims of aggression into liberty. Above all, the Athenians must regard Philip as 'an irreconcilable enemy of your free constitution and democracy'.[53]

Such sentiments as these would surely have struck a resonant and sympathetic chord in the hearts of his audience. For the Athenians of the fourth century not only were proud of their democracy and egalitarian spirit, but were convinced that they had always been the champions of the Hellenes against the oppression of despots and tyrants, whether foreign or home-grown. Indeed, it was firmly believed that the Athenian empire of the fifth century had been precisely the instrument for securing and guaranteeing the liberty and equality of the Hellenes; and it is instructive to compare the hard reality of fifth-century Athenian imperialism as expressed by the Athenian Euphemus at Camarina in 415 with the sentiments of fourth-century authors such as Lysias in his *Funeral Oration* of *c.*390 or Isocrates in his *Panegyricus* of 380.[54] This theme permeates what is surely the finest of all Demosthenes' speeches, *On the Crown* (18), and especially the superb passage which culminates in the famous 'Marathon' oath (196–208).

How effective an orator was Demosthenes in his public speeches? Dionysius of Halicarnassus obviously found him to be most effective, if we may gauge from his remarks in his essays *On Demosthenes* and *On Thucydides*.[55] If Dionysius, at a remove of three hundred years, could be so affected, would not the live impact of the orator on his own audience have been even greater? Or, was Dionysius capable of whipping himself into a frenzy because of his idolisation of Demosthenes? Such questions, of course, must remain speculative. What can be said is that at least from the time of the first *Philippic*, the Athenians increasingly, if not immediately and totally, adopted the policies and strategies which Demosthenes advocated and which he constantly hammered away at. Does this mean that they were persuaded by Demosthenes or that Demosthenes saw the way the wind was blowing and followed it? Again, any answer must be speculative, but I suspect that the most brilliant oratory will not persuade an audience to adopt a position with which it is not already to some extent sympathetic. In my opinion, Demosthenes was correct in his assessment of the threat posed by Philip, at least from 351 onwards, as were more and more of his fellow citizens; and it would be absurd to think of him as a mere opportunist, trying to create fear and hostility for his own advantage. Demosthenes' speeches, like those of Winston Churchill, were a powerful factor in clarifying and crystallising the thoughts and attitudes of his fellow citizens and urging them along a course which they already knew instinctively was the right one. In this respect, the speeches were supremely effective and Demosthenes deserves all the praise heaped on him by later critics. He was indeed 'by a long way the most eminent and virtually the canon of public speaking' (Quintilian, *Institutio Oratoria* 10.1.76).

NOTES

* I thank Ian Worthington for his comments on an earlier draft.
1 See R.D. Milns, 'Hermias of Atarneus and the Fourth Philippic Oration' in C. Questa (ed.), *Filologia e Forme Letterarie: Studi Offerti a Francesco della Corte* 3 (Urbino: 1987), pp. 287–302. This paper cites several modern discussions of the authenticity of the speech, to which should now be added L. Pearson, *The Art of Demosthenes* (Meisenheim am Glan: 1976), pp. 133–7, and Ian Worthington, 'The Authenticity of Demosthenes' Fourth Philippic', *Mnemosyne*[4] 44 (1991), pp. 425–8. See also the remarks on the authenticity of Demosthenes' speeches of Badian, Chapter 1.
2 For example, the reference in section 32 to the decrees passed against the Megarians when they had appropriated the holy meadow land. On this see J.R. Ellis and R.D. Milns, *The Spectre of Philip* (Sydney: 1970), pp. 96–7.
3 For *On Halonnesus*, see Libanius' *Hypothesis*, Harpocration, s.v. Hegesippus, and the Scholiast on Demosthenes 17, 2.6. For *On the Treaty with Alexander*, see Libanius' *Hypothesis*, Harpocration, s.v. Pro-bolas, Scholiast on Demosthenes 17, 1, and Dion. Hal. *Demosthenes* 35.

4 For *On Halonnesus*, see S. Michaelson and A.Q. Morton, 'The New Stylometry: A One-Word Test of Authorship for Greek Writers', *CQ*[2] 22 (1972), pp. 576–88, and D.F. McCabe, *The Prose Rhythm of Demosthenes* (New York: 1981), pp. 186–99.

5 Scholiast on Demosthenes 17, 2, 18–19.

6 Nobody, however, would accept Dionysius' division of *Philippic* 1 into two speeches, with the first finishing at the end of section 29; on this and on the dating see Badian, Chapter 1; cf. Ryder, Chapter 2.

7 'Demosthenes' erste Philippika' in P. Jors, E. Schwartz and R. Reitzenstein (eds.), *Festschrift Theodor Mommsen zum fünfzigjährigen Doctorjubiläum* (Marburg: 1893), pp. 1–44.

8 W. Jaeger, *Demosthenes: The Origin and Growth of his Policy* (Berkeley: 1938; repr. New York: 1977), pp. 115–24, accepts Schwartz's date, but argues that the reference to an attack on Olynthus is evidence of a late revision of the speech after the fall of Olynthus.

9 *Spectre of Philip*, pp. 37–8.

10 R. Sealey, 'Dionysius of Halicarnassus and Some Demosthenic Dates', *REG* 68 (1955), p. 89. J.E. Sandys, *The First Philippic and The Olynthiacs of Demosthenes* (repr. London: 1950), pp. xlix–li, believes that Dionysius is wrong to place the speech earlier than the Aristocrates speech, but correct to assign both speeches to the same year.

11 See especially the discussion of Sandys, *First Philippic and The Olynthiacs*, pp. lxiv–lxvii and Sealey, 'Dionysius of Halicarnassus', p. 89.

12 *Spectre of Philip*, pp. 37–8.

13 On the question of revision and publication of the public speeches, see most recently, J. Trevett, 'Did Demosthenes Publish his Deliberative Speeches?', *Hermes* 124 (1996), pp. 425–41. The view that the speeches were in fact political pamphlets was first put forward by Schwartz, 'Demosthenes' erste Philippika', pp. 1–44. C.D. Adams contested this view in 'Are the Political Speeches of Demosthenes to be Regarded as Political Pamphlets?', *TAPA* 43 (1902), pp. 5–22. See also L. Hudson-Williams, 'Political Speeches in Athens', *CQ*[2] (1951), pp. 68–73 and, especially on the question of revision, Ian Worthington, 'Greek Oratory, Revision of Speeches and the Problem of Historical Reliability', *C&M* 42 (1991), pp. 55–74. M.H. Hansen, 'Two Notes on Demosthenes' Symbouleutic Speeches', *C&M* 35 (1984), pp. 55–70, has some interesting suggestions as to why our speeches, out of what must have been a much larger number of speeches delivered in the Assembly, should have been published or circulated. See also the chapters by Buckler, especially his Appendix (Chapter 4), and Golden (Chapter 5).

14 'Did Demosthenes Publish', p. 426. Cf. also the story in Pseudo-Plutarch about Philip II's reaction on reading a copy of the speeches spoken against him by Demosthenes (*Mor.* 845c).

15 For an excellent discussion of the text of *Philippic* 3, see J.E. Sandys, *Demosthenes, On the Peace* (London: 1953), pp. lix–lxvii. For the argument that the shorter version was intended for an Hellenic audience and the longer for the Athenians, see Sealey, 'Dionysius of Halicarnassus', p. 102, who accepts this argument.

16 Cf. Hansen, 'Two Notes on Demosthenes', pp. 57–60.

17 'Did Demosthenes Publish', p. 437. The weak point of this argument is, of course, the highly polished nature of the speeches as we have them; they can hardly be called 'drafts'. See further on this aspect Worthington, 'Greek Oratory' and 'History and Rhetorical Exploitation' in Ian Worthington (ed.), *Persuasion: Greek Rhetoric in Action* (London: 1994), pp. 109–29.

18 'Two Notes on Demosthenes', pp. 60–70.

19 F. Blass, *Die attische Beredsamkeit* 3.1 (Leipzig: 1893), p. 49.

20 The question of 'barracking' (*thorubos*) in the law-courts and the Assembly is dealt with by V. Bers, 'Dikastic Thorubos' in P. Cartledge and F.D. Harvey (eds.), *Crux: Essays Presented to G.E.M. de Ste. Croix on his 75th Birthday* (London: 1985), pp. 1–15. See also P.E. Harding, 'Rhetoric and Politics in Fourth-Century Athens', *Phoenix* 41 (1987), pp. 25–39, on the difficulties of speaking in the Assembly.

21 For organised groups of supporters, see M.H. Hansen, *The Athenian Assembly* (Oxford: 1987), pp. 69–81.

22 For the size of the quorum for the Assembly, see Hansen, *Athenian Assembly*, pp. 14–19. On p. 128, Hansen estimates that Pnyx II (*c.*400–340) could hold a maximum of 6,500 citizens. J. Ober, *Mass and Elite in Democratic Athens* (Princeton: 1989), p. 132, gives a slightly higher estimate.

23 In addition to the alleged reaction of King Philip referred to in note 14, there is the famous story relayed with variations by Cicero (*De Oratore* 3.213), Quintilian (*Institutio Oratoria* 11.3.7), Pliny the Elder (*Natural History* 7.110) and Pliny the Younger (*Epistles* 2.3) of Aeschines' reply to the amazed reaction of his students at Rhodes when he read his *Against Ctesiphon* speech to them: 'What then, if you had heard the beast himself?'

24 C.W. Wooten, 'Dionysius of Halicarnassus and Hermogenes on the Style of Demosthenes', *AJP* 110 (1989), pp. 576–88. On the assessment of the later rhetoricians see especially Cooper, Chapter 8; for Demosthenes' style and artistry in his private orations see Mirhady, Chapter 6.

25 'What then was the cause of this? For it is not without reason and just cause that the Hellenes of that time were so ready for freedom while the Hellenes of today are ready for slavery. There was something, men of Athens, something in the minds of the majority which is no longer there – something that vanquished the wealth of Persia and kept Hellas free. It was not defeated either in a sea-battle or a land-battle, but now it has perished and so has ruined everything and turned our affairs upside down. What then was this? It was nothing complicated or clever, but the fact that everybody hated those who accepted money from those who wished to rule or destroy Hellas; and it was the most dangerous thing to be convicted of taking bribes; and they punished such a person with the greatest penalty; and there was no begging off or pardon.'

26 See especially *Art of Demosthenes*, ch. 4, and 'The Development of Demosthenes as a Political Orator', *Phoenix* 18 (1964), pp. 95–109. On Demosthenes' earlier career, with discussion of his earlier political speeches, see Badian, Chapter 1; on Demosthenes' political speeches

during the reign of Philip II, see Ryder, Chapter 2 and Buckler, Chapter 4.

27 'Development of Demosthenes' p. 97. A Thucydidean element of Demosthenes' style not noted by Pearson is his fondness for the articular infinitive. Sandys, in his commentary on *Philippic* 1 at p. 130, states that: 'The articular infinitive is extremely common in Demosthenes, as also in Thucydides. The average number of examples per Teubner page is in Thucydides 0.45, in his 'speeches' nearly 1; in the 'public orations' of Demosthenes 1.25 and in the first *Olynthiac* as high as 2.75.' There is no doubt that there is a higher proportion of such infinitives in the speeches up to and including *On the Peace* (with the significant exception of *Philippic* 1). *Philippic* 2, *On the Chersonese* and *Philippic* 3 show a dramatic drop in the proportions.

28 'Development of Demosthenes', p. 96.

29 See C. Carey, 'Rhetorical Means of Persuasion' in Ian Worthington (ed.), *Persuasion: Greek Rhetoric in Action* (London: 1994), pp. 26–45, especially pp. 33–4.

30 See sections 24 for Philip, 31 and 32 for traitors, and 17–21 for democracy and oligarchy. This last topic will be treated later in this chapter, but mention may be made now of the well-argued article of J.W. Leopold, 'Demosthenes on Distrust of Tyrants', *GRBS* 22 (1981), pp. 227–46.

31 I say this despite the fact that after 346 the political tide increasingly flowed in Demosthenes' direction, with the Peace being regarded merely as an opportunity to rebuild Athens' military strength. But at the time of the speech's delivery, Demosthenes had to tread a delicate line between provoking an Amphictyonic war against Athens and appearing to be pleading Philip's cause. Caution and cool-headed reason were more important than fiery anti-Philip passion.

32 See Pearson, *Art of Demosthenes*, p. 126, and 'Development of Demosthenes'. This rhetorical ploy may well be borrowed from the tactics of the law-courts. For a really good example from an earlier orator see Andocides 1.101, for the imaginary interrogation of Andocides by Charicles. For a Demosthenic example of an imaginary dialogue in a law-court case, see 54.35.

33 For further comments on Demosthenes' use of anaphora see C.D. Adams, *Demosthenes* (London, 1927), pp. 86–7. For Demosthenes' supreme mastery of the 'figures' of speech (*schēmata* in Greek, *sententiae* in Latin) and their contributions to his oratory's power, see Cicero, *Brutus* 141 and *Orator* 39.136.

34 See Adams, *Demosthenes*, pp. 82–5. G.O. Rowe, 'Demosthenes' First Philippic: the Satiric Mode', *TAPA* 99 (1968), pp. 361–74, notes that this speech 'contains an unusual proportion of metaphors and similes'. Metaphor and simile are amongst the *sententiae* mentioned by Cicero, *Orator* 39.136.

35 'But now all these things [*sc.* the right moment for action, concord amongst citizens and distrust of tyrants and barbarians] have been sold and exported as though from an open market and in their place have been imported the things by which Hellas has been ruined and has become diseased.'

36 *Art of Demosthenes*, p. 154.

37 See the excellent note of Sandys, *First Philippic and The Olynthiacs*, p. 208 n. 40, where the full significance of the verb *propinein* ('to drink a person's health') is explained.

38 See the note of Sandys on this passage, *First Philippic and The Olynthiacs*, pp. 210–16, with a reference to the corresponding simile in Plato, *Republic* 411b.

39 This same paradox reappears in Demosthenes 9.5.

40 On the use of historical examples in the orators generally, see L. Pearson, 'Historical Allusions in the Attic orators', *CP* 36 (1941), pp. 209–29, S. Perlman, 'The Historical Example, Its Use and Importance as Political Propaganda in the Attic Orators', *SH* 7 (1961), pp. 150–66, Worthington, 'Greek Oratory'. For Demosthenes' use of historical examples, see R.D. Milns, 'Historical Paradigms in Demosthenes' Public Speeches', *Electronic Antiquity* 2.5 (1995).

41 The former must be the so-called Peace of Callias (*c.*448) and the latter the detested Peace of Antalcidas or King's Peace (387). On the 'known to you all' topos, see Ober, *Mass and Elite*, p. 181.

42 See Sandys, *On the Peace*, pp. 116–17 n. 45, for Demosthenes' perhaps deliberate historical error in this example. For an amazing example of the conflating of two totally different events in a paradigm, see Andocides 1.107.

43 For the Arthmius decree, see Sandys, *On the Peace*, pp. 220–1 n. 45. Arthmius was something of a topos in the Attic orators. He is used as a paradigm by Aeschines (3.258) and Dinarchus (2.24), who, like Demosthenes, refers to the relevant stele on the Acropolis. On Arthmius, see further Ian Worthington, *A Historical Commentary on Dinarchus* (Ann Arbor: 1992), pp. 309–11.

44 Sandys, *First Philippic and The Olynthiacs*, p. lxxiii.

45 At pp. xiii–xiv. Cf. also his comment on Demosthenes' adherence to Blass's law: 'To such an extent does he devote himself to the needs of the situation or his own convenience that the rule is almost overwhelmed by the frequent exceptions.' The essence of Blass's law is that Demosthenes allegedly avoided as far as possible the consecutive use of three or more short syllables.

46 'The Virtuoso Passages in Demosthenes' Speeches', *Phoenix* 29 (1975), pp. 214–30. See also his 'Hiatus and Its Purposes in Attic Oratory', *AJP* 96 (1975), pp. 138–59.

47 Cf. 2.13, 3.23–8, 36, 4.7, 24, 35, 6.8–12, 8.50–1, and 9.41–6.

48 1.16, 3.32, 4.51, 8.69, and 9.63–5.

49 See especially 3.22, 27–32, 8.34, 69; cf. 70–2; for the qualities of a good citizen, see 9.2–5.

50 Traitors: 2.4, 4.18, 5.12, 8.20, 53, 61–6, and 9.14, 36–47, 49, 53, 63–7. Philip's character: 1.12–13, 2.5–8, 15–21, 4.49, 6.20–5, and 9.10, 56–62.

51 1.15, 25, 3.8–9, 6.35, and 8.43–7.

52 See above and Leopold, 'Distrust of Tyrants'.

53 It is interesting that Aristotle (*Politics* 5.10), himself no lover of democracy, argues that the reason why tyranny and democracy are so hostile to each other is because they are so similar and 'potter quarrels with potter', as Hesiod says (*Works and Days* 25).

54 Thucydides 6.83, Lysias 2.55–7, Isoc. 4.103–9.

55 *Demosthenes* 22. In *Thucydides* 55, Dionysius states that Demosthenes is the best of orators, that *On the Crown* (18) is the best of his forensic speeches and *Philippic* 3 (9) is the greatest of his political speeches against Philip. Probably few today would disagree with this judgement.

8

PHILOSOPHERS, POLITICS, ACADEMICS

Demosthenes' rhetorical reputation in antiquity*

Craig Cooper

1 Introduction

This chapter concerns Demosthenes' reputation as an orator in antiquity. Hellenistic biographers who wrote about his life were less concerned with Demosthenes' political achievements than with his literary accomplishments. They wanted to know about his early childhood and education, his training regimen and the works he left behind. Political events were mentioned but they were incidental to the real story: Demosthenes the orator. This Demosthenes was very much the product of Alexandrian scholarship and Peripatetic research to which these biographers were deeply indebted. It was not until Plutarch composed his own biography that Demosthenes was treated as a real political figure.

The Demosthenes who emerges from the shadows of Hellenistic research is a remarkable figure of great accomplishment. By the first century, he was regarded as the best of the Attic orators. Dionysius of Halicarnassus noted that Demosthenes' *deinotēs* ('forcefulness') was 'oratory in its most perfect form' (*Isaeus* 20; cf. 3), and Roman rhetoricians agreed. According to Cicero (*Brutus* 35), Demosthenes was the perfect orator who lacked nothing; nothing was more elevated than the sublime, passionate and ornate dignity of his words and thoughts. For Quintilian (*Institutio Oratoria* 10.1.76), though Athens may have produced ten remarkable orators, Demosthenes was by far the leading representative; he was the *lex orandi* ('the standard of oratory'), so great was his *vis* ('force'). For rhetoricians, of the late Republic and early imperial period,

224

Demosthenes was the consummate orator, whose skill was especially seen in his *deinotēs* or *vis dicendi* ('force of speaking').[1]

Demosthenes' achievement was all the more remarkable given his frail constitution and a stutter which in normal circumstances would have prevented anyone from succeeding in public speaking. Despite his handicaps, Demosthenes' determination, his hard work, and countless hours of speech preparation and practice on his delivery enabled him to achieve a level of rhetorical proficiency that surpassed all his contemporaries – or so the tradition goes. But the orator was not always so highly regarded. As I shall argue in this chapter, the tradition which these later rhetoricians so readily accepted is hardly reliable: it was invented by the Peripatetics, who were, in fact, highly critical of Demosthenes' political and rhetorical integrity, and it was shaped by a political controversy that raged between Demochares and the Peripatetics, who tended to regard Aeschines, Demades and Phocion as the better orators. The three were either more honest in what they said or more naturally skilled at speaking than Demosthenes. To compete with these better orators, the Peripatetics claimed that Demosthenes had to work on his speeches and perfect his delivery but they were by no means being complimentary and in fact were being quite critical. Yet despite their criticism, this image of the 'practised' orator became the accepted tradition in antiquity; what would change, however, was Demosthenes' reputation, which would be rehabilitated over the course of the Hellenistic period and, by Cicero's time, would reach a stature unsurpassed by all other Attic orators.

2 Philosophers and rhetorical reputation: orator as craftsman

At chapter 90 of *Orator*, Cicero concludes his discussion of the plain style by remarking that whatever is *salsum* ('witty') is peculiar to the Attic orators. Lysias and Hyperides, he notes, were adequate; Demades excelled all others, but Demosthenes was inferior. Cicero attempts to defend Demosthenes' lack of ability by insisting that he was not so witty (*dicax*) as humorous (*facetus*); the former demands a keener genius, the latter greater art.

Cicero's last remark echoes the *phusis/techne* debate that was first raised by Peripatetics in connection with Demosthenes' rhetorical skill, and repeated by later rhetoricians and biographers.[2] According to Dionysius of Halicarnassus (*Demosthenes* 53), Demetrius of Phalerum (fr. 165 Wehrli),[3] the Peripatetic, and all other writers of

Demosthenes' life, related that Demosthenes worked hard on the intonation of his voice and his gestures, despite being naturally ill-suited to such exertion. That this, in fact, became the accepted tradition among biographers is confirmed by the *Suda*, who records that the third-century biographer Hermippus, who was himself labelled a Peripatetic, had characterized Demosthenes in precisely the same terms, when he described him as a 'practised rather than natural orator' (*Suda*, s.v. Demosthenes 454). All later biographers followed suit.[4] Demetrius himself claimed, allegedly based on first-hand knowledge,[5] that Demosthenes stuttered (Plut. *Dem.* 11.1, Demetrius, fr. 167 Wehrli) and could not pronounce his rhos (Cicero, *De Divinatione* 2.46.96, Demetrius, fr. 168 Wehrli), but that he corrected this stutter by reciting speeches with a mouthful of pebbles. More than that, he exercised his voice by discoursing as he ran, strengthened his breathing by reciting speeches in single breaths and practised his gesturing before a mirror. Later biographers described even more bizarre practices: retiring to a cave, like Euripides, shaving half his head to shame himself into not coming out, and hanging a sword or knife over his shoulder to correct a shoulder spasm ([Plut.] *Mor.* 844d–e, Plut. *Dem.* 7.5). Pomeroy is right to say that 'Demosthenes became a celebrated example of overcompensation for a physical handicap.'[6] But it is hardly credible, as she believes, that 'an adolescent would invent bizarre devices' such as these. These are the romantic fictions of biographers who were simply elaborating on what the Peripatetics themselves had reported and there is little in their report that should be trusted.

This characterization of Demosthenes as a 'practised rather than natural orator' grew out of Peripatetic discussions on the orator's inability to compete with naturally gifted orators, like Aeschines and Demades. At one point in his discussion on whether rhetoric was a *techne*, Philodemus repeats the view of Critolaus, who claimed that Demosthenes was 'a craftsman', whereas Aeschines and Demades never studied (*On Rhetoric* 2.97). Critolaus, who was head of the Peripatos in the second century, cited Aeschines and Demades as examples of orators who could succeed without rhetorical training. The former was an actor, the latter a boatman.[7] By contrast, Demosthenes' success as an orator depended solely on his training.

Critolaus was certainly not the first to voice this opinion. Earlier Peripatetics, like Theophrastus, were highly critical of Demosthenes' skill as an orator, and showed a clear preference either for

Demades, who had a natural talent for extemporizing, or for Phocion, who was noted for his rhetorical simplicity. Theophrastus' views are preserved for us in Plutarch's *Life of Demosthenes*. At the beginning of chapter 10 Plutarch remarks that 'the general consensus was that Demades was invincible when he used his natural talent, and when he extemporized he surpassed the studied preparations of Demosthenes'. Plutarch then cites the philosopher Ariston of Chios for Theophrastus' judgement on the two orators. When asked what sort of orator he considered Demosthenes, Theophrastus replied: 'Worthy of the city'. What sort was Demades? One 'too good for the city'. That this evaluation came from a rhetorical work in which Theophrastus contrasted the different styles of the two orators seems assured from what Plutarch says next in the chapter. Apparently in the same work Theophrastus had also recorded the remark of Polyeuctus the Sphettian, who had once 'declared that Demosthenes was the greatest orator but Phocion the most powerful speaker, since the latter expressed the most sense in the fewest words'.[8]

Polyeuctus' comparison of the two orators is also repeated in Plutarch's *Life of Phocion* (5.2–3), where, as Tritle argues, Plutarch preserves some of the technical language used by Theophrastus to describe Phocion's style of oratory.[9] Theophrastus attributed two qualities to Phocion's oratory, 'brevity' and 'forcefulness' (*deinotēs*), and the anecdotal evidence of Polyeuctus offered by Theophrastus indicates that in his estimation Phocion surpassed Demosthenes in *deinotēs*, which was achieved not through carefully contrived speech, as Demosthenes used, but through brevity. Indeed, Plutarch (*Phocion* 5.2), again perhaps drawing indirectly on Theophrastus, identifies three facets of Phocion's speech that resulted from such brevity: 'imperious', 'severe' and 'unsweetened'. However we define these terms, it would seem that Phocion, with Theophrastus' approval, preferred simple and unadorned speech that was direct and to the point, the very opposite of Demosthenes, who was criticized by Peripatetics, like Demetrius of Phalerum, for his rhetorical affectation (frs. 161–2 Wehrli).[10] Elsewhere we learn that Theophrastus himself believed that the language of deliberative oratory, which is the subject of discussion in Plutarch, should be free of all forms of affectation (Quintilian, *Institutio Oratoria* 3.8.61). Even if, as Tritle argues, the term *deinotēs* did not carry for Theophrastus the idea of 'forcefulness', as it did for later rhetoricians, but simply meant rhetorical skill,[11] Phocion was regarded as the better orator because of his rhetorical simplicity, something which Demosthenes' speech apparently lacked. Perhaps now we may better understand what Theophrastus was getting at when he ranked Demades above Demosthenes. It was something in his oratory that marked him out as too good for his city.

At 8.2 of his biography of Demosthenes, Plutarch remarks that whatever speech Demosthenes heard delivered he would reduce to propositions and periods and introduce various corrections and changes in expression: 'Consequently he possessed a reputation for not being naturally gifted but for deriving his forcefulness and power from hard work.' Here again we have the Peripatetic contrast between natural ability and practice. The evidence that Plutarch provides to substantiate his claim was that 'Demosthenes was rarely heard to speak at a critical moment (*epi kairou*; that is, to extemporize). Although the people would frequently call upon him by name as he sat in the Assembly, he would not come forward until he had given thought to the matter and prepared his words.'[12] For this, we are told, he was ridiculed by Pytheas, who once remarked that Demosthenes' arguments smelled of the lamp-wick. There is an obvious insinuation that Demosthenes had to prepare his speeches and could not extemporize.[13]

Plutarch concludes chapter 8 by offering further proof of Demosthenes' lack of courage *pros kairon*: 'Often when he became confused by the clamour in the Assembly, Demades would rise in support and speak off the cuff, but Demosthenes never did the same for Demades' (5). This concluding remark anticipates the opening statement of chapter 10, with which Plutarch introduces Theophrastus' judgement of the two orators. There, we recall, Plutarch noted that the general consensus was that when Demades relied on his natural abilities he was invincible, and his skill at extemporizing surpassed Demosthenes' studied preparations. Theophrastus' evaluation of the two orators must be seen in light of this statement. He had contrasted Demosthenes unfavourably to Demades: the latter was naturally talented at extemporizing, but the former was not, and so needed to practise and prepare his speeches. In this context Theophrastus may have suggested, as later Peripatetic writers do (Demetrius, *On Style* 282–6), that Demades' witty remarks delivered extemporaneously contained a measure of *deinotēs* that could not be imitated, not even by Demosthenes' carefully crafted speeches. Demades was just 'too good for the city', Demosthenes 'deserved his city'. Contained in this evaluation may also be a moral judgement that we find other Peripatetics making about Demosthenes in connection with his rhetoric.

The content of chapters 8–10 of Plutarch's *Life of Demosthenes* seems to be based ultimately on the rhetorical discussions of the Peripatetics.[14] In the mind of Theophrastus Demosthenes was clearly an inferior orator. He could not match Phocion's rhetorical simplicity or Demades' skill for extemporization. Rather he had to rely on carefully prepared speeches, and on this point the Peripatetics were highly critical. What they noted about these speeches, but what later rhetoricians and biographers admired most about them, were the rhetorical flourishes that were aimed at entertaining the masses. In particular, the Peripatetics were critical of Demosthenes' delivery and elaborate use of figures, two things, however, that were so much admired in him by later rhetoricians and contributed, so these rhetoricians argued, to this quality that they called *deinotēs*. But these later admirers were approaching Demosthenes not as philosophers but as rhetoricians, and this point needs to be kept in mind.

3 Philosophers and rhetorical reputation: orator as actor

For later rhetoricians like Dionysius of Halicarnassus, Cicero and Quintilian, what made Demosthenes great was this quality which they called *deinotēs*, and it was this quality which came to be identified specifically with Demosthenes' oratory. Our clearest understanding of it is given by a certain Demetrius, the author of a work of literary criticism entitled *On Style*. The work was written some time between 270[15] and the early first century[16] and shows clear Peripatetic influence.[17] Demetrius identified four types of style: the plain, the elevated, the elegant and the forceful. He is the only critic to introduce *deinotēs* as a separate style, which he notes is now all the rage (245). More than any other author Demetrius cites Demosthenes for examples of the forceful style, and rarely, if ever, in connection with any of the other styles. Already by the middle of the third century, and certainly by the second century, Demosthenes was beginning to be characterized solely for his *deinotēs*, and, as Rhys Roberts suggests, in creating this separate category, Demetrius was trying to find an independent place for Demosthenes' style of oratory, which was now becoming so fashionable.[18] But Demetrius clearly lacks the enthusiasm for Demosthenes felt by later rhetoricians of the first century. He criticizes the orator for his excessive use of antithesis (250). Nor is Demosthenes the only orator cited for examples of this style: Aeschines is mentioned, as is

Demades, and even Lysias, who is cited for an example of how *deinotēs* is achieved from a dash of playfulness (259). Witness his remark to an old woman's lover: 'It was easier to count her teeth than her fingers.' This is precisely the kind of playfulness and wit which even later admirers like Cicero had to admit that Demosthenes lacked. But playfulness was not something that they felt created *deinotēs*.[19]

There were two things in particular which rhetoricians identified with *deinotēs*, a dramatic delivery and intricate use of figures of speech.[20] And in the case of figures they were indispensable for an effective delivery. At section 269 of *On Style*, Demetrius notes that 'above all, disjunction or asyndeton (*dialusis*)[21] produces forcefulness' (cf. 301), and he proceeds to cite an example from Demosthenes 19.314. At section 271 he reiterates the point, making this time a connection between debate, delivery and forcefulness. 'In general', he says, 'figures of speech help a speaker in histrionic delivery and in debate, that is for forcefulness, and this is especially true of the disjointed style (*to dialelumenon*)'. And again in an earlier passage the same thing is said, and the same connection is made by Demetrius between asyndeton and delivery. At 193 he tells us that 'the disjointed style (*dialelumenē lexis*) lends itself better to debate, and this style is called histrionic, since looseness (*lusis*) stimulates an actor's delivery. A written style, on the other hand, is best read.' In all these passages forcefulness or *deinotēs* is closely associated with debate, delivery and the disjointed style, that is the orator who wants to debate will use the forceful style, which is especially achieved through the use of figures such as asyndeton, which in their turn produce an effective delivery.

This association between delivery and debate is Aristotelian. It should be noted that in section 193 Demetrius draws the same distinction between agonistic and written styles, which we find in Aristotle's *Rhetoric* 3.12, and it is there that Aristotle also gives us his most extensive treatment of delivery. 'The written style', according to Aristotle (3.12.2), 'is more precise; the agonistic more histrionic or suited to delivery.' The latter is of two types, ethical and emotional. 'It is for this reason,' he notes, 'that actors go after plays of this kind and poets after actors competent in such plays.' Aristotle continues by saying 'speeches by writers appear meagre in debate; those by orators, however well read, look amateurish. The reason is that they are only suited to debate; for this reason the histrionic features, when delivery is absent, do not fulfil their function.' The histrionic features which Aristotle mentions are asyndeton and repetition, and as we have seen it was the disjointed style which Demetrius labelled as histrionic, and it was Demosthenes whom Demetrius noted for his use of disjunction or asyndeton.

The Peripatetic influence on Demetrius is further evident from the fact that, like Aristotle, Demetrius connects rhetorical delivery with acting. Like Aristotle, he draws his examples from comedy and tragedy. Menander, he says (193), can be delivered on stage because his style is disjointed, but Philemon is best read, and to illustrate the effects of *lusis* on delivery he quotes a passage from Menander (194): 'I conceived you, I bore you, I nursed you, dear.' In rhetorical discussions, *hupokrisis* meant both the delivery of the orator and the actor, and there was much overlap between the two. This fact was already hinted at by Aristotle in *Rhetoric* and was probably made clear by Theophrastus in his book *On Delivery*, where he noted how the two shared many features and techniques in common.[22]

Aristotle himself had noted a direct correlation between recent developments in drama and in contemporary rhetoric. According to Aristotle (*Rhetoric* 3.1.3), 'delivery had only lately appeared in tragedy and rhapsody, since poets first used to act themselves'. And the same phenomenon, he notes, is also happening in rhetoric. According to Aristotle, those who master all aspects of delivery (volume, pitch and rhythm) win all the prizes at the dramatic contests, and 'just as the actors now have greater influence than the poets, so it is in political contests because of the corruption of the forms of government'. The implication here is that in Aristotle's day the orator's performance was more important than what was actually said. The packaging was what counted, not the substance of the speech. Although Aristotle himself felt (*Rhetoric* 3.1.5) that the whole subject of delivery was in itself vulgar, it was necessary, since the business of rhetoric was all about persuading public opinion. And delivery, he notes (*Rhetoric* 3.1.5), has this power to persuade because of the corruption of the listener.

As the greatest proponent of the forceful style, we would expect to see Demosthenes excel in delivery, particularly of a theatrical kind. And in fact we do. The story is repeatedly told by later rhetoricians, when they came to discuss the importance of delivery in persuasion, how in response to the question of what was the first thing in oratory, Demosthenes answered delivery. What was the second, he again replied delivery; the third, again delivery.[23] In Quintilian's rendition (*Institutio Oratoria* 11.3.6), the importance which Demosthenes placed on delivery is specifically connected with his training under the tragic actor Andronicus, and, as we shall see, this connection between Demosthenes' style of delivery and acting, and particularly his training under an actor, was first made by the Peripatetics, who were highly critical of Demosthenes' style of delivery.

For these Peripatetics, Demosthenes embodied precisely the kind of corruption that Aristotle talked about in his *Rhetoric*. What counted most for Demosthenes was the presentation, not the substance. According to Plutarch (*Dem.* 11.3), Demosthenes 'thought that the tone and the delivery of the speaker was so very important for persuasion. Accordingly his delivery was marvellously pleasing to the masses, but men of refinement, like Demetrius of Phalerum [fr. 161 Wehrli], considered his affectation mean, ignoble and soft.' In Plutarch's text Demetrius' criticism is directly related to the importance that Demosthenes attached to delivery as a means of persuasion. The same criticism is preserved in Philodemus (*On Rhetoric* 1.197.24), who reports that Demetrius of Phalerum (fr. 162 Wehrli) regarded the orator's delivery as 'overly intricate and affected, not simple and of a noble fashion, but rather inclined to what is soft and mean'. At one level, Demetrius' evaluation carries with it a moral condemnation of Demosthenes, whose delivery appealed to the lower classes, and as such looks back to Aristotle, who connected the rise in the importance of delivery in political contests first to the corruption of government and second to the corruption of the listener (*Rhetoric* 3.1.3–5). Elsewhere Demetrius himself had charged Demosthenes with such corruption, with cowardice and corruptibility in contrast to the brave and honest Phocion, who was also the more able speaker (fr. 133 Wehrli Plut. *Dem.* 14.1; cf. 10.2).

Demosthenes' affectation appeared in the highly theatrical manner of his delivery, and to make this point Demetrius cited a number of examples from comedy that illustrated the theatrical nature of the orator's delivery, which, he argued, showed the influence of the stage. These notices are preserved in four parallel texts.[24] In all four texts mention is made of a metrical oath that Demosthenes is said to have sworn once in the Assembly. Photius attributes this particular notice to Demetrius, and Pseudo-Plutarch adds the important detail that the oath appeared in the comedies of Antiphanes and Timocles, indicating the direction from which Demetrius drew his information. Wehrli is right when he suggests that the iambic form of the oath originated from comic travesty.[25] He argues that Demetrius would have used the comic poets as evidence for the affected manner of Demosthenes' delivery, which was due to his theatrical training. At the beginning of his text, Plutarch cites Eratosthenes, Demetrius and the comic poets as his sources, but again specifically attributes the oath to the testimony of Demetrius. Although Plutarch cites Eratosthenes for the notice that Demosthenes often assumed a 'frenzied' or 'theatrical appearance' when he spoke, this is no more than a variation of what Demetrius himself said, when he noted, according to Plutarch, that Demosthenes swore the metrical oath 'as if he were possessed'. At the end of Plutarch's extract come two comic notices; again, Antiphanes is named, this for a comic rendering of Demosthenes' abuse of antithesis. This once more points to the comic origin of many of these notices from Demetrius.

The same is true of the Andronicus anecdote, which is preserved in Pseudo-Plutarch and Photius.[26] As Wehrli suggests,[27] the joke lies in the fact that rhetorical affectation could only be achieved from a real actor, and as a successful student Demosthenes' confession of the importance of delivery suits the context of comic invention.[28] The confession itself may have been a parody of a philosophical discourse in which the actor asked his student what were the three divisions of rhetoric. Aristotle (*Rhetoric* 3.1) had divided the study of rhetoric into three areas: proofs, style and arrangement. He had further subdivided style into three parts of which delivery was only the third, but with the 'greatest power'. As a student of an accomplished tragic actor, the only right answer Demosthenes could give was 'delivery'. Like contemporary tragedy, political drama was now all about acting. Demosthenes' exclusive praise of delivery was a perversion of Aristotle's view, and explains Demetrius' criticism of Demosthenes' affectation. His criticism looks back to Aristotle, who suggested that delivery was having the same corrupting effect on oratory as acting had on drama. It was, no doubt, from this analogy that it was first suggested to Demetrius that Demosthenes had himself been trained by an actor, particularly when he found a number of theatrical features in his delivery parodied in comedy.

The problem with Demetrius' assessment is that Demosthenes' political rivals never make the same criticism, as we suspect they would if it were true. By contrast, Demosthenes does not hesitate to warn the Athenians about Aeschines' acting abilities and the beguiling qualities of his voice. He frequently refers to Aeschines' fine voice.[29] He is said to be loud-sounding, which allows him to express clearly and emphatically whatever he wants with his voice (Dem. 19.206; cf. 18.260, 19.216, 338). Aeschines is compared to a gust of wind, who can string together words clearly 'without taking a breath' (*apneusti*). Ironically this is what later biographers said Demosthenes could not do; he could not speak *apneusti* (Zosimus 299.64; [Plut.] *Mor.* 844f), and it was Demetrius who noted how Demosthenes would exercise his breathing. Demosthenes charges that Aeschines places great stock in his voice, expecting to subdue the audience with his histrionic talent (Dem. 19.337). On more than one occasion he connects Aeschines' fine voice with his training in the theatre (Dem. 18.127, 287, 313, 19.189, 246–7). He notes that his rival exercises his voice and practises (Dem. 18.280, 308, 309, 19.255, 336). This is precisely the picture of Demosthenes found in the biographical and rhetorical traditions: he practised his orations, trained his voice, and put great import on its tone (Plut. *Dem.* 11.3). The irony in all this is that Demosthenes, who so sharply criticized Aeschines for his naturally fine voice and histrionic talent, suffered according to Demetrius from a poor voice and turned to an actor for help. Aeschines, who was regarded both by himself and later writers as naturally talented,[30] was himself an actor; but the orator who lacked natural talent took up theatrical training. It all sounds too specious, particularly since Aeschines never criticized Demosthenes for such training or for having a poor voice.[31] It all appears to be the invention of Demetrius of Phalerum, who was highly critical of the orator's style of delivery.

4 Politics and rhetorical reputation

On the other hand, there can be no question, if we accept what the comic poets tell us, that Demosthenes could at times be melodramatic. But at the same time he was highly popular with the Athenian audience to which he played. Both contemporary comic poets, who parodied his speech, his striking antitheses and dramatic delivery, and critics like Demetrius of Phalerum, who picked up on what these comedians had to say, are testimony to his popularity. Whereas the comedians were simply making fun of a political contemporary, who at times went over the top in emphasizing his points, at the heart of Demetrius' criticism of Demosthenes' style of rhetoric, was the very corruption of the political actor and of the political audience. His philosophical assessment, as we have noted, looked back to Aristotle, who had regarded a discussion of delivery as relevant only because of such corruption. There was a direct correlation suggested by the Peripatetics between an orator's style of oratory and his political honesty. Theophrastus had judged Phocion a better orator for his brevity and simplicity of style that did not mask the truth, and not surprisingly, in the Peripatetic tradition, Phocion emerges, perhaps through the invention of Demetrius of Phalerum, as a philosopher-like figure who outdoes Demosthenes not only in rhetorical aptitude but in political integrity.[32] Like a second Socrates, he goes barefoot and can be found lost in thought, considering just how he can shorten the speech which he is about to deliver in the Assembly (Plut. *Phocion* 4.2, 5.3). He is honest and brave, and, according to Demetrius of Phalerum (fr. 133 Wehrli), because of this courage and honesty Phocion was ranked with the great statesmen of the past, Ephialtes, Aristides and Cimon. But Demosthenes, who was cowardly and corruptible, was only capable of praising the virtues of the older generation, not of imitating them (Plut. *Dem.* 14.1). The account of Phocion's death at the hands of a vengeful Athenian jury is replete with Socratic motifs.[33] By contrast, Demosthenes dies a cowardly death, ingesting poison concealed in his pen (Plut. *Dem.* 29.3–4), the very pen with which he composed his speeches.[34] Peripatetics, like Demetrius, who questioned Demosthenes' political integrity, also criticized his overly affected style of oratory which aimed at mass appeal.

But does such criticism ring true? Demetrius may in fact be responding to the severe criticism which he himself had received at the hands of Demochares, who attempted to rehabilitate his uncle's memory at Demetrius' own expense. He had proposed and received honours (280/79) commemorating the memory of Demosthenes ([Plut.] *Mor.* 847d, 850f). But long before he had won this recognition, the battle to rehabilitate and honour his uncle's memory had been waged by the pen. Demochares had written a history of his own times, which was apparently more rhetorical than historical (Cicero, *Brutus* 286); that is to say, it contained a good deal of polemic and eulogy. It is likely that it was in this history that he described the death of Demosthenes, which he attributed not to poison, as all other accounts reported, but to the honour and kind favour of the gods who had rescued his uncle from the cruelty of the Macedonians by granting him a speedy and painless death (Plut. *Dem.* 30.4). There seems to be an obvious attempt at apology, which included not only a defence of Demosthenes' life but also vicious attacks on Demosthenes' political enemies. Demochares reported how as a third rate actor in the role of Oenomaus Aeschines fell flat on his face on stage and had to be helped up by the Chorus leader (*Vita Aes.* 2.7). The hostile tradition about Phocion preserved by Nepos (*Phocion* 2.2–3) seems to derive from

Demochares.[35] There we are told how Phocion, even after Demosthenes had provided him with political and legal support to promote and sustain his career, betrayed Demosthenes by conspiring with Demades to hand over Athens to Antipater and by proposing the very decree that called for Demosthenes' exile.[36]

Demades' and Phocion's complicity with the Macedonians would certainly explain Demochares' hostility toward them. It was their complicity that led directly to Athens' loss of freedom and Demosthenes' death. After Athens' defeat at the battle of Crannon (322), the city came under direct Macedonian control; Antipater installed a garrison in Piraeus and modified Athens' constitution to an oligarchy. In this he was supported by Demades, Phocion and Demetrius of Phalerum, all of whom had served on the legation that negotiated the terms of surrender. Demades had himself proposed the decree calling for Demosthenes' death, and later Phocion resisted all calls to negotiate with Antipater about removing the garrison. Even after Antipater's death (319), when Polyperchon, the regent of Macedon, and Cassander, Antipater's son, were jockeying for control of Athens, Phocion refused to push for the removal of the garrison, though he had the opportunity. Consequently, when the democracy was restored in 318, Phocion was condemned to death, and his supporter Demetrius of Phalerum was forced to take refuge with Nicanor, the garrison commander in Piraeus. But the new democracy was short-lived, and in the following year Cassander defeated Polyperchon and won control of Athens. The Athenians were forced to negotiate and a leading role in the talks was taken by Demetrius of Phalerum, who was rewarded by Cassander with control of Athens' government, a position which he would hold for the next ten years (317–307). Soon after Demetrius' instalment, Phocion's body was returned to Athens and honoured with a state burial. His rehabilitation had begun.[37]

Demochares' attack on Demetrius of Phalerum, who was so closely associated with Phocion, was also vicious. Polybius (12.13.7–8) suggests that a great deal of the polemic in Demochares' history was directed at Macedonian associates like Demetrius. He took direct aim at Demetrius' government, in which the Phalerian had expressed such pride. As Walbank notes, Polybius' words indicate that Demochares was responding to a statement that Demetrius had made justifying his ten-year rule, perhaps in one of his apologies.[38] Demochares had characterized Demetrius' term as something only a vulgar tax collector would pride himself in – all Demetrius could boast about was cheap food and entertainment. The outlandish ostentation that he displayed and apparently described without any shame in his apology, according to Demochares, only underscored Athens' humiliation and subjection to Cassander. Demetrius did not remain silent. Polybius (12.13.12) implies that he had responded to Demochares' criticism in a subsequent work but not in kind.[39] His criticism took a different form. What form it may have taken we do not know precisely but it obviously involved criticism of Demosthenes. Demetrius was certainly hostile; he had, as we have seen, charged Demosthenes with corruption and cowardice in direct contrast to Phocion, who was the more able and more honest orator. And just as Phocion's honesty was reflected in his speech, so Demosthenes' corruption showed through in his oratory – his over-the-top delivery was purposely designed to pander to a corrupt Athenian audience.

Nor was Demetrius the only Peripatetic to criticize Demosthenes' oratory. Theophrastus, Demetrius' teacher, had ranked Demades above Demosthenes. Nor may it be inconsequential that Theophrastus himself had felt Demochares' wrath. In 307/6, after the departure of Demetrius of Phalerum, Theophrastus was forced to leave Athens, when Sophocles of Sunium introduced a law banning all philosophical schools which had not received official permission.[40] The law was directed at the Peripatetic school, and there can be no question that Demochares was behind the action. When Sophocles was indicted by Philon, a member of the Peripatetic school, he was defended in court by Demochares, who apparently heaped all kinds of abuse on philosophers (Athenaeus 11.509a–b). Though Sophocles was convicted and Theophrastus subsequently returned to Athens, the first salvo had been fired, and in the literary war that followed between Demochares and the Peripatetics, one of the casualties was Demosthenes.

In the Peripatetic tradition, which would have such a profound influence on how later rhetorical and biographical writers conceived of Demosthenes, the image that emerges is that of the 'practised rather than natural orator', who cannot compete with Demades' skilful extemporization, Aeschines' natural ease at speaking or Phocion's simple unaffected oratory. These three were the orators of choice for the early Peripatetics, and not surprisingly all three were pro-Macedonians. The image of Demosthenes that was created by these Peripatetics and emerged from the controversy, however, stuck; every biographer included some description of how Demosthenes overcame his physical deficiencies by practising tirelessly his declamation, something that was first described in detail by Demetrius of Phalerum (frs. 165–8 Wehrli). Every rhetorical work included some account of the important emphasis that Demosthenes placed on delivery as a means of persuasion, again something that was detailed by Demetrius (frs. 161–4 Wehrli). But biographers celebrated what the Peripatetics criticized. Demosthenes' physical handicaps and the hard work and careful speech preparation that went into overcoming his deficiencies only enhanced his greatness. Rhetoricians were taken with Demosthenes' powerful use of figures and his theatrical delivery and regarded them as the source of his *deinotēs* and not some attempt by a corrupt politician to titillate his audience. The image had not really changed but what was made of it. By the second century, Demosthenes would become the darling of rhetoricians, whose own reputations depended on successfully teaching rhetoric and on showing how the skill could be learned. Demosthenes, whom tradition claimed learned his rhetoric, was just the ticket to sell their wares. But Demosthenes was now in the hands of literary critics and rhetoricians, not philosophers.

5 Academics and rhetorical reputation: Demosthenes' rehabilitation

The literary image of Demosthenes that has come down to us was shaped in controversy and cannot help but be distorted. How much of that image is real and how much of it is fiction is anyone's guess. I suspect there is a good deal more fiction than reality. But however distorted that literary image may be, and however far removed from the real Demosthenes who acted on a real political stage, it was immortalized in writing. Once in writing it became fixed for all time, and then the accepted reality. Hellenistic society, certainly as it was embodied in the Museum at Alexandria, was antiquarian in nature and of course depended on earlier literary sources for much of its knowledge. Demetrius of Phalerum may have had a hand in organizing the library along Peripatetic lines;[41] certainly his works were well known to biographers like Hermippus who wrote about Demosthenes. Much of what we know and what they knew about the orator and his rhetorical style came from the Peripatetics, who were, as we have seen, hostile to Demosthenes. Although by the time Hermippus came to write his biography (200), the immediate political controversy that created this negative image of Demosthenes was long forgotten, the image itself, however distorted, was accepted without question and even celebrated in Hermippus' biography. By the second century, Demosthenes' reputation had been rehabilitated, perhaps in large part through the scholarly efforts of the Alexandrians. His speeches had been catalogued by Callimachus, and Hermippus, Callimachus' student, provided a popular biographical supplement to the reading of Demosthenes, who was by now a famous literary figure.

In the third century, when the Asianic style of oratory flourished and Hegesias of Magnesia was the best-known orator, Demosthenes' style was not fashionable.[42] But by the middle of the third century, if we accept Grube's date for Demetrius' *On Style*, or by the early part of the second century, the date I prefer for the publication of the work, and certainly by the first century, if we accept Kennedy's date, Demosthenes was in vogue, and according to Demetrius his forceful style was all the rage. His popularity may in large part be due to a number of commentaries and other exegetical works now available on his speeches. Didymus, who was active in the second half of the first century, wrote on the Attic orators. In his *Peri Demosthenous*, he refers to earlier commentators with whom he disagreed. These commentaries belong to the later part of the second century,[43] and such activity may have been going on for some time. Aristophanes of Byzantium, who was active in the last quarter of the third and first quarter of the second centuries, provided selected lists of approved authors, including the orators, and wrote a supplement to Callimachus' catalogue.[44] By the turn of the second century, then, Demosthenes' speeches were widely available, critically analysed and assessed. His biography had been written. He was emerging as an important literary figure, whose speeches could be studied and appreciated in their own right as any other literary work; by this point, the study of rhetoric was the preferred pastime and education of the leisured class.

Despite his growing popularity Demosthenes the orator and literary figure was never far removed from controversy, and he would be co-opted for different battles in different contexts. Throughout the third century, the study of rhetoric was in the hands of philosophers. That would change by the second century, when higher education passed from philosophers to rhetoricians, who were eagerly sought after by the Romans. By 150 Hermagoras was a celebrated teacher, who offered and published a systematic study of rhetoric.[45] Rhetoric was regarded as a *techne* that could be taught and mastered through careful study, and with every aspect covered in detail. After his time advanced studies in rhetoric became common and schools abounded both in Greece and Asia and later in Rome. The growing popularity of rhetorical studies at the expense of the philosophical schools elicited a response from philosophers. Regardless of their philosophical affiliation, all the leading philosophers of Hermagoras' day denied that rhetoric was a *techne* and so worthy of study.[46] Carneades, the Academic, and his student Charmadas maintained that rhetoric was simply an innate aptitude to coax (Cicero, *De Oratore* 1.90). The tenor of what was at times a very acrimonious debate between philosophers and rhetoricians is captured in Cicero's *De Oratore* 1.85–90. At the centre of the controversy is what to make of Demosthenes. In the debate that Antonius reports, Menedemus, the rhetorician, tried to refute Charmadas' charge that rhetorical handbooks were paltry treatises stuffed full of maxims and rules devoid of wisdom. To this end he quoted passages from Demosthenes' speeches that showed that rhetoric achieved the very ends that Charmadas claimed for philosophy. The philosopher, we are told, could not deny that Demosthenes possessed the highest wisdom and greatest *vis dicendi* ('force of speaking'). But Demosthenes, he maintained, owed this ability either to natural talent or, as is generally agreed, to studying under Plato. Since the tradition was now well established that Demosthenes lacked such natural talent but had achieved his rhetorical skill through study, the only conclusion to be drawn by Charmadas was that he was a student of the Academy.

Critolaus the Peripatetic reached a similar conclusion. For him rhetoric was a *kakotechnia*, 'a base art' (Sextus Empiricus, *Against the Professors* 2.12) rather than a *techne*; in his mind, it was neither a faculty, a science nor an art, but a 'knack' (Quintilian, *Institutio Oratoria* 2.15.23; cf. 2.17.15). He could point to Demades and Aeschines who succeeded without instruction but through natural talent (Philodemus, *On Rhetoric* 2.97.2–2.98.21; cf. 2.71.1), and although he conceded that Demosthenes was a *technites*, 'a craftsman', he must have suggested, as one later Peripatetic did (Dion. Hal. *To Ammaeus* 1), that Demosthenes' success as an orator came from his study of philosophy. This later Peripatetic claimed that Demosthenes had learned his rhetoric from Aristotle, and it has been suggested that this view originated with Critolaus.[47] Demosthenes was by now a formidable literary figure, whose style was imitated, whose success through hard work and training was celebrated in biography and rhetorical works. Critolaus could not deny what was now the accepted and popular image of Demosthenes; instead he enlisted that Demosthenes to fight in a new literary war that waged between his school and the rhetorical schools. Unwittingly and unknowingly he perpetuated an image that had been invented by earlier hostile Peripatetics in a different context for a different war.[48]

The ebb and flow of Demosthenes' political career finds a parallel in the rise and fall and subsequent rise of his rhetorical reputation. By the time of the Harpalus affair (324/3) Demosthenes had reached the pinnacle of his career, and the charges of corruption that led to his political exile also led to an exile into the wilderness of rhetorical ignominy.[49] At the hands of philosophers, Demosthenes' reputation as an orator was greatly tarnished; his political dishonesty, they argued, was reflected in the dishonesty of words and the theatrics of his delivery. Demosthenes would languish in that wilderness for most of the third century. It was not until academics got hold of him that he would acquire a reputation as a great speaker. By this time the study of rhetoric had passed into the hands of rhetoricians, who could present Demosthenes as an example of one who could succeed through hard work and careful speech preparation.

NOTES

* I would like to thank Mark Golden, Phillip Harding and Ian Worthington for reading various drafts of this chapter and for their insightful comments.

1 Harding, Chapter 9, also highlights Demosthenes' reputation in antiquity, although he is more concerned with Demosthenes' reputation from the Middle Ages especially to the present day. On Demosthenes' style see also Milns, Chapter 7; cf. Mirhady, Chapter 6.

2 Beginning with the sophists of the later fifth century, the question was debated among philosophers whether certain skills, like rhetoric, were innate (a matter of *phusis*) or acquired through learning (a matter of *techne* or 'art').

3 All fragments of Demetrius of Phalerum are cited from F. Wehrli, *Die Schule des Aristoteles* 4 (Basel and Stuttgart: 1968).

4 The same idea is found preserved in nearly every extant biography; it is repeatedly stated that Demosthenes suffered naturally (*ek phuseōs*) from a stutter, a shortness of breath, an awkward shoulder movement and an inability to project his voice. All of these problems he corrected through practise (*meletē*). In each account there is a clear contrast made between *phusis* and *meletē*, between natural ability and training. See Libanius 295.62, Zosimus 299.60, Anonymous *Vita* 305.66, *Suda* 311.51, [Plut.] *Mor.* 844d–e. All of the minor biographers (for example, Libanius 295.62) are cited by page and line number from A. Westermann, *Biographi Graeci Minores* (Braunschweig: 1845; repr. Amsterdam: 1964).

5 These anecdotes were found in Demetrius' work *On Rhetoric*, which I suspect took the form of a dialogue in which one of the interlocutors reported what he heard from Demosthenes as an old man.

6 S. Pomeroy, *Families in Classical and Hellenistic Greece: Representations and Realities* (Oxford: 1997), pp. 173–4.

7 See Quintilian, *Institutio Oratoria* 2.17.12, Sextus Empiricus, *Against the Professors* 2.16. Both authors mention Critolaus. For a full discussion see H.M. Hubbell, 'The Rhetorica of Philodemus', *Transactions of the Connecticut Academy of Arts and Science* 23 (1920), pp. 371–4.

8 It is not absolutely clear whether this citation was derived from Ariston or Theophrastus, since Plutarch simply writes 'and the same philosopher records'. Cf. L. Tritle, *Phocion the Good* (London: 1988), pp. 23 and 165 n. 35.

9 Tritle, *Phocion*, pp. 23–4.

10 According to Tritle (*Phocion*, p. 23), *austērē* ('severe') meant lack of euphony, which was a quality of speech recognized by Theophrastus and included under the category of composition. Whether this is the sense Plutarch means here is uncertain; for later literary critics and rhetoricians, it was a technical term to describe a particular style of composition (*harmonia*) (Polybius 9.1.2, Dion. Hal. *On Composition* 22 and *Demosthenes* 38), which could avoid euphony but also parallelisms and polished rhythms. According to Dionysius, this style was not florid but generally unadorned. I would agree with Tritle that *anēduntos* ('unsweetened') obviously refers to a lack of embellishment (*akosmetos*) which was discussed by Theophrastus under the category of figures, but I cannot accept that *deinotēs* does not mean here 'forcefulness' but only rhetorical cleverness. Both Plato and Aristotle use the term in a sense of passionate force or intensity (see G.M.A. Grube, *A Greek Critic: Demetrius on Style* [Toronto: 1961], pp. 136–7), and I would suspect so too did Theophrastus. Indeed Demetrius, the writer of *On Style*, who was greatly influenced by the Peripatetics, identifies brevity, lack of smoothness (241–4), an avoidance of parallelism (247) and lack of euphony (255–6) as elements of the forceful style.

11 Tritle, *Phocion*, pp. 24–5; cf. W. Rhys Roberts, *Demetrius On Style*, Loeb Classical Library (Cambridge, Mass.: 1922), p. 266 and note b, Grube, *A Greek Critic*, pp. 136–7.

12 Cf. [Plut.] *Mor.* 848c, where we are told that Epicles reproached Demosthenes for always preparing his speeches, to which Demosthenes replied he would never offer advice off the cuff to such an important body.

13 The tradition is consistent on this point. There is only one notice to the contrary ([Plut.] *Mor.* 848c), which claims that most of Demosthenes' speeches were delivered extemporaneously, as he was naturally gifted for it. Whatever the value of this notice, the important point here is the connection between natural talent and extemporization, both of which the Peripatetics claimed Demosthenes did not possess.

14 The repeated use of this phrase *epi kairou* in the context of the contrast between Demades' ability and Demosthenes' inability to extemporize suggests that Plutarch's account in chapter 8 derives from Theophrastus' *Peri kairōn*, which dealt not with political crises but with the opportune moment of speaking. And in fact the catalogue of his works

preserved in Diogenes Laertius distinguishes two such works, a *Politikon pros tous kairous* (5.45) in four books and a *Peri kairōn* in two books (5.50), the latter being listed alongside other rhetorical works. Likewise, Demetrius of Phalerum is known to have written a treatise *Peri kairou*, which may have been a rhetorical work rather than an ethical or political work. See Grube, *A Greek Critic*, p. 52. David Mirhady, however, takes issue with my position and believes the citations come from a political work by Theophrastus; *contra* Tritle, *Phocion*, pp. 23 and 165 n. 37, who suggests Theophrastus' *On Style*.

15 So Grube, *A Greek Critic*, pp. 39–56 and G. Kennedy, *The Art of Persuasion in Greece* (Princeton: 1963), p. 286, who follows Grube. But in his revised and abridged edition, *A New History of Classical Rhetoric* (Princeton: 1994), Kennedy suggests the first century. Three Peripatetic writers are quoted in the work, Theophrastus, Demetrius of Phalerum and Praxiphanes. All three were active in the first half of the third century, which inclines me to suggest the latter half of the third or early part of the second century for the date of composition, precisely the time when Demosthenes' popularity was on the rise.

16 Kennedy, *A New History*, p. 88.

17 Grube, *A Greek Critic*, pp. 32–9.

18 Roberts, *Demetrius On Style*, p. 267.

19 On comic invective in oratory see P.E. Harding, 'Comedy and Rhetoric' in Ian Worthington (ed.), *Persuasion: Greek Rhetoric in Action* (London: 1994), pp. 196–221.

20 See especially Quintilian, *Institutio Oratoria* 6.2.24 and Cicero, *Brutus* 141, where Antonius is compared to Demosthenes, who surpassed all other orators in his use of figures and delivery.

21 By this term Demetrius clearly means asyndeton, the lack of connectives between clauses and phrases in a sentence, and indeed elsewhere (192) he connects the two terms: 'Asyndeton and disjunction (*dialelumenon*) makes everything completely obscure, because the beginning of each clause is obscured by the looseness (*lusis*)'. But as Grube points out, the terms *dialusis* or *lusis* also have a more general meaning of loose, non-periodic structure (*A Greek Critic*, p. 105 n. 192).

22 W. Fortenbaugh, 'Theophrastus on Delivery', *Rutgers University Studies* 2 (1985), pp. 281–3. At 195, Demetrius notes that other aspects of delivery must be considered. As an example he refers to the scene in Euripides' *Ion*, in which the hero threatens the swan with his bow. The fetching of the bow, the address to the swan and all other stage business provide the actor with a variety of movements. Realizing that he has digressed, Demetrius concludes abruptly: 'but our discussion at present is not about delivery (*peri hupokriseōs*)'. As Fortenbaugh notes, this last comment suggests that under the phrase 'on delivery' a Peripatetic writer would include dramatic delivery ('Theophrastus on Delivery', p. 282).

23 Cicero, *De Oratore* 3.3, *Brutus* 142, *Orator* 56, Philodemus, *On Rhetoric* 1.196.3, Quintilian, *Institutio Oratoria* 11.3.6, [Plut.] *Mor.* 845b.

24 Plut. *Dem.* 9.4–5 (Demetrius, fr. 163 Wehrli), Photius, *Bibliotheca* 493 a 41 (fr. 164 Wehrli), [Plut.] *Mor.* 845a–b, G. Vitelli (ed.), *Pubblicazioni della Società italiana per la ricerca dei papiri greci e latini in Egitto*

(*PSI*), *Papiri Greci e Latini* 2 (Florence: 1913), no. 144. In one text or another we find notices on Demosthenes' training under the actor Andronicus (Pseudo-Plutarch, Photius), on his famous testimonial that delivery was the first, second and third thing in rhetoric, on the theatrical or frenzied manner of his speaking (Plutarch, *PSI*), on his mispronunciation of the name Asclepius (Pseudo-Plutarch, Photius, *PSI*), and on his misuse of antithesis (Plutarch).

25 Wehrli, *Schule des Aristoteles* 4, p. 82.

26 Photius is essentially an extract of Pseudo-Plutarch. On the relationship of the two authors see A. Zucker, 'Quae ratio inter vitas Lysiae, Dionysiacam, Pseudo-Plutarchean, Photianam intercedet', *Acta Seminarii Philologici Erlangensis* 1 (1878), pp. 289–315, A. Prasse, *De Plutarchi quae feruntur Vitis Decem Oratorum* (Marburg: 1891), G. Shoemaker, *Dinarchus: The Tradition of His Life and Speeches with a Commentary on the Fragments of the Speeches* (diss. Columbia University: 1986), pp. 41, 82, R. McComb, *The Tradition of 'The Lives of the Ten Orators' in Plutarch and Photius* (diss. Chapel Hill: 1991), pp. 31–85.

27 Wehrli, *Schule des Aristoteles* 4, p. 81.

28 J.O. Meerwaldt, 'De comicorum quibusdam locis ad ludendum Demosthenem pertinentibus', *Mnemosyne* 55 (1927), p. 300, attempts to reconstruct the comic verse.

29 A. Schaefer, *Demosthenes und seine Zeit*^{2} 1 (Leipzig: 1885), p. 240 n. 2, collects all the references; for a discussion of Demosthenes' criticism of Aeschines see J.F. Kindstrand, *The Stylistic Evaluation of Aeschines in Antiquity* (Uppsala: 1982), pp. 17–23.

30 Aes. 2.241, 3.228, Anonymous *Vita Aeschines* 268.11, *P. Oxy.* 1800 1.48, Dion. Hal. *On Imitation* 212.20 and *Demosthenes* 35, Photius, *Bibliotheca* 61 20b.

31 In fact, Aeschines claims that Demosthenes has a shrill and loud voice: 2.86, 157.

32 See C. Bearzot, *Focione tra storia e trasfigurazione ideale* (Milan: 1985); cf. the review of Bearzot by P.E. Harding, *JHS* 108 (1987), pp. 233–4; see also Tritle, *Phocion*, pp. 29–32.

33 Tritle, *Phocion*, pp. 30–1.

34 Cf. fr. 134 Wehrli (Plut. *Dem.* 28.3–4), where we are told Demetrius had reported that Archias was a student of Anaximenes. Archias was Antipater's henchman, who had been dispatched to track down Demosthenes, Hyperides and others who had fled the city. It is likely that Demetrius had described Demosthenes' death.

35 Tritle, *Phocion*, pp. 5–6.

36 Other sources indicate that Phocion was involved in the embassy that was sent to Antipater to negotiate peace that resulted in the surrender of Demosthenes and others, but the decree itself was proposed by Demades. See Plut. *Dem.* 28.2–4, *Phocion* 26.3, 27.3–5, Diod. 18.18.1–2.

37 For full discussion of events leading up to and including the rule of Demetrius see C. Habicht, *Athens from Alexander to Antony* (transl. D.L. Schneider, Cambridge, Mass.: 1997), pp. 36–66, and W.S. Ferguson, *Hellenistic Athens* (London: 1911), pp. 1–94.

38 Either in *On the Ten Years* (Diogenes Laertius 5.81) or *On the Constitution* (Strabo 9.398). See F.W. Walbank, *A Historical Commentary on Polybius* 2 (Oxford: 1967), pp. 358–9.

39 Walbank, *Commentary on Polybius* 2, pp. 359–60.

40 Pollux 9.42, Diogenes Laertius 5.38, Athenaeus 13.610f. See Ferguson, *Hellenistic Athens*, pp. 103–7.

41 P.M. Fraser, *Ptolemaic Alexandria* 1 (Oxford: 1972), pp. 314–21, R. Pfeiffer, *History of Classical Scholarship* (Oxford: 1968), pp. 98–102.

42 Kennedy, *A New History*, p. 96; cf. *Art of Persuasion*, pp. 302–3, G.M.A. Grube, *The Greek and Roman Critics* (Indianapolis: 1995), pp. 122–3.

43 Pfeiffer, *Classical Scholarship*, p. 278.

44 Dates: Pfeiffer, *Classical Scholarship*, p. 172, Fraser, *Ptolemaic Alexandria* 1, pp. 332–3; literary activity: Pfeiffer, *Classical Scholarship*, pp. 133, 204–6, 278, Fraser, *Ptolemaic Alexandria* 1, pp. 456, 460.

45 For Hermagoras see Kennedy, *Art of Persuasion*, pp. 303–21 and *A New History*, pp. 97–101, and Grube, *Greek and Roman Critics*, pp. 142–4.

46 On the quarrel between the philosophical and rhetorical schools see Kennedy, *Art of Persuasion*, pp. 321–30, and Grube, *Greek and Roman Critics*, pp. 142–3.

47 A.H. Chroust, 'The Vita Aristotelis of Dionysius of Halicarnassus (1 *Ep. Ad Amm.* 5)', *AAntHung* 13 (1965), pp. 369–77; cf. G. Kennedy, *The Art of Rhetoric in the Roman World* (Princeton: 1972), p. 345 n. 65.

48 Kennedy, *A New History*, p. 88, suggests that Critolaus was not familiar with Theophrastus' work.

49 On the Harpalus affair see Worthington, Chapter 3.

9

DEMOSTHENES IN THE UNDERWORLD

A chapter in the *Nachleben* of a *rhētōr*

Phillip Harding

1 Introduction

Charting the tradition regarding an author or theme[1] from classical antiquity has become one of the most popular and fruitful fields for scholars to exploit in the last few decades.[2] It has interest not only for those who wish to follow the ups and downs of classical scholarship itself, but also for social and intellectual historians, who can often find reflections of contemporary attitudes in the views a given generation holds of the individual or idea concerned. Indeed, in many cases these shifts and changes tell us more about ourselves than about the subject.[3] In this context, a brief review of the history of scholarship on Demosthenes, his Afterlife (*Nachleben*), has more to tell than many such studies, since he was both orator and politician,[4] two pursuits which were and have been embroiled in controversy.

During his lifetime Demosthenes practised two professions, speech-writer (*logographos*) and politician. In the first capacity he either composed for himself or, more usually, aided another litigant in the composition of a speech for a lawsuit in the *dikasteria* (*dikanikoi logoi*).[5] This aspect of his career (i.e. as an advocate) has been discussed by David Mirhady (Chapter 6). As a politician he composed speeches exclusively for himself, for presentation of policy issues before the Assembly (*symbouleutikoi logoi*) – this aspect of his career has been discussed by Bob Milns (Chapter 7). At times, he composed his own speeches for prosecution or defence in political trials in the lawcourts. These latter include his two most famous speeches, *On the False Embassy* and *On the Crown* (on behalf of

Ctesiphon). In the course of this activity he honed his rhetorical skills to a high degree, which was appreciated to an extent in his own day, but subsequently, from the time of Cicero, became for both Greeks and Romans the very model of excellence in rhetoric. His *Nachleben* to this point and in this respect has been treated by Craig Cooper (Chapter 8). The reception of Demosthenes, the orator, from Rome to the present will be one part of the subject of this chapter. The other part will assess the reaction of later generations to his career as a politician, about which a few words need to be said as background.

Demosthenes was in many ways the very model of modern democratic politicians. Like them, he needed to find an issue and create an image for himself. The issue that he seized upon was the rise of Philip of Macedon and the threat he supposedly represented to the liberty of the Greek city-states. For his *persona* he chose to project himself as the people's counsellor (*symboulos*), whose main qualities were wisdom; that is, he saw what others did not see and gave advice that was always right, and integrity, which, in the context of ancient Athenian democracy, meant that he was not susceptible to bribes (*adōrodoketos*). By contrast, of course, he had to claim that his opponents in politics were blind to the dangers that beset the state and for that reason gave bad advice; further, he asserted that their blindness had been bought by bribes.[6] His blistering attacks were directed against anyone who disagreed with him, but the especial butt of his rhetoric was Aeschines, against whom he employed shameless invective (*loidoria*) and slander (*diabolē*).[7]

Eventually, Demosthenes was victorious and drove Aeschines from Athens, but his victory was ephemeral. Like Demosthenes, Aeschines published his speeches and three of them (*Against Timarchus*, *On the False Embassy* and *Against Ctesiphon*) have survived. In these Aeschines challenged every charge Demosthenes made against him in diametrically opposite terms and created a counter-image that has haunted the tradition. This rhetorical counter-image of a Demosthenes who worked for peace with Macedon (Aes. 2.18–20), who lost his voice when he had a chance to speak to Philip (Aes. 2.34–5) and who ran like a coward from the battle of Chaeronea (Aes. 3.152, 159), was given real support late in Demosthenes' life by the Harpalus affair (324/3), in which Demosthenes was found guilty of accepting bribes and exiled from Athens (see Worthington, Chapter 3). It is immaterial whether he was guilty or not; what was important was that the credibility of his claim to incorruptibility (and by extension his whole political *persona*) was destroyed. The Harpalus affair has been a millstone around the neck of Demosthenes' reputation ever since.

The other great opponent in Demosthenes' lifetime was, of course, Philip of Macedon, who was vilified by the orator as immoral, both politically (perfidious and unjust, see for example 2.5) and personally (sexually depraved and bibulous, see for example 2.17–20). He has not left any speech in his own defence, but perhaps more effective were his actions. By his success at Chaeronea and after, and furthermore through the great career of his son, Philip transformed the Greek world that Demosthenes had fought so hard to save. Even during Demosthenes' lifetime, Philip's success called into question the wisdom of the policy of confrontation and, although Demosthenes vindicated himself in the eyes of his fellow citizens through his masterpiece, *On the Crown*, subsequent generations have seen the issue otherwise.

In short, when Demosthenes went down to the underworld, he carried with him some heavy baggage in the form of Aeschines, Harpalus and Philip of Macedon. And the next generation added another bugbear in the form of Phocion ('the chopper'), a man who appears to have become significant only after Demosthenes' death, but whom the Peripatetics elevated into their version of excellence in politics and rhetoric (see Cooper, Chapter 8). Phocion, also, has dogged Demosthenes through the tradition. But the harsh truth is that for ghosts like these Demosthenes had only himself to blame. He created his own image in such stark and uncompromising terms that it was (and is) necessary for his opponents (or critics) to respond in kind. Demosthenes' rhetoric leaves little room for compromise. It is at this point that the orator and the politician coincide.

2 The orator

Probably the best way to describe Demosthenes' rhetorical style is that it is inimitable. This fact was first publicly proclaimed by Cicero, as Cooper has shown (Chapter 8). But Cicero wisely chose to develop his own style,[8] and therein lies the paradoxical influence he has wielded upon the tradition. In theoretical studies, even those written by practising orators, Demosthenes is acknowledged as 'the master' and the model to be followed, but in practice the more fulsome, balanced style of Cicero has been the one favoured by most of those who have attempted to express their ideas in a form elevated above the ordinary.[9] Probably this has something to do with the fact that oratory has been the preserve of gentlemen, for Demosthenes was not of that kind. His *deinotēs* was too passionate for that. But, it is also beyond question that it is easier to analyse the excellence of Demosthenic rhetoric in theory, than it is to put it into practice.

Cicero's appraisal of Demosthenes was picked up by several subsequent commentators, not least Quintilian, and became the standard for the Latin-speaking world in the late Roman and Mediaeval period, when, of course, no text of Demosthenes in the original existed. In the Greek domain of the Byzantine empire his reputation stood just as high, and there, by contrast, it had the support of his speeches, which were extensively studied, especially in the schools. Demosthenes had not been neglected by Alexandrian scholars,[10] but it was a contemporary of Cicero, Dionysius of Halicarnassus, who had established in Greek the fact that Demosthenes was the greatest of the Attic orators and his opinion was confirmed and reinforced by Hermogenes of Tarsus in the second century after Christ. By his time rhetoric had become a discipline in its own right (if not *the* discipline) and his manuals on the subject, especially those on *staseis* (issues) and *ideai* (styles), emerged as the textbooks for the study of the subject in Byzantium.[11] Hermogenes defined seven types of style, the greatest of which was *deinotēs*. In every type Demosthenes surpassed all other orators and *deinotēs* was his special quality. Throughout the two books on *ideai*, passages of Demosthenes were used to illustrate points. In this way his reputation as the greatest of the orators was secured and perpetuated in the Greek East.[12] From there it was brought back to the West in 1397 by the Byzantine diplomat and scholar, Chrysoloras, and the two strands of the tradition (Greek and Latin) were once again united.

Manuel Chrysoloras was invited to Florence to teach Greek.[13] He arrived in 1397, bringing with him the manuscripts of several Greek authors. Among these was probably a text of Demosthenes, since he lectured on the orator, and one of his pupils, Leonardo Bruni, was the first to translate him into Latin. Bruni's Latin version of the speech *On the Crown*[14] and Aeschines' *Against Ctesiphon*, produced in 1406, became the standard for other early humanists to match, and several tried their hand. Before the end of the fifteenth century five other Latin versions of *On the Crown* were produced by scholars like George of Trebizond and Lorenzo Valla.[15] These scholars were competing not only with Bruni, but with

Cicero, who was also known to have attempted the task, and thus aligning themselves with the two greatest orators of antiquity.[16]

Chrysoloras was only the first in a veritable stream of Greek professors who came to the West to make a living by teaching Greek. Others worth mentioning are George of Trebizond, Theodorus Gaza and Janus Lascaris, the last of whom had the distinction of bringing the oldest and best of our manuscripts (S) to Italy in 1490. Not surprisingly, given the importance of Demosthenes in Byzantine education, he played a significant role in their lectures, and as a consequence his popularity was increased incidentally. Perhaps the most influential of these Byzantine scholars was George of Trebizond. George came to the West (Venice) in 1416 to teach Greek, but he eventually emerged (by mid-century) as a master of Latin rhetoric and language, as is evidenced by the fact that he is one of those who translated *On the Crown* into Latin. By that time he had already published his *Rhetoricorum Libri V*, a handbook on rhetoric that analysed Latin oratory in Byzantine terms and integrated Greek authorities with their Latin counterparts.[17] His handbook became the standard for humanistic rhetoric in the fifteenth and early sixteenth centuries in both Italy and northern Europe.[18] As a result of his work, and that of the other Byzantine scholars, Demosthenes became in the West, as he had been in the East, a fundamental part of the educational curriculum. This is nowhere more apparent than in the school directed by Vittorino da Feltre at Mantua,[19] where the primary authors were Vergil, Homer, Cicero and Demosthenes.

It was in this same company that Demosthenes was introduced to a larger reading public after the invention of printing. The first printed text of Demosthenes' speeches was produced by the publishing house of Aldus Manutius at Venice in 1504.[20] The dedication opened with these words: 'There is no one who disputes that Demosthenes holds the top position in oratory amongst the Greeks and Homer in poetry; likewise, amongst the Romans Marcus T. is easily *princeps* in oratory and in poetry the Mantuan poet.'[21] And, as Nigel Wilson points out, these same four authors were still the mainstay of instruction in classics at Oxford five hundred years later at the beginning of the Second World War.[22] The dedication to this first printed edition continues with a comparison of Demosthenes with Cicero, in which it is emphasised that, although they were similar in many ways, Demosthenes was the more unfortunate. He had been born with defects, which he had overcome only by hard work: 'But of the two Demosthenes was the more unlucky. For he was also born with certain defects, which he needed a great deal of effort to alleviate. For which reason Valerius Maximus (says): "Nature made one Demosthenes, hard work made the other".[23] In this way, the representation of Demosthenes as a man who was not a natural orator but succeeded only through industry was perpetuated in print.

Over the next one hundred years the complete works of Demosthenes were re-edited by the best scholars of the sixteenth century and published by the most famous printing houses of Europe. In 1532 Johannes Hervagius brought out an edition at Basel, in the introductory material to which is a letter from Erasmus stating that: 'The great consensus of educated men holds that amongst Greek orators Demosthenes is so far and away the first that you would not find anyone whom you could compare with him.'[24] In 1543 a new edition was published at Venice by Felicianus, only this time in three volumes. This new format was followed by Hervagius in his second publication of 1547, which was largely plagiarised from Felicianus. But the Basel press vindicated itself in 1572 with its bilingual (Greek and Latin) edition that was the work of the great scholar Hieronymus Wolff. This edition, amplified especially by a huge number of laudatory letters and poems from all the leading scholars of the time, was republished in Frankfurt in 1604 by the house of Marinus and Aubrii. It became the definitive edition for well over a century. But one other publication of the complete works in the sixteenth century deserves mention; this was the elegant volume produced at Paris in 1570 by Johannes Benenatus.[25] The text was largely the work of Guillaume Morel, though he had died before it was finished and Dionysius Lambinus had completed it at the request of Benenatus. Morel had made a serious attempt at establishing the text by collating the Aldine and eight manuscripts from the Royal Library against the first Basel edition. It was his great misfortune to be just a few years too early, for in 1594 the Royal Library acquired from Catherine de Medici the great manuscript *Parisinus Graecus* 2934. This was the text that had been brought to Italy over a century earlier by J. Lascaris and is now recognised as the earliest and best manuscript of Demosthenes. It arrived too late for Morel to use and ended up languishing in the Library, unexploited for over two hundred years. The French scholar Auger used it for some part of his edition of 1790, but it was first given prominence by Immanuel Bekker in his edition (Oxford: 1823).[26]

In addition to these great editions of the complete works the sixteenth century witnessed the production of numerous 'selections' and translations. A good conspectus of these publications (for northern Europe, at least) can be seen in the tables at the end of Schindel's study of the eighteenth-century tradition.[27] They present the same general picture as their Italian counterparts. On the whole, far and away the favourite works to select were the *Philippics*, the *Olynthiacs*[28] and the speeches of Demosthenes and Aeschines in the cases of the *False Embassy* and the *Crown*. Less popular, but also represented, were the speeches against Leptines, Meidias and Androtion. In other words, the focus was upon Demosthenes' nationalistic speeches and, besides those, the speeches that reflected on his career. This remained the template for Demosthenic studies, whether in the school or out, until very recently.

But it was not enough to edit the text. Just like the early humanists of the fifteenth century, so the scholars of the sixteenth tested (or proclaimed) their knowledge of Greek by translating the major authors, of whom Demosthenes was amongst the foremost, into various languages, but especially Latin. Such well-known scholars as Philip Melanchthon, Desiderius Erasmus, Johannes Sturm, Joachim Camerarius and, of course, Hieronymus Wolff (all from northern Europe, where the passion for the study of Greek burned warmest) translated some or all of Demosthenes' speeches into Latin. But the enthusiasm to render his eloquence into the vernacular did not lag far behind. Already in 1495 Johannes Reuchlin had translated the *First Olynthiac* into German. In 1550 in Italy we have a translation into Tuscan, and only one year later Louis Le Roy translated the *Timaeus* of Plato and Demosthenes' *Olynthiacs* into French.[29] More interesting than these, however, is the first translation into English that was made by Thomas Wylson in 1570.[30]

Though the teaching of Greek was first established in England at the University of Oxford as early as 1491, during much of the sixteenth century it flourished more vigorously at Cambridge. Interestingly, the first Reader in Greek there, Richard Croke, was also appointed the first Public Orator, a position in which he was succeeded by Sir John Cheke, the first Regius Professor of Greek. Thus, from the very beginning, instruction in Greek at Cambridge was closely allied with the practice of oratory. Demosthenes was at the centre of things. Cheke's own fondness for Demosthenes is evidenced by his translation into Latin of several of the speeches.[31] Further evidence comes from his students, so many of whom had a special affection for Demosthenes. One of these was Roger Ascham, who succeeded Cheke as Public Orator. He became the private tutor of Elizabeth I, as Cheke had been to Edward VI, and the story of his reading Demosthenes and Aeschines with her is well known: 'Queen Elizabeth and I read together in Greek the orators Aeschines and Demosthenes *On the Crown*. She explicated (the text) to me, and at first glance comprehended so knowledgeably not only the peculiar quality of the language and the meaning of the speech, but also the whole argument of the case, the resolutions of the people (and) the habit and character of that city, that you would have been absolutely amazed.'[32] Another of his students was Thomas Wylson, the author of the first English translation of Demosthenes. Like so many of his contemporaries, not least at Cambridge, Wylson saw him as a model for the orator. His own interest in the subject is demonstrated by his work *The Art of Rhetorique, for the use of all suche as are studious of eloquence sette forthe in Englishe* (London: 1553). He also perceived him as a useful precursor of his own political position at the court of Elizabeth I.

I shall return to this point later, but for now it is worth noting that his was not the only translation of Demosthenes made at this time. Only a year after Wylson's English version came out, the same publisher, Henry Denham, produced a Latin version of the *Olynthiacs* and *Philippics* by Nicholas Carr, who before his death in 1568 had been Regius Professor of Greek at Cambridge.[33] Wylson had seen this translation before it appeared and to him was addressed the preface to Carr's translation, written by Thomas Bing. Also in the dedicatory paraphernalia to this translation was a laudatory poem by Sir Anthony Cooke, whose daughter Ann was the mother of Francis Bacon. So, it is ironic to find Bacon later writing, not approvingly, in his *Advancement of Learning* of 'the almost deification of Demosthenes by Car of Cambridge' (1.iv.2.).

Behind these briefly stated details lie some important facts. All the above named English scholars, and several that have not been named, were Protestants and reflected the Lutheran idea of education, especially as it was propagated by the educationalist John Sturm.[34] In the Lutheran view, precise study of language was essential to the correct interpretation, understanding and presentation of the text. For the study of Greek prose and eloquence (presentation) Demosthenes was, for obvious reasons, the model of excellence. The Lutheran viewpoint was readily espoused by non-Catholic forces in England, hence his prominence at the court of Elizabeth I. But, by the beginning of the seventeenth century, the enthusiasm for the authority of the ancients was being challenged, and Bacon's criticism of Carr should be seen in this context.

In the seventeenth century there was a considerable decrease in the popularity of Demosthenes. This can be seen in the dearth of editions of any of his works in Italy, France and England, and in the great decline in production in Germany.[35] This may be attributed in part to a natural exhaustion following the huge output of the previous century; particularly, in the case of Demosthenes, the monumental Frankfurt edition of his works by Hieronymous Wolff was the culmination of sixteenth-century textual criticism and was the authoritative text for the next century and a half. But, in fact, Demosthenic studies were suffering a setback that was experienced by scholarship in general and the classics in particular, the reasons for which are too complex to treat here.[36] The most famous reflection of this change in attitudes in the post-Renaissance period was the Battle of the Books, or the Quarrel of the Ancients and the Moderns, in which the authority of the classical writers was called into question in ways that are not totally different from those of the twentieth century. But whereas in our time the art of rhetoric is quite neglected, in the seventeenth and eighteenth centuries it was still a fundamental part of the school curriculum.

The revival of interest in Demosthenes as an orator in the eighteenth century is evidenced first in England. France was still actively involved in the Battle of the Books for the first part of the century, and even those who valued the ancient orators as models preferred Cicero's elegance and urbanity to Demosthenes' vehemence. Only in the pulpit was there a place for his style of rhetoric.[37] There was no place for political oratory. The same attitudes were to a large extent to be found in Germany, where Demosthenic scholarship is exemplified by the work of Reiske, whose energy produced a compendium of all previous scholarship on the ancient orators (not without many additions of his own).[38] In England, however, political rhetoric flourished and the instruction that men received in the schools could be put into practice in public life.

So, as early as 1702 we find Jacob Tonson publishing a collection of translations of speeches of Demosthenes by a group of gentlemen, amongst whom were the Right Honourable Earl of Peterborough and the Honourables George Granville and Colonel Stanhope.[39] From this date onwards there is no part of the world that eulogised Demosthenes as a model for the art of persuasion to the same extent as England, the home of parliamentary democracy, though the United States had his admirers, too, in the nineteenth century.

Given the limitation of space, it is this tradition that I shall follow for the rest of this section.

The gentlemen who boldly published their renderings of Demosthenes' *Olynthiacs* and *Philippics*, all men of public affairs, were following in the wake of the Elizabethan scholar-courtiers, like Wylson, Cheke and Ascham, and were the precursors of such eminent parliamentarians of the next century as the elder Pitt, George Canning, Lord Brougham, who himself translated the speeches *On the Chersonese* and *On the Crown*, and William Gladstone.[40] Indeed, the spirit of the Renaissance, when scholarship infused and informed public affairs, was best preserved in England from the eighteenth century onwards. In the particular case of Demosthenes, no other country witnessed the same extent of intercourse between the school and the forum as did England. That rhetoric was still a fundamental element of the school curriculum was an inheritance from the past. English students, who had access to education in the schools and the universities in the eighteenth and, more extensively, the nineteenth centuries, were exposed to Cicero and Demosthenes as a matter of course.[41]

These students were from the élite, as always. They were trained for public life. From Eton to Oxford or Cambridge the ruling class of the British Isles was moulded in the classical tradition. The influence of the classics on the educational system reached its peak during the Victorian period. The way the élite exploited the classics to secure their own exclusivity is now well known,[42] and their fondness for Demosthenes may well be a contributing factor in his unpopularity today. But I find a graphic indication of the way in which he was promoted as a model in the dedication written on the inside of the cover of my own copy of the beautiful edition of some of Demosthenes' and Aeschines' speeches by the eighteenth-century lawyer, John Taylor. Signed by Clarendon, at the Grove, 15 February 1799, it reads: 'These two volumes were given to me in the year 1771 upon my leaving Eton school by my excellent Tutor and valuable friend (now alas! no more) the Rev. Robert Deane. He left this world, and all who had the happiness of his friendship, to regret their loss on the sixth day of February 1799. *Nulli flebilior quam mihi.*'

This is a touching token of respect from student to tutor and an expensive gift from teacher to pupil, but no doubt it was taken for granted that an Earl of Clarendon would need a text of Demosthenes. Indeed, until after the First World War, Demosthenes remained an integral part of the education of the English élite in the art of public speaking. Even across the Atlantic, in that other home of democratic government, Demosthenes was not without influence on affairs, as has been well shown by Adams.[43] Probably the most illustrious example of this is Hugh Swinton Legaré, whose *Demosthenes: The Man, the Statesman, and the Orator* revealed an erudition quite as sophisticated as Lord Brougham's.[44] Much of this essay was, in fact, directed against Brougham's *A Dissertation on the Eloquence of the Ancients* (Edinburgh: 1838), as can be seen from the following passage, which at the same time demonstrates Legaré's admiration for Demosthenes:

> Considering, as we do, the masterpieces of this great orator [sc. Demosthenes] as the true and only models of popular eloquence – as its *beau idéal* – not Greek, not Attic, not ancient, not local or transitory or peculiar as Lord Brougham vainly imagines them to be, but made like the Apollo or the Parthenon for all times and all nations, and worthy of study and imitation wherever genius shall be called to move masses of men by the power of the *living word*, we know not how we can do anything more profitable or more acceptible to our readers, than to fix their attention, for a few moments, upon the excellencies which distinguish him beyond every other orator that has ever appeared in any period of the world's history.[45]

But the influence of Demosthenes on public affairs in the United States was not as extensive as it was in England, because already by Legaré's time the American universities were making that turn towards German *Wissenschaft*, so vehemently defended by W.M. Calder III,[46] that saw the removal of the classics from the arena of real life and their isolation in the Academy.

This is not, however, to denigrate the value of such scholarship, nor to undervalue the contribution of German scholars to the study of Demosthenes. Whilst the eighteenth and nineteenth centuries saw the publication of several editions of his works in England and France,[47] it was in Germany that the most important advances were made. J.J. Reiske's multi-volume edition of the *Oratores Graeci* (1770–5) has already been mentioned; the Demosthenic portion of it was soon reworked and revised by G.H. Schaefer in three volumes (London: 1822), which he followed by his five-volume *Apparatus criticus et exegeticus ad Demosthenem* (London: 1824–7). But, maybe the most important contributions to the text of Demosthenes were made by Immanuel Bekker, whose *Oratores Attici* was published first at Oxford (1823), then in Berlin (1824). Bekker was the first editor to give pride of place to the manuscript S, as has already been noted. Bekker was also responsible for the numbering of the paragraphs that are in use today. In a sense, therefore, his text rendered all its predecessors obsolete, and the history of the modern text of Demosthenes begins with him. It would be otiose to list all the editions that followed, but Wilhelm Dindorf's nine-volume Oxford publication deserves mention, because volumes 8 and 9 contained the best text of the scholia that was available until very recently, when they have been re-edited by Mervin Dilts.[48] It was only at the beginning of the twentieth century that English scholarship re-asserted itself with the publication of the Oxford Classical Text of S.H. Butcher (vols. 1–2.1: 1903 and 1907) and W. Rennie (vols. 2.2 and 3: 1921 and 1931). Today, this remains the most accessible modern text of the works of Demosthenes, since the Teubner of K. Fuhrs and J. Sykutris is incomplete. The Budé by Georges Matthieu and others represents French scholarship of the twentieth century.

It would, of course, be incorrect to suggest that the contribution of German scholars was solely to the establishment of the text. During the nineteenth century several masterful works of interpretation resulted from their erudition. Pride of place amongst these for any student of Demosthenes must be taken by Arnold Schaefer's *Demosthenes und seine Zeit*, published in Leipzig.[49] Even today, it would be unwise to begin discussion of any issue related to Demosthenes and his career without reference to Schaefer. And the same is no less true of Friedrich Blass's study of Greek oratory, *Die attische Beredsamkeit* (3 vols., second edition, Leipzig: 1887–98), the first part of the third volume of which is devoted to Demosthenes.

To conclude this section on the tradition concerning Demosthenes as an orator, it is quite fair to say that the view inherited from antiquity, namely that Demosthenes was the greatest of the Greek orators, held good right into the first decades of the twentieth century. That he was the model for public speakers to follow was also commonly argued, though in that case he had competition from Cicero, and professionals, like Brougham, might be found to argue that they had surpassed the model. Yet, it was particularly in nineteenth-century England, where great practitioners of parliamentary debate abounded, that Demosthenes' influence upon the art of persuasion was most enthusiastically recognised and felt.

3 The politician

A statement that I have encountered several times during the years I have been teaching Demosthenes goes somewhat as follows: 'Demosthenes! I like his Greek, but I cannot stand his politics.' That such a sentiment should be expressed by a citizen of a free democracy, especially considering the horrors that have been perpetrated by the autocratic dictators of the twentieth century, is baffling and will require examination. But it is not unfamiliar to the story of Demosthenes, the politician. This should not be surprising, since, with the brief exception of Demochares and the Nationalists in the generation after his death, there was little sympathy for Demosthenes or his cause either in antiquity or for a large part of modern history. In the time of the Hellenistic monarchs and the Roman emperors there was little place for the champion of democracy and the critic of autocracy. To be sure, Cicero felt himself a sort of kindred spirit, but he also turned out to be a loser. And, as has been seen, he bequeathed to the early humanists the view that Demosthenes was the greatest Greek practitioner of the art of rhetoric and nothing more, a view that was reinforced by the Greek scholars who came west from Constantinople. It is this tradition that has justified his fame throughout the following centuries and that I have traced above: a model for the orator and for the student of Greek, but not an ideal for the statesman or politician.

One might have thought that his cause would have struck a chord with a statesman like the Florentine Leonardo Bruni, himself a leader of an embattled city-state, but Athens and Macedon were too unfamiliar at that time, and Cicero's defence of Republican Rome against Caesar was better suited to Florentine Republican propaganda of the late fourteenth and early fifteenth centuries. There were exceptions. In 1470 Cardinal Bessarion had ended the introduction of his translation of the *First Olynthiac*, delivered to the princes of Italy in an attempt to arouse them to fight against the Turks, with the following comparison: 'Philip at that time threatened Greece in the same way as the Turk now threatens Italy. So, let Philip assume the part of the Turk, the Italians of the Athenians, we of Demosthenes. In this way you will easily understand that his whole speech agrees with our cause.'[50] Only twenty-five years later, in 1495, Johannes Reuchlin had used his German translation of the same speech to incite the German princes to unite behind the emperor Maximilian against Charles VIII's invasion of Italy.[51] But these are generic uses of his call to arms against the invader, rather than specific uses of his themes. The first such use was in Elizabethan England.

I have already mentioned Thomas Wylson as the first person to translate Demosthenes into English, and given the title in full in note 30. That provocative title, with its claim that the speeches are 'most nedeful to be redde in these daungerous dayes, of all them that love their Countries libertie' has caused many to conclude that Wylson saw the Armada coming a full eighteen years before it did. The fact that the book was 'seene and allowed according to the Queenes Maiesties Injunctions' and that it was dedicated to her minister, Sir William Cecil, and that, in it, he was encouraged to 'compare his (i.e. Demosthenes') time with this time: "Countrie with Countrie, neighbours with neighbours: and king with king" ' also seems to confirm the view that 'Wylson was employed by the government to translate Demosthenes with a view to rousing a national resistance to Spanish invasion.'[52] There may be a grain of truth to this, but, as I have shown elsewhere,[53] there were other motives behind Wylson's translation. Wylson was the first, and most explicit, exploiter of Demosthenes' self-declared role as wise and incorruptible counsellor (*symboulos*), which he used to advance the position of his group – the Reformation, scholar-courtiers at the court of Elizabeth. As he said to Cecil in his dedication 'the Orator himself, having bene a Counsellor in his Countrie as you now are in this Realme, he is your glasse I am well assured whereupon you do often loke'.

These new ministers recognised the value of Demosthenes' call to unity against the foe, but for them the foe was the Catholic element within England (i.e. Mary, Queen of Scots and her followers). They appreciated him as the voice of civil obedience and loyalty to the state, especially the new 'concept of order' that was evolving from the breakdown of the seigneurial system. In this new vision of the relationship between ruler and ruled the mediating role was played by the new, supposedly impartial, magisterial class, to which Wylson, Cecil, Smith, Cheke, Ascham and others belonged. The themes of loyalty to the state and respect for its magistrates was the main concern for the 'Administration' to get out. From the abundance of evidence for this to be found in the paraphernalia to Wylson's translation, perhaps the most illustrative is his adaptation of a famous passage from Sophocles' *Antigone* (175–90), in which Creon contrasts the loyal with the treacherous citizen. Wylson re-titles it A *playne declaration of a just magistrate and true subject to his*

Countrie. Thus, there was a very interesting relationship between Elizabeth and her advisers, and Demosthenes was the key.

But we have not quite finished with Wylson or Elizabethan England. To Wylson can be attributed the first equation of England with Athens, a theme which will reappear. In his introduction he says: 'And nowe most gentle Reader thinke that when I was occupied about this work: to make Athens and the government thereof to be knowne to my Countriemen: my meaning was that every good subject according to the levell of his witte, should compare the time past with the time present, and even when he heareth Athens or the Athenians to remember England and the Englishmen.' Probably more important than this is the appeal for increased instruction in rhetoric by Nicholas Carr, which he justifies by the claim that the study of rhetoric preserves liberty. His argument equates the extinction of the liberty of Republican Rome by Caesar (already a popular theme with fifteenth-century Florentines) with the end of freedom in Athens. In his claim that the orator is the champion of popular liberty against autocracy[54] he was out of step with his contemporaries, but the forerunner of a debate that would rage from the eighteenth century onwards.

After a hiatus in the seventeenth century, interest in Demosthenes' political *persona* resurfaced in the eighteenth. Since I am limited in space, and since this century has been so thoroughly treated by Ulrich Schindel in the monograph referred to above (note 2), I shall confine myself to two points (both of which happen to be people) of special relevance: Phocion and Philip. The man who brought Phocion to life (literally) was Guy Bonnot, Abbé de Mably. In his *Entretiens de Phocion* (Zurich: 1763) he posed as the translator of a work by Phocion that had recently been discovered in Monte Cassino. This discourse purported to be Phocion's criticism of fourth-century Athens as degenerate, and of the policy of Demosthenes as disastrous. These were, of course, charges that had been made in antiquity, the first by Demosthenes, the second against him. But they were neatly combined by Bonnot with the tradition that Phocion had been a friend of the Macedonian rulers into a depiction of Phocion as the truly wise statesman, who realistically recognised the limitations of the possible and counselled peaceful co-operation with the kings. This was a vision most congenial to the political ethos of absolute monarchy in France before the Revolution.

It found a very sympathetic ear in Germany, where Phocion suddenly became the man of the moment, and Demosthenes was, by contrast, either denigrated or ignored.[55] The reason can easily be found in the long and often successful reign of Frederick II (the Great) of Prussia. Indeed, that king's career prompted an increased interest in Philip of Macedon as a nation-builder, with consequent diminution of the reputation of his opponent, Demosthenes. It was to reappear in a stronger form in German writings of the later nineteenth century. This attitude was even found in England.[56] But, far more influential in late eighteenth century and early nineteenth century English thought were the ideas of William Mitford, whose multi-volume *History of Greece* was produced between 1784 and 1810, and was many times reprinted.

Mitford was a harsh critic of Athenian democracy. His objections were rooted in his own ideological fondness for the English parliamentary constitution of his day. He felt threatened by the movement towards liberal reform and saw the precedent for the evils of liberalism in the irrationality of the Athenian demos, whose fickleness he described in more than Thucydidean terms. His peculiar bias has been well analysed in recent works,[57] but his view of Demosthenes can bear repeating, since it has an interesting legacy. It stands to reason that he could not speak well of the 'champion of democracy', and follows inevitably that he found good things to say about his opponents, Aeschines, Phocion and Philip. Of Aeschines he says: 'Aeschines, to balance the disadvantage of birth, possessed, with great mental abilities, a superior figure, a voice uncommonly melodious and powerful, a reputation for courage repeatedly shown in his country's cause, a private character without stain, and manners that made him generally acceptable. Demosthenes had nothing of all these.'[58] His characterisation of Demosthenes, by contrast, reads as follows: 'Even his admirers seem to have acknowledged that his temper was uncertain, his manners awkward, that he was extravagant in expense and greedy of gain; an unpleasant companion, a faithless friend, a contemptible soldier, and of notorious dishonesty in his profession of an advocat.' (6, p. 342)

And, finally, his opinion of that profession, at least as it was practised by Demosthenes, is worth quoting. This can best be seen in his discussion of the authorship of the speech *On Halonnesus*, which he attributes to Hegesippus. His reasoning is revealing in its perversion (7, p. 28):

> That oration differs widely in character, not only from the *Second Philippic*, but from everything remaining from De-mosthenes. Not only is it inferior, as the critics have ob-

served, in style, but wholly wants the neatness of delusive reasoning, the subtilty of insinuation, avoiding assertion, the wonderfully ingenious texture of phrase, calculated to infuse falsehood into the hearer's belief without pledging the speaker, the whole art, in which Demosthenes has so singularly excelled, of making the worse appear the better cause, disguising with fair colours the foulest forms, and recommending monsters by the grace and splendour of the robes with which he could veil their hideousness.

Mitford may be misguided, but he is significant. As Turner points out, he 'more than anyone else legitimized the use of Athenian history as a vehicle for debating in detail the wisdom and viability of modern democratic government.' As a result, the debate over, Demosthenes' political career entered a new and more intense phase. The first to take up the challenge, on behalf of liberalism, was George Grote, whose great history was written specifically to refute Mitford. Grote rehabilitated Demosthenes in a rousing obituary:

> The violent deaths of these illustrious orators [sc. Demosthenes and Hyperides], the disfranchisement and deportation of the Athenian demos, the suppression of the public Dikasteries, the occupation of Athens by a Macedonian garrison, and of Greece generally by Macedonian Exile-Hunters – are events belonging to one and the same calamitous tragedy, and marking the extinction of the autonomous Hellenic World ... Throughout the whole career of Demosthenes as a public adviser, down to the battle of Chaeroneia, we trace the same combination of earnest patriotism with wise and long-sighted policy ... But what invests the purposes and policy of Demosthenes with peculiar grandeur, is, that they were not simply Athenian, but in an eminent degree Panhellenic also.[59]

In the battle for the hearts of the English Grote carried the victory, at least until after World War II. His revival of the view of Demosthenes as a champion of liberty against autocracy, who died nobly fighting a worthy, but losing, cause, was the dominant view well into the next century, as can be seen, for example, from the title of A.W. Pickard-Cambridge's book, *Demosthenes and the Last Days of Greek Freedom* (New York and London: 1914).

This view of Demosthenes was well suited to the growing tendency of the late Victorian and early twentieth-century English to see their country not only as a new Rome, but as a reincarnation of Athens, especially as their self-confidence weakened in the face of the emerging power of Germany. This has been well shown by Jenkyns in the last chapter of *The Victorians and Ancient Greece*. But he, like others, has missed an insignificant work by a significant individual that both sums up the Victorian attitude to Demosthenes and foreshadows this change in national identity.[60] In 1871, Wyman and Son of London published a short versified drama about the death of Demosthenes, entitled *The Exile of Calauria, or the last days of Demosthenes*. Though the author's name was not acknowledged, a signature on the copy in the British Museum, combined with the revealing preface, makes his name clear. The author was Stratford Canning, first cousin of the famous prime minister, George Canning, and himself a renowned British diplomat, who earned the nickname 'the Great Ambassador'. One of Canning's greatest diplomatic achievements was the part he played in the negotiations on the island of Poros (ancient Calauria) in autumn 1828 that led to Greek independence. He was in a true sense a Philhellene.

Stratford Canning was a typical nineteenth-century upper-class Englishman. As a child, he had a close relationship with his cousin, the prime minister, who called him by the diminutive 'Stratty'. George Canning himself was a man familiar with the classical authors, not least Demosthenes. His use of sections 49–50 of *On the Chersonese* in a speech in 1789, *Respecting Peace with France*, was introduced in the following words: 'Sir, they were wise words, that were spoken by a great statesman and orator of ancient times under circumstances not wholly unlike the present circumstances of the world.' He was, of course, referring to the conquests of Napoleonic France. His cousin, Stratford, would have been equally familiar. He was educated at Eton, where Demosthenes was a standard part of the curriculum. From there he went on to Cambridge. This background and training prepared his mind for the inspiration that struck him on Poros, that autumn of 1828. As he says in his preface: 'The idea of Demosthenes, so circumstanced as to have his mind of necessity dwelling constantly on his past career and the disastrous condition of his country, ... caught my fancy and clung to my recollection.... At last ... the latent, long-cherished thought became a desire, a resolution, an attempt: and finally, at the end of a fortnight, an entire performance.'

The Exile of Calauria focuses upon the theme of the extinction of the flame of Hellenic freedom, and its author has rightly seen the dramatic potential of the lonely exile and eventual suicide of a once proud Athenian politician, who was previously capable of arousing a whole people to do battle for liberty. With his death the flame of liberty is extinguished in Greece. This is all rather standard stuff. More interesting is a passage in which the chief priest laments the death of Demosthenes and, as he does so, has a vision of a new Athens, guided by a new Athena, to which will pass the torch of liberty and the task of championing it:

I turn away, – I turn, and a scene, –
A golden scene, far-shadowed in the loom,
Before me spreads, and glories 'round it float.
An island rises from the briny waste:
White are its cliffs and green its ample meads,
By nature lovely, by the generous arts
Made lovelier still; and o'er its teeming glades
In peaceful, busy occupation rove
All shapes of life; nor is there lack throughout
Of cities vaste as Nile or Phrates owns,
House link'd to house, street interlaced with street,
And column, dome, and tow'r, half lost in cloud,
All proudly telling forth the pomp beneath;
And statues shaped in marble pure as ours
Seem by the waving arm and parted lips
To show how earth's remoter sons will prize
Our own best art, and, haply, make it theirs.
Anon, with smiles, th'inspiring God presents
One vision more; behold! on some tall peak,
Rear'd from the waves, an awful image stands,
Colossal, like our own Palladian maid,
And in her grasp the trident, firmly poised,
Emblem of ocean pow'r, Poseidon's gift:
She points – and lo! strange ships of monster size
Instinct with life, through surge and billow rush,
While lightnings dart and smokewreaths round them curl.

This vision of England as a new Athens was the one for which two generations of Englishmen would fight in two world wars. Still, in 1941, Gilbert Murray could make an address entitled 'Greece and England' to the Royal Society of Arts, in which he could say, 'Free speech, Liberty, Equality before the Law, all the familiar Greek watchwords are our watchwords also.'[61] And in the same year Adela Adams published an article entitled 'Philip *alias* Hitler'.[62] Even in France, where the attitude towards Athens and Demosthenes was, on the whole, more restrained,[63] we find the phenomenon of Georges Clemenceau's passionate address to and about Demosthenes as a 'burning furnace of irresistible powers' who 'would have saved his country had it consented to be saved'.[64]

The reason for all this excitement was, of course, the rise in the power of Germany and the attitude towards Demosthenes that accompanied it. John Knipfing[65] has well demonstrated the reasons, both philosophical and ideological, behind the change that took place in the nineteenth century in the attitude of German historians towards Macedonian imperialism and Athenian democracy in the time of Demosthenes. At the beginning of that century Barthold Niebuhr had dedicated his translation of the *First Philippic* to the Tsar of Russia, Alexander, with the clear purpose of inciting him to resist Napoleon.[66] But increasingly through the century, thanks to the influence of Hegel and the rise of Prussian imperialism, German scholars of distinction argued that Demosthenes had been wrong to defend Greek particularism against the rise of the nation state, offered by the unifier, Philip of Macedon. This denigration of Demosthenes culminated in the very Mitfordian vision, 'Demosthenes, that master of the tuneful phrase and the solemn gesture', of Engelbert Drerup in his polemical tract against democracy ancient and modern, *Aus einer alten Advokatenrepublik*.[67]

4 Epilogue

What is the state of Demosthenic studies today? It should come as no surprise that as an orator Demosthenes no longer enjoys the status he has held for so many centuries. The decline in the teaching of rhetoric is one reason for this. The decrease in the influence of the classics is another. But amongst the classical authors Demosthenes has suffered a worse reversal of fortune than most. From being one of the top four and mandatory reading for all students in the field, he has fallen into almost total neglect. Maybe this is only his due, having been over-popular, especially with the élite, before. Maybe also, after two world wars, we are tired of nationalistic rhetoric. For there are signs of a revival of interest in his works, but not in the speeches that were formerly so popular, the *Philippics* and the *Olynthiacs* (though this generation has seen the publication of the most detailed and thorough commentary on the speech *On the Crown*).[68] Now, following a trend that was begun by the great German scholars of the ancient economy, law and society (like Boeckh and Schaefer), and promoted in England by Sandys and Paley with their two volumes of *Demosthenes' Private Orations* (Cambridge: 1886), we find new editions of these speeches by, for example, Carey and Reid, prompted by a lively interest in Greek law.

As in so many other ways, the classical authors no longer live for us, but we are picking over the bones of antiquity. Yet one can still find the occasional flash. For example, the English politician Denis Healey could appreciate that a speech made by Enoch Powell 'had all the moral passion and rhetorical force of Demosthenes'.[69] Of course, these men were both classically trained. More surprising, perhaps, might be to find a reference to Demosthenes in a speech by Margaret Thatcher in 1984 on the subject *Why Democracy Will Last*:[70] 'Doubtless consensus politicians mocked Demosthenes when he warned that the blandishments of King Philip of Macedon had only one object – the extinction of freedom in the Greek cities. But he was right.' This is, however, an isolated example; more typical of the current attitude towards Demosthenes is the representation of him in Mary Renault's novel, *Fire from Heaven*, where he is depicted as a weak-voiced, vain and cowardly man, ineffective in private and public intercourse.

More difficult to understand is the open hostility to Demosthenes the politician amongst scholars. Since World War II there has been very little written about him, and even what has has a negative tone to it. For example, a recent attempt to update Arnold Schaefer by Raphael Sealey, entitled *Demosthenes and his Time* (Oxford: 1993) bears the subtitle *A Study in Defeat*. By contrast, there have been numerous books about Philip of Macedon, praising him as a nation-builder.[71] This is hard to understand, since, as we have seen throughout this chapter, the changing attitudes towards Demosthenes or his opponents have always reflected contemporary conditions, and the circumstances that explained the popularity of Philip in the eighteenth century and again in the period of Prussian imperialism do not pertain today. It is even more perplexing, because in so many ways Demosthenes is a man for our times – the very model of a modern democratic politician. Could it be that his unpopularity reflects our own feelings about the politicians of our day?

NOTES

1 Such as, for an example that is pertinent to this volume, J.T. Roberts's study of the reception of Athenian democracy in *Democracy on Trial* (Princeton: 1995).

2 This is not a new phenomenon, of course. Most readers will be familiar with Gilbert Highet's comprehensive study, *The Classical Tradition* (Oxford: 1949). More recent studies have focused on specific periods or issues, especially on the use or abuse made of the classics by the Victorian élite. See, for example, Richard Jenkyns, *The Victorians and Ancient Greece* (Cambridge, Mass.: 1980) and Frank Turner, *The Greek Heritage in Victorian Britain* (New Haven: 1981). Demosthenes has not been neglected; from early in the twentieth century we have E. Drerup's *Demosthenes im Urteile des Altertums* (Würzburg: 1923), then C.D. Adams' *Demosthenes and his Influence* (London: 1927), and more recently the monographs by Manfred Lossau, *Untersuchungen zur antiken Demosthenesexegese*, *Palingenesia* 2 (Berlin: 1964) and Ulrich Schindel, *Demosthenes im 18. Jahrhundert*, *Zetemata* 31 (Munich: 1963). Now, since the foundation in 1991 of The International Society for the Classical Tradition, with its own publication (the *International Journal of the Classical Tradition*), this field has become a separate discipline.

3 See now the provocative study by Christopher Stray, *Classics Transformed* (Oxford: 1998).

4 Though these roles were not, of course, distinct in his time and *rhētōr* was one of the titles by which an Athenian politician was known: see M.H. Hansen, 'The Athenian Politicians, 403–322 B.C.', *GRBS* 24 (1983) pp. 33–55.

5 For the process see K.J. Dover, *Lysias and the Corpus Lysiacum* (Berkeley and Los Angeles: 1968), pp. 148–74.

6 On this and what follows see P. Harding, 'Rhetoric and Politics in Fourth Century Athens', *Phoenix* 41 (1987), pp. 25–8.

7 For a discussion of these terms and some analysis of the way they were used by Demosthenes, see P. Harding, 'Comedy and Rhetoric' in Ian Worthington (ed.), *Persuasion: Greek Rhetoric in Action* (London: 1994), pp. 196–221.

8 He does, however, claim to have translated the speeches of both Demosthenes and Aeschines for the lawsuit *On the Crown*, though only the preface, the *de optimo genere oratorum*, not the translation has survived. Maybe he found Demosthenes truly inimitable.

9 This point is well stated by Adams, *Demosthenes and his Influence*, p. 111.

10 Their work culminated in the prodigious scholarship of Didymus Chalcenterus, part of whose huge monograph *On Demosthenes* has survived on papyrus, a new edition and translation of which I am preparing for Oxford University Press.

11 See the detailed presentation in H. Hunger, *Die hochsprachliche profane Literatur der Byzantiner* 1 (Munich: 1978), pp. 75–91.

12 An indication of the extent to which Demosthenes was favoured over other orators, including Isocrates, is to be seen in the number of manuscripts (8) that have survived of his works (complete or partial) from the Byzantine period. See Drerup, *Demosthenes im Urteile*, p. 147.

The best discussions of the manuscript-tradition of Demosthenes as a whole are by D. Irmer. See his *Zum Primat des Codex S in der Demostheneskritik* (diss. Hamburg: 1961), 'Beobachtungen zur Demosthenes-überlieferung', *Philologus* 112 (1968), pp. 43–62, and *Zur Genealogie der jüngeren Demostheneshandschriften*, *Hamburger philologische Studien* 20 (Hamburg: 1972).

13 On Chrysoloras see now N.G. Wilson, *From Byzantium to Italy* (London: 1992), pp. 8–12, and J. Monfasani, 'The Byzantine Rhetorical Tradition and the Renaissance' in J. Murphy (ed.), *Renaissance Eloquence: Studies in the Theory and Practice of Renaissance Rhetoric* (Berkeley: 1983), pp. 174–87.

14 He also translated the *Third Olynthiac* and *On the Chersonese*.

15 For the details and the dates see J. Monfasani, *George of Trebizond* (Leiden: 1976), pp. 61–8.

16 See Monfasani, *George of Trebizond*, p. 62.

17 Monfasani, 'Byzantine Rhetorical Tradition', p. 179.

18 Monfasani, ibid., and *George of Trebizond*, pp. 241–99.

19 On this see Wilson, *Byzantium to Italy*, pp. 34–41.

20 *Demosthenis Orationes duae et sexaginta, Venetis in aedibus Aldi*, MDIIII.

21 *Summum locum in oratoria tenere apud Graecos Demosthenem, et in poetica Homerum, nemo est qui ambigat, sic apud Latinos in oratoria Marcum T. esse facile principem, in poetica vero Mantuanum poetam.*

22 *Byzantium to Italy*, p. 35.

23 *Verum ex duobus his infelicior Demosthenes fuit. Nam et cum vitiis quibusdam natus est, quae industria non mediocri tolli oportuit. Unde Valerius Max(imus) 'Alterum Demosthenem natura, alterum industria fecit'.*

24 *Demosthenem inter Graecos rhetores sic esse primum, ut ne invenies quem cum illo possis conferre, magnus eruditorum omnium consensus est.*

25 Though it appears to have been published by various houses at the same time. As well as that by Benenatus himself, we have copies by Jacob Dupuys and Michael Sonnius.

26 See H. Wankel, *Demosthenes: Rede für Ktesiphon über den Kranz* 1 (Heidelberg: 1976), p. 66 and N.G. Wilson, *Scholars of Byzantium* (London: 1983) p. 219.

27 Schindel, *Demosthenes im 18. Jahrhundert*, pp. 207–24.

28 Even the earliest Spanish edition, by Franciscus Vergara (published at Complutum in 1524 by Michael de Guia), was of the three *Olynthiacs*.

29 Each part has a separate title page; that for Demosthenes reads: *Trois oraisons de Démosthène prince des Orateurs, dittes Olynthiaques, pleines de matières d'éstat, déduittes avecques singulière prudence et éloquence, translatées pareillement de grec en françois, avec une préface contenant la conionction de l'éloquence et de la philosophie. A Paris. De l'imprimerie de Michel de Vascosan. MDLI.*

30 *The three Orations of Demosthenes chiefe Orator among the Grecians, in favour of the Olynthians, a people in Thracia, now called Romania: with those his fower Orations titled expressely and by name against King Philip of Macedonie: most nedeful to be redde in these daungerous dayes, of all them that love their Countries libertie, and desire to take warning for their better avayle, by example of others. Englished out of the Greek by Thomas Wylson, Doctor of Civill Lawes.* H. Denham, London: 1570.

31 Those were the three *Olynthiacs*, three *Philippics*, and the speeches of
   Demosthenes and Aeschines against each other.
32 *R. Aschami Epistolarum libri quatuor* (Oxford: 1703), bk. 1, letter 11: *D.
   Elizabètha et ego una legimus Graece oratores Aeschines et Demosthenis
   περὶ Στεφάνου. Illa praelegit mihi et primo aspectu tam scienter intelligit, non
   solum proprietatem lingue, et orationis sensum: sed totam caussae contentionem,
   populi scita, consuetudinem et mores illius urbis, ut summopere admirareris.*
33 *Demosthenis, Graecorum Oratorum Principis Olynthiacae orationes tres et
   Philippicae quatuor, e Graeco in Latinum conversae, a Nicolao Carro, Anglo
   Novacastrensi, Doctore medico, et Graecorum literarum in Cantabrigiensi
   Academia professore Regio.* Londini apud Henricum Denham: 1571.
34 See P. Harding, 'Orations ... most nedeful to be redde in these
   daungerous Dayes', *Classical News and Views* 23 (1979), pp. 51–63.
35 See the tables in Schindel, *Demosthenes im 18. Jahrhundert*, pp. 209, 222
   and 224.
36 There is a useful, though brief, statement of the issues in Highet,
   Classical Tradition, chs. 13 and 14.
37 As was stated most graphically by Cardinal Maury in his *Principes de l'
   éloquence pour la chaire et le barreau* (Paris: 1777).
38 J.J. Reiske, *Oratores Graeci*, 12 vols. (Leipzig: 1770–5).
39 *Several Orations of Demosthenes, to encourage the Athenians to oppose the
   exorbitant power of Philip of Macedon: Englished from the Greek by several
   hands* (J. Tonson, London: 1702).
40 A brief overview can be found in Adams, *Demosthenes and his Influence*,
   pp. 153–64.
41 For example, in the first examinations given at Oxford after the
   revision of the undergraduate programme by the Royal Commission of
   1850, 'more honours candidates brought up Demosthenes than any
   other author except Virgil ...': R. Jenkyns, 'The Beginning Of Greats,
   1800–1872. 1, Classical Studies' in M.G. Brock and M.C. Curthoys
   (eds.), *The History of the University of Oxford* 6 (Oxford: 1997), p. 518.
42 See Stray, *Classics Transformed*, pp. 7–113.
43 *Demosthenes and his Influence*, pp. 164–74.
44 Mary Legaré (ed.), *Writings of Hugh Swinton Legaré* 1 (New York and
   Boston, Mass.: 1846), pp. 443–501.
45 *The Man, the Statesman, and the Orator*, p. 444.
46 Most recently in a review article, 'How are American Universities
   German?', in the *International Journal of the Classical Tradition* 5 (1998),
   pp. 97–102. It is, of course, only fair to note that English educational-
   ists of the mid-nineteenth century also admired German scholarship.
   See O. Murray, 'The Beginning Of Greats, 1800–1872. 2, Ancient
   History' in M.G. Brock and M.C. Curthoys (eds.), *The History of the
   University of Oxford* 6 (Oxford: 1997), p. 525.
47 In eighteenth-century England editions were produced, for example,
   by P. Foulkes and J. Friend, *Aeschines Against Ktesiphon and Demosthenes
   On the Crown* (Oxford: 1715), by Richard Mounteney, *Demosthenis,
   Selectae Orationes* (Cambridge: 1731), notable for its dedication to
   Robert Walpole, in which he is compared to Demosthenes, much to
   the latter's disadvantage, by William Allen, *Demosthenis, Orationes de
   republica duodecim*, 2 vols. (London: 1755), and by John 'Demosthenes'
   Taylor, *The Surviving Works of Demosthenes, Aeschines, Deinarchus and*

Demades, in Greek and Latin 3 (Cambridge: 1748) and 2 (Cambridge: 1757). The last was certainly the most scholarly in its study of the manuscripts. The strange details of its publication are explained by the fact that Taylor was following the ordering of the works used by Wolff in his 1572 and 1604 editions. He produced volume 3 first. It contains speeches 20–6, 58, 59 and 57. Volume 2 contains the three extant speeches of Aeschines and Demosthenes *On the False Embassy* and *On the Crown*. The edition was dedicated to John Carteret, Earl Granville, an outspoken opponent of Walpole and one of the best orators of his day.

In the nineteenth century most texts of Demosthenes published in England were the work of German scholars like Bekker and Dindorf. There was, however, the ten-volume collection by William Dobson, *Demosthenis et Aeschinis, quae exstant omnia* (London: 1828), but this contained little by the way of original scholarship and derived its text from various predecessors.

The most distinguished text to come out of France in this period was the work of Athanasius Auger, *Demosthenis et Aeschinis, quae exstant omnia* (Paris: 1790). This was important for two reasons: it marked the first text of Demosthenes printed in the new stereotype of Firmin Didot, and it made use of the important manuscript *Parisinus Graecus* 2934 (S), though only in places.

48 M.R. Dilts, *Scholia Demosthenica*, 2 vols. (Leipzig: 1983–6).

49 First produced in the 1850s, but subsequently partly revised and re-published 1885–7. A series of essays that were part of the original edition of 1858 were not republished in the second edition. The whole work can be found reproduced by G. Olms of Hildesheim (1966–7).

50 *Ita enim tunc Graeciae Philippus imminebat, ut nunc Turcus Italiae. Sustineat igitur Philippus Turci personam, Itali Atheniensium, nos Demosthenis. Iam facile intelliges totam orationem causae nostrae convenire. Reverendissimi Cardinalis Nicaeni ad illustrissimos, inclitosque Italiae principes contra Turcos exhortatio* (Antonius Bladus Asulanus, Rome: 1537) part IV, *Eiusdem ad eosdem persuasio ex authoritate Demosthenis.*

51 See F. Poland, *Reuchlins Verdeutschung der ersten olynthischen Rede des Demosthenes* (Berlin: 1899), pp. v–xi.

52 It is suspected that this quotation derives from Dr Johnson. It appeared in *The Literary Magazine* of 1758. I owe the reference to J.F. Pollard in *Dictionary of National Bibliography* 21 (London: 1922), p. 605.

53 'Orations ... most nedeful', pp. 51–63.

54 Ibid., pp. 60–61.

55 For the treatment of Phocion by German historians of the late eighteenth century see Schindel, *Demosthenes im 18. Jahrhundert*, pp. 61–9.

56 For example, in John Gillies, *A View of the Reign of Frederick II of Prussia: with a parallel between that Prince and Philip II of Macedon* (London: 1789).

57 See Turner, *Greek Heritage in Victorian Britain*, pp. 187–263, and Roberts, *Democracy on Trial.*

58 For citations from Mitford, I am using the eight-volume edition of 1838. This passage comes from volume 6, pp. 339–40.

59 For citations from Grote I am using the eight-volume edition, produced in London by John Murray in 1862. This passage comes from volume 8, pp. 525–6.

60 Though it did have Elizabethan antecedents, as we have seen in the above discussion of Wylson.

61 G. Murray, *Greek Studies* (Oxford: 1946), p. 192.

62 *Greece and Rome* 10 (1941), pp. 105–13.

63 See N. Loraux and P. Vidal-Naquet, 'La formation de l'Athènes bourgeoise: Essai d'historiographie 1750–1850' in J. Bolgar (ed.), *Classical Influences on Western Thought* (Cambridge: 1979), pp. 169–222.

64 G. Clemenceau, *Demosthenes* (transl. C.M. Thompson, London: 1926), p. 10.

65 J. Knipfing, 'German Historians and Macedonian Imperialism', *AHR* 26 (1921), pp. 657–71.

66 B.G. Niebuhr, *Demosthenis erste philipp. Rede im Auszug übers* (Hamburg: 1805).

67 Published in Paderborn in 1916. The quotation is on p. 189.

68 Herman Wankel's two-volume work, *Demosthenes: Rede für Ktesiphon über den Kranz* (Heidelberg: 1976).

69 He made this comment about Powell's speech in 1959 over the Hola Camp massacre in Kenya. See Denis Healey, *The Time of my Life* (Harmondsworth: 1990), p. 146.

70 The speech was the Second Carlton Lecture in Robin Harris (ed.), *The Collected Speeches of Margaret Thatcher* (London: 1997), pp. 227–55. The passage cited is on p. 231. The context is somewhat forced: the threat to democracy posed by powerful producers 'who would impose on people systems of production and distribution based on compulsion'. I owe this and the previous reference to my colleague R. B. Todd.

71 For example, J.R. Ellis, *Philip II and Macedonian Imperialism* (London: 1976), G.L. Cawkwell, *Philip of Macedon* (London: 1978) and N.G.L. Hammond, *Philip of Macedon* (London: 1994).

BIBLIOGRAPHY

Accame, S., *La lega ateniese del sec. IV. a.c.* (Rome: 1941)

Adams, A., 'Philip *Alias* Hitler', *G&R*² 10 (1941), pp. 105–13

Adams, C.D., 'Are the Political Speeches of Demosthenes to be Regarded as Political Pamphlets?', *TAPA* 43 (1902), pp. 5–22

—— *Demosthenes and his Influence* (London: 1927)

Adcock, F.E. and D.J. Mosley, *Diplomacy in Ancient Greece* (London: 1975)

Allen, William, *Demosthenis, Orationes de republica duodecim*, 2 vols. (London: 1755)

Archibald, Z.H., *The Odrysian Kingdom of Thrace* (Oxford: 1998)

Ascham, R., *Epistolarum libri quatuor* (Oxford: 1703)

Auger, Athanasius, *Demosthenis et Aeschinis, quae exstant omnia* (Paris: 1790)

Badian, E., 'Harpalus', *JHS* 81 (1961), pp. 16–43

—— 'A Comma in the History of Samos', *ZPE* 23 (1976), pp. 289–94

—— 'Philip II and Thrace', *Pulpudeva* 4 (1983), pp. 51–71

—— 'The King's Peace' in M.A. Flower and M. Toher (eds), *Georgica: Greek Studies in Honour of George Cawkwell* (London: 1991), pp. 25–48

—— 'Jaeger's Demosthenes: An Essay in Anti-History' in W.M. Calder (ed.), *Werner Jaeger Reconsidered* (Atlanta: 1992), pp. 289–313

—— 'Agis III: Revisions and Reflections' in Ian Worthington (ed.), *Ventures Into Greek History: Essays in Honour of N.G.L. Hammond* (Oxford: 1994), pp. 258–92

—— 'The Ghost of Empire: Reflections on Athenian Foreign Policy in the Fourth Century' in W. Eder (ed.), *Die athenische Demokratie im 4. Jahrhundert v. Chr.* (Stuttgart: 1995), pp. 79–106

—— 'Alexander the Great between Two Thrones and Heaven: Variations on an Old Theme' in A. Small (ed.), *Subject and Ruler: The Cult of the Ruling Power in Classical Antiquity* (Ann Arbor: 1996), pp. 11–26

—— 'Philip II and the Last of the Thessalians', *Ancient Macedonia* 6 (Thessaloniki: 1999), pp. 109–22

Barnes, J.A., *A Pack of Lies: Towards a Sociology of Lying* (Cambridge: 1994)

Bearzot, C., *Focione tra storia e trasfigurazione ideale* (Milan: 1985)

Beloch, K.J., *Theopomps Hellenika* (Halle: 1909)

—— *Griechische Geschichte*² 3.1 (Berlin and Leipzig: 1922)

Bengtson, H., *Die Staatsverträge des Altertums*[2] 2 (Munich: 1975)

Bers, V., 'Dikastic Thorubos' in P. Cartledge and F.D. Harvey (eds.), *Crux: Essays Presented to G.E.M. de Ste. Croix on his 75th Birthday* (London: 1985), pp. 1–15

—— 'Tragedy and Rhetoric' in Ian Worthington (ed.), *Persuasion: Greek Rhetoric in Action* (London: 1994), pp. 176–95

Berve, H., *Das Alexanderreich auf prosopographischer Grundlage*, 2 vols. (Munich: 1926)

Bessarion (Cardinal), *Reverendissimi Cardinalis Nicaeni ad illustrissimos, inclitosque Italiae principes contra Turcos exhortatio*, Part IV: *Eiusdem ad eosdem persuasio ex authoritate Demosthenis* (Rome: 1537)

Bickerman, E., *Chronology of the Ancient World* (Ithaca: 1968)

Blass, F., *Die attische Beredsamkeit*[2], 3 vols. (Leipzig: 1887–98)

Bonner, R.J., *Evidence in Athenian Courts* (Chicago: 1905)

—— *Lawyers and Litigants in Ancient Athens: The Genesis of the Legal Profession* (Chicago: 1926)

Bosworth, A.B., *A Historical Commentary on Arrian's History of Alexander* 1 (Oxford: 1981)

—— *Conquest and Empire: The Reign of Alexander the Great* (Cambridge: 1988)

Brunt, P.A., 'Euboea in the time of Philip II', *CQ*[2] 19 (1969), pp. 245–65

Buckler, J., *Philip II and the Sacred War* (Leiden: 1989)

—— 'Philip II, the Greeks, and the King 346–336 B.C.', *ICS* 19 (1994), pp. 99–122

—— 'Philip II's Designs on Greece' in R.W. Wallace and E.M. Harris (eds.), *Transitions to Empire: Essays in Honor of E. Badian* (Norman: 1996), pp. 77–97

Burke, E.M., '*Contra Leocratem* and *De Corona*: Political Collaboration?', *Phoenix* 31 (1977), pp. 330–40

—— 'Lycurgan finances', *GRBS* 26 (1985), pp. 251–64

Burstein, S.M., '*IG* I[3] 61 and the Black Sea Grain Trade' in R. Mellor and L. Tritle (eds.), *Text and Tradition* (Claremont: 1999), pp. 93–104

Busolt, G. and H. Swoboda, *Griechische Staatskunde* 2 (Munich: 1926)

Calder, W.M., III, 'How are American Universities German?', *International Journal of the Classical Tradition* 5 (1998), pp. 97–102

Calhoun, G.M., 'Oral and Written Pleading in Athenian Courts', *TAPA* 50 (1919), pp. 177–93

Carey, C., 'Artless Proofs in Aristotle and the Orators', *BICS* 39 (1994), pp. 95–106

—— 'Legal Space in Classical Athens', *G&R*[2] 41 (1994), pp. 172–86

—— 'Rhetorical Means of Persuasion' in Ian Worthington (ed.), *Persuasion: Greek Rhetoric in Action* (London: 1994), pp. 26–45

—— 'Rape and Adultery in Athenian Law', *CQ*[2] 45 (1995), pp. 407–17

—— 'The Witness's *Exomosia* in the Athenian Courts', *CQ*[2] 45 (1995), pp. 114–19

—— '*Nomos* in Attic Rhetoric and Oratory', *JHS* 116 (1996), pp. 33–46

Carey, C. and R.A. Reid, *Demosthenes: Selected Private Speeches* (Cambridge: 1985)

Cargill, J., *The Second Athenian League* (Berkeley: 1981)

—— 'IG II² 1 and the Athenian Kleruchy on Samos', *GRBS* 24 (1983), pp. 321–32

Carr, N., *Demosthenis, Graecorum Oratorum Principis Olynthiacae orationes tres et Philippicae quatuor, e Graeco in Latinum conversae* (London: 1571)

Cartledge, P., P. Millett and S. Todd (eds.), *Nomos: Essays in Athenian Law, Politics and Society* (Cambridge: 1990)

Cawkwell, G.L., 'The Defence of Olynthus', *CQ²* 12 (1962), pp. 122–40

—— 'Eubulus', *JHS* 83 (1963), pp. 47–67

—— 'Demosthenes' Policy after the Peace of Philocrates I and II', *CQ²* 13 (1963), pp. 120–38 and 200–13

—— 'The Crowning of Demosthenes', *CQ²* 19 (1969), pp. 163–80

—— *Philip of Macedon* (London: 1978)

—— 'Notes on the Failure of the Second Athenian Confederacy', *JHS* 101 (1981), pp. 40–55

—— 'The Deification of Alexander the Great: A Note' in Ian Worthington (ed.), *Ventures Into Greek History: Essays in Honour of N.G.L. Hammond* (Oxford: 1994), pp. 293–306

—— 'The End of Greek Liberty' in R.W. Wallace and E.M. Harris (eds.), *Transitions to Empire: Essays in Honor of E. Badian* (Norman: 1996), pp. 98–121

Christ, M.R., *The Litigious Athenian* (Baltimore: 1998)

Chroust, A.H., 'The Vita Aristotelis of Dionysius of Halicarnassus (1 *Ep. Ad Amm.* 5)', *AAntHung* 13 (1965), pp. 369–77

Clemenceau, G., *Démosthènes* (transl. C.M. Thompson, London: 1926)

Cloché, P., *Démosthène et la fin de la démocratie athénienne* (Paris: 1957)

Cohen, D., *Law, Sexuality, and Society* (Cambridge: 1991)

—— *Law, Violence and Sexuality in Classical Athens* (Cambridge: 1995)

Cohen, E.E., *Athenian Economy and Society: A Banking Perspective* (Princeton: 1992)

Connor, W.R., 'Tribes, Festivals and Processions: Civic Ceremonial and Political Manipulation in Archaic Greece', *JHS* 107 (1987), pp. 40–50

Cook, M.L., 'Timokrates' 50 Talents and the Cost of Ancient Warfare', *Eranos* 88 (1990), pp. 69–97

Daitz, S.G., 'The Relationship of the *De Chersoneso* and the *Philippika quarta* of Demosthenes', *CP* 52 (1957), pp. 145–62

Danov, C.M., *Altthrakien* (Berlin: 1976)

Davies, J.K., *Athenian Propertied Families* (Oxford: 1971)

—— 'Documents and "Documents" in Fourth-Century Historiography' in P. Carlier (ed.), *Le IVᵉ siècle av. J.-C.: Approches historiographiques* (Paris: 1996), pp. 29–39

de Ste. Croix, G.E.M., 'The Alleged Secret Pact between Athens and Philip II concerning Amphipolis and Pydna', *CQ²* 13 (1963), pp. 110–19

Develin, R., *Athenian Officials, 684–321 BC* (Cambridge: 1989)

Dilts, M.R., *Scholia Demosthenica*, 2 vols. (Leipzig: 1983–86)

Dobson, William, *Demosthenis et Aeschinis, quae exstant omnia*, 10 vols. (London: 1828)

Doherty, F.C., *Three Private Speeches of Demosthenes* (Oxford: 1927)

Dover, K.J., *Lysias and the Corpus Lysiacum* (Berkeley: 1968)

—— *Greek Popular Morality in the Time of Plato and Aristotle* (Berkeley and Los Angeles: 1974)

Drerup, E., *Aus einer alten Advokatenrepublik. Demosthenes und seine Zeit* (Paderborn: 1916)

—— *Demosthenes im Urteile des Altertums* (Würzburg: 1923)

Easterling, P.E., 'Actors and Voices: Reading between the Lines in Aeschines and Demosthenes' in S. Goldhill and R. Osborne (eds.), *Performance Culture and Athenian Democracy* (Cambridge: 1999), pp. 154–65

Edmonds, J.M., *The Fragments of Attic Comedy* 2 (Leiden: 1957)

Eichler, E., 'War Demosthenes' erste Philippica doch eine Doppelrede?' in J. Hauser (ed.), *Jahresbericht über das k.k. Staatsgymnasium im II. Bezirke von Wien* (Vienna: 1883), pp. 1–29

Ekman, P., M. O'Sullivan and M.G. Frank, 'A Few Can Catch a Liar', *Psychological Science* 10 (1999), pp. 263–6

Ellis, J.R., *Philip II and Macedonian Imperialism* (London: 1976)

Ellis, J.R. and R.D. Milns, *The Spectre of Philip* (Sydney: 1970)

Errington, R.M., 'Samos and the Lamian War', *Chiron* 5 (1975), pp. 51–7

Ferguson, W.S., *Hellenistic Athens* (London: 1911)

Fiehn, K., 'Timarchos', *RE* 6A (1936), cols. 1234–6

Finley, M.I. (ed.), *Slavery in Classical Antiquity: Views and Controversies* (Cambridge: 1960)

Fisher, N., 'Gymnasia and the Democratic Values of Leisure' in P. Cartledge, P. Millett and S. von Reden (eds.), *Kosmos: Essays in Order, Conflict and Community in Classical Athens* (Cambridge: 1998), pp. 84–104

—— '"Workshops of Villains": Was there much Organised Crime in Classical Athens?' in K. Hopwood (ed.), *Organised Crime in Antiquity* (London: 1999), pp. 53–96

—— 'Masculinity and the Law in Classical Athens' in L. Foxhall and J. Salmon (eds), *When Men Were Men: Masculinity, Power and Identity in Classical Antiquity* (London and New York: 1999), pp. 68–97

—— 'Symposiasts, Fisheaters and Flatterers: Social Mobility and Moral Concern in Old Comedy' in D. Harvey and J. Wilkins (eds.), *Aristophanes and His Rivals* (London: 2000), pp. 355–96

Fortenbaugh, W., 'Theophrastus on Delivery', *Rutgers University Studies* 2 (1985), pp. 269–88

Foulkes, P. and J. Friend, *Aeschines Against Ktesiphon and Demosthenes On the Crown* (Oxford: 1715)

Fox, R.L., 'Aeschines and the Athenian Democracy' in R. Osborne and S. Hornblower (eds.), *Ritual, Finance, Politics* (Oxford: 1994), pp. 135–55

Foxhall, L., 'The Law and the Lady: Women and Legal Proceedings in Classical Athens' in L. Foxhall and A.D.E. Lewis (eds.), *Greek Law in its Political Setting: Justifications not Justice* (Oxford: 1996), pp. 133–52

Fraser, P.M., *Ptolemaic Alexandria* 1 (Oxford: 1972)

Gagarin, M., 'The Torture of Slaves in Athenian Law', *CP* 91 (1996), pp. 1–18

—— *Antiphon: The Speeches* (Cambridge: 1997)

Gallo, I., *Frammenti Biographi da Papiri* 1 (Rome: 1975)

Garland, R., *The Piraeus* (Ithaca: 1987)

Garner, R., *Law and Society in Classical Athens* (London: 1987)

Gentlemen, a group of, *Several Orations of Demosthenes, to encourage the Athenians to oppose the exorbitant power of Philip of Macedon: Englished from the Greek by several hands* (London: 1702)

Gernet, L., *Démosthène, Plaidoyers civils* 1 (Paris: 1954)

Gillies, J., *A View of the Reign of Frederick II of Prussia: with a parallel between that Prince and Philip II of Macedon* (London: 1789)

Golden, M., 'Demosthenes and the Age of Majority at Athens', *Phoenix* 33 (1979), pp. 25–38

—— *Children and Childhood in Classical Athens* (Baltimore and London: 1990)

—— *Sport and Society in Ancient Greece* (Cambridge: 1998)

Goldstein, J., *The Letters of Demosthenes* (New York: 1968)

Goodwin, W.W., *Demosthenes On the Crown* (Cambridge: 1957)

Gribble, D., 'Rhetoric and History in [Andocides] 4, *Against Alcibiades*', CQ^2 47 (1997), 367–91

Grote, G., *History of Greece*, 8 vols. (London: 1862)

Grube, G.M.A., *A Greek Critic: Demetrius on Style* (Toronto: 1961)

—— *The Greek and Roman Critics* (Indianapolis: 1995)

Habicht, C., *Athens from Alexander to Antony* (transl. D.L. Schneider, Cambridge, Mass.: 1997)

Hall, E., 'Lawcourt Dramas: The Power of Performance in Greek Forensic Oratory', *BICS* 40 (1995), pp. 39–58

Halliwell, A.S., 'The Uses of Laughter in Greek Culture', CQ^2 41 (1991), pp. 279–96

Hammond, N.G.L., *Philip of Macedon* (London: 1994)

Hammond, N.G.L. and G.T. Griffith, *A History of Macedonia* 2 (Oxford: 1979)

Hammond, N.G.L. and F.W. Walbank, *A History of Macedonia* 3 (Oxford: 1988)

Hansen, M.H., 'The Athenian Politicians, 403–322 B.C.', *GRBS* 24 (1983) pp. 33–55

—— 'Two Notes on Demosthenes' Symbouleutic Speeches', *C&M* 35 (1984), pp. 55–70

—— *The Athenian Assembly in the Age of Demosthenes* (Oxford: 1987)

—— *The Athenian Democracy in the Age of Demosthenes* (Oxford: 1991)

—— *The Athenian Democracy in the Age of Demosthenes*^{2} (Norman: 1999)

Harding, P., 'Androtion's Political Career', *Historia* 25 (1976), pp. 186–200

—— 'Orations ... most nedeful to be redde in these daungerous Dayes', *Classical News and Views* 23 (1979), pp. 51–63

—— *From the End of the Peloponnesian War to the Battle of Ipsus* (Cambridge: 1985)

—— 'Rhetoric and Politics in Fourth Century Athens', *Phoenix* 41 (1987), pp. 25–39

—— Review of C. Bearzot, *Focione tra storia e trasfigurazione ideale* (Milan: 1985), *JHS* 108 (1987), pp. 233–4

—— 'Comedy and Rhetoric' in Ian Worthington (ed.), *Persuasion: Greek Rhetoric in Action* (London: 1994), pp. 196–221

Harrel, H.C., *Public Arbitration in Athenian Law* (Columbia: 1936)

Harris, E.M., 'Demosthenes' Speech against Meidias', *HSCP* 92 (1989), pp. 117–36

—— 'Did the Athenians Regard Seduction as a Worse Crime than Rape?', *CQ*² 40 (1990), pp. 370–7

—— '*Apotimema*: Athenian Terminology for Real Security in Leases and Dowry Agreements', *CQ*² 43 (1993), pp. 73–95

—— 'Law and Oratory' in Ian Worthington (ed.), *Persuasion: Greek Rhetoric in Action* (London: 1994), pp. 130–50

—— 'Demosthenes Loses a Friend and Nausicles Gains a Position: A Prosopographical Note on Athenian Politics after Chaeronea', *Historia* 43 (1994), pp. 378–83

—— *Aeschines and Athenian Politics* (New York: 1995)

Harris, Robin (ed.), *The Collected Speeches of Margaret Thatcher* (London: 1997)

Harrison, A.R.W., *The Law of Athens* 2 (Oxford: 1971)

Healey, Denis, *The Time of my Life* (Harmondsworth: 1990)

Heskel, J., *The North Aegean Wars 371–360 B.C.* (Wiesbaden: 1997)

Highet, Gilbert, *The Classical Tradition* (Oxford: 1949)

Hornblower, S., Review of J. Cargill, *The Second Athenian League* (Berkeley: 1981), *CR* 32 (1986), pp. 235–9

—— 'Introduction' in S. Hornblower (ed.), *Greek Historiography* (Oxford: 1994), pp. 1–72

Hubbell, H.M., 'The Rhetorica of Philodemus', *Transactions of the Connecticut Academy of Arts and Science* 23 (1920), pp. 243–382

Hudson-Williams, L., 'Political Speeches in Athens', *CQ*² 1 (1951), pp. 68–73

Humphreys, S.C., 'Social Relations on Stage: Witnesses in Classical Athens', *History and Anthropology* 1.2 (1985), pp. 313–69

Hunger, H., *Die hochsprachliche profane Literatur der Byzantiner* 1 (Munich: 1978)

Hunter, V., *Policing Athens: Social Control in the Attic Lawsuits, 420–320 B.C.* (Princeton: 1994)

Irmer, D., *Zum Primat des Codex S in der Demostheneskritik* (diss. Hamburg: 1961)

—— 'Beobachtungen zur Demosthenesüberlieferung', *Philologus* 112 (1968), pp. 43–62

—— *Zur Genealogie der jüngeren Demostheneshandschriften, Hamburger philologische Studien* 20 (Hamburg: 1972)

Isager, S. and M.H. Hansen, *Aspects of Athenian Society in the Fourth Century B.C.* (Odense: 1975)

Jaeger, W., *Demosthenes: The Origins and Growth of His Policy* (Berkeley: 1938; repr. New York: 1977)

Jenkyns, R., *The Victorians and Ancient Greece* (Cambridge, Mass.: 1980)

—— 'The Beginning of Greats, 1800–1872. 1, Classical Studies' in M.G. Brock and M.C. Curthoys (eds.), *The History of the University of Oxford* 6 (Oxford: 1997), pp. 513–20

Johnstone, S., 'Cracking the Code of Silence: Athenian Legal Oratory and the Histories of Slaves and Women' in S.R. Joshel and S. Murnaghan (eds.), *Women and Slaves in Greco-Roman Culture: Differential Equations* (London and New York: 1998), pp. 221–35

—— *Disputes and Democracy: The Consequences of Litigation in Ancient Athens* (Austin: 1999)

Jones, A.H.M., 'The Economic Basis of the Athenian Democracy', *Past and Present* 1 (1952), pp. 13–31

—— 'The Social Structure of Athens in the Fourth Century B.C.', *Economic History Review* 8 (1955), pp. 141–55

—— 'Slavery in the Ancient World', *Economic History Review* 9 (1956), pp. 185–99

—— *Athenian Democracy* (Oxford: 1960)

Just, R., *Women in Athenian Law and Life* (London: 1989)

Kahrstedt, U., *Studien zum öffentlichen Recht Athens* 2 (Stuttgart: 1936)

Kase, E.W., G.J. Szemler, N.C. Wilkes and P.W. Wallace (eds.), *The Great Isthmus Corridor Route* 1 (Dubuque: 1991)

Kennedy, G., *The Art of Persuasion in Greece* (Princeton: 1963)

—— *The Art of Rhetoric in the Roman World* (Princeton: 1972)

—— 'Oratory' in P.E. Easterling and B.M.W. Knox (eds.), *Cambridge History of Classical Literature* 1 (Cambridge: 1985), pp. 498–526

—— *A New History of Classical Rhetoric* (Princeton: 1994)

Kindstrand, J.F., *The Stylistic Evaluation of Aeschines in Antiquity* (Uppsala: 1982)

Knox, R.A., '"So Mischievous a Beaste"? The Athenian *Demos* and its Treatment of Politicians', *G&R*[2] 32 (1985), pp. 132–61

Kyle, D.G., 'The First Hundred Olympiads: A Process of Decline or Democratization?', *Nikephoros* 10 (1997), pp. 53–75

—— 'Games, Prizes, and Athletes in Greek Sport: Patterns and Perspectives (1975–1997)', *CB* 74 (1998), pp. 103–27

Lanni, A., 'Spectator Sport or Serious Politics? οἱ περιεστηκότες and the Athenian Lawcourts', *JHS* 117 (1997), pp. 183–9

Lefèvre, F., *L'Amphictionie pyléo-delphique: histoire et institutions* (Paris: 1998)

Legaré, Mary (ed.), *Writings of Hugh Swinton Legaré* 1 (New York and Boston: 1846)

Lentz, T.M., *Orality and Literacy in Hellenic Greece* (Carbondale: 1989)

Leopold, J.W., 'Demosthenes on Distrust of Tyrants', *GRBS* 22 (1981), pp. 227–46

Londey, P., 'The Outbreak of the 4th Sacred War', *Chiron* 20 (1990), pp. 239–60

Loraux, N. and P. Vidal-Naquet, 'La formation de l' Athènes bourgeoise: Essai d' historiographie 1750–1850' in J. Bolgar (ed.), *Classical Influences on Western Thought* (Cambridge: 1979), pp. 169–222

Lossau, Manfred, *Untersuchungen zur antiken Demosthenesexegese*, *Palingenesia* 2 (Berlin: 1964)

MacDowell, D.M., *Demosthenes Against Meidias (Oration 21)* (Oxford: 1990)

Mackendrick, P., *The Athenian Aristocracy 399–31 B.C.* (Cambridge, Mass.: 1969)

Mactoux, M.-M., 'Lois de Solon sur les esclaves et formation d'une société esclavagiste' in T. Yuge and M. Doi (eds.), *Forms of Control and Subordination in Antiquity* (Leiden: 1988), pp. 331–54

Mann, C., 'Krieg, Sport und Adelskultur. Zur Entstehung des griechischen Gymnasions', *Klio* 80 (1998), pp. 7–21

Maury (Cardinal), *Principes de l' éloquence pour la chaire et le barreau* (Paris: 1777)

McCabe, D.F., *The Prose Rhythm of Demosthenes* (New York: 1981)

McComb, R., *The Tradition of "the Lives of the Ten Orators" in Plutarch and Photius* (diss. Chapel Hill: 1991)

McEwan, I., *Enduring Love* (London: 1997)

Meerwaldt, J.O., 'De comicorum quibusdam locis ad ludendum Demosthenem pertinentibus', *Mnemosyne* 55 (1927), pp. 287–303

Meiggs, R. and D.M. Lewis, *A Selection of Greek Historical Inscriptions to the End of the Fifth Century* B C[2] (Oxford: 1989)

Michaelson, S. and A.Q. Morton, 'The New Stylometry: A One-Word Test of Authorship for Greek Writers', *CQ*[2] 22 (1997), pp. 576–88

Mikalson, J.D., *Religion in Hellenistic Athens* (Berkeley and Los Angeles: 1998)

Miller, Stephen G., 'Naked Democracy' in P. Flensted-Jensen and T.H. Nielsen (eds) *Polis and Politics* (Copenhagen: 2000), pp. 277–96

Millett, P.C., *Lending and Borrowing in Ancient Athens* (Cambridge: 1991)

Milns, R.D., 'Hermias of Atarneus and the Fourth Philippic Oration' in C. Questa (ed.), *Filologia e Forme Letterarie: Studi Offerti a Francesco della Corte* 3 (Urbino: 1987), pp. 287–302

—— 'Historical Paradigms in Demosthenes' Public Speeches', *Electronic Antiquity* 2.5 (1995)

Mirhady, D.C., 'Aristotle on the Rhetoric of Law', *GRBS* 31 (1990), pp. 393–410

—— 'Non-Technical *pisteis* in Aristotle and Anaximenes', *AJP* 112 (1991), pp. 5–28

—— 'The Oath-Challenge in Athens', *CQ*² 41 (1991), pp. 78–83

—— 'Torture and Rhetoric in Athens', *JHS* 116 (1996), pp. 119–31

—— 'The Athenian Rationale for Torture' in J. Edmondson and V. Hunter (eds.), *Law and Social Status in Classical Athens* (Oxford: 2000), pp. 53–74

—— 'Athens' Democratic Witnesses' in E.M. Harris and L. Rubenstein (eds.), *The Law and the Courts in Ancient Greece* (London: 2001)

Mitchel, F., 'Athens in the Age of Alexander', *G&R*² 12 (1965), pp. 189–204

—— 'Lykourgan Athens: 338–322', *Semple Lectures* 2 (Cincinnati: 1970)

Mitford, W., *History of Greece*, 8 vols. (London: 1838)

Monfasani, J., *George of Trebizond* (Leiden: 1976)

—— 'The Byzantine Rhetorical Tradition and the Renaissance' in J. Murphy (ed.), *Renaissance Eloquence: Studies in the Theory and Practice of Renaissance Rhetoric* (Berkeley: 1983), pp. 174–87

Morris, J., 'A.H.M. Jones', *Past and Present* 47 (1970), pp. 147–50

Mosley, D.J., *Envoys and Diplomacy in Ancient Greece* (Wiesbaden: 1973)

Mossé, C., *Athens in Decline* (transl. J. Sewart, London: 1973)

—— 'The "World of the *Emporium*" in the Private Speeches of Demosthenes' in P. Garnsey, K. Hopkins and C.R. Whittaker (eds.), *Trade in the Ancient Economy* (London: 1983), pp. 53–63

Mounteney, Richard, *Demosthenis, Selectae Orationes* (Cambridge: 1731)

Murray, A.T. (transl.), *Demosthenes III–V* (Cambridge, Mass.: 1936–39)

Murray, G., *Greek Studies* (Oxford: 1946)

Murray, O., 'The Beginning Of Greats, 1800–1872. 2, Ancient History' in M.G. Brock and M.C. Curthoys (eds.), *The History of the University of Oxford* 6 (Oxford: 1997), pp. 520–42

Niebuhr, B.G., *Demosthenis erste philipp. Rede im Auszug übers* (Hamburg: 1805)

Nightingale, A.W., 'Plato's Lawcode in Context: Rule by Written Law in Athens and Magnesia', *CQ*² 49 (1999), pp. 100–22

Nouhaud, M., *L'Utilisation de l'histoire par les orateurs attiques* (Paris: 1982)

Ober, J., *Mass and Elite in Democratic Athens* (Princeton: 1989)

—— 'Power and Oratory in Democratic Athens: Demosthenes 21, *Against Meidias*' in Ian Worthington (ed.), *Persuasion: Greek Rhetoric in Action* (London: 1994), pp. 85–108

Osborne, M.J. and S.G. Byrne (eds.), *Lexicon of Greek Personal Names* 2 (Oxford: 1994)

Osborne, R.G., 'Law in Action in Classical Athens', *JHS* 105 (1985), pp. 40–58

Ostwald, M., *From Popular Sovereignty to the Sovereignty of Law* (Berkeley: 1986)

Paley, F.A. and J.E. Sandys, *Select Private Orations of Demosthenes* Part 1³ (Cambridge: 1898), Part 2⁴ (Cambridge: 1910)

Papillon, T.L., *Rhetorical Studies in the Aristocratea of Demosthenes* (New York: 1998)

Parke, H.W., 'Notes on Some Delphic Oracles', *Hermathena* 52 (1938), pp. 71–8

Pearson, L., 'Historical Allusions in the Attic orators', *CP* 36 (1941), pp. 209–29

—— 'The Development of Demosthenes as a Political Orator', *Phoenix* 18 (1964), pp. 95–109

—— *Demosthenes: Six Private Speeches* (Norman: 1972)

—— 'The Virtuoso Passages in Demosthenes' Speeches', *Phoenix* 29 (1975), pp. 214–30

—— 'Hiatus and Its Purposes in Attic Oratory', *AJP* 96 (1975), pp. 138–59

—— *The Art of Demosthenes* (Meisenheim am Glan: 1976)

Perlman, S., 'The Historical Example: Its Use and Importance as Political Propaganda in the Attic Orators', *SH* 7 (1961), pp. 158–66

—— 'Quotations from Poetry in Attic Orators of the Fourth Century B.C.', *AJP* 85 (1964), pp. 156–72

—— (ed.), *Philip and Athens* (London: 1973)

Pfeiffer, R., *History of Classical Scholarship* (Oxford: 1968)

Pickard-Cambridge, A.W., *Demosthenes and the Last Days of Greek Freedom* (London: 1914)

Poland, F., *Reuchlins Verdeutschung der ersten olynthischen Rede des Demosthenes* (Berlin: 1899)

Pomeroy, S., *Families in Classical and Hellenistic Greece: Representations and Realities* (Oxford: 1997)

Porter, J.R., 'Adultery by the Book: Lysias 1 (*On the Murder of Eratosthenes*) and Comic *Diegesis*', *EMC* 41 (1997), pp. 421–53

Prasse, A., *De Plutarchi quae feruntur Vitis Decem Oratorum* (Marburg: 1891)

Pratt, L.H., *Lying and Poetry from Homer to Pindar: Falsehood and Deception in Archaic Greek Poetics* (Ann Arbor: 1993)

Preuss, S., *Index Demosthenicus* (Leipzig: 1892)

Reiske, J.J., *Oratores Graeci*, 12 vols. (Leipzig: 1770–75)

Rhodes, P.J., *The Athenian Boule* (Oxford: 1972)

—— *A Commentary on the Artistotelian Athenaion Politeia* (Oxford: 1981)

Rhys Roberts, W., *Demetrius On Style*, Loeb Classical Library (Cambridge, Mass.: 1922)

Roberts, J.T., *Democracy on Trial* (Princeton: 1995)

Roebuck, C., 'The Settlements of Philip II with the Greek States in 338 B.C.', *CP* 43 (1948), pp. 73–92

Roux, G., *L'Amphictionie, Delphes, et le temple d'Apollon au IVe siècle* (Lyons: 1979)

Rowe, G.O., 'The Portrait of Aeschines in the Oration *On the Crown*', *TAPA* 97 (1966), pp. 397–406

—— 'Demosthenes' First Philippic: The Satiric Mode', *TAPA* 99 (1968), pp. 361–74

Roy, J., 'An Alternative Sexual Morality for Classical Athenians', *G&R*[2] 44 (1997), pp. 11–22

Le Roy, Louis, *Trois oraisons de Démosthène prince des Orateurs, dittes Olynthiaques, pleines de matières d'éstat, déduittes avecques singulière prudence et éloquence, translatées pareillement de grec en françois, avec une préface contenant la conionction de l'éloquence et de la philosophie* (Paris: 1551)

Rue, L., *By the Grace of Guile: The Role of Deception in Natural History and Human Affairs* (New York and Oxford: 1994)

Ruschenbusch, E., 'Demosthenes' erste freiwillige Trierarchie und die Datierung des Euböaunternehmens vom Jahre 357', *ZPE* 67 (1987), pp. 158–9

Russell, D.A., '*Ethos* in Oratory and Rhetoric' in C. Pelling (ed.), *Characterization and Individuality in Greek Literature* (Oxford: 1990), pp. 197–212

Ryder, T.T.B., *Koine Eirene* (Oxford: 1965)

—— 'Demosthenes and Philip's Peace of 338/7 B.C.', *CQ*[2] 26 (1976), pp. 85–7

—— 'Ambiguity in Aeschines', *LCM* 2 (1977), pp. 219–23

—— 'The Diplomatic Skills of Philip II' in Ian Worthington (ed.), *Ventures Into Greek History: Essays in Honour of N.G.L. Hammond* (Oxford: 1994), pp. 228–57

Ryder, T.T.B. and A.N.W. Saunders, *Demosthenes and Aeschines* (Harmondsworth: 1975)

Sandys, J.E., *The First Philippic and The Olynthiacs of Demosthenes* (repr. London: 1950)

—— *Demosthenes, On the Peace* (London: 1953)

Sawada, N., 'Athenian Politics in the Age of Alexander the Great: A Reconsideration of the Trial of Ctesiphon', *Chiron* 26 (1996), pp. 57–84

Scafuro, A., 'Witnessing and False-Witnessing: Proving Citizenship and Kin Identity in Fourth-Century Athens' in A.L. Boegehold and A.C. Scafuro (eds.), *Athenian Identity and Civic Ideology* (Baltimore: 1994), pp. 156–98

—— *The Forensic Stage: Settling Disputes in Graeco-Roman New Comedy* (Princeton: 1997)

Schaefer, A., *Demosthenes und seine Zeit*[2], 3 vols. (Leipzig: 1885–7; repr. Hildesheim: 1966–7)

Schaps, D., 'The Woman Least Mentioned: Etiquette and Women's Names', *CQ*[2] 27 (1977), pp. 323–30

Schiappa, E., *The Beginnings of Rhetorical Theory in Classical Greece* (New Haven: 1999)

Schindel, Ulrich, *Demosthenes im 18. Jahrhundert*, Zetemata 31 (Munich: 1963)

Schwartz, E., 'Demosthenes' erste Philippika' in P. Jors, E. Schwartz and R. Reitzenstein (eds.), *Festschrift Theodor Mommsen zum fünfzigjährigen Doctorjubiläum* (Marburg: 1893), pp. 1–44

Sealey, R., 'Dionysius of Halicarnassus and Some Demosthenic Dates', *REG* 68 (1955), pp. 77–120

—— 'Athens after the Social War', *JHS* 75 (1955), pp. 74–81

—— 'Callistratos of Aphidna and His Contemporaries', *Historia* 5 (1956), pp. 178–203

—— *Essays in Greek Politics* (New York: 1967)

—— *Demosthenes and His Time* (Oxford: 1993)

Sherwin-White, S.M., *Ancient Cos* (Göttingen: 1978)

Shoemaker, G., *Dinarchus: The Tradition of his Life and Speeches with a Commentary on the Fragments of the Speeches* (diss. Columbia University: 1986)

Sickinger, J.P., *Public Records and Archives in Classical Athens* (Chapel Hill: 1999)

Slater, W.J., 'The Theatricality of Justice', *CB* 71 (1995), pp. 143–57

Stählin, F., *Das hellenische Thessalien* (Stuttgart: 1924)

Stray, C., *Classics Transformed* (Oxford: 1998)

Szemler, G.J., W.J. Cherf and J.C. Kraft (eds.), *Thermopylai: Myth and Reality in 480 BC* (Chicago: 1996)

Taylor, John 'Demosthenes', *The Surviving Works of Demosthenes, Aeschines, Deinarchus and Demades, in Greek and Latin* 3 (Cambridge: 1748) and 2 (Cambridge: 1757)

Thomas, R., *Oral Tradition and Written Record in Classical Athens* (Cambridge: 1989)

Thür, G., *Beweisführung vor den Schwurgerichtshöfen Athens. Die Proklesis zur Basanos* (Vienna: 1977)

Tod, M.N., *Greek Historical Inscriptions* 2 (Oxford: 1948)

Todd, S., 'The Use and Abuse of the Attic Orators', *G&R*[2] 37 (1990), pp. 159–78

—— 'The Purpose of Evidence in Athenian Courts' in P. Cartledge, P. Millett and S. Todd (eds.), *Nomos: Essays in Athenian Law, Politics and Society* (Cambridge: 1990), pp. 19–39

—— *The Shape of Athenian Law* (Oxford: 1993)

Trevett, J. *Apollodorus the Son of Pasion* (Oxford: 1992)

—— 'Did Demosthenes Publish his Deliberative Speeches?', *Hermes* 124 (1996), pp. 425–41

Tritle, L., *Phocion the Good* (London: 1988)

Tuplin, C.J., 'Demosthenes' *Olynthiacs* and the Character of the Demegoric Corpus', *Historia* 47 (1998), pp. 276–320

Turner, Frank, *The Greek Heritage in Victorian Britain* (New Haven: 1981)

Vitelli, G. (ed.), *Pubblicazioni della Società italiana per la ricerca dei papiri greci e latini in Egitto (PSI), Papiri Greci e Latini* 2 (Florence: 1913)

Walbank, F.W., *A Historical Commentary on Polybius* 2 (Oxford: 1967)

Wallace, R.W., *The Areopagos Council, to 307 B.C.* (Baltimore and London: 1989)

Wankel, H., *Demosthenes, Rede für Ktesiphon über den Kranz*, 2 vols. (Heidelberg: 1976)

—— 'Demosthenes' erste freiwillige Trierarchie und die Datierung des Euböaunternehmens vom Jahre 357', *ZPE* 71 (1988), pp. 199–200

Wehrli, F., *Die Schule des Aristoteles* 4 (Basel and Stuttgart: 1968)

West, W.C., 'The Public Archives in Fourth-Century Athens', *GRBS* 30 (1989), pp. 529–43

Westermann, A., *Biographi Graeci Minores* (Braunschweig: 1845; repr. Amsterdam: 1964)

Wilcken, U., *Alexander the Great* (transl. G.C. Richards, New York: 1967)

Wilson, N.G., *Scholars of Byzantium* (London: 1983)

—— *From Byzantium to Italy* (London: 1992)

Wilson, P.J., 'Demosthenes 21 (*Against Meidias*): Democratic Abuse', *PCPS* 37 (1991), pp. 164–95

—— 'Tragic Rhetoric: The Use of Tragedy and the Tragic in the Fourth Century' in M.S. Silk (ed.), *Tragedy and the Tragic: Greek Theatre and Beyond* (Oxford: 1996), pp. 310–31

Wirth, G., *Philipp II* (Stuttgart: 1985)

Wolff, H.J., *Demosthenes als Advokat. Funktionen und Methoden des Prozesspraktikers im klassischen Athen*, Schriftenreihe der juristischen Gesellschaft e.V. 30 (Berlin: 1968)

Wooten, C.W., 'Dionysius of Halicarnassus and Hermogenes on the Style of Demosthenes', *AJP* 110 (1989), pp. 576–88

Worthington, Ian, '*IG* ii^2 370 and the Date of the Athenian Alliance with Aetolia', *ZPE* 57 (1984), pp. 139–44

—— 'The Chronology of the Harpalus Affair', *SO* 61 (1986), pp. 63–76

—— 'The Duration of an Athenian Political Trial', *JHS* 109 (1989), pp. 204–7

—— 'Greek Oratory, Revision of Speeches and the Problem of Historical Reliability', *C&M* 92 (1991), pp. 55–74

—— 'The Authenticity of Demosthenes' Fourth Philippic', *Mnemosyne*[4] 44 (1991), pp. 425–8

—— *A Historical Commentary on Dinarchus* (Ann Arbor: 1992)

—— 'History and Oratorical Exploitation' in Ian Worthington (ed.), *Persuasion: Greek Rhetoric in Action* (London: 1994), pp. 109–29

—— 'The Harpalus Affair and the Greek Response to the Macedonian Hegemony' in Ian Worthington (ed.), *Ventures Into Greek History: Essays in Honour of N.G.L. Hammond* (Oxford: 1994), pp. 307–30

—— *Greek Orators 2: Dinarchus 1 and Hyperides 5 & 6* (Warminster: 1999)

Wüst, F.R., *Philipp II von Makedonien und Griechenland* (Munich: 1938)

Wylson, Thomas, *The three Orations of Demosthenes chiefe Orator among the Grecians, in favour of the Olynthians, a people in Thracia, now called Romania: with those his fower Orations titled expressely and by name against King Philip of Macedonie: most nedeful to be redde in these daungerous dayes, of all them that love their Countries libertie, and desire to take warning for their better avayle, by example of others* (London: 1570)

Zucker, A., 'Quae ratio inter vitas Lysiae, Dionysiacam, Pseudo-Plutarchean, Photianam intercedet', *Acta Seminarii Philologici Erlangensis* 1 (1878), pp. 289–315

SELECT INDEX

Aeschines: indicts Ctesiphon (in
330) 96–7, 99–100, 146–7;
Speech *Against Ctesiphon* 146–7,
148–54, 170–1; and
Demosthenes 96–100, 114–58,
247; and First Embassy to Philip
61–3, 120–2, 138; Second
Embassy to Philip 66–68, 124–9,
169; and Fourth Embassy to
Philip 69–70; Speech *On the False
Embassy* 137–40, 148–54;
emergence in political life
116–19; family connections
with Demosthenes 14–15; and
Fourth Sacred War 80–1, 142–4;
oratorical style of 233–4; and
Peace of Philocrates 58–71,
117–29; Speech *Against
Timarchus* 133–4; trial of in 343
76, 134–40; *see also* Ctesiphon;
Demosthenes; Philip II;
Speeches
Agis III 91, 93, 95–6, 97–8, 100;
see also Demosthenes; Sparta
Alexander the Great: and
deification 102–3; and
Demosthenes 90–113; and
Exiles Decree 102–3, 104–5,
106, 108; in Persia 94, 96, 99;
destroys Thebes 92; possible

effect of absence on
Demosthenes' oratory 93–4; *see
also* Demosthenes; Speeches
Amphipolis 19–20, 45–6, 62, 74,
121; 'secret treaty' over 20; *see
also* Philip II
Androtion 20–3; *see also*
Demosthenes; Social War
Antipater 63, 64–5, 92, 95–6, 98,
100, 102, 106–7, 123–4, 236
Aphobus 16–18, 162; *see also*
Demosthenes
Aristocrates 24–5, 50; *see also*
Charidemus; Demosthenes
Aristodemus 59
Athenian democracy abolished
(322) 106–7

Cardia 74, 77, 125; *see also*
Chersonese; Diopeithes; Philip II
Cersebleptes 35, 47, 49, 50, 52,
62, 65, 66–7, 76, 116, 120–1,
122, 123, 125; *see also* Philip II;
Thrace
Chares 47, 48, 55, 57, 60, 116, 123
Charidemus 24–5, 50, 52, 56; *see
also* Aristocrates
Chersonese 49–50, 62, 74, 76–7,
79, 116, 121, 125; *see also* Philip
II; Thrace

Cicero: on Demosthenes' style 248–9, 224, 225, 229–30; *see also* Demosthenes; Speeches

Corinth; League of 83–4, 92, 95, 98, 102; *see also* Philip II; Thebes

Ctesiphon: proposes crown for Demosthenes (in 336) 83, 145–6; treats with Philip (in 346) 59, 117; trial of (in 336) 96, 146; *see also* Aeschines; Speeches

Demades 83, 92, 100, 106, 227–9, 236; *see also* Demosthenes; Philip II

Demetrius: on Demosthenes' style 229–31, 232–4; *see also* Demosthenes; Speeches

Demosthenes: and Aeschines 14–15, 76, 96–100, 114–58, 247; resists Agis III's war (331–30) 95, 97–8, 99–100; and Alexander the Great 4, 90–113; Speech *Against Androtion* 21–2, 23–4; prosecutes Aphobus and Onetor 16–18, 162, 186–98; Speech *Against Aristocrates* 24–5, 50; early career of 3–4, 15–44; Chaeronea and aftermath 82–3, 91, 92–3; Speech *On the Chersonese* 76, 77–8, 94, 211–12, 216–17; Speech *Against Conon* 199–200; Crown trial of 330 91, 96–7, 99–100, 146–7; Speech *On the Crown* 147, 148–54; death of 107; and First Embassy to Philip 61–3, 120–22; and Second Embassy to Philip 66–8, 71, 124–9; Speech *On the False Embassy* 135–7, 148–54; family of 12–15; and Harpalus affair 102–6, 108, 247–8; inheritance of squandered 15–18;

Speech *Against Leptines* 27–8, 173–4; Speech *For the Megalopolitans* 30–1, 32–3, 48, 211; *Olynthiac* speeches of 49, 54, 55–6, 57, 206–7, 211, 212–13, 214, 216; oratorical style of 93–4, 104, 182–201, 209–18, 224–45; Speech *On the Peace* 71, 211; use of Persia against Alexander 93, 94–5, 98–9; and Philip II 4, 5, 20, 33–4, 45–89, 91, 107, 115–45, 246–7, 248; *Philippic* 1 speech 33–6, 50–2, 160–1, 207–8, 211–12, 213, 214, 216; *Philippic* 2 speech 72–3, 208, 214–15, 216–17; *Philippic* 3 speech 76, 78, 94, 208, 213, 215, 216; and Peace of Philocrates 58–71, 117–32; private speeches of 5, 181–204; public speeches of 5, 205–23; reaction of to Philip's death 84, 91; reputation of in antiquity 5, 9–10, 224–45, 248–9; reputation of in post antiquity 3, 5–6, 246–71; reputation as an orator in post antiquity 248–67; reputation as a politician in post antiquity 258–66; Speech *For the Liberty of the Rhodians* 31–3, 52–3, 211, 214, 216; and social history 4–5, 159–80; spurious speeches of 1, 10–11, 16–17, 205–6; statue of 1–2; Speech *On the Symmories* 28–30, 32, 46–7, 210–11, 214; texts of 9–10, 239, 249–57; alliance with Thebes (339) 81, 91, 143–5; Speech *Against Timocrates* 23–4, 159–60, 162; *see also* Aeschines; Philip II; Speeches

Dionysius: on Demosthenes' style 210, 217–18, 224, 225–6, 229; *see also* Demosthenes; Speeches

Diopeithes 77–8, 79; *see also* Chersonese; Philip II; Thrace

Euboea: and Philip (in 348) 56–7, 117; after 346 75, 76, 78, 134, 140–1

Eubulus 30, 47, 60, 64, 65, 117–18; *see also* Demosthenes

Euctemon 21–2

Exiles Decree 102–3, 104–5, 106, 108; *see also* Alexander the Great; Demosthenes; Harpalus affair

Gymnasium 4–5, 170–5; *see also* Demosthenes; Speeches

Halonessus 74–5; *see also* Philip II

Halus 120–1, 125–6, 129; *see also* Philip II

Harpalus affair 91, 102–6, 108, 247–8; *see also* Alexander the Great; Exiles Decree

Hegesippus 74–5, 76, 134; *see also* Philip II

Heraion-Teichos 49, 50, 51, 52; *see also* Philip II

Hyperides 78, 82, 100, 106, 107, 108, 134, 142; *see also* Demosthenes; Harpalus affair

Lamian War 106

Leptines 27–8, 173–4; *see also* Demosthenes; Social War

Lycurgus 100–1, 107

Macedonian hegemony of Greece 100–1, 104, 107–8

Mausolus 29, 32

Methone 34, 46, 51; *see also* Philip II

Nausicles 49, 116, 199; *see also* Philip II; Thermopylae

Olynthus 34, 35, 46, 53–8, 59, 60, 74, 116–17; *see also* Demosthenes; Philip II

Onetor 16–18; *see also* Demosthenes

Parmenion 63, 120–1, 123–4

Peace of Philocrates 58–71, 117–32; *see also* Aeschines; Demosthenes; Philip II

Persia: in Demosthenes' strategy against Alexander 93, 94–5, 98–9; in Demosthenes' *For the Liberty of the Rhodians* 32–3, 53; in Demosthenes' *On the Symmories* 29–30, 46–7; projected invasion of by Philip 58, 83–4, 98–9

Philip II: Chaeronea and aftermath 82, 83, 91, 92–3; and the Chalcidic campaign 53–8, 116–17; death of 84; and Demosthenes 20, 33–7, 45–89, 91, 107, 115–45, 246–7, 248; and Euboea 56–7, 75, 76, 78, 117, 140; and Greece 19–20, 22, 24–5, 33–5, 46–89, 115–44; and Peace of Philocrates 58–71, 117–29; and Persian invasion 58, 83–4, 98–9; and Sacred War 116–17, 126–9, 132; *see also* Aeschines; Corinth, League of; Demosthenes

Philocrates 59–60, 61–3, 63–6, 66–8, 76, 117, 119, 126, 130, 134; *see also* Aeschines;

Demosthenes; Peace of Philocrates; Philip II

Phocion 56–7, 75, 83, 100, 227–9, 236

Phocis: 47, 49, 60, 136; fate of in 346 69–70, 128–9; in negotiations over Peace of Philocrates 63–70, 122, 124, 126–7; *see also* Philip II; Sacred War

Plutarch: on Demosthenes' style 227–9, 233–4; *see also* Demosthenes; Speeches

Potidaea 34, 46–7, 51, 74; *see also* Philip II

Pydna 34, 46; *see also* Philip II

Python 73–4, 75, 134; *see also* Philip II

Quintilian: on Demosthenes' style 224, 229, 231–2; *see also* Demosthenes; Speeches

Sacred War (against Phocis) 47–9, 60, 62, 63–70, 115–29; *see also* Demosthenes; Philip II; Phocion; Thebes

Sacred War (fourth) 80–1, 142–4; *see also* Aeschines; Philip II; Thebes

Samos 102, 104, 105

Second Athenian Naval Confederacy 26–7, 63–4, 119–20

Social War 26–7, 29, 34; *see also* Androtion; Leptines; Philip II

Sparta: Agis III's war (331–30) 91, 93, 95–6, 97–8, 100; in Demosthenes' *For the Megalopolitans* 31, 33; and Peace of Philocrates 124; penalty in Sacred War 70; *see also* Alexander the Great; Demosthenes; Philip II

Speeches: revision of 148–54, 207–9; veracity of 6, 114–15, 148–54, 160–9

Thebes: ally of Athens (in 339) 81–2, 143–5; battle of Chaeronea and aftermath 82, 83, 92–3; in Demosthenes' *For the Megalopolitans* 31; razing of (in 335) 91, 92; in Sacred War 52, 60, 65, 69, 70, 126–8; in Fourth Sacred War 142–4; *see also* Philip II

Thermopylae 49, 51, 52, 60, 68–9, 80, 116, 119, 125, 126, 129, 143; *see also* Philip II

Thessaly 34–5, 48–9, 50, 52, 55, 65, 69, 71, 72, 116, 119–20, 124; *see also* Philip II; Sacred War

Thrace 76–7, 79, 116, 120; *see also* Philip II

Timarchus 133–4; *see also* Aeschines; Speeches

Timocrates 23–4, 159–60, 162; *see also* Demosthenes